CW00340815

The Welsh
at War

The Welsh
at War

FROM MONS TO LOOS
AND THE GALLIPOLI TRAGEDY

Steven John

Pen & Sword
MILITARY

First published in Great Britain in 2018 by
PEN & SWORD MILITARY
an imprint of
Pen and Sword Books Ltd
47 Church Street
Barnsley
South Yorkshire S70 2AS

Copyright © Steven John, 2018

ISBN 978 1 47383 209 1

Printed and bound in England by
CPI Group (UK) Ltd, Croydon, CR0 4YY

Typeset in Times New Roman
by CHIC GRAPHICS

Pen & Sword Books Ltd incorporates the imprints of
Pen & Sword Archaeology, Atlas, Aviation, Battleground, Discovery, Family
History, History, Maritime, Military, Naval, Politics, Railways, Select, Social
History, Transport, True Crime, Claymore Press, Frontline Books, Leo Cooper,
Praetorian Press, Remember When, Seaforth Publishing and Wharncliffe.

For a complete list of Pen and Sword titles please contact
Pen and Sword Books Limited
47 Church Street, Barnsley, South Yorkshire, S70 2AS, England
E-mail: enquiries@pen-and-sword.co.uk
Website: www.pen-and-sword.co.uk

Contents

Acknowledgements

Much of the material within these pages comes from a wide-ranging variety of sources, while details of the casualties themselves come from over a decade of research by the author into Welsh casualties and award-winners. The author is grateful for all the help he has received while carrying out his research into war memorials in west Wales over the past twelve years but is especially grateful to all at Pen & Sword Books, especially Roni Wilkinson, for showing continued support in publishing my work and to Nigel Cave for having the patience to proof-read and correct my last two works; to John Dart, former curator of the now-extant Welsh Regiment Museum at Cardiff, for allowing the author to copy several of their excellent photographs; and also to Bob Pike who, over the last decade, has supplied the author with countless photographs of war graves in France, Italy, Gallipoli and Israel.

The author did originally start out with the intention of writing a chapter on touring battlefield sites that are of interest to anyone following the Welsh troops during the war but, as work on the book continued, it became obvious that there were too many stories to try to fit into the confines of this book and also that almost every part of every battlefield of the Great War was visited by Welsh troops at one time or another.

It is therefore recommended that anyone considering the idea of visiting the battlefields, especially those of France and Belgium, which the author knows well, should gain encouragement from the fact that if he can make the trip in his usual disorganized manner then anyone can, but that good maps and guide books, particularly the ones written by Major and Mrs Holt and the more specialized books in the fantastic Battleground Europe series; all of which are available from Pen & Sword, are invaluable and packed with interesting facts. These books also contain tips on travelling, places to stay and must-see places to visit that may otherwise be missed. A list of publications particularly recommended for battlefield touring, from the author's personal experience, can be found below in the Bibliography section.

While the CWGC publishes a very useful pocket-sized book with maps of France and Belgium overlaid with locations of cemeteries and memorials, it should also be noted that for anyone with a Sat-Nav a free download is available from http://www. poigraves.uk that contains the locations of almost every war grave in Britain, Belgium and France and makes life for the battlefield tourist so much easier. The download is also available through the Tom Tom updater itself. This excellent resource has proved to be a massive time-saver for the author on his last few trips to France and is highly recommended in preventing domestic disputes!

Introduction

Prior to the outbreak of the Great War on 4 August 1914, Wales was home to three fine regular infantry regiments: the Royal Welsh Fusiliers (23rd Regiment); the South Wales Borderers (24th Regiment); and the Welsh Regiment (41st/69th Regiment).

As well as these infantry units, the country was also home to several Yeomanry regiments: the Montgomery Yeomanry, the Pembroke Yeomanry, the Glamorgan Yeomanry and the Denbighshire Hussars. This was in addition to having its own Royal Horse, Field and Garrison Artillery units; the Royal Anglesey and the Royal Monmouth Royal Engineers and the Welsh Field Company Royal Engineers; as well as Welsh medical units and units of the St John's Ambulance Brigade, the latter set up for work in the mines.

Wales was also home to a Royal Naval Dockyard at Pembroke Dock, situated on the banks of Milford Haven, one of the finest and safest anchorages for Royal Navy warships in Britain as well as being a manufacturing and repair facility. The dockyard built three cruisers – *Cambrian*, *Cordelia* and *Curacoa* – and also four submarines during the war, as well as several other smaller craft. Milford Haven and the forts surrounding the waterway were the home of the Pembroke Battery, Royal Garrison Artillery (RGA), while Caernarfonshire, Glamorgan and Cardiganshire also had their own RGA and Royal Field Artillery (RFA) batteries, and Glamorgan had a Royal Horse Artillery Battery (RHA). In addition, the Shropshire RHA was attached to the Welsh Border Mounted Brigade.

In general British infantry regiments were made up of two front-line battalions and a third reserve or depot battalion that was used to supply reinforcements and new recruits to either of the front-line units. There were also Territorial battalions affiliated to each regiment. These battalions were numbered 1st, 2nd and 3rd Battalion of their parent regiment and the Territorial battalions numbered 4th, 5th, 6th and 7th Battalion. The outbreak of the Great War led to a massive programme of expansion in the army and as a result each regiment formed several new battalions that would become known as 'Service' or war-time-only battalions during the course of the war.

The Great War also saw the birth of two new regiments for Wales: the Welsh Horse Yeomanry and the Welsh Guards. The Welsh Horse Yeomanry would only survive the Great War and was never re-formed; but the Welsh Guards have retained their proud history and are still an active service regiment today.

Of course, Welsh men and women did not only serve in Welsh units but in almost every regiment of the British army. Many, especially those from seafaring towns such as Cardiff, Newport, Barry, Llanelli, Pembroke, Milford, Cardigan, Holyhead, Fishguard and Aberystwyth, served in the Merchant and Royal Navy; many enlisted in the Royal Flying Corps (RFC), which became the Royal Air Force after merging with the Royal Naval Air Service in 1918; while countless others had made their homes overseas in the colonies and would serve the Australian, Canadian, New Zealand, South African and the United States forces. Many of the Welsh regiments contained a considerable number of non-Welsh soldiers in their ranks, with many English, Scottish and Irishmen who were working in the Welsh coal mines prior to the war enlisting into these local units.

Welshmen would fight and die in every major action and every theatre of the war, but several actions would become synonymous with Welsh troops during the conflict: notably the epic Welsh and Worcester defence of the Menin Road in 1914; the landing of the 53rd (Welsh) Division at Gallipoli in August 1915; the attack of the 38th (Welsh) Division on Mametz Wood in July 1916 and its capture of the Pilckem Ridge in July-August 1917; and the campaign of the Welsh Yeomanry and Territorial units in Palestine that year. Welsh units were also heavily involved during the Battle of Cambrai and the heroic fighting that followed the German offensives of spring 1918, as well as the drive that eventually won the war during the hundred-day offensive of 1918.

In total over 272,000 Welsh men and women served during the course of the war, while around 49,000 lost their lives.

The Welsh at War tells the story of the Welsh units that fought in every theatre of this first truly global war and of the new units raised in order to participate in the conflict. Interspersed with the actions in which these units fought are stories of great tragedy, such as the sinking of the *Lusitania*; the deaths of Welsh sportsmen and members of the Welsh aristocracy; and of some of the Welshmen killed with other units. *The Welsh at War* was originally intended to comprise only one volume but with the vast number of actions fought, combined with the large number of men and women involved, the author could not contain such tales within just one book. As a result the work has been extended to three volumes that can be read together or as an individual volume that may be of particular interest to the reader.

This volume covers the story of the *The Welsh at War* from the first rush to enlist in August 1914, the movement of Welsh units to France, and from the Battle of Mons until the Battle of Loos and the winter of 1915–16, when the 38th (Welsh) Division arrived. Subsequent volumes will be – under the main title of *Welsh at War* – Volume II, *The Grinding War: The Somme and Arras* and Volume III, *Through Mud to Victory: Third Ypres and the 1918 Offensives*.

This trilogy is not intended to be an encyclopaedic or academic record of all of the Welsh units and is not intended to claim that the Welsh were the finest fighting race or that Wales won the Great War, but only to tell as many stories as possible that illustrate the heroic efforts of some of our Welsh forefathers during the epic conflict, to commemorate the actions fought by Welsh units and to highlight major battlefields soaked with Welsh blood and sweat.

Chapter 1

1914
The Outbreak of War and the
Response in Wales

With the centenary of the Great War during 2014–18, most people will now be familiar with the events leading up to the outbreak of that destructive conflict. Tensions had been growing for some time beforehand, but it is generally accepted that the war was sparked by the assassination by a member of the Serbian Black Hand organization on 28 June 1914 of the heir to the Austro-Hungarian Empire, Archduke Franz Ferdinand, and his wife Sophie while they rode in an open carriage through Sarajevo.

This assassination set in motion a catastrophic chain of events after being viewed by Germany as the ideal opportunity to begin the war that its Emperor craved. Austria blamed Serbia for their part in the assassination and was backed by Germany in any action deemed necessary in dealing with the Serbs. The situation thus swiftly deteriorated, with Serbia and Austro-Hungary mobilizing their armies. Germany rushed a division to seize vital railheads in Luxembourg, and France and Russia moved quickly to mobilize their vast armies and the scene was then set for a European war.

On 2 August 1914, Germany insisted upon right of way to advance their now massed armies through Belgium to northern France. The Belgian King Albert refused and on the following day Germany declared war on France and their troops entered Belgium.

Britain had a treaty with Belgium which tied her fate to that of the smaller country and so at 11 pm on 4 August 1914 the British government solemnly declared war on Germany. Instantly the call to mobilize the troops was issued and posters went up on every notice board around the country. Troops stationed in Britain were rapidly mobilized for war and the call went out for other units stationed throughout the Empire to return home. With the army mobilizing, the Territorial and Yeomanry regiments were automatically embodied, while Royal Naval Reservists around Wales made for their war stations.

So far as the army was concerned, the regular army was the first to be mobilized; next was the Special Reserve, formerly known as the Militia; the Territorial Forces comprised three different groups: the Special Reserve (Territorial) Section was composed of men who received an annual payment in return for which they were liable to be called upon at any moment to fill vacancies caused by the movement of units of the regular army from their home stations; then the Territorial Force, which was liable on a general mobilization order for defence duty in Great Britain; and finally the Territorial Force Reserve, composed of men who had served on the active list of the force for their full period and had retired but who wished to remain at their country's disposal in time of urgent need. The *Brecon County Times* reported:

> Mobilisation Order at Brecon. A telegram was received by the Chief Constable of Breconshire (Capt. Cole Hamilton, D.S.O.), at 6.30 p.m. on Tuesday, announcing that a General Mobilisation of all the Forces of the Crown had been ordered, including the Army Reserve and the Territorials, and within a few minutes telegrams were being despatched to various centres in the county, and arrangements were being made for proclamations to be posted.

Within days of the outbreak of war thousands of men streamed into their respective depots to re-enlist: Hightown Barracks, Wrexham for the RWF; the Barracks, Brecon for the SWB; and Maindy Barracks, Cardiff for the Welsh Regiment. Frank Richards of the RWF wrote about the mobilization of the reserves in his classic book *Old Soldiers Never Die*:

Your King and Country need YOU!

MOBILISATION.

FLINTSHIRE TERRITORIALS.

The Association desire to ascertain the names of **MEN** between the ages of **17** and **35**, not serving in the National Reserve, who are anxious to enlist in any Branch of the Territorial Force.

Notices will be posted throughout the County, giving information as to where men can apply.

One of many mobilization orders published in the Welsh newspapers during the first week of August 1914. Flintshire Observer, 6 August 1914 ordering mobilization of the Flintshire Territorials (5th RWF).

> On the fourth of August, 1914, I was at Blaina, Mon., having a drink in the Castle Hotel with a few of my cronies, all old soldiers and the majority of them reservists. One had took us around South Africa; there wasn't a Boer left in South Africa by the time he had finished his yarn. Next I had took them around India and Burma and there wasn't a Pathan or Dacoit left in the world by the time I had finished mine... when someone happened to come in with a piece of news. He said that war had broken out with Germany and that the Sergeant of Police was hanging up a notice by the post office, calling all reservists to the Colours. This caused a bit of excitement and language, but it was too late in the evening for any of us to proceed to our depots so we kept on thinking and yarning until stop-tap. By that time we were getting a little top-heavy and an old artilleryman wound up the evening by dropping howitzer shells over the mountain and destroying a mining village in the valley beyond.
>
> The next day I proceeded to the Regimental Depot at Wrexham, arriving there about 9 pm. On my way to barracks I called at a pub which I used to frequent very often when I was a recruit and found it full of Royal Welch reservists.

Newspapers all over the country told stories of hundreds of reservists assembling at railway stations throughout Wales to rejoin their units: 'A large number of Reservists who had just arrived at Nevin, Morfa Nevin, Abersoch, Pwllheli, Criccieth and Porthmadog for a holiday were called to the colours on Tuesday and left on Wednesday.' (*North Wales Chronicle*, 7 August 1914.)

Swansea, as in the case of all other towns in the country, was the scene of considerable activity last night, when Territorials and Military Reservists were called up. The Proclamation of the King ordering a mobilisation of all His Majesty's Forces was posted up near the Market and elsewhere on Tuesday evening and until a late hour large crowds gathered round the notice boards. The streets were crowded with an expectant throng and the whole air was permeated with pent-up excitement. (*Cambrian Daily Leader*, 5 August 1914.)

There were stirring scenes in Brecon on Tuesday night when it became known that the Territorials were to be mobilised and sent to their War Station for duty. The mobilisation order included the whole of the Reserves, who have to come to the Depot, but many of these live some distance away and they came in gradually. Not so with the Territorials. They had just come from camp with the expectation of being mobilised, and before midnight Tuesday probably every man in the county had had his order... The orders were for departure of the battalion in two trains to Pembrokeshire in the evening, and at the time of writing practically everything was ready for the start. A number of Brecon men have already come forward to join the Territorials. The Special Reserves of the S.W.B. (the old Militia) are coming in, and it is expected they will be ready to leave, in command of Colonel Stuart Morgan, on Friday. (*Brecon County Times*, 6 August 1914.)

On Sunday the order was given out for the mobilisation of the Naval Reserve (trawler section) of whom there are about 150 men in the port, including skippers, mates, deck hands, engineers, etc. A naval officer was busy all day serving notices on all the men in from sea. This was not all, for orders were given for the handing over to the Admiralty of certain steam trawlers for the mine sweeping service, the vessels to be manned. The stream trawler *Abelard* was stripped of her gear and prepared at once, leaving the port on Sunday afternoon. The *Falmouth* was obliged to discharge her fish at eleven o'clock on Sunday night, and left on Monday morning. The destination of the trawlers is said to be Dover, but it is probable that they sail under sealed orders. The *Cleopatra* and *Marloes* were getting ready on Monday, and the number of ships likely to be commissioned is 16 to 20. (*Haverfordwest and Milford Haven Telegraph*, 5 August 1914.)

There were also reports of Germans leaving Wales to take up arms for their mother country:

The German Consul at Swansea (Mr Dahne) on Tuesday received the first notice from his Government re the German Army reservists in the town and many assembled for departure at once. About 200 are affected in the district. Amongst those going back to Germany are the two sons of Mr Roeder, manager of the Mannesmann Tube Works, Landore. (*Llais Llafur*, 8 August 1914.)

The men were required to go through formalities. Each man had to be medically examined to pass as fit for overseas service and, if passed fit, was issued with uniform, boots, rifle and equipment and, with an abundance of seasoned soldiers to pick from, the first units that were soon to embark for France with the British Expeditionary Force (BEF) would be the most well-trained and physically capable units of the British army during the war. Men not picked to go to France with the first drafts joined their regiment's 3rd Battalions: the 3rd RWF had been at Pembroke but on 9 August returned to Wrexham; the 3rd SWB moved to Pembroke Dock for garrison duty on 8 August; while the 3rd Welsh remained in Cardiff, with a detachment guarding the Severn tunnel.

Based in Britain at this time were three Welsh front-line battalions: the 2nd Battalion, Royal Welsh Fusiliers had just returned from Malta and was training at Wool under Lieutenant Colonel Henry Delmé Radcliffe; the 1st Battalion, South Wales Borderers under Lieutenant Colonel Henry Edmund Burley Leach was at Camp Bordon; and the 2nd Battalion, Welsh Regiment was at Aldershot under Lieutenant Colonel Charles Bernard Morland. The 2nd Welsh and 1st SWB were attached to 3 Brigade 1st Division, commanded by Major General Lomax, while the 2nd RWF was unallocated to a division, having just returned to Britain.

The 2nd Battalion, Welsh Regiment marching to their embarkation port in August 1914.

The original officers of the 1st Battalion, South Wales Borderers prior to embarking for France.

The three other front-line battalions were stationed around the Empire: the 1st Battalion, Royal Welsh Fusiliers (RWF) was in Malta under Lieutenant Colonel Henry Osbert Samuel Cadogan; the 2nd Battalion, South Wales Borderers (SWB) was in Tientsin, China under Lieutenant Colonel Hugh Gilbert Casson; and the 1st Battalion, Welsh Regiment was in Chakrata, India under Lieutenant Colonel Thomas Owen Marden.

According to *Soldiers Died in the Great War* (SDGW), the first official Welsh casualties occurred on 5 August 1914 when two men of the 4th RWF – Private Caradog Pritchard (6850) of Rhosddu, Denbigh and Private Bertie Price (7255) of Rhosllanerchrugog, Denbigh – died.

However, Caradog Pritchard, a 26-year-old collier from Park Street, Rhosddu was in fact killed in an accident at Gresford Colliery on 11 April 1914 and is buried in Wrexham Cemetery. According to a contemporary news report he was engaged as an onsetter near the pit bottom and appeared to have taken out the locks from the wheels of the first four full tubs. When eight other full tubs came against the four that he was attempting to hold back they overpowered him and he was crushed against the cage, which in the meantime had descended behind him. The young man was a well-known footballer and on the day before the accident took part as goalkeeper of the Wrexham Wednesday Club in the final tie for the Denbighshire Wednesday Cup against Buckley.

Herbert 'Bertie' Price, a 20-year-old waggoner from Hall Street, Rhos was also killed in an accident at the nearby Hafod Colliery. He was leading a pit pony taking a full tub of coal from an underground seam on 28 May 1914 when the roof collapsed upon him and the pony, killing Price instantly.

Why these men are commemorated on *SDGW* as having died on 5 August 1914 remains a mystery.

Therefore, first Welsh casualties of the Great War occurred on 6 August 1914. In 1910 the Royal Naval Dockyard at Pembroke Dock received an order for an *Active-*class scout cruiser. The ship, HMS *Amphion*, was launched on 4 December 1911 and commissioned on 2 April 1913, joining the 4th Battle Cruiser Squadron of the First Fleet. By the outbreak of war *Amphion* was serving as the flotilla leader of the 3rd Destroyer Flotilla and was assigned to the Harwich Force, defending the eastern approaches to the English Channel, under the command of Captain Cecil H. Fox. During the morning of 5 August the 3rd Flotilla steamed into the North Sea to patrol the area between Harwich and the Dutch island of Terschelling. During the morning a ship was spotted throwing items overboard. *Amphion* steamed towards the ship and saw that these objects being dropped were mines. The ship was the German vessel SS *Königin Luise*, which had been converted by them for minesweeping duties. The British force fired several salvoes at the German boat, which began to sink and the British stopped to pick up survivors. While returning to Harwich *Amphion* struck one of the mines, which detonated beneath her bridge and led to her forward magazine exploding before she sank.

One officer and 131 ratings were killed, including at least seven Welshmen, all but one of whom is commemorated on the Plymouth Naval Memorial: Chief Stoker William Bowen (276237) of Carmarthen; Petty Officer Stoker Alfred Ernest Simmonds (289127) of Pembroke Dock; Leading Seaman David Craig (161407) of St Dogmaels; Leading Stoker William John Hughes (286027) of Chepstow; 1st Class Stokers Albert Martin (K/9641) of Milford Haven; James Henry Skyrme (296150) of Llangwm; and William Welton (K/16747) of Cardiff. The only one of these men with a known grave is Albert Martin, whose body was recovered and buried in St Mary's Cemetery, Shotley, Suffolk.

Within a week of mobilization the three Welsh front-line battalions in Britain had moved to the south coast and on 13 August the 1st SWB and 2nd Welsh disembarked in France. The 2nd RWF had embarked from Southampton at 2 pm on 10 August and landed at Rouen the following day, where it was put to work as Lines of Communications troops. These three battalions thus became the first Welsh units to arrive on the Western Front and men in both units mentioned the language barrier being overcome by an old soldier (Frank Richards) having a fluent mixture of Hindustani, Welsh and coarse language!

The grave marker of 1st Class Stoker Albert Martin in St Mary's Cemetery, Shotley, Suffolk.

While the BEF was assembling in France, a well-known sportsman, Major Arthur Hughes-Onslow, of Linda Vista, Abergavenny became the first Welsh casualty of the war in France when he died at Le Havre on 17 August. Hughes-Onslow was born on 24 August 1862 and was commissioned in the 10th Hussars, serving in Sudan and India for several years. He was a renowned horseman and won the Grand Military Gold Cup at Sandown in 1888, subsequently winning it twice more. He had served with his regiment during the Boer War of 1899–1902, where he commanded A and B Troops, surviving a shipwreck before falling ill and returning to England in July 1900. In 1902 he retired from the army and pursued a successful horse-racing career, gaining several victories in Britain and Ireland. He volunteered to rejoin the army at the outbreak of war and embarked for France to command the Army Remount Depot in Le Havre. For reasons known only to himself, while aboard the transport ship SS *City of Edinburgh*, on 17 August Hughes-Onslow shot himself dead. The 51-year-old is buried in Ste. Marie Cemetery, Le Havre.

Back in Wales a wave of khaki had spread over the country. The garrison town of Pembroke Dock, due to its strategic importance, was packed with troops of several units: the Heavy & Siege Signals Training Centre Royal Artillery formed at Pembroke Dock; 3rd (Reserve) Battalion, King's Liverpool Regiment; 2nd Battalion, Border Regiment; 1st, 2nd and 3rd Battalions, the Monmouthshire Regiment; 1st Battalion, Hereford Regiment; 3rd (Reserve) Battalion, Royal Welsh Fusiliers; 3rd (Reserve) Battalion and the 9th (Service) Battalion, King's Shropshire Light Infantry; 1st and 3rd (Brecknockshire) Battalions, South Wales Borderers; 3rd and 9th (Reserve) Battalions, South Wales Borderers; the 44th and 57th companies, Royal Garrison Artillery; 16th and 19th Siege Batteries, Royal Garrison Artillery; Pembrokeshire Royal Garrison Artillery; Cardiganshire Battery, Royal Field Artillery; and elements of the 4th, 5th and 7th Battalions, Welsh Regiment were among the units that moved to the town during August 1914 prior to being posted elsewhere.

Throughout Wales the local Territorial and Yeomanry units assembled after receiving orders on 4 August. The Territorial battalions are dealt with in a later chapter that covers the raising of the two Welsh divisions. The Yeomanry regiments consisted of four squadrons each and were distributed as follows:

Welsh Border Mounted Brigade
Shropshire Yeomanry: A Squadron at Shrewsbury; B Squadron at Oswestry; C Squadron at Ludlow; D Squadron at Wellington.
Cheshire Yeomanry: A Squadron at Knutsford; B Squadron at Eaton; C Squadron at Northwich; D Squadron at Macclesfield.
Denbighshire (Hussars) Yeomanry: A Squadron at Wrexham; B Squadron at Denbigh; C Squadron at Bangor; D Squadron at Birkenhead.
Brigade troops: Shropshire RHA, Shrewsbury; Ammunition Column, Church Stretton; Transport and Supply Column, ASC, Chester; Field Ambulance, RAMC, Chester.
South Wales Mounted Brigade
Pembroke Yeomanry: A Squadron at Tenby; B Squadron at Haverfordwest; C Squadron at Carmarthen; D Squadron at Lampeter.
Montgomeryshire Yeomanry: A Squadron at Llanfyllin; B Squadron at Welshpool; C Squadron at Newtown; D Squadron at Llandrindod Wells.
Glamorganshire Yeomanry: A Squadron at Swansea; B Squadron at Bridgend; C Squadron at Cardiff; D Squadron at Pontypridd.

Brigade troops: Glamorganshire RHA, Port Talbot; Ammunition Column, Port Talbot; Transport and Supply Column, ASC, Swansea; Field Ambulance, RAMC, Hereford.

Meanwhile, other reserve units, many of which were still taking part in their summer camps, also began to mobilize:

The Welsh (Caernarfonshire) RGA Heavy Batteries whose headquarters are at Bangor (the right section, by the way, is stationed at Bangor, the left section at Caernarfon and the ammunition column at Llandudno), have been embodied and posted to the station allotted to them for home defence. The order to mobilise was received at 5.30 pm on Tuesday, August 4, the operations necessary to carry out the order were immediately initiated and the troops fell in at 7 am on Wednesday. Whilst the stores were being collected and packed, Captain Savage, as the official purchasing officer, was busy buying horses, waggons and harness and with such success was the whole work carried on, that the battery was able to start from Bangor to the minute of the time laid down in the mobilisation scheme... A message was received from headquarters asking what percentage of the men would volunteer for service abroad. Steps were taken at once to ascertain this, with the result that practically the whole battery has volunteered.

The men of the Royal Anglesey Royal Engineers Special Reserve, who disbanded on Saturday, have all too soon been recalled for real service. Mobilisation commenced immediately on the issue of the Royal Proclamation. The men made a ready response to the call. Accommodation was found for them, in the various public buildings in the town. Several young townsmen, members of the Denbighshire Hussars Yeomanry, also left for the depot at Bangor on Wednesday morning. (*North Wales Chronicle*, 7 August 1914.)

Within weeks of mobilization the Yeomanry units moved via Hereford to Suffolk (Welsh Border Mounted Brigade) and Norfolk (South Wales Mounted Brigade) to guard the coast against enemy invasion. Their time for glory would really come in Palestine in 1917, but some of the Yeomanry units would also take part in the Gallipoli campaign in 1915.

While the majority of people were concerned about the men leaving for war, the departure of the Yeomanry led to other concerns in some parts of Wales:

From all over the country comes news of the interruption to hunting which is likely to result from the war. Yeomanry officers have been warned for active service and hunters in many districts have been commandeered, while apart from these considerations few members of the hunting world would like to persevere with sport while the nation has such serious business in hand. We have not heard how it will affect the local hunt, but if the War proves a protracted one it is improbable that our hounds will be seen in the field. (*Haverfordwest and Milford Haven Telegraph*, 12 August 1914.)

The Territorial battalions throughout Wales also began their mobilization:

> The North Wales Infantry Brigade camp at Aberystwyth was broken up on Monday. At 6.15 in the morning the troops received orders to break up their camp, return all stores and ordnance and proceed to their peace headquarters forthwith. Under ordinary circumstances the camp would not have concluded until Saturday next. However, in view of the gravity of affairs and the rate at which events were moving, the military authorities decided to break up all Territorial camps. The news travelled round the camp at once and aroused intense interest, the uppermost feeling in the minds of all – officers and men alike – being one of enthusiasm at the prospect of being called up for service... A large number of Reservists who had just arrived at Nevin, Morfa Nevin, Abersoch, Pwllheli, Criccieth and Portmadoc for a holiday were called to the colours on Tuesday and left on Wednesday... The Pwllheli Territorials were ordered to Chatham on Wednesday and the Portmadoc Territorials to Caernarfon... On Wednesday the police authorities at Pwllheli and Portmadoc were searching for the members of the old Volunteer Corps. According to some reports these retired volunteers, if under a certain age, are to be called out to join the Territorial Forces. (*North Wales Chronicle*, 7 August 1914.)

Royal Naval and Marine Reservists had also been recalled, with many Welsh sailors entraining for Pembroke Dock to join their ships. Stationed with the 3rd Fleet at Pembroke Dock were the pre-dreadnought battleships HMS *Ocean*, HMS *Goliath*, HMS *Albion*, HMS *Jupiter*, HMS *Canopus* and the cruiser HMS *Terrible*. Each ship had been crewed by a skeleton staff, but within days of the outbreak of war had taken aboard thousands of sailors between them (700–800 men per battleship). *Goliath* and *Ocean* would be lost in tragic circumstances off Gallipoli within months. Across the Haven the townspeople of Milford were saddened to see many of their men steam away in their trawlers, a large number of which had been requisitioned by the Admiralty for conversion to minesweepers, mine-layers and (later in the war) decoy Q-ships. Many of these men were also Royal Naval Reservists and would perform some terrific acts of bravery in their small vessels during the course of the war.

In fact the number of reservists was so great that the Admiralty decided to form the excess number into battalions to fight on land. These battalions were originally named after one of the major naval depot ports: Chatham, Portsmouth, Plymouth and Deal. Winston Churchill then decided to embody two more naval brigades with surplus Naval Reservists to join with the Royal Marine Brigade to produce a Royal Naval Division. A few petty officers and ratings were transferred from the navy to provide a cadre and some officers were provided by the army; but most of the recruits were reservists or men who had volunteered on the outbreak of war. The eight battalions were named after naval commanders: Drake, Benbow, Hawke, Collingwood, Nelson, Howe, Hood and Anson. Men of the Welsh Division of the Royal Naval Reserve and Royal Naval Volunteer Reserve were conspicuous by the prefix to their service numbers, 'Wales Z/'; well over 200 of these men would be killed during the course of the war.

While recruiting in Wales was going well, many people around the country felt that not enough of their menfolk were stepping forward to serve their nation. Open letters appeared in many newspapers around Wales during the weeks following the declaration of war, such as the following in the *North Wales Chronicle* of 4 September 1914:

> Sir, The heavy toll of war is being too sadly levied at the front, but where is the esprit de corps, the patriotism and the sense of duty of the youth living in the northern counties of Wales? Why cannot they emulate the miners of Cardiff or the yeomanry of Montgomeryshire, who have volunteered to a man for active service? What are the hundreds of Caernarfonshire quarry men doing, only able to work half-time? What about the idlers along our coast apparently reaping an easy harvest out of a belated tourist season? What about the able-bodied country-youths inland with a harvest being swiftly garnered? What about the members of Parliament for North Wales, can they not rouse some sense of patriotism in their various constituencies? Where are the ministers of religion of all denominations, who could be preaching on odd occasions the duty of encouraging the weak and of the honour of our country? Perhaps they have all had sedative draughts administered to them by the Germans and are awaiting a clarion call in the shape of a Zeppelin dropping bombs in our midst. Apparently they are not ashamed by the stalwart Canadian men. Will not the young men recruit as fast as they can and wipe out the disgrace that would other-wise be written in the annals of these parts? They have forgotten how their forefathers poured their hordes down our peaceful mountain sides to withstand for generations the far stronger hosts of the English from the East. I am a great lover of peace and am not a suffragette, but I blush for my countrymen and am forced to subscribe myself – a disgusted and disappointed WELSH WOMAN.

Another rousing letter was published in the *Carmarthen Journal* of 9 September 1914, written by Major Delmé Davies-Evans of the Pembroke Yeomanry:

> Sir, I appeal to the young men in the agricultural districts of West Wales to come forward more readily as recruits for the Pembroke Yeomanry. I have spent a week doing my best to get recruits and I can only say, with deep regret, that the response has been most disheartening. There are scores of young men who ought to come forward willingly unless they wish to be forever branded as cowards. Is it possible that young Welshmen in the agricultural districts are going to refuse to come to their country's help, when thousands of men from India, Canada, Australia, New Zealand and all other colonies are volunteering so readily? For the honour of Wales do not let it be said that our young men are afraid. If we

look through the recruiting returns for West Wales, we find a higher percentage is made up of the English boys, who have been working on the Welsh farms. More honour to them! Is this as it ought to be? Is the old Welsh spirit dead? Are Welshmen in the agricultural districts going to stand by and do nothing?

Indeed, certain areas of Wales did seem to suffer from a lack of patriotism as far as volunteering for service was concerned. Although there was some lack of response in Pembrokeshire and Carmarthenshire, the men of Cardiganshire did not seem so hesitant, while industrial areas in south Wales like Port Talbot, Swansea, Llanelli, Cardiff and the valleys saw floods of men rushing to enlist. This was perhaps due to the fact that life was extremely difficult for those working in industry and the thought of life in the army was not such a frightening prospect compared to leaving a more idyllic, yet still hard-working country lifestyle. In North Wales it appears that the men of Denbighshire enlisted in great numbers yet, as the letter above states, the quarrymen were slower to enlist. Some of this apathy was credited to the Welsh Baptist ministers who were reluctant to press their congregations to enlist for war, yet many other church leaders worked hard to aid recruitment throughout the country. Many men of the cloth had also felt the sense of patriotism deeply, leading to a crisis in the Welsh Anglican Church due to the large numbers of ministers volunteering to serve as chaplains and even in the ranks. Reverend Alfred George Edwards, the Bishop of St Asaph, was among the first to volunteer for service, becoming chaplain to the Denbighshire Yeomanry, while at least two of his sons also gained commissions into the army and would later die as a result of the war. Reverend John Owen, the Bishop of St David's, saw several of his nephews join the colours, some of whom would also fall in battle.

While the entire country was in the grip of this recruiting frenzy, the regular troops were about to make their move to France.

Chapter 2

The Battle of Mons and the Retreat from Mons

After moving to France the elements of the BEF, comprising around 80,000 men and 300 guns under the command of Sir John French, entrained for Leschelles before marching to Étreux, splitting into two corps. The men marched the final 20 miles to the Belgian city of Mons by 22 August, taking up defensive positions along the Mons-Condé Canal and the River Sambre. The French were on their right flank on a front north of the town of Maubeuge and covered the front from there to the border. The 1st Division, with the 1st SWB and 2nd Welsh, was positioned south-east of Mons around the village of Givry as part of I Corps under the command of Sir Douglas Haig, while II Corps was on the banks of the canal due south of Mons under Sir Horace Smith-Dorrien.

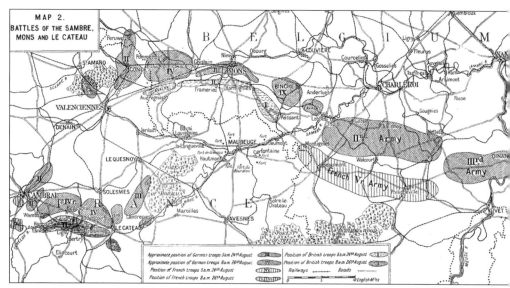

Map showing the dispositions of the armies between 21 and 23 August 1914 on the Franco-Belgian border.

Advancing towards the British was the German First Army under Alexander von Kluck, which comprised 160,000 men and 600 guns (these guns were mostly the

Nimy Bridge, the defence of which resulted in the award of the first two Victoria Crosses of the Great War.

lightweight 13-pdr and the standard 18-pdr artillery pieces), and the scene was set for the first major engagement that the British army would be involved in during the Great War.

While the BEF was digging in, the Germans attacked the French across the River Sambre, while British cavalry took part in the fighting by the BEF on 22 August when the 4th Dragoons attacked a numerically-superior force of German lancers. (The first minor engagement had been a day earlier, when Private John Parr of the Middlesex Regiment became the first British combat casualty of the war.)

At dawn on 23 August the Germans attacked the BEF under an artillery bombardment, sending men against each of the four bridges over the canal. During the fierce fighting that followed, the first two Victoria Crosses of the Great War were won by Lieutenant Maurice Dease and Private Sidney Godley of the Middlesex while defending Nimy Bridge. Dease was mortally wounded during the action and his VC was awarded posthumously.

Although the BEF put up a good fight, with the well-drilled soldiers using their .303" Lee Enfield rifles to good effect, the Germans had superiority in numbers and, after suffering heavy casualties, at 3 pm were unexpectedly ordered to retreat. Neither the 1st SWB nor 2nd Welsh had been directly involved in the Battle of Mons as I Corps had only been faced by German cavalry, but both battalions were now in retreat along with the remainder of I Corps and the rest of 23 August was spent marching to what was thought to be a new defensive line. The flanking French were already in retreat. Captain Hubert Conway Rees of the 2nd Welsh wrote in his diary:

> Melville with one machine gun was posted on the railway line to sweep with his gun the approaches from Merbes St Marie (i.e. E. towards the gap between the B.E.F. and the French). We had a very disturbed night, having at the most three-quarters of an hour's sleep on the track. On three occasions during the night did the German Army open rifle fire. It appeared as if tens of thousands of men were all firing as fast as they could. They could not have been very far away as a few, very much spent, bullets reached us.

Captain (later Major) Hubert Charles Rees of the 2nd Welsh.

> 24th August. In addition to the cannonade from Mons a still heavier roar of firing began at dawn about the outskirts of Charleroi and the French were steadily driven back, as far as we could judge, through Merbes St Marie on Merbes Le Chateau. By 9 am we seemed to run the risk of being cut off. About 9.30 am we got orders to retire on Croix and Rouveroy and at the same moment a German cavalry patrol appeared from the Bees (Bois) Houdiez (about 1,000 yards distant). When we had quite decided they were really Germans a section opened fire and brought down the whole patrol, both men and horses.

Among the first Welshmen to fall in France, although three Welshmen had been killed at Mons on the previous day, was Alban Henry Gaunt, a driver with the Army Service Corps and a well-known man throughout south Wales, who was killed at Le Cateau. He was the son of George and Harriet Gaunt of Burton Joyce, Notts. He resided at Haverfordwest prior to 1907 and married Jessie Evelina John in 1907. The couple then spent periods living at Skewen, Coedfranc, Swansea and Llanelli prior to the outbreak of war due to his work as a driver for Buckley's Brewery. When war erupted, Gaunt enlisted at Llanelli as a driver with the Base MT (Mechanical Transport) Depot, Army Service Corps and most probably drove one of the Buckley's Brewery trucks that had been requisitioned by the army for use by the BEF. Jessie moved with their children to the Bull Inn at Prendergast, Haverfordwest, to be back with her family. Henry moved to France with the BEF and was wounded by shell fragments at Mons. He died of wounds on 24 August 1914, aged 28. Gaunt was buried where he fell on the battlefield, but his body was lost and so he is today commemorated on the La Ferté-sous-Jouarre Memorial in France and on the Felinfoel War Memorial in Wales. His wife was informed of his death by telegram on 28 August. Two days later she was shocked to receive his last letter home:

British troops had a splendid reception all along the route. The French people gave us almost everything. We had fruit in abundance and really, I am almost getting tired of it... The French make a tremendous fuss of us and it is surprising where all the food and cider comes from. We had as many as four bottles in the car at a time. The dust on the roads is chronic and we look more millers than car drivers at the end of a day's journey. It is very exciting. How are the little children getting on? Do they call for dad now? Every little child I see brings back to me memories of home and I am thinking about all of you in all my spare moments. I am praying to God to grant us a speedy return to England, home and beauty, for, after all, there is no place like home.

Driver Alban Henry Gaunt, a brewery worker from Llanelli.

As well as the awards of the VC to Godley and Dease on the opening day of the battle, on the following day an officer of Welsh heritage, well-known in Swansea, gained his own award of the coveted Victoria Cross.

Captain Francis Octavius Grenfell was born on 4 September 1880, the twin brother of Riversdale Nonus Grenfell and the eighth son of Pascoe Du Pré Grenfell and Sophia Grenfell. He was the grandson of Pascoe St Leger Grenfell, a wealthy industrialist and philanthropist from Swansea, who later became Baron Grenfell. The twin brothers had spent large parts of their childhood at Merthyr House, Swansea prior to being educated at Eton and went their separate ways afterwards. Francis was commissioned in the Seaforth Highlanders on 13 December 1899. He served with the regiment during the Boer War and in 1905 transferred to the 9th (Queen's Royal) Lancers, embarking for France with the regiment in August 1914. On 24 August Grenfell's regiment charged a large body of German infantry in an effort to check their advance against the 5th Division. His CO was killed in the charge, so Grenfell assumed command of the survivors, continuing the charge before volunteering to assist in the withdrawal of field guns belonging to the 119th Battery, Royal Field Artillery (RFA).

For his gallant work throughout the day, Grenfell was awarded the VC. The citation was published in the *London Gazette* of 16 September 1914 and read: 'For gallantry in action against unbroken infantry at Andregnies, Belgium, on 24th August 1914 and for gallant conduct in assisting to save the guns of the 119th Battery, Royal Field Artillery, near Doubon the same day.'

Grenfell continued to fight bravely with the regiment until his death at Ypres on 24 May 1915 and is buried in Vlamertinghe Military Cemetery. His twin brother, Captain Riversdale Nonus Grenfell of the same regiment, was killed at Vendresse on 14 September 1914 and is buried in the churchyard there. Two older brothers, Pascoe and Robert, had been killed in earlier wars.

A Welsh soldier, Private William Bryan, fought under Grenfell during the action and related his experiences to a reporter while at home at 24 Silver Terrace, Burry Port, recovering from wounds:

Captain Grenfell was in charge of four squadrons of 120 men each. Fighting had been going on from Sunday till Wednesday, and we must have been outnumbered by at least three to one. On the fourth day the squadron, to which I had the honour and privilege of belonging, first received orders to dismount and fill up the trenches, but afterwards we were ordered to re-mount and charge right across the German guns in order to allow our infantry to retire. Captain Grenfell, whose heroism made the pulse beat quicker and the heart throb faster, shouted: 'Go down on your knees and pray before God, as I do not know whether I can bring you back again, but for the honour of our country we must make this charge.'

There was no time for praying, so we rushed off straight away, and we were only too glad to get at the Germans. We fought left and right with sword, sabre and lance. The scene was too fearful to describe and I would rather try to forget it.

Captain Grenfell was galloping in front of the 'A' Squadron when two of his fingers were shot off, and both his legs wounded, but that was not the time to falter, and like a great hero he led us on. 'Come on!' he shouted with indomitable pluck and courage: 'we must win here. Remember that our country is threatened with destruction. I am myself badly wounded, and I cannot say whether I can bring you back, but whatever befalls us we must think of the honour and glory of dear old England.' He nobly led us through that charge. We got lost and when the roll was called only twenty out of the 120 answered. All the seventy were wounded in that terrible charge, and the others were missing. We retired to Compiegne and were eventually sent from Amiens to Forgesleau, where we rested for a short time... While we were proceeding from Amiens to Rouen my thoughts were turned to Llanelly by seeing one of Buckley's motor lorries which had been commandeered by the Government at the outbreak of the war. Among those who accompanied me in a railway Carriage was one of the Turcos, wearing baggy trousers and a red cap. As a prize of war he proudly carried the head of a Uhlan, which he had severed from the body. On the head was a helmet with the chain and strap around the chin.

The retreat of the BEF, later known as 'the Great Retreat' or 'the Retreat from Mons', continued over the coming days, with the 1st SWB and 2nd Welsh crossing the River Sambre above Maubeuge on the 25th and the Germans following closely behind. The withdrawal so far was not without incident, as noted by Captain Rees:

The artillery fire was only a distant matter of sound and I don't imagine anyone was considering the possibility of being attacked. The pandemonium, which ensued when a sharp rattle of musketry broke out from the Queen's, beggars description. The Frenchmen leapt on their horses bareback, firing their pistols, a bolting two-horsed limber charged down the road and all the men scrambled over the hedges to get out of its way, whilst a 60-pounder Battery somehow got off the road into action and opened fire at a range of 800 yards on a herd of frightened cows, which were mistaken in the dusk for a Battery of German artillery coming into action.

The retreat saw the death of one of the first members of the Welsh aristocracy to be lost during the war, who was also the first top-class cricketer to be killed. The Honourable Archer Windsor-Clive was born at Hewell Grange, Redditch, Worcestershire on 6 November 1890, the son of Robert Clive, 1st Earl of Plymouth and Viscount Windsor, of St Fagans. Windsor-Clive spent the summers of his early years living in St Fagans Castle (now the home of the National Museum of Wales) before being educated at Eton and at Trinity College, Cambridge. He was a talented cricketer and made his debut for the Eton XI in 1907 and later played for his university side, the Glamorgan county team and the village team at St Fagans. Upon leaving Cambridge, he gained a commission in the Coldstream Guards on 8 September 1911.

Lieutenant the Honourable Archer Windsor-Clive, 3rd Battalion, Coldstream Guards.

Windsor-Clive embarked for France with the 3rd Battalion, Coldstream Guards on 13 August 1914. The battalion was attached to 4 (Guards) Brigade, 2nd Division and had taken part in the Battle of Mons before joining the great retreat. On 25 August 4 (Guards) Brigade was ordered to make a stand at the town of Landrecies in order to stem the advance of the Germans and allow the remainder of the BEF to continue its retreat. During the late evening sentries of the battalion spotted an officer appearing in French uniform, who informed them that a column of French troops was approaching and not to fire upon their allies. It was a devious trick: as the column, the front rows dressed in a mixture of French and Belgian uniforms, appeared, they spread out and opened fire on the Coldstream Guards, supported by artillery fire, and inflicted a number of casualties on the surprised battalion. Windsor-Clive was reportedly killed by shell fragments during the engagement. The 20-year-old officer was buried by the Germans in Landrecies Communal Cemetery, where he lies today.

Another Welshman, Sergeant Whittaker of Brecon, was serving with the Lancashire Fusiliers during the retreat and spoke of his experience of the retirement while back in hospital in England:

A little later I was wounded in the head, and the Germans being now only about 200 yards away and our ammunition being pretty nearly all gone, I gave the order to retire. While we were retiring I was knocked down by a second bullet in the head, and this left me practically unconscious for a short time. When I came round I scrambled on hands and knees through several turnip fields, with a few more wounded men, until we came across some soldiers, who directed us to the field hospital. I had lost my cap, which a bullet had sent flying, and some of my tackle. Whilst we were crawling along a lane in search of the hospital, to our surprise there came a shower of bullets, but we took cover, and were not further molested. By this time we had lost all trace of the remainder of the regiment, and after a dreary march across rough country we came to a first-class road. Here we met a mechanical transport waggon and were conveyed on this to the base hospital, which we reached after riding through the whole of the afternoon and night.

The two corps of the BEF had split either side of the mighty Forest of Mormal, intending to reform south of the forest; however, II Corps had been forced into a shorter march than I Corps and reached Le Cateau on 24 August while I Corps was still some miles away, so Smith-Dorrien ordered his men to make a stand. On the morning of 26 August the Germans attacked Le Cateau. The BEF again put up a stout resistance they were forced to withdraw after suffering heavy casualties and losing a number of their guns. The German advance had been temporarily halted but soon began again.

A view inside the imposing Forest of Morma; the BEF was split in two by the Great Retreat from Mons.

Gunner William Roy Davies (69890) of Derri Mountain, Abergavenny later told of his experiences while fighting with the 121st Battery, Royal Field Artillery (27th Brigade) at Le Cateau:

We came into action about 9 o'clock on Sunday morning, August 23rd, and we had a pretty rough time of it. We were fighting till about three o'clock in the afternoon, when the order came to retire, and so we retired – but at what a cost. The Germans were following us up and were shelling both our troops and the town continually. We retired all that night and until Tuesday evening. On Wednesday morning we came into action again at Le Cateau, and we fought there from 9 till half-past 12. The order again came to retire, but the 121st Battery did not get the word until half an hour later, when a Major came galloping up with instructions. We had four German maxim guns on us and about 2,000 infantry. The German marksmanship was so poor, however, that when the horses came up to take our guns away there was not a gun or a horse hit, except my own. I felt my horse going from me, and I flung myself clear. Seeing that my only chance of escape was in going across two fields and making for cover, I ran as hard as I could under a perfect hail of shot from maxims and bullets from rifle fire. My hat was knocked off with a bullet, and my great coat was riddled with bullets. I got behind cover and was walking along the road, thinking there was no danger, when two maxim guns again opened fire. There was no-one about but myself. Naturally, I ran as hard as I could. I got into the main street, and heard someone shouting 'Get up.' There was a limber waggon coming along, and I scrambled on the top.

Meanwhile I Corps had retreated south and east of the Forest of Mormal through Landrecies and was passing southwards in earshot of the fighting at Le Cateau. A gallant rearguard action by the 2nd Battalion, Royal Munster Fusiliers on 27 August at Étreux prevented I Corps from coming under attack, but the Munsters were almost wiped out. Rations had been dumped by the roadside for the men, who loaded themselves up with tins of hard tack biscuits, bully beef, Oxo, cheese, jam, sugar and bacon, but as the day drew on C.S.M. Joshua of 2nd Welsh noticed that this bounty was slowly being dropped on the roadside by the tiring men. The 1st SWB were ordered to take up positions on high ground south-west of the village of Iron while the remainder of I Corps marched on, falling in to the rear once the bulk of the troops had passed.

In the meantime the 2nd RWF had been enjoying a warm French welcome at Rouen and had acted as a guard of honour after the death of the original commander of II Corps, Lieutenant General James Grierson, who had died of heart failure near Amiens on 17 August, as well as attending the burial in St Acheul Cemetery of two British airmen who had crashed near Amiens on 16 August (Air Mechanic Herbert Edward Parfitt and Second Lieutenant Evelyn Copland Walter Perry, the first British officer killed on active service). The battalion was then despatched to join the BEF, joining the forces at Le Cateau, after merging with the 1st Middlesex, 1st Cameronians and

An isolated grave on the 1914 battlefield, with a ruined farmhouse on the horizon.

the 2nd Argyll and Sutherland Highlanders to form 19 Brigade. Frank Richards wrote of their arrival at Le Cateau:

> We arrived in Le Cateau about midnight, dead-beat to the world. I don't believe any one of us at this time realized that we were retiring, though it was clear that we were not going in the direction of Germany. Of course the officers knew, but they were telling us that we were drawing the enemy into a trap. Le Cateau that night presented a strange sight. Everyone was in a panic, packing up their stuff on carts and barrows to get away south in time. The Royal Welch [sic] camped on the square in the centre of the town. We were told to get as much rest as we could. The majority sank down where they were and fell straight asleep. Although dead beat, Billy, Stevens and I went on the scrounge for food and drink. We entered a café, where there were a lot of officers of other battalions, besides a couple of staff officers, mixed up with ordinary troops, all buying food and drink. For three days officers and men had been on short rations. This was the only time during the whole of the War that I saw officers and men buying food and drink in the same café. I slept the sleep of the just that night, for about three hours. I could have done with forty-three, but we were roused up at 4 a.m. and ordered to leave our packs and greatcoats on the square... Everyone was glad when that order was issued; the only things we had to carry now, besides rifle and ammunition, were an extra pair of socks and our iron rations which consisted of four army biscuits, a pound tin of bully beef, and a small quantity of tea and sugar. Iron rations were carried in case of emergency but were never supposed

to be used unless orders came from our superior officers. Haversacks were now strapped on our shoulders and each man was issued with another fifty rounds of ammunition, which made two hundred and fifty rounds to carry.

Within weeks of the outbreak of war the first three Welsh infantry battalions to move to France were finally together, taking part in the retirement from Mons. There were several brief engagements during the coming days: all the Welsh units encountered German cavalry patrols at some point, leading to exchanges of fire, while men from all the regiments noted the pitiful plight of French refugees fleeing from the battle area.

On 26 August the 1st SWB lost their first man killed in France, 26-year-old Lance Corporal Robert Mayersbeth (9857) of Lambeth. His grave was lost during the war and Mayersbeth is commemorated on the La Ferté-sous-Jouarre Memorial. (His brother Joseph was killed while serving as a captain in the 48th Battalion, Australian Imperial Force (AIF) at Ypres in 1917.)

The Germans had fallen behind by now: von Kluck had moved his army south-west, mistakingly thinking that this was the direction of the BEF's retreat, so 29 August saw the men take a day's welcome rest from the hot march when it was realized that the Germans were some way distant. General Joffre, the French commander in chief, had been planning an attack on the Germans but, realizing that the BEF had moved too far south, decided on a withdrawal to the south banks of the River Marne. The 1st SWB reached Bertaucourt via La Fère by 29 August and Lieutenant Colonel Collier wrote in the battalion War Diary:

A rest day and we need it. Men are able to get a wash and air their clothes and lie down and sleep in barns though all roads are picketed... Orders come at 11 pm to say that our retirement shall continue. This is sickening news; we were all hoping that at last we shall turn about and go for the enemy.

The consensus among all of the men in the BEF, especially those men of I Corps who had not yet seen proper action, was overwhelming: they were getting disheartened by this constant retreat and wanted to stand and fight. Their chance to prove themselves would soon come. (The retreat to the Marne, where the allies would eventually make a stand, took several further days and 200 miles in total and included several minor actions, notably St Quentin and the Affairs at Cérizy and at Néry, the latter the gallant stands of the 1st Cavalry Brigade and of the Royal Horse Artillery, but these three Welsh units saw little more than the odd skirmish during the retreat.)

The BEF crossed the Marne on 3 September and on the following day received orders to stand firm after thirteen days of retreat and to be ready for an attack in conjunction with the French. Within days the first batches of reserves were reaching the front, to take the places of men who had fallen by the wayside during the march. (Casualties had not been very heavy, except many men taken prisoner at Le Cateau; whilst numbers of men had fallen behind on the march and were captured by the Germans.)

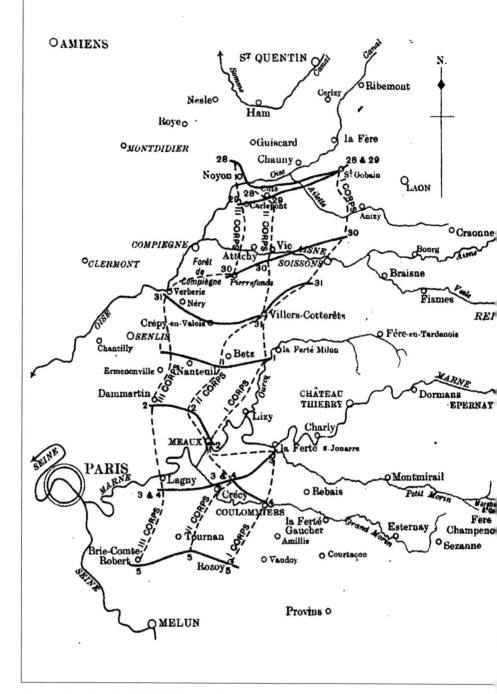

A map taken from the Official History *showing the retreat of the BEF from 28 August until 5 September 1914.*

A draft for the 2nd Welsh leaves Cardiff in November 1914.

One Welshman who was serving with the 1st Battalion, Duke of Cornwall's Light Infantry during the retreat, Private Daniel Moriarty (7831) of Ammanford, had just arrived home after being wounded at Mons. An issue of the *Amman Valley Chronicle* wrote of his experience:

> Private D. Moriarty, of the Duke of Cornwall's Light Infantry, who has been invalided home at Ammanford, is a hero of the Battle of Mons and is now rapidly recovering from shell wounds in both legs and will this week again be ready for service. Moriarty, it may be mentioned, had experience of active service in the South African war, but the fighting there (he says) pales into insignificance compared to the Battle of Mons. The horrors which he there witnessed weighed upon him like a nightmare. The German artillery wrought havoc upon his regiment and no less than 600 of them, he computes, were mowed down within an hour. The roar of the cannon and the screaming overhead of the shells made the scene indescribable. It was hellish. Nevertheless, he is anxious to get at 'em again.

Another Welshman, Lance Corporal Stanley Thomas, 1st SWB, of Pontycymmer, was scathing about the behaviour of the Germans:

> We entered Mons just in the nick of time. A regiment of Uhlans were attacking the rear of a convoy and we soon got to work, hundreds of Germans being killed by the fire of our artillery at close range. We found that they had been looting

our dead and some of the dead Germans wore our khaki, with full equipment. The next day we were relieved by the South Lancashires and it was officially reported to us that we had not been relieved more than two hours before the enemy were all shelled to pieces, hardly any escaping. After that we were caught in a death trap. We got into a village and we were surrounded by a brigade of Uhlans, but we were saved by the timely arrival of the Scots Greys and the 1st Lancers, who put about 1,500 out of mess in six hours, charging them through and through... Of course, we were not losing one-sixth of what the Germans were. But I will never forget it. The Germans came so unexpectedly. Whilst we guarded the right flank, the Guards charged the centre square, killing about 850 in ten minutes. The Germans don't like cold steel. They were falling on their knees and praying, but our blood boiled at the way they were treating the civilians and we had no mercy. The Germans are worse than brutes. After wounding a soldier, if he was unable to get up again, they would all make a stab at him as they passed. That's the German way... I have done my best to sweep as many Germans as I can off the face of the earth, but they very nearly swept me off. However, I am longing for the time when I will be well enough to have another pop at them. (The *Glamorgan Gazette*, 18 September 1914.)

Chapter 3

The Home Front and the Expansion of the Army

While the BEF was preparing to make its stand on the Marne, back in Wales the expansion of the armed forces was in full swing and the civilian population was also beginning to react. One of the main developments in Wales at this time was the obvious need to cater for what could be a large number of casualties returning home for medical care. Members of the St John's Ambulance Brigade in Wales received orders for mobilization on 6 August and during the first few days of war local detachments of the Red Cross had also mobilized around the country. Dozens of auxiliary hospitals, staffed by many members of the Red Cross, began to be set up to run in conjunction with existing civilian and military hospitals. They included the following:

Anglesey: Beach Auxiliary Hospital, Holyhead; Holborn Auxiliary Hospital, Holyhead; Bodlondeb Auxiliary Hospital, Menai Bridge Road, Bangor; Darien Auxiliary Hospital, Trearddur Bay, near Holyhead; Hill Auxiliary Hospital, Holyhead; Isallt Fawr Auxiliary Hospital, Trearddur Bay, near Holyhead; Bungalow Auxiliary Hospital, Trearddur Bay, near Holyhead.

Breconshire: Red Cross Auxiliary Hospital, Builth Wells; Llyswen Auxiliary Hospital, Penoyre, Brecon.

Caernarfonshire: Plas VAD Auxiliary Military Hospital, Llanfairfechan; Bodlondeb, Bangor Road, Menai Bridge; Wern Auxiliary Military Hospital, Porthmadog; Plas Tudno Nursing Home, Llandudno; Plas Tudno and St Tudno Auxiliary Military Hospital, Llandudno; Red Cross Hospital, Red Court, Church Walks, Llandudno; Belmont; Balmoral Red Cross Hospital, Llandudno; Penrhyn Cottage VAD Hospital, Bangor.

Cardiganshire: Cardiganshire Red Cross Hospital, Aberystwyth; The Old Bank, Bridge Street, Aberystwyth; Red Cross Hospital, Aberayron.

Carmarthenshire: Auxiliary Military Red Cross Hospital, Church House, Llandovery; The St John Auxiliary Hospital, 1 Penlan Road, Carmarthen; Red Cross Auxiliary

Hospital, Parc Howard, Llanelli; Auxiliary Military Red Cross Hospital, Dolygarreg, Llandovery.

Denbighshire: Ruthin Auxiliary Hospital, Ruthin; Llandernog Auxiliary Hospital, Llandernog; Roseneath, Auxiliary Hospital, Wrexham; Croes Howell Auxiliary Hospital, Rossett; Colwyn Bay Auxiliary Hospital, Colwyn Bay; Brynkinalt Auxiliary Hospital, Chirk; Ystrad Isaf Auxiliary Hospital, Denbigh.

Flintshire: Talardy Auxiliary Hospital, St Asaph; Leeswood Hall Auxiliary Hospital, Mold; Rhyl and District Auxiliary Hospital, Rhyl; Pentrefyon Convalescent Home, Holywell.

Glamorganshire: Beaupre, Cowbridge; Baglan Hall, Briton Ferry; Horton, Porteynon; Llwynypia, Rhondda; Hendrefoilan, Sketty; Aberpergwn, Glynneath; Mirador Officers' Hospital, Swansea; Pontyclun Red Cross Hospital; Windsor Road Red Cross Hospital, Barry; St John Hospital, Pontardawe; Brynmill, Swansea; Glanrhyd, Pontardawe; Red Cross Hospital, Maesteg; Llwynarthern, Castleton, Cardiff; Radyr Red Cross Hospital; Bridgend Red Cross Hospital; The Rest, Porthcawl; Gnoll Park, Woodland Road, Neath; Coytrahen Park, Tondu; Dock View Road, Barry; Victoria Red Cross Hospital, Mumbles; Court Sart, Briton Ferry; Lan Wood, Pontypridd; Llwyncelyn, Porth; The Laurels, Neath; The Lodge, Llandaff; Rookwood Officers' Hospital, Llandaff; Dunraven Castle, St Brides Major; Officers' Hospital, Llandaff; Stanwell Road, Penarth; Aberdare and Merthyr Red Cross Hospital; Lavernock House, near Penarth; St Fagan's Red Cross Hospital; Danycoed, Blackmill; YMCA Red Cross Hospital, Swansea; Tuscar House, Southerndown; Samuel House, Cardiff; St Pierre's, Cardiff; Dinas Powis Red Cross Hospital, Old Mansion House, Cardiff; Heddfan, Sketty; Caerphilly Red Cross Hospital, Kelvin, Penarth; Clyne House Officers' Hospital, Cardiff; Ash Hall, Cowbridge; Parc Wern Red Cross Officers' Hospital, Swansea; The Quarr, Clydach; St John Hospital, Barry Island; St John Hospital, Penarth.

Merionethshire: Aber Artro, Llanbedr; Caerynwch, Dolgelly; Pale Auxiliary Military Hospital, Pale, Corwen; Officers' Hospital, Nannau, Dolgelly.

Montgomeryshire: Red Cross Hospital, Machynlleth; VAD 14 Hospital, Broadway, Church Stoke; Red Cross Hospital, Clive House, Welshpool; Red Cross Hospital, Maenol, Llanidloes.

Monmouthshire: Walker Memorial Red Cross Hospital, Portskewett; Baldwins Auxiliary Hospital, Griffithstown; Gwy House Red Cross Hospital, Chepstow; Brynslas Red Cross Hospital, Newport; Llanwern Park Red Cross Hospital, Llanwern; The Coldra, Newport; Red Cross Hospital, Ebbw Vale; Maindiff Court Red Cross Hospital, Abergavenny; Red Cross Hospital, Monmouth; Wrenford Memorial Hall, Newport; Llwynasthen Red Cross Hospital, St Mellons.

Pembrokeshire: Angle VA Hospital, Angle; Tenby Auxiliary Hospital, Somerset House, Esplanade, Tenby; Cottesmore Auxiliary Hospital, Haverfordwest.

Radnorshire: Highland Moors Red Cross Hospital, Llandrindod Wells; Red Cross Hospital, Offas Lodge, Knighton; Corton Hospital, Presteign; Military Auxiliary Hospital, Llyswen, Boughrood; Auxiliary Hospital, Knighton 2, The Cottage, Knighton. (Source: the British Red Cross.)

These Red Cross hospitals were usually run by volunteers, with the local groups chaired by ladies such as Mrs Pryse Rice of Llwynybrain, Llandovery, Lady Magdalen Williams Bulkeley of Anglesey and Lady Glanusk of Brecon. There was also a large Welsh National Hospital at Netley, in Hampshire, that was funded by Welsh patronage and had a large number of Welsh staff, some of whom had seen active service with the Welsh Hospital during the Boer War.

The Red Cross also provided staff for base hospitals outside Wales to supplement the work of the stretched Royal Army Medical Corps. The *North Wales Chronicle* of 6 November reported on the numbers of local members posted for service:

The following were despatched on the undermentioned dates and posted for service at the places named: October 29th, Servia [Serbia], six doctors and 12 orderlies. October 31st, Rennes, six doctors and 12 dressers. November 1st, Boulogne, eight doctors; Rouen, two dressers. November 2nd, four doctors, November 3rd, Boulogne, two doctors and 15 dressers. October 31st, Rennes, 28 nurses. November 1st, Boulogne, 36 nurses. The following nurses were also supplied for home service: October 30th, Mansfield, four. October 31st, Angar, three. Southampton, six; Wigan, one. November 2nd, Bristol, one; Louth, Lincolnshire, one; Margate, two; Winchester, two. November 3rd, Bicester, one; Gerrards Cross, five; Perth, one; Reigate, three.

Nurses of the Anglesey Red Cross, November 1914.

The people of Wales were also keen to throw their money into the expansion of the Red Cross. The *Brecon and Radnor Express* of 3 December 1914 published a thank-you letter from one society whose donors had been especially generous to the cause:

Sir,

Please spare me a few lines to express, on behalf of the Llandrindod Wells Red Cross Society, their deep sense of gratitude for the generous response which has been made to their appeal for help. The Red Cross Hospital was begun in a spirit of faith, except for the promise of the maintenance of sixteen beds nothing was certain at all, but the appeal made towards the maintenance of thirty-five beds showed that the committee had been wise in trusting to the liberality of the county. Not only was there a considerable sum of money collected, but week by week each district has helped to supply the wants of the hospital with provisions, garden produce, game and butchers' meat. I would like to mention especially the districts of Rhayader, Cwmdauddwr, Nantmel, Llanyre, Llanfihangel, Doldowlod, Newbridge, Builth Road, Llanelwedd and Disserth. From all these districts regular supplies have been collected and while it is impossible to thank every donor personally, I would ask them to accept the very grateful thanks of the committee for their continued kind contributions. Without their help the hospital could not have been run on its present lines and we could not have offered to the War Office the substantial assistance which we have already rendered.

Yours faithfully,

JOHN MURRAY,

Chairman of the Llandrindod Wells Red Cross Society.

As well as this vast mobilization by the Red Cross and also the St John's Ambulance Brigade, as we have already seen, the Welsh Territorial and Yeomanry units began mobilization on 6 August.

At the start of the Great War, the regular British army consisted of six divisions and one cavalry division based in Britain and a further four divisions serving overseas. There were fourteen Territorial Army divisions and 300,000 men in the Army Reserve. There was widespread excitement around the country regarding the prospect of facing the Germans in battle and almost all believed that the British army was unbeatable and that the war would be over by Christmas 1914. As a result, many young men enthusiastically rushed to enlist after reading in the newspapers of heroic deeds done by the soldiers in France so that they too could see action before the war ended.

Lord Kitchener, the new Secretary of State for War, thought otherwise and visualized a lengthier campaign. He considered the Territorial Army untrained and useless and believed that the regular army should be used to help train a new army with seventy divisions, which he thought would be needed to help win a war that would prove to be long and protracted and therefore a serious drain on manpower and resources.

The result of this far-sighted thinking was Kitchener's call to arms: a public cry for men to enlist into Kitchener's New Army or 'Kitchener's Mob', as it would become known. On 14 August all the local newspapers printed large advertisements for an extra 100,000 soldiers to create this first New Army. Recruitment in the first few weeks of war was high, but the real boom began in the last week of August, when news of the British retreat following the Battle of Mons reached Britain. By the end of September 1914 over 750,000 men had enlisted and by January 1915 over 1 million.

As part of this expansion, a growing political force in Wales had come to see the chance of creating a Welsh Army Corps. The first steps towards this came into being as a result of a speech made by David Lloyd George, the Chancellor of the Exchequer, at the Queen's Hall, London on 19 September 1914:

> I should like to see a Welsh Army in the Field. I should like to see the race that faced the Norman for hundreds of years in a struggle for freedom, the race that helped to win Crécy, the race that fought for a generation under Glyndwr against the greatest Captain in Europe – I should like to see that race give a good taste of their quality in this struggle in Europe; and they are going to do it!

This patriotic speech helped to set the wheels in motion, ultimately leading to the formation of the Executive Committee with its dream of raising a Welsh Army Corps of two divisions that would take to the field together.

The inaugural meeting to form the committee was held at Cardiff on 24 September 1914 and invitations were sent out to various peoples of high standing throughout Wales. The new committee knew that enough Welshmen had already been recruited to form an army corps and it was soon realized that to raise another large number of men to fulfil the requirements for a complete army corps of their own would take a lot of hard work.

Nonetheless, this work involved in the first stages of recruiting the men began and in addition to the men already serving with the regular army and the men of the 53rd (Welsh) Division (Territorial Army), a further army corps of between 40,000 and 50,000 men was asked for.

Over the coming months the first part of the dream of a Welsh Army Corps turned into reality and thus part of Lloyd George's dream came into being with the formation of the 43rd (Welsh) Division, which assembled in North Wales for its initial training. (For a more in-depth description of the raising of the Welsh Division see the end of this chapter.)

A new Welsh unit, the Welsh Horse Yeomanry, was by now up to full strength and was in a tented camp at Sophia Gardens, Cardiff. The Welsh Horse was the brainchild of a man who was a living legend in Wales, Arthur Owen Vaughan, known by his bardic name of Owen Roscomyl. Vaughan was born in Southport, Merseyside and raised in Lancashire, but had been strongly influenced by his grandmother, who was from Tremeirchion in Denbighshire. He ran away from home at the age of 15 and found work as a miner and cowboy in America before returning to Britain and enlisting in the 1st

Royal Dragoons in 1887. During the Boer War he served with Rimington's Guides and with Damant's Horse and was awarded the Distinguished Conduct Medal (DCM) for bravery. He later joined Ross's Canadian Scouts, reaching the rank of captain. He returned to Britain in 1902 and became prominent in Welsh cultural life. When war broke out in August 1914, Vaughan was prominent in forming a Welsh cavalry regiment, the Welsh Horse Yeomanry, but was never given command of it; instead he became a major with the 14th Battalion, Northumberland Fusiliers. He was promoted to lieutenant colonel on 21 March 1915 and given command of the 21st Division Cyclists.

Command of the Welsh Horse Yeomanry was instead given to Lieutenant Colonel Hugh Edwardes, 6th Baron Kensington, of St Bride's. It was he who became the key figure of the training of the Welsh Horse during its time at Sophia Gardens after the new regiment had been given official sanction on 15 August.

The remainder of the officers originally commissioned in the Welsh Horse, all well-known men at the time, were as follows:

Arthur Owen Vaughan, DCM, later Lieutenant Colonel Arthur Owen Vaughan, MBE, DSO, DCM.

Colonel LORD KENSINGTON, D.S.O.
(Commanding Officer).

Major the HON. W. BAILEY
(Second in Command).

Major GOLDTHORP.

Major A. O. VAUGHAN
(Owen Rhoscomyl).

The original officers of the Welsh Horse Yeomanry during their formation in Cardiff.

Serg.-major GRIFFITHS, R.A.M.C. (T.).

Captain the EARL OF LISBURNE.

Captain J. GORDON.

38

Second-in-Command: Major the Hon. William Bailey, Glanusk Park, Crickhowell. Late 11th Hussars.

Lieutenant and Quartermaster: Owen Thomas. 26. Park Court, Clapham Park Road, London. S.W. Independent means. Late Eastern Mounted Rifles.

Majors (four): Francis Herbert Goldthorp. Elmsfield, Newport Road, Cardiff. Retired major (Indian Cavalry); Herbert Owain Pugh, DSO, of Mount Hill, Carmarthen, secretary to the United Counties Territorial Association. Late Lumsden's Horse (Indian Forces) and South African Constabulary; Arthur Owen Vaughan of The Vron, Dinas Powis, Glamorgan. Late Rimington's Scouts; George Robert Powell, of Tynewydd, Hirwain, Glamorgan. Twenty years' experience in Regular and Militia Forces.

Captains (four): John Gordon Rees, of Penydarren Park, Crickhowell, mining engineer. Late 10th Hussars. Reserve of Officers; Alexander Ernest Burchardt-Ashton, of Llandogo Priory, Chepstow. Late 4th Dragoon Guards and Royal Gloucester Hussars (Yeomanry). Reserve of Officers; James Job Pugh Evans of Lovesgrove. Aberystwyth. Late 2nd Battalion Royal Welsh Fusiliers (West India); Ernest Edmund Henry Mallet, the Earl of Lisburne, of Crosswood, Aberystwyth. Peer of the Realm. Late Scots Guards.

Lieutenants: Cyril Roderick Roch of Tenby Club. Tenby. Gentleman. Independent means. Late Imperial Yeomanry; George Rice Pryce of Peihtyll, Bow Street, near Aberystwyth. Late Cape Mounted Rifles.

Second Lieutenants: William Prothero Roch, MFH, of Plasybridell. Cilgerran. Late Bihar Light Horse; John Garbutt Hutchinson of Hillside, Whitland. Late Officers' Training Corps and Field Artillery (Volunteers); Gerald Stratton, DCM, of Plas Machen, Newport, Monmouthshire, late Glamorgan Yeomanry and Highland Light Infantry; Arthur Gunn of Ty To Mawr, St Mellon's, Cardiff; John Julian Boyd Harvey of Maesteg, Glamorgan, late Glamorgan Yeomanry; Geoffrey Hall of Vraeside, Dyserth, late Bedfordshire Yeomanry; Douglas Henry Neale of Dryngarth, Fforest Road, Penarth, Glamorgan; Pence Overton Ward of Caenewydd, Clydach Vale, Glamorgan, late Glamorgan Yeomanry.

Medical Officer: Major J. Griffiths, RAMC, of Llandrindod Wells.

Veterinary Surgeon: Lieutenant Thomas Charles Howatson, AVC, of Hafod Elwy, St Asaph.

This list of officers changed dramatically throughout the war; indeed it was even somewhat different from the officers who proceeded overseas with the regiment the following year, but is given here for historical interest.

The men, many with previous military service, trained hard in Sophia Gardens and at Blackweir Farm, grounds that had been given over by the Marquis of Bute. By 22 September the first horses, mainly Welsh cobs, arrived and the men began training further afield, notably around the Caerphilly hills. On 2 October Lord Kensington assembled the men and asked for volunteers to go overseas on active service. The response was astonishing: these were men with a desire to prove the mettle of the new regiment and the entire assembly volunteered.

The Welsh Horse moved by road from Cardiff to Margam Park on 28 October and the proud men were greeted by huge crowds along their route until reaching the grounds that were usually used for the summer camp of the Glamorgan Yeomanry. In the meantime, however, there had been a public outcry in Cardiff earlier in the month, following the news that the HQ would be moved from its spiritual home at Cardiff to a more central place at Newtown, enabling men from the whole of Wales to be able to volunteer. Lord Kenyon had initially publically raised this idea in order to gain more support from the Welsh-speaking areas of Wales.

As well as the rush to recruit men to enable the expansion of the army, Wales would also see the creation of several new military air bases during the course of the war. RFC Shotwick in Flintshire became the very first military airfield in Wales when its civilian airfield was requisitioned by the RFC in 1916. The airfield was used as a training base with Sopwith Pups, Camels and Avro 504s and was eventually joined by another airfield that opened on the other side of the nearby railway line, the two being named Shotwick North and Shotwick South. The first squadron to train at the aerodrome was 95 Squadron. The two sites eventually merged in 1924 and took the name of RAF Sealand, seeing further service during the Second World War.

A site near the village of Sageston, known as RNAS Pembroke and later RAF Carew Cheriton, was opened in August 1915, situated just off the main road between Carmarthen and Pembroke. The site was used for the operation of Coastal-class and Sea Scout Zero SSZ-type airships that patrolled the Western Approaches and were housed in large airship sheds on the site. In April 1917 the aerodrome was extended with the erection of three hangars to house Sopwith 1½ Strutter and Airco DH-4 flights. The aerodrome was used again during the Second World War.

Fishguard Harbour was deemed to be the ideal location for a Royal Naval Air Service (RNAS) seaplane station. Three buildings were erected to house the seaplanes and a single slipway was built, along with a launching crane. The base opened for operations in March 1917, equipped with the Sopwith Baby and Short Type 184 seaplanes. The unit became 245 Squadron on 20 August 1918 and was disbanded on 10 May 1919.

Milford Haven was the ideal location for the RNAS to operate a balloon section, which worked in conjunction with Carew Cheriton and operated from 1917 until the end of the war. The base was the HQ of the Special Duties Flight of 77 Wing and carried out coastal defence operations.

Near the village of Llangefni on Anglesey, a large site was requisitioned by the RNAS to create RNAS Anglesey. An airship shed and aircraft hangar were erected, together with several huts to form a base for Sea Scout SS type, Pusher SSP type and Zero Type SSZ airships. On 6 June 1918 521 and 522 Coastal Patrol Flights were formed as part of 255 Squadron, equipped with Airco DH-4 aircraft. The site later moved to RNAS Bangor, as it was deemed unsuitable for aircraft, and was renumbered 244 Squadron. The station closed in 1919 but was used again during the Second World War.

A site located on the coastal strip between Bangor and Abergwyngregin, which formed part of Glan y Mor Isaf Farm, was identified as an ideal location to build RNAS Bangor. Four hangars were erected and the farm buildings were requisitioned by the RNAS. Part of 244 Squadron moved to the aerodrome in August 1918, equipped with Airco DH-6 aircraft for coastal patrol duties. The squadron was disbanded on 22 February 1919 and the land reverted to farming.

Towards the end of the war Swansea aerodrome was also licensed by the Air Ministry as being deemed suitable for use by Avro aircraft, while a nearby aerodrome at Llanelli was deemed to be a suitable emergency landing site. However, due to the Armistice, Swansea aerodrome, on ground known as Fairwood Common, was not taken over by the military until the Second World War.

Chapter 4

The Battles of the Marne and the Aisne

While recruitment was the main topic in Wales, back in France the BEF was taking stock of its war so far, the main point of interest for the Welsh troops being the retreat from Mons. Captain Rees of the 2nd Welsh wrote:

The determination of the men during the Retreat passed all belief. The reservists, as I remarked before, were not in any way fit for such a terrific test of endurance. Between 22nd August and 5th September, we marched about 240 miles and only on one day did we have any semblance of rest. The men were absolutely tired out before the actual retreat began on 24th. At the end of some of the marches it was impossible to maintain our formation and the column became merely a crowd flowing very slowly along the road, the men looking as if they neither saw nor felt anything. Almost without exception their feet were raw and bleeding and many marched with puttees wrapped round their feet. Their one desire was to halt and fight the enemy and not being allowed to do so was the cause of bitter complaint.

Some Welsh soldiers wounded during the retreat to the Marne had by now arrived home to pay a fleeting visit to their families. One of these men, Gunner Phil Davies, had related some of his worst experiences to his father, who worked for the *Carmarthen Journal*. He had been wounded by fragments from a 'Jack Johnson' shell that had killed all the rest of his detachment and was lying in hospital in Sheffield when he spoke to his father. Tales of German atrocities filled his tale, which was recounted by his father:

Those who are reluctant to believe the horrible stories of German barbarity published in the newspapers should listen to those of our own soldiers. Here are some that are told by Gunner Davies; they are not things that he has heard of but things that he himself has seen. What would people say in this country if when walking out in the country they saw a little dead baby pinned to a tree with a bayonet? That is what Gunner Davies has seen in Belgium and chalked above the poor little mangled body was the motto 'Kaiser Wilhelm'... Gunner Davies was lying in hospital at Sheffield. In the next bed was a surgeon who had been attending to a wounded officer on the battlefield, already wounded himself, when he was surprised by several Germans, who got hold of him, cut off both his hands and threw him back into the trench... There is hardly a man in the British Army who has not seen women and children lying dead in the streets, shot and bayoneted, or hanging dead from trees. One night Gunner Davies was in the trenches on duty when two French girls from 18 to 19 years of age crawled up to them. They had been attacked by the Germans and both of them had their breasts cut off. One of our Tommies, horrified, took off his shirt to protect them from the rain which was pouring down. The girls were at once attended to, but they died in half an hour.

Private Samuel Knight (8069) of the 2nd Welsh wrote of this period of the retreat:

Sunday, August 30th–September 5th. Marching, marching, marching. Pass through delightful country. Picturesque villages resound to the tramp of our feet. Not an inhabitant do we see. All have fled. Children's toys left in the middle of play here and there strew the gardens of their homes. Marching, marching, marching. We overtake a long line of refugees, a pitiable sight. Oxen draw heavy-laden waggons. On one of these sits an old woman nursing a babe about a month old. On the same waggon are packs, boxes and a pig. Behind this same waggon trudges the young mother, presumably the daughter of the aged dame with three children clinging to her skirt. Similar sights meet us as we pass along. All in the same direction. They look very hungry. We are in the same plight, but we hand them a few tins of bully beef. They try to keep up with us. We leave them behind. Marching, marching, marching. I have forgotten the day; too weary to make further notes.

In France, by early September, the German First Army was headed to the south-east to outflank the left of the French Fifth Army, which was falling back to avoid envelopment, while the French Sixth Army to the east and north-east of Paris, together with the BEF to the south, threatened the right flank and rear of the German First Army. General Joffre realized that the time was now right to attack the Germans.

The order to advance reached Sir John French quite late, at 3 am on 5 September, so the BEF began its move a day after the French, advancing north-east so as to attack the right flank of the German First Army. The battle itself began in earnest that day when the French Sixth Army attacked from the direction of Paris over the Ourcq towards Château Thierry as the BEF moved up towards Montmirail, while the French Fifth Army attacked northwards, with its right flank protected by the Ninth Army along the St Gond marshes.

Although the French attack momentarily stalled following a German counter-attack, the Germans began falling back to the north bank of the River Marne under intense pressure from the French. The 1st Division of the BEF was at the centre of the pivot of the move north-east and the 1st SWB and 2nd Welsh moved towards the village of La Chapelle-Iger, coming into earshot of the sound of fighting somewhere ahead. The

A blown bridge over the River Marne at La Ferté-sous-Jouarre

2nd RWF, along with 19 Brigade, were moving forwards through beautiful countryside and bivouacked at La Haute Maison on the night of 5–6 September.

The attack from the BEF commenced on the following morning; but very little fighting was seen during that first day. The Battle of the Marne proved to be a turning-point of the war, with the combined French and BEF assault stemming the German drive on Paris and forcing the enemy to withdraw northwards, although none of the Welsh units in action had yet seen any real fighting.

On 6 September the BEF began crossing the Marne, securing a bridgehead 5 miles deep; and with reinforcements now flowing into the French armies and to the BEF, the Germans retreated to the River Aisne, marking the abandonment of the Schlieffen Plan. Casualties suffered by the Germans amounted to 11,717 prisoners, 30 guns and 100 machine guns to the French and 3,500 prisoners to the British.

Another member of the Welsh aristocracy was killed during the day. Walter de Winton was born on 21 February 1893, the son of Major Walton De Winter and Hylda Teresa Jane de Winton of Maesllwch Castle, Radnorshire. De Winton was educated at Eton and Sandhurst before being commissioned in the 3rd Battalion, Coldstream Guards on 5 February 1913. His 'coming of age' celebrations were held in Maesllwch on 10 June 1914 and were attended by hundreds of villagers and tenants of the estate. He embarked for France with the battalion and was killed in action on 6

Lieutenant Walter de Winton, 3rd Battalion, Coldstream Guards, heir to the Maesllyn Estate in Radnorshire.

September. De Winter was originally buried in the gardens of Monsieur Muraband at La Fortelle, Royosen Brie, Seine et Marne, but his remains were exhumed after the war and reburied in Bouilly Crossroads Military Cemetery.

On 10 September, Joffre issued orders for the French and the BEF to advance; four days later the German withdrawal to the Aisne had halted and the Germans began to dig in. The BEF moved towards the German defensive positions south of the Chemin des Dames Ridge between Soissons and Reims, the 1st Division crossing the River Vesle near Bazoches on the 12th, yet encountered only sporadic resistance.

The 2nd Welsh then took the duty of Advanced Guard for the 1st Division and spent a cold, miserable night in Longueval. On 13 September Sir John French issued orders to the BEF to advance and the British crossed the Aisne later that day on a 10-mile front. No. 3 Brigade took up positions north of the village of Bourg that night, with the BEF under orders to attack at 6 am on the following day.

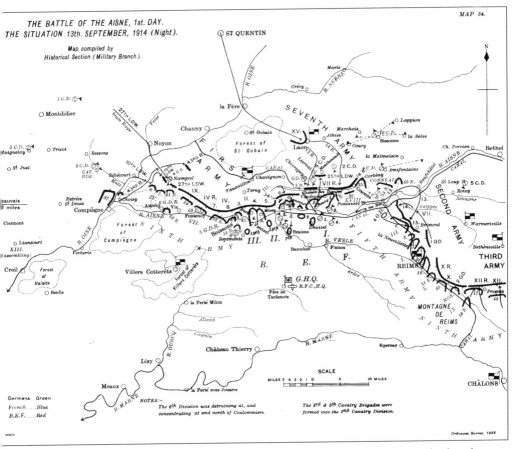

A map taken from the Official History *showing the dispositions of the forces involved in the* Battle of the Aisne.

Private Samuel Knight (8069) of the 2nd Welsh wrote of the entry into Bourg:

The Germans have blown up the main bridge. Find a small one higher up the river. Evidence here of attempts to blow up this also. We cross this bridge and mount the hill overlooking the town. Rest. Five miles to our right the French artillery is booming away. We can see the spitting flames. Night has fallen. We are taken to billets in the town. Rations follow, but the hour is too late for distribution. They decide to give us what we consider to be needed most. The tobacco is doled out. Biscuits can remain till the morning.

At long last the two Welsh battalions would see action, while the 2nd RWF remained in reserve with 19 Brigade, the men spending their time idly playing games:

During the time we were on the Aisne our brigade were in reserve and during our leisure hours we played Kitty Nap, Pontoon, Brag and Crown and Anchor. A pukka old soldier's Bible was his pack of cards. Corporal Pardoe of my section and I won quite a lot of money. Mine came in handy afterwards for having a good time, but Corporal Pardoe was thrifty with his winnings and didn't spend hardly a penny. (Frank Richards.)

In the meantime Gunner William Roy Davies (69890) of Abergavenny was in action again with the 121st Battery, Royal Field Artillery:

We retired for a week without encountering any sign of the enemy. We saw a Taube aeroplane overhead being chased by about 20 French aeroplanes. It was brought down by an anti-aircraft gun mounted on a motor-car. The flight of the refugees towards Paris as we went along was terrible to witness. Women were wheeling barrows containing mothers, who were too old to walk. We were 23 kilometres from Paris on the Sunday morning when we received orders to advance. We advanced for three or four days before we encountered the enemy at Landrecies. We found the towns and villages as we went along had been ransacked by the Germans, who had written on the windows: 'The traitorous English – they die.' The people in the town cheered us to the echo, and we never had such a reception in our lives.

After leaving Landrecies we did not see any more of the enemy until we got into action on Saturday night, Sept. 12, just south of the river Aisne. We shelled the enemy for three days before they discovered our whereabouts. On the Wednesday morning, however, the big guns of the Germans began to play on us and caused terrible havoc. There were only two officers and three men who escaped out of about 70 gunners and five officers. The next thing I knew was that I was being carried away by two comrades from a deep trench where I had been struck by a shrapnel shot in the right side. The wounded were taken to the village, which was being constantly shelled by the Germans, and the wounded were removed to the cellars for safety. One man left his own gun-pit and went to the next gun-pit, thinking he would be safer, but he had not been there two minutes when a fragment of shell came and took one of his arms and part of his head away. In that condition he walked to the village, about 200 yards distant, and when he was put on the stretcher it was found that he was dead.

The combination of his wounds and shellshock put an end to Davies' active service for almost three years. After recuperating at the 1st Eastern General Hospital, Cambridge, he was promoted to sergeant and remained in Ireland until sailing for Mesopotamia on 26 August 1917. He was eventually discharged at Shanghai on 14 June 1920 after service with the British Military Mission at Vladivostok; he appears to have deserted his wife and child who lived at Abergavenny.

At 6 am on the 14th the 1st Division began its assault on the Chemin des Dames, its objective being to secure the ridge westwards from Cerny. The first assault was made by 2 Brigade, whose task it was to clear the roads to the ridge of the enemy. The attack soon became held up, so 1 (Guards) Brigade was sent up to support the left of the attack and outflank the Germans. Meanwhile, 3 Brigade, including 1st SWB and 2nd Welsh, was ordered to advance from Moulins towards the Beaulne Spur and prolong the line held by 1 (Guards) Brigade.

The time had come for the first major engagement by Welsh troops in the Great War. The 1st SWB were on the right, the 2nd Welsh on the left and the 1st Gloucesters in reserve; the advance began in a north-westerly direction. No sooner had it begun when a German counter-attack developed on the opposite ridge, towards the left flank of 1 Brigade, so 3 Brigade changed direction to catch the flank of the Germans. This change of direction opened up a gap between the 2nd Welsh and 1st SWB, who were being slowed due to having to advance through wooded ground; but the 2nd Welsh carried the advance, establishing positions on the south-eastern slopes of the Beaulne Spur, where the 1st SWB caught up.

Both battalions then advanced down into the Chivy Valley, across the river and up the slope of Chivy Ridge, all the while under heavy artillery and rifle fire. Lieutenant George David Melville of the 2nd Welsh wrote:

I, with my machine gun section in extended order, followed closely behind the leading Company in the attack. The machine gun section of the SWB and the Brigade machine gun officer (Arthur Geoffrey Lyttelton) were with the supporting Company. The advance was a most unhealthy one as, owing to the nature of the ground, we were fired at, not only from the front, but also from the right flank, and, to make it even more unpleasant, some shots from our covering artillery fire fell on our own troops. Halfway across the valley, my section Sergeant, next to me, was shot through the leg and I saw him no more that day.

The 2nd Welsh bore the brunt of the attack, suffering a large number of casualties from rifle and machine-gun fire and came face-to-face with the Germans in a cornfield. The Welsh rushed the Germans, who fled; while advancing further they came under direct artillery fire. D Company of the 2nd Welsh was now on the top of Chivy Ridge, but the situation was desperate. Ammunition was low, so men were sent to crawl back over the battlefield to collect ammunition from their dead comrades. Private Knight wrote of the attack:

> At 5 am move off. After proceeding about two miles we are greeted by the enemy's artillery fire. Shrapnel shells burst over our heads. Roofs of neighbouring barns rattle like kettle drums. I hear a peal of laughter from my comrades near me, for, as the result of an unconscious action, I had raised the collar of my coat. I laugh myself. We are now in the thick of it. The effect of the shrapnel is beginning to tell, as my comrades fall out to the roadside to be bandaged. We continue to advance up a gradient. Upon the horizon we open out in extended order. A valley opens out before us. Beyond it is a hill whose sides are clothed with a dense wood. This hill and wood are held by the enemy. B Company under Captain Haggard is ordered to advance to drive out the enemy from this position. We have orders to lie down. Our comrades' advance is greeted by the enemy with a heavy rifle fire. Their firing is high. The bullets missing the intended billets, 'pizz' 'pizz' 'pizz' about us in the rear. The Welsh return with vigour. I hear the rattle of the enemy's machine guns. The Welsh make a dash for the hill, but on its summit are met with heavy shellfire. They retire a little. Rifle fire ceases somewhat and I see the Germans like a grey cloud attempt an advance on the other side of the same hills. When on the brow, our artillery on my left lets go. The first shell finds the range to a nicety. Almost immediately the whole battery speaks and with destructive effect. Shattered bodies and limbs dance in the air.

The 2nd SWB had lost their first officer killed during this advance: Lieutenant Mervyn Taylor Johnson, the 28-year-old son of Captain William and Rosina Johnson of Fern Bank, Oddington, Moreton-in-Marsh was mortally wounded shortly after the advance began. He died soon afterwards and is buried in Vendresse British Cemetery.

The 2nd SWB were advancing from Chivy when Major Moore ordered the 2nd Welsh to withdraw some 250 metres to the bank of the river, Lieutenant Gabriel Roy Fitzpatrick being killed during the move. From there the men watched the battle raging around them while the BEF artillery poured fire down on the Chemin des Dames Ridge.

The grave of Lieutenant Mervyn Taylor Johnson in Vendresse British Cemetery.

In the meantime, one man of the 2nd Welsh, Lance Corporal William Fuller, was about to carry out an act of gallantry that would see him become the first Welshman to be awarded the Victoria Cross during the Great War.

Captain Mark Haggard of the 2nd Welsh found that his company had been held up by a German machine gun. Determined to save his men and to carry on the advance, Haggard rose to his feet and charged the machine gun, armed only with his pistol, reportedly cheering his men on with the now famous words: 'Stick it, the Welsh!'.

The gallant Haggard outran his men and fired several shots into the Germans before falling to the ground, mortally wounded in the stomach. One of his men, Lance Corporal William Fuller, kept up with Haggard as he fell, ran forward and, after dressing his wounds and discarding his kit, picked up the dying Haggard and dragged him back to shelter in a barn about three-quarters of a mile away where he died at 4.30 pm the following day. Haggard is buried in Vendresse British Cemetery.

William Charles Fuller was born on 24 March 1884 in Newbridge Road, Laugharne, the son of William and Mary Fuller. His father was a butcher and moved the family to Swansea around 1891, setting up home at 47 Orchard Street. Fuller was educated at Swansea

Lieutenant Gabriel Roy Fitzpatrick. He was born in Chelsea on 20 October 1883 and was commissioned in the 3rd Welsh in August 1909. Fitzpatrick has no known grave and is commemorated on the La Ferté-sous-Jouarre Memorial.

before he took up work in Swansea Docks. On 31 December 1902, he enlisted in the 1st Welsh and served in South Africa. He spent several years in India with the regiment and was discharged to the reserve in 1909, joining the 2nd Welsh from the reserves in August 1914. He died in Swansea on 29 December 1974 and is buried in the town at Oystermouth Cemetery.

Lance Corporal William Charles Fuller VC, the first Welshman to be awarded the Victoria Cross during the Great War.

Captain Mark Haggard of the 2nd Welsh, who died of wounds on 15 September 1914 and is buried in Vendresse British Cemetery.

The *Carmarthen Journal* carried Fuller's account of the action:

We were supposed to be the advance party for the South Wales Borderers, but instead formed a bit to the left and made an advance ourselves. We marched from a wood in the direction of a ridge and on the way we came across a wire fence. Instead of waiting to use our wire-cutters, Captain Haggard pulled one of the posts out and we continued our advance to the top of the ridge. On reaching that point we saw the enemy and Captain Haggard and myself and two other men who were in front started firing. On proceeding a little further we were faced by a Maxim gun. There was a little wood on the top and a hedge about 50 yards long. It was not long before the men on Captain Haggard's left were both shot and the man on the right was wounded. [This quote appears verbatim and there may be some confusion regarding the number of men involved.]

At the same time Captain Haggard was struck in the stomach and he fell doubled, the shot coming out through his right side. Thus I was the only one uninjured. Our company was met with such an enfilading fire that the right part of the platoon had to retire back and make an attack towards the right. That left Captain Haggard, myself and the wounded man below the ridge and it became necessary for me to carry Captain Haggard back to cover. This was done by him putting his right arm around my neck, while I had my right arm under his legs and the left under his neck. I was only from 10 to 20 yards behind him when he was shot and as he fell he cried, 'Stick it, Welch!' With the shots buzzing around us I bandaged him, the while our fellows were mowing down the Germans and Captain Haggard asked me to lift up his head so that he could see our big guns firing at the Germans as they were retiring from the wood.

The citation that appeared in the *London Gazette* of Monday, 23 November 1914 reads:

No. 7753 Lance-Corporal William Fuller, 2nd Battalion, The Welsh Regiment, for conspicuous gallantry on 14th September, near Chivy on the Aisne, by advancing about 100 yards to pick up Captain Haggard, who was mortally wounded and carrying him back to cover under very heavy rifle and machine gun fire.

Fighting continued throughout the remainder of the day, but the 1st Division managed to keep control of the ground gained, spending a miserable night on the battlefield surrounded by dead men. The artillery maintained accurate fire on the Germans whenever they dared to attempt to counter-attack, but on the following day a determined enemy attack saw the division pushed back to a new line north of Chivy and the Germans firmly established on top of the Chemin des Dames Ridge, a position they would hold for much of the war.

Fuller was not the only Welshman to show gallantry during the day. Corporal Derry of the 2nd Welsh later recounted how he had been saved by one of his men:

Taken from Deeds That Thrill the Empire, *this image depicts the rescuing of Captain Mark Haggard by William Fuller.*

On the 14th of September the Welsh were at Chivy and were being shelled by the German artillery. It was suicide to remain where we were and it was just at this time that I was struck down. Davies, seeing me lying wounded, at great risk to himself ran out, and, although the shells were falling all around us, he picked me up and carried me to cover and went back to fetch my brother, who was also wounded. We, together with a lot more wounded officers and men, were conveyed to a barn of a farm, and, there being no doctor available, Davies alone attended to the wounds for 76 hours without a rest. We should have been in a terrible plight had it not been for his untiring efforts. When we felt a bit downhearted your son soon put us right with a few songs... I owe him a debt of gratitude which I can never repay.

The hero was Private David John Davies (8003), 2nd Welsh, a Reservist who was working at the Anthony Pit (Naval Collieries), Penygraig, when he rejoined the colours. He gained no official recognition in the form of decorations for his actions, even though the act of gallantry was exactly the same as Fuller's. The only difference was that Fuller had rescued an officer.

During the same day that Corporal Derry was being carried to safety, three Welsh officers were killed serving with non-Welsh units. One was Captain Algernon Foulkes Attwood of the 4th Battalion, Royal Fusiliers.

Attwood was born on 17 May 1880, the only son of Llewellyn Carless Foulkes Attwood, JP, of Pandy, Monmouth and of Llay, Denbigh and his wife, Rachel Edith Attwood. He was educated at Haileybury and Christ Church Oxford and was commissioned in the 4th Battalion, Royal Fusiliers on 4 May 1901. During the spring of 1914 he undertook a course of aviation at Upavon and was recommended for a commission in the RFC, but instead embarked for France with his battalion in the rank of captain. On 14 September 1914 he was reported severely wounded and missing but was later found to have been mortally wounded after having been shot twice while skilfully and gallantly withdrawing his men from an advanced position near Vailly that could not be held. He died that same day and is commemorated on the La Ferté-sous-Jouarre Memorial.

The other two officers killed were Captain Riversdale Nonus Grenfell of the 9th (Queen's Royal) Lancers, and Lieutenant Rhys Ivor Thomas MC of the 1st Battalion, Connaught Rangers.

Grenfell was the twin brother of Francis Octavius Grenfell. The twins were born on 4 September 1880, the sons of Pascoe Du Pré Grenfell and Sophia Grenfell, and had spent much of their childhood with their guardian, Baron Grenfell, at Kilvey, Swansea. The twins were educated at Eton, as were their three older brothers. Francis left Eton to join the Seaforth Highlanders, while Riversdale became a clerk for the Bank of England. He

The Grenfell twins Francis and Riversdale of the 9th Lancers, grandsons of Baron Grenfell of Kilvey, Swansea.

later spent much time travelling in South Africa and North America before returning to England in 1913 and spent some time training with the Buckinghamshire Hussars. He joined the 9th Lancers at the outbreak of war, meeting up with his brother, who had joined the regiment in 1905, and embarked for France with the regiment in August. Francis had been awarded the Victoria Cross for his gallantry on 24 August and had been invalided home. On 14 September Riversdale was shot and killed while directing fire on enemy positions. He is buried in Vendresse churchyard. His brother Francis later returned to duty and was killed at Ypres on 24 May 1915. John Buchan, the celebrated author, later wrote a book on the lives of the twins, *Francis and Riversdale Grenfell: A Memoir*.

Fighting continued on a lesser scale on the following day and the BEF took stock of its casualties while mounting a defence against several German counter-attacks. The 1st Division stood firm, both Welsh battalions suffering heavy casualties, yet both Welsh units had been largely instrumental in saving the situation in the 1st Division area. The Germans had suffered heavy casualties, but had been considerably reinforced over the preceding days and were now strongly entrenched.

The next five days brought no further change in the position of the 1st Division but casualties continued on a regular basis, especially when the 1st SWB became involved in heavy fighting on the 18th when it was attacked by a force of 150 to 500 German infantry, suffering a further 15 men killed. During the day a veterinary surgeon who was well-known in both north and south Wales died of wounds suffered at the Marne three days earlier.

Stuart Kirby Jones MRCVS, was born at Wavertree, Liverpool in 1888, the son of William and Alexandrina Jones. He had graduated from Liverpool University while serving a four-year apprenticeship with Rowland S. Rowlands, veterinary surgeon of The Laurels, Pensarn, near Abergele, prior to gaining a post as Pembroke Council's Veterinary Inspector. Jones was commissioned in the Army Veterinary Corps Reserve on 18 November 1911 after attending a course at the Army Veterinary School at Aldershot. When war broke out he was sent to France as a lieutenant attached to the 25th Brigade, Royal Field Artillery, which was one of the original units of the BEF and attached to the 1st Division, alongside the 1st SWB and 2nd Welsh.

Lieutenant Stuart Kirby Jones MRCVS, Army Veterinary Corps. Pembroke Council's veterinary inspector and one of the first Welsh veterinary casualties of the war.

On 15 September he was riding along the Moulins to Bourg road when a German shell crashed nearby, sending red-hot fragments of metal hurtling through the air. One large fragment caught Jones in the thigh, shattering his leg. He was taken to the nearest Field Ambulance, which patched him up and evacuated him to Number 2 General Hospital near Versailles, where he died two days later on 18 September 1914. He was buried with full military honours in Les Gonards Cemetery, Versailles. The chaplain who conducted the service took the time to write the following to his mother:

You will have heard already from here of the death of your brave son who has given his life for his country; but I think you will like me to write and tell you of his funeral which took place this morning, September 21st. It was carried out with full military honours, and a large crowd was present of French Dragoons and infantry. A large number of French officers were also there and also the Colonel commanding and the Major of this Hospital. At the close of the service a French Colonel spoke a few touching words as to the services rendered by your son to his own country and to ours. I know, too, that you will be touched to hear that several wreaths of flowers were sent by French people here. The grave is in a beautiful cemetery on the outskirts of this town, the Cimetière des Gonards, which lies on the slope of a hill, and is surrounded by trees. It is in a portion in the cemetery which has been reserved for the British soldiers, and will be marked with a plain wooden cross bearing your son's name. I am enclosing a small piece of heather which I plucked this morning within a few yards of the grave. May I be allowed to express my deep sympathy with you in your sorrow? It is my earnest prayer that the God of all comforts will Himself comfort you. (*Pembroke County Guardian.*)

Also killed during the same day were one officer, Captain Marwood Edwards Yeatman, and four men of the 1st SWB. Yeatman was born on 29 September 1883, the son of Marwood Shuttleworth Yeatman and Caroline Yeatman of Holwell Manor, Dorset. He was educated at Winchester before being commissioned in South Wales Borderers on 10 October 1903 and had forged a reputation as a good shot, having won several prizes at Bisley in July 1914. He had married Gwladys Mary Koe in 1909 and had a son, Marwood John Richard. The family lived at Glamorgan Street, Brecon where Yeatman took advantage of the splendid fishing in the River Usk. On 15 September, while his men were digging in among some woodland by the river, he was seen to have taken several pot shots at the Germans with his pistol, killing at least four of them, before he fell to the ground, shot in the heart by a sniper. Yeatman has no known grave and is commemorated on the La Ferté-sous-Jouarre Memorial.

Captain Marwood Edward Yeatman of the 1st SWB. H was shot through the heart while picking off Germans with his revolver.

By 20 September it had become clear that the BEF could do no more than hold its ground, so Major (General) Lomax decided to withdraw the 1st Division to Vendresse Ridge, where there was more cover from the constant shelling and behind which he could safely maintain his reserves; so on the night of 20/21 September, both Welsh battalions slipped away without attracting attention, the 2nd Welsh to Beaulne and the 1st SWB to hold the southern end of the Vendresse spur, with the 1st Gloucesters on their right.

Between 15 and 21 September, the Germans made several attacks at various points to attempt to drive the allies back across the Aisne, without success. The French, meanwhile, had failed to envelop the right flank of the German First Army on the River Oise. A stalemate had been reached that would herald the end of the mobile war that had been fought thus far and heralded the beginning of the period that would later become misleadingly known as the 'Race to the Sea'; a period in which the line known as the 'Western Front' would form.

The southern flanks of both armies now rested on the Swiss frontier, while the northern flanks were open. The lines of communication of the German First Army lay north through St Quentin to Belgium, while the most convenient ports for the BEF – Calais and Boulogne – were undefended. As a result, both warring parties, the allies and the Germans, decided to make a move in the north, the allies hoping to link up with the Belgians in an attempt to break out of Antwerp and the Germans hoping to drive through Belgium to take the Channel ports, thus cutting off the lifeline of the BEF; and threatening to outflank the allies.

As a result, on 26 September the Germans launched a fresh assault on the Aisne to prevent the allies moving north and the two Welsh battalions again saw heavy fighting, the 1st SWB in particular suffering heavy casualties. Once again, though, the attack was stemmed and the Germans were forced to withdraw after encountering strong opposition.

A Welshman serving with another unit, Corporal J. Davies of the King's (Liverpool) Regiment, took the opportunity to write of his experiences to his parents at 7 Conway Street, Mold from his bed in the 1st Southern General Hospital, Birmingham:

On Monday, September 14th, the first day of the battle of the Aisne, we were under heavy German shell fire, when a piece of shell hit me right in the mouth and broke my teeth. In the firing line we are fed mostly on biscuits and they are terribly hard. I used to manage the biscuits all right before my teeth were broken, but afterwards I was sickened. At any rate, I did not give way. I remained in the trenches from September 14th until September 22nd on bully beef, with the exception of two days when I had a little bread... It was doing nothing but rain. Our trenches were half full of rain and we had to stick in them night and day. I was at last carried in a weak state to hospital. That is how I am in England now, but I am pleased to say that I am getting quite strong again. I have been recommended for a new set of teeth and when I get them I expect I will be off to the front again.

Another Welshman, Private Frank Hill, 2nd Welsh, of Llangadock, who was wounded when a German shell struck his billet, later recounted his experience of the retirement from Mons and the Battle of the Aisne:

We sailed from Southampton on August 11th, not knowing where we were going to. We reached Havre, then entrained to a place unknown to us, where we remained till the order came that we had to do a long march, that was to Mons. There we met our opponents.

After a lot of fighting we had to retire, that was the retirement from Mons, which was a very tiresome one, lasting nine days, till we were within 15 miles of Paris. Then we started to advance, not having lost a man up to that time. We marched towards the Aisne; the advances were easier than the retirements. At a village on the Aisne we began to get the German shells. We had orders to stand fast; we were the brigade in reserve of the division of that day.

Then we advanced to Chivy. It was something cruel to see how the people were shot, hundreds of them. We had 12 of our officers wounded on the first day, including Lieut. Fitzroy and Lieut. Ford, two of my company commanders.

Fighting went on all day. In the evening we made a move to our right, where we captured 150 Germans and practically no end of guns. We lay down on the side of the road all night, and, to our surprise, in the morning found maxim guns put upon us. Several comrades were wounded and we had to retire that morning back to where we were the night before. But about 12 noon we returned and there we started to entrench. Trenches were dug and we lay in them, having sentinels on the alert. We had to fetch water from a village, a dangerous job, owing to so many shells flying about and snipers in the woods.

We remained in those trenches for about 14 days; then one night had orders to move on to another village. We lay down by the side of a church wall until the morning, when we had some more shells from the Germans. In the evening we went in to some trenches that had been dug by B Company of the 2nd Welsh. We were in the trenches till 4.0 am, then returned to the village once more. We had all that night off in a farmhouse close by. We were well treated, plenty of the best food and everything. We lay down till night, then went back once more to the trenches to find that several 90lb. shells had been fired at our trenches during the day. We left the trenches by day and returned to them at night.

One night we went out to find that the Germans had taken one of our trenches. We returned to the village, remaining in a shed. About half-past twelve mid-day a shell crashed through the roof. Then I received my wounds and there were two others, one in the ankle, the other in the muscles of the arm.

Two of us were able to walk to the field hospital, 50 yards away. Shells were bursting by our side and we were very lucky to miss them. We were seen to at once by the medical officers and treated very well. About 8 o'clock that night we were taken to a village unknown to me and sent down next morning to Rheims and from there to a camp hospital at Rouen.

There we remained until the order came to return home, to the Royal Herbert Hospital at Woolwich.

The BEF began to redeploy from the Aisne from 1 October, its place being taken by the French, and over the next two weeks its units entrained for northern France via Abbeville.

Casualties had been heavy among the two Welsh battalions on the Aisne. The 2nd Welsh had lost the following:

The ruined village of Paissy, on the Chemin des Dames.

Killed: Major J.H. Kerrich; Captains Mark Haggard and H.C. Davies; Lieutenants C.R. Fitzpatrick and C.O. Birch; and fifty Other Ranks.
Wounded: Captain F.H. Gaskell; Lieutenants C.A.S. Carleton, Hon. W. Fitzroy Somerset, F.W. Ford, W. Owen and H.A. Walker; and 132 Other Ranks.
Missing: Twenty-eight Other Ranks.

The following had been lost from the 1st SWB:

Killed: Major G.E.E. Welby; Captain M.E. Yeatman; Lieutenants G.P. Blackhall-Simmonds, J.C. Coker, M.T. Johnson and C.C. Sills; and 110 Other Ranks.
Wounded: Five officers and 267 Other Ranks.
Missing: Thirty-five Other Ranks.

Chapter 5

China:
The Landings at Lao Shan Bay
and the Siege of Tsingtao

Throughout the late nineteenth century, Imperial Germany became one of several other European powers who had seized territory in the Far East from a weak China. Its power there was centred in the city and port of Tsingtao, which by 1914 had become the home base of the German navy's East Asia Squadron, which operated in support of the German colonies in the Pacific. Britain had leased the Chinese port of Weihaiwei to counter this German threat in China and also began forging close ties with neighbouring Japan.

When the war in Europe began in August 1914, Britain requested Japanese assistance in the Far East and on 15 August Japan issued an ultimatum to Germany stating that she must withdraw her warships from Chinese and Japanese waters and transfer control of its port of Tsingtao to Japan. On 23 August Japan declared war on Germany and preparations for a military operation against the German colonies began, with the Japanese navy beginning to bombard the port almost immediately. The Japanese army began preparations to take Tsingtao by force and so the 2nd SWB, under

The landing-place for the 2nd SWB at Lao Shan Bay, Tsingtao, China in September 1914.

On the deck of HMS Triumph, *en route to Lao Shan Bay.*

Lieutenant Colonel Hugh Gilbert Casson, was despatched to the area to aid in any ensuing action, embarking on 19 September aboard three small transport ships that steamed for Lao Shan Bay, escorted by HMS *Triumph* and HMS *Usk*.

Soon after the declaration of war, on 8 August Private Wallace Baker (10722) wrote home to his parents at Aberavon:

This may be my last letter, as we are under active service conditions and ready to move at a moment's notice. We have not taken our boots or clothes off for the last ten days. The Germans who were at this station went to their base at Tsingtao, about 40 miles from here, as soon as the war broke out. They have 5,000 troops and five war boats there. We are expecting to move south to Tsingtao any moment, but I believe they are waiting for the Germans' first move. We receive about half-a-dozen cablegrams from England every day, giving us all the news of the war in Belgium and on the other frontiers. Of course, there is great rejoicing here over it.

In another letter, dated 22 August, he wrote:

Our battalion has concentrated here, all mobilised, ready to move at any moment. The Gloucester Regiment are under orders to sail. The Germans are still holding up our shipping. All the troops are very excited and talking about war, but I think the Germans will surrender, as it appears hopeless for them to try and hold out against such tremendous odds. I suppose our first battalion at Borden has gone to the front long ago. I expect you think I am lucky being out here, but I don't. I would like to be there in the thick of it. They are all grumbling out here over it. But never mind, I might have a hand in it out here next week, when the fighting will be in full swing, or else it will be the surrender of the Germans.

Baker would soon get his wish to be 'in the thick of it'. On 23 September 1914 the 2nd Battalion, South Wales Borderers (2nd SWB) landed at Lao Shan Bay and over the coming days marched overland via Puh-li, Chimo, Liuting, Litsun and Yang-chia-chung in preparation for a combined attack with the Japanese against the German garrison at Tsingtao. The sounds of heavy naval guns firing in the distance brought some realization to the men that their war had begun for them; by 30 September they had reached Yang-chia-chung, where the battalion dug in on a reverse slope so that German artillery fire would not reach them.

Private Trevor Mabbett (10470) of the 2nd SWB took the opportunity to write a brief letter home to his mother at 44 Powell Street, Swansea:

We are working in conjunction with the Imperial Japanese Army and Navy at a place called Tsingtao or 'the German Gibraltar of the East'. We have been very successful up to the present and I think this is about the last crow Germany will have. About 200 Germans made an attack on the Japanese outpost, but they got cut to pieces. The next morning the Japanese sent in a flag of truce to enable the Germans to take away their wounded and bury the dead. The Germans sent back a reply that dead men eat no rations and if the Japanese went forward and attempted to attend to them the Germans would fire on them. About four days later the Germans asked for four hours' armistice to bury the brave men that were killed and starved to death but they were afraid to come out after they had their wish granted and the Japanese had to bury them.

Private Mabbett was wounded soon after and returned to England for treatment, dying at Netley Hospital of his wounds on 5 March 1915.

On 2 October an aide to the Emperor of Japan visited the 2nd SWB, bringing presents of *sake*, sugar cakes and cigarettes, before thanking the battalion for its co-operation with the Japanese troops. These gifts were welcomed by the men, as rations were in short supply due to the nature of the country prohibiting the battalion transport from reaching them. On 10 October orders finally reached the battalion to move into the front line and two companies then took up positions on Shibosan Ridge, where preparations began for the attack on the port. The battalion suffered one of its first casualties here when Private James Thomas (10406) died on 2 November of wounds suffered from shellfire. (Private William Henry Hopkins (9886), the 25-year-old son of Henry and Anne Hopkins of 3 Griffin Street, Newport, Monmouth had become the 2nd SWB's first casualty in China when he died there on 13 September.)

A map taken from the History of the South Wales Borderers *showing the dispositions of the 2nd SWB at Tsingtao.*

Preparations for the attack proved to be slow, but the battalion luckily suffered few casualties in their advanced position, spending some of their time looking on as the Germans were bombarded by battleships anchored offshore. The first men of the 2nd SWB killed in action occurred on the night of 5/6 November when digging an advanced 'Third Attack Position' after the men made contact with a German sniper's post, which they attacked and captured. The skirmish prompted a German party on the left flank to pour fire into the 2nd SWB and the ensuing action killed Sergeant Arthur George Payne (7235) and Privates Edward James Bettis (10019), George Parkes (10202), Joseph Williams (9763) and Herbert Evans (10614). Private Leslie Craske (9327) wrote of the gallantry of Lance Corporal Sydenham during the night's action:

Three journeys he made to the danger zone, each time returning with a wounded man and he had just returned and picked up a fourth, when a machine gun opened fire and he fell on the comrade he sought to save. He was riddled with bullets and his body acted as a shield for his comrade, who was rescued alive. Lance Corporal Sydenham, who was mortally wounded, showed rare courage on his way to the hospital. Private Gibbons, who was one of the stretcher party, recounts that one of Sydenham's legs was blown off, but he sang several songs as he was borne along, two having reference to his parents and home and one to the fact that he would need a wooden leg. As the bearer party was taking him off Gibbons saw that the white flag was hoisted and said, 'It's all over, Sydenham.' The wounded man replied 'Let's get up and have a look' and, his wish gratified, he expired. As they were marching in after the surrender the Borderers saw on the roadside a Japanese and a German locked on each other's bayonets. Death overtook both at the same time and they still grasped their rifles.

These would be the first of many men of the battalion who would fall during the war. Another daily hazard came from German aircraft dropping bombs made of coffee cans with tin propellers onto the Borderers' trenches. Private Smale wrote of these bombs: 'Captain Collier, of the Australian Intelligence Staff, who was in charge of the transport, fired at one and exploded it.'

The Japanese pressed their attack on Tsingtao the following morning, capturing a fort on the western side of the port, and at 7 am on 7 November the Germans ran up a white flag to signify their surrender of the port along with 4,042 German officers and men. During the afternoon the Borderers marched into the town. Private Smale wrote:

Well, we paraded and marched to Tsingtao and it was a sight I don't want to see again. On the road alone there were hundreds of dead and wounded Germans. Some must have been there for days. There were broken rifles, Maxim-guns, bayonets and swords. You could see where one of those brave men had tried to get cover, but caught it before they got there. One fellow on the road still had his rifle up to his shoulder and over 200 spent cartridges around him.

The 2nd South Wales Borderers at Tsingtao, November 1914.

Although a limited operation, the 2nd SWB were rewarded handsomely for their efforts. In his despatch, General Barnardiston reported the following officers and men of the 2nd SWB as deserving of special mention for their services: Lieutenant Colonel H.G. Casson; Major E.C. Margesson; Captain J. Bradstock; Captain and Adjutant G.H. Birkett; Captain D.G. Johnson; Lieutenant R.L. Petre; Lieutenant H.J. Simson, Royal Scots (Japanese interpreter, attached); Captain G.H. Dive, Royal Army Medical Corps, attached; No. 2/10423 Sergeant J.J. Ward (killed); No. 2/9972 Private G.C. Snow; No. 2/9004 Private A. Green; No. 2/9980 Private T. Jenkinson; No. 10171 Drummer W.I. Jones (killed); No. 10634 Private C.J. Foley; No. 10614 Private H. Evans (killed); No. 2/9952 Private J. West (died of wounds); No. 2/4528 Drummer C.W. Lewis; No. 2/9244 Company Sergeant Major G.A. Davies; No. 7309 Sergeant H. Leach (died of wounds); and No. 3/10849 Corporal (Acting Sergeant) W.S. Rosier. Some of these gained awards as a result of their actions: Lieutenant Colonel Casson was made Commander of the Order of St Michael and St George (CMG); Captain Dudley Graham Johnson was awarded the Distinguished Service Order (DSO); Captain John Bradstock the Military Cross (MC); and five men – C.J. Foley, A. Green, G.C. Snow, J.J. Ward and J. West – the Distinguished Conduct Medal (DCM) for gallantry in rescuing wounded men while under heavy fire.

The 2nd SWB left Tsingtao on 17 November and were given a rousing send-off by Japanese troops who lined the streets as the battalion marched out to embark for Hong Kong aboard the SS *Delta*. The families of the married men then met up with the battalion in Hong Kong before re-embarking aboard *Delta* to sail back to England, escorted by HMS *Ocean*. On 12 January 1915 the *Delta* dropped anchor in Plymouth Sound.

Chapter 6

The First Battle of Ypres

On 4 October the 1st Battalion, Royal Welsh Fusiliers (1st RWF), which had returned to England from overseas service, embarked aboard HMT *Winifredian* and landed in the Belgian port of Zeebrugge on 7 October, attached to 22 Brigade, 7th Division. Oddly, the battalion suffered its first man killed on 4 October: Private John William Davies (11139) of Tyn yn Celyn Farm, Llanfihangel Glyn Myfyr, is recorded as having been presumed dead on or since that day, three days before the battalion actually landed! He is commemorated on the Nieuport Memorial, so possibly drowned during the crossing. Zeebrugge was in the process of being overrun by the Germans, so the division marched via Bruges towards Ostend and entrained for Ghent two days later to assist in the defence of the city; but due to the withdrawal of the beleaguered Belgian and French troops, along with countless scores of refugees, was forced to join their retreat.

From 11 October a general retirement was carried out by the Fusiliers, who marched from Ghent via Tronchiennes to Hansbeke on the following day. Three companies of the 1st RWF were ordered to hold important crossings along the German line of advance from Ghent over the canal between Hanime and Neyele. During the evening the three companies received orders to move to Thielt to rejoin the remainder of the battalion and were relieved by troopers of the Northumberland Hussars. On the following day the retirement continued, with Roulers being reached during the afternoon and on 14 October, once the withdrawal of the Belgian army to the Yser had been completed, the 7th Division moved to the Flemish town of Ypres, spending the night of 14/15 October there. The following morning the division moved out to positions at Zonnebeke, east of Ypres, where it began to dig in. The 1st RWF therefore became the first Welsh unit to defend the city.

To understand how the war had developed so that the 7th Division was now in Ypres, an overview of the events on the Western Front is necessary.

Between 17 September and 17 October the allies and the Germans made mutual attempts to turn the northern flank of their opponent. On 2 September Joffre ordered the French Second Army to move to the north of the French Sixth Army, which prompted von Falkenhayn to move the German Sixth Army from the Franco-German border area to the northern flank on 17 September.

By the next day French attacks north of the Aisne led to von Falkenhayn ordering the Sixth Army to secure the flank. Further north, during the Battle of Picardy from 22 to 26 September, the French met a German attack east of Albert. Further fighting continued northwards during the Battle of Arras between 1 and 4 October and so the

French soldiers of the 103rd Infanterie Regiment.

outflanking manoeuvres continued northwards. By 6 October the French needed the BEF to defend against German attacks around Lille, thus necessitating the BEF to move north to Flanders, assembling on the left flank of the French Tenth Army, which had been formed from the left flank units of the French Second Army on 4 October.

From 8 October the BEF began arriving in Flanders, joining the British forces already there and there were now four regular Welsh battalions at the front. The 1st RWF along with the 7th Division held a line stretching in an arc to the east of Ypres. North of them lay the Belgian army. The BEF line stretched south from Ypres to La Bassée. This also brought the BEF much closer to its supply lines.

The scene was now set for the First Battle of Ypres.

During Friday 16 October the 7th Division moved out of Ypres along the Menin Road, with orders to occupy the villages of Zonnebeke, Gheluvelt and Zandvoorde. By Sunday 18 October the 2nd RWF had moved into reserve positions west of Ypres, along with the remainder of 19 Brigade, taking up positions west of Vlamertinghe after having become temporarily attached to the 6th Division on 6 October. Interestingly, it was deemed fit to post sentries on all the estaminets in the area in order to save the men from themselves! The 1st RWF was in line with 22 Brigade, just north of the Menin Road at Becelaere, and to the rear of the main line that was held by 21 Brigade. The 3rd Cavalry Division held the line on the left flank of the division.

The 1st Division, including the 1st SWB and 2nd Welsh, was around Cassel and in reserve, after moving from the La Bassée sector.

North of Ypres, the Battle of the Yser opened on 18 October following the launch of an attack by the Germans against the French and Belgian army's position east of

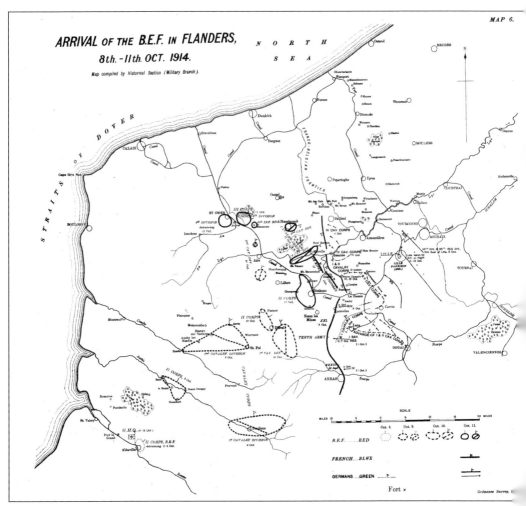

MAP 6.

ARRIVAL OF THE B.E.F. IN FLANDERS,
8th.-11th. OCT. 1914.
Map compiled by Historical Section (Military Branch).

A map taken from the Official History *showing the dispositions of the BEF during its first deployment in Flanders.*

the Yser Canal. To the south II and III Corps of the BEF were already fighting around La Bassée and on the 19th had captured Aubers Ridge from the Germans and were just 5 miles from Lille. There was still a chance of turning the flank of the Germans and forcing an end to the war.

On the morning of 18 October, 7th Division HQ received reports that the enemy was strongly entrenched on the line Wervicq to Menin, with fortified outposts at Kleythoek and south of Gheluwe. An attack by the 7th Division had been planned by Major General Rawlinson for the following day: 22 Brigade was to advance on Kleythoek; 20 and 21 Brigade were to advance on Gheluwe; then the entire division would combine to advance upon Menin from Kleythoek and Gheluwe.

At 5 am on 19 October the 1st RWF began its move forward from Becelaere and proceeded to its rendezvous point at Strooiboomhoek. Advance parties reported that

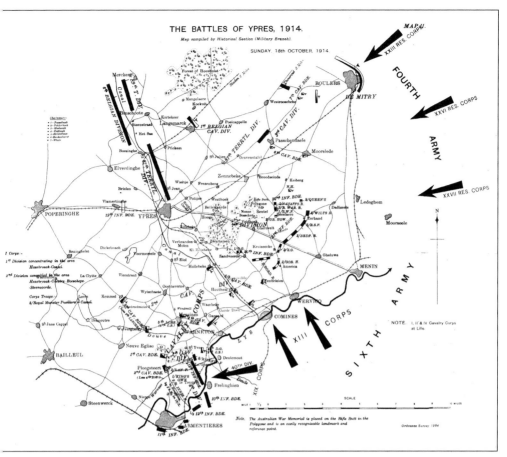

THE BATTLES OF YPRES, 1914.

Map compiled by Historical Section (Military Branch).

SUNDAY, 18th OCTOBER, 1914.

A map taken from the Official History *showing the dispositions of the BEF, including 1st and 2nd battalions RWF, just prior to the advance of the 7th Division.*

the area south of Dadizeele was clear of the enemy and, as a result, 22 Brigade advanced towards the town.

Upon reaching positions around Dadizeele, the 1st RWF advanced towards Kleythoek and launched their attack on the village just after 11.15 am. No sign of the enemy was to be found, but the battalion came under heavy shrapnel fire from German artillery. By 12.40 pm the battalion was ordered to retire towards Dadizeele after a pilot of the RFC had reported seeing massed German infantry; but they came into contact with the enemy, making the withdrawal a difficult one. Heavy fighting continued over the coming hours, necessitating the division to begin a general withdrawal back to its starting positions and at around 4 pm the 1st RWF began withdrawing towards Becelaere. During this first day's fighting the battalion lost Captain John Henry Brennan, Lieutenant Guy Ogden de Peyster Chance and seventeen other ranks killed; Major R.E.P. Gabbett, Captain W.H. St John, Captain S. Jones, Second Lieutenant R.E. Naylor and eighty-four other ranks wounded, and eleven men

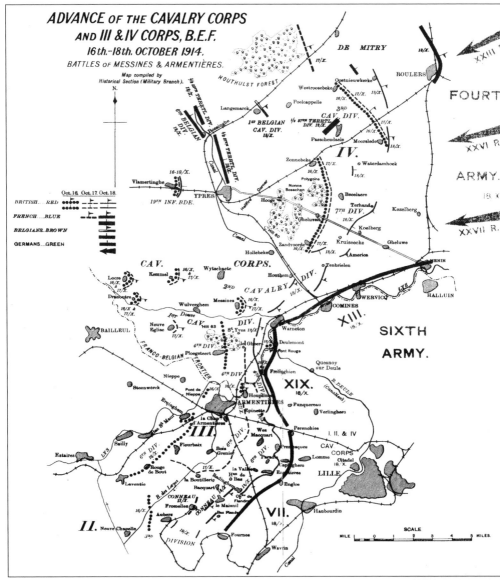

ADVANCE OF THE CAVALRY CORPS
AND III & IV CORPS, B.E.F.
16th.-18th. OCTOBER 1914.
BATTLES of MESSINES & ARMENTIÈRES.

Map compiled by
Historical Section (Military Branch).

A map taken from the Official History *showing the advance of the 7th Division.*

missing. Also thought killed was Captain Eric Ommanney Skaife, but he had in fact escaped death after being taken prisoner by the Germans, becoming a brigadier during a distinguished post-war career that also saw him knighted.

Captain Eric Ommanney Skaife, taken prisoner by the Germans on 19 October 1914. He became a prominent member of Welsh society after the war, rising to the rank of brigadier before being knighted

While touring the battlefields several years ago the author came across a row of thirteen graves of unknown men of the Royal Welsh Fusiliers buried in Harlebeke New British Cemetery who were killed in October 1914. These graves would have been relocated here from the local area during post-war clearances and the only possible conclusion is that these graves belong to some of the men of the 1st RWF killed around Dadizeele on 19 October 1914, as this was the only time the regiment fought in this area during that month. The graves include seven inscribed as follows:

'A SOLDIER OF THE GREAT WAR/ROYAL WELSH FUSILIERS/ OCTOBER 1914'; one to 'A SOLDIER OF THE GREAT WAR/UNKNOWN LANCE CORPORAL/ROYAL WELSH FUSILIERS/ OCTOBER 1914'; three to 'A SOLDIER OF THE GREAT WAR/UNKNOWN CORPORAL/ROYAL WELSH FUSILIERS/OCTOBER 1914'; one to 'A SOLDIER OF THE GREAT WAR/UNKNOWN SERGEANT/ROYAL WELSH FUSILIERS/OCTOBER 1914'; and another among them to a 'A SOLDIER OF THE GREAT WAR/UNKNOWN OFFICER/OCTOBER 1914'.

Of the nineteen men killed on that day, four are buried in named graves at Harlebeke, one man at Perth (China Wall) Cemetery and another at Tyne Cot Cemetery. Thirteen men are commemorated on the Ypres (Menin Gate) Memorial. There are thirteen unknown RWF graves at Harlebeke, so these 'missing' men must be buried there and at least one of the following is positively identifiable: Private Harry Barnett (9016) of

The thirteen graves to 'unknown' members of the 1st RWF in Harlebeke British Cemetery. These men are identifiable, but solid evidence is required by the CWGC.

Kenilworth; Corporal Ernest Blake (6479) of Burton-on-Trent; Captain John Henry Brennan of Montreal; Private Samuel Brotherton (10805) of Birmingham; Lieutenant Guy Ogden de Peyster Chance of Bury St Edmunds; Private Richard Stanley Dier (10572) of Pembroke Dock; Private Henry James Hooper (11036) of Cardiff; Corporal Walter Guy Jones (6766) of Birmingham; Private James Long (10730) of Sydenham, London; Sergeant Alfred Martin (5169) of Whitechapel, London; Private William John Penney (10131) of Chester; Private James Sant (6583) of Liverpool; and Private William Worsford (6557) of Northwich.

It is always worth making notes of graves of any unknown soldiers during any battlefield tour as modern referencing techniques sometimes make identification of these men possible. The problem then is of producing enough evidence to enable the Commonwealth War Graves Commission (CWGC) to properly commemorate these men on a named headstone but, as the author knows from experience, that is a very difficult task, with many hurdles to overcome.

The operation was a failure, but some success was claimed by the staff of the 7th Division who realized how hard the operation had been. It was purely a matter of overwhelming odds that had forced the division to retreat, but the large numbers of German forces in the area foretold what was about to come, whilst the constant stream of refugees from the burning town of Roulers passing through the area told their own sad story.

Soon after 9 am on the following morning of 20 October, German artillery fire began raining down on the positions occupied by the division, followed by an attack by large numbers of German infantry. The 1st RWF bore the brunt of the onslaught that followed, although the 3rd Cavalry Division on the left flank around Passchendaele also suffered badly. Suffering terrible casualties, the battalion was reinforced by a company of Royal Warwicks and somehow managed to survive the day, heavy fighting carrying on until 10 pm, when the German attacks became more sporadic.

Over the preceding days I Corps had moved up into support behind Ypres and 4 (Guards) Brigade came into the line during the night of 20/21 October, relieving the 3rd Cavalry Division, while the Guards also reinforced the battered 7th Division, taking the line to the left of the 1st RWF. The battalion had suffered three officers and thirty-two men killed during the day, the three officers being Captain William Miles Kingston DSO, Lieutenant Edwin Cecil Leigh Hoskyns and Second Lieutenant Geoffrey Phillip Joseph Snead-Cox.

In the meantime I Corps had been concentrating in Flanders and the 1st Division had begun its march towards the front on the 20th. The 1st SWB and 2nd Welsh were billeted in Poperinghe overnight, before the division renewed its march the following day with the sound of battle within earshot. With the holding of the front held by the 7th Division, Sir John French proposed to attempt to attack again and proposed that this attack should head towards Roulers, headed by the 1st and 2nd divisions, while the 7th Division held their ground in front of Polygon Wood. Thus on 21 October the 2nd Division advanced on Passchendaele while the 1st Division, on the extreme left, moved on Langemarck.

Captain William Miles Kington DSO. He was the son of Lieutenant Colonel William Miles Napier Kington of Wroxall, Somerset and Sophia Kington, née Baker. He was educated at Winchester and at the Royal Military College, Sandhurst before being commissioned in the RWF and was awarded the DSO during the Boer War. He was killed in action at Becelaere on 20 October 1914.

Lieutenant Edwin Cecil Leigh Hoskyns. Born on 22 September 1890, the son of Sir Leigh Hoskyns, he was educated at Eton and at the Royal Military College, Sandhurst before being commissioned in the RWF. He was killed in action at Becelaere on 20 October 1914.

Second Lieutenant Geoffrey Phillip Joseph Snead-Cox. Born on 20 February 1895, he was the son of the lord of the manor of Broxwood. Snead-Cox was educated at Downside School, Bath and at the Royal Military College, Sandhurst before being commissioned in the 1st RWF. He was killed in action at Becelaere on 20 October 1914. Two of his brothers also fell during the war: Herbert Arthur and Richard Mary Snead-Cox.

After a particularly unpleasant night for the defenders of Ypres, the Germans attacked again on the following morning, throwing large numbers of troops into wave upon wave of attack on the beleaguered lines of the 7th Division. The 1st RWF held trenches across the Broodseinde to Passchendaele road in front of the village of Zonnebeke and on the morning of 21 October came under an intense artillery bombardment. The men crouched low in their trenches while fire rained about them and when the guns ceased firing at around 11 am the German infantry attack began. Accurate rifle fire soon stemmed the German advance and at about 4 pm the German artillery opened up again. The left flank of the 1st RWF came under enfilade fire from the Germans and suffered heavy casualties throughout the day, some thirty-nine men being killed, making a total of almost 100 officers and men killed in just a few days. Total casualties for the battalion amounted to twenty-three officers and 750 other ranks killed, wounded or missing. The battalion had been almost wiped out in its first major action of the war and following its relief on 22 October, the roll-call of survivors amounted to just six officers and 206 other ranks. The gradual destruction of Ypres and its surrounding villages had begun in earnest and the war was now in danger of being lost by the allies, who were under terrible pressure. However, despite its losses, the 7th Division had stood firm.

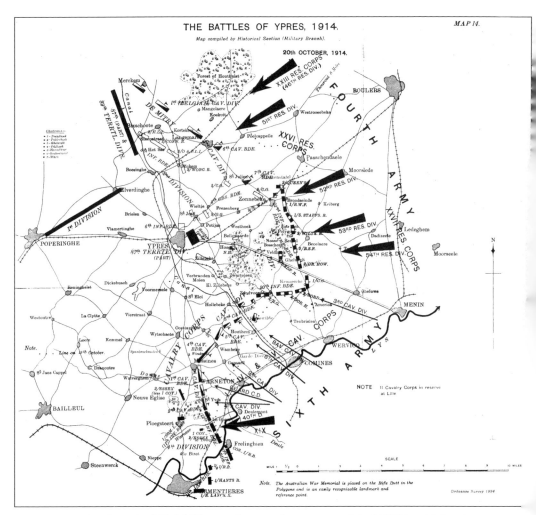

A map taken from the Official History *showing the situation of the 1/RWF on 21 October.*

The attack of the 1st Division that same day was led by 3 Brigade, comprising the 1st SWB and the 1st Gloucesters with the 2nd Welsh in reserve, and by 9 am Langemarck had been captured. Pushing through the village, the Germans were found in greater strength and an attack developed from the German lines, driving the French cavalry from the Houthulst Forest, so the 1st Gloucesters were sent to push the line to the left. Following further pressure from the Germans, the 2nd Welsh were also sent forward through the village, taking up positions to the left of the 1st SWB. Of these two battalions the 1st SWB had suffered the brunt of the fighting so far, suffering heavy casualties from artillery and rifle fire before digging into positions in front of Langemarck, where the 2nd Welsh joined them.

The Germans were now throwing huge numbers of men into the attack but the British held firm, the well-drilled soldiers using their Lee Enfield rifles to great effect

A group of young German soldiers, possibly some of the many student soldiers killed during the fighting at Langemarck.

to knock down the hordes of grey-clad Germans who were reported to have been singing as they advanced. This action later became known by the Germans as the *Kindermord von Ypren* or the Massacre of the Innocents at Ypres, due to the large number of student soldiers in their ranks. The 1st SWB War Diary contains a brief but interesting note about this: 'The Germans come on in great masses, silly idiots.'

With Houthulst Forest now evacuated by the French, 1 (Guards) Brigade was sent forward to hold a defensive line to the left flank of the 2nd Welsh, facing north. To the right of the 1st SWB lay the 2nd Division, while the French re-formed on the west bank of the Ypres Canal, turning the line into a series of angles that created a position in which the 1st SWB and 2nd Welsh could be enfiladed from both sides.

This was obviously not an ideal situation to be in, especially when the ground had been so hard-won by the 1st SWB and the 1st Queen's, but common sense dictated that a tactical withdrawal should occur and that 3 Brigade should withdraw closer to Langemarck. At dusk the brigade pulled back 300 metres to form a new line just in front of the village. It was now obvious to the allies that, far from advancing, they would struggle even to maintain their present positions and the situation was at a critical point.

As night closed in, the 1st SWB counted their losses. Captain William Charles Curgenven, Second Lieutenant Horace Holmes Watkins and sixty other ranks had been killed, as was also one of the first Americans to be killed during the war: Private Edgar Lewis Delan (10827), a New Yorker serving with the 1st SWB. Over 100 men had

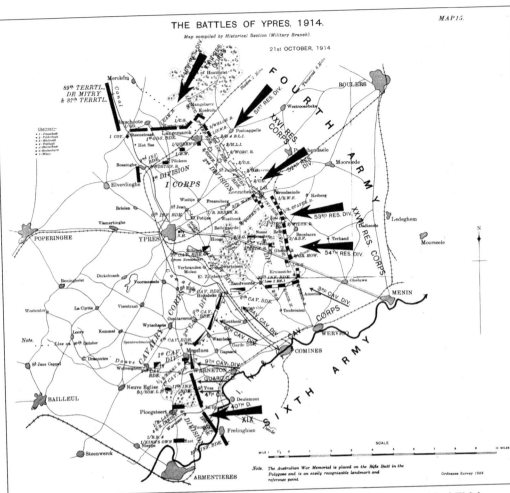

A map taken from the Official History, *showing the situation of the 1st SWB and 2nd Welsh on the left flank of the BEF at Langemarck on 21 October.*

also been wounded in the battalion. The feeling among the survivors was one of desperation; the men could see their fallen comrades lying on the battlefield but couldn't bring them in. As a result, badly-wounded men died where they lay, while a large proportion of them never received a decent burial, instead being commemorated on the Ypres (Menin Gate) Memorial after the war.

William Charles Curgenven of the 1st SWB was a gallant man who had been wounded at Bloemfontein during the Boer War. He was born on 7 November 1876, the son of Charles James Curgenven, Paymaster-in-Chief, Royal Navy, and was a talented sportsman, especially good at football and hockey, and had played cricket for Newport. He was a well-respected officer and was well-known throughout south Wales during many years of service, having been stationed for long periods at Pembroke Dock and at Newport. Curgenven had taught topography at the Royal Military College, Sandhurst prior to rejoining the regiment for its move to France in August 1914.

Following his death at Langemarck, he became one of the very few members of his battalion to receive a burial and now lies next to a private from his battalion in Perth Cemetery (China Wall), near Ypres.

The 2nd Welsh had fared much better, having only advanced from the reserve to support the remainder of 3 Brigade, just losing one man killed that day, Private John Rees (1159) of Penyrheol, Glamorgan.

It must be remembered that Welshmen were also in action with other regiments along the line during this trying time. For example, on 21 October alone: one officer, Second Lieutenant Philip Lloyd Elliott of Henllan, Cardiganshire and two Welshmen of the 1st DCLI were killed near Cuinchy; Captain Athol Thomas Gibson of Penarth was killed with the 2nd South Lancs near Neuve Chapelle; and six more Welshmen were killed with other units – two with the 1st KSLI and one apiece with the 3rd Worcesters, the 2nd Essex, the 4th Royal Fusiliers and the 2nd Lancashire Fusiliers.

Captain William Charles Curgenven, a former instructor at Sandhurst, killed at Langemarck with the 1st SWB on 21 October 1914. He is one of very few men killed that day to have been afforded a proper burial and lies in Perth Cemetery (China Wall).

Athol Thomas Gibson was born in Penarth in 1878, the son of Thomas and Alice Gibson. He was a shipping storage agent at Porthcawl prior to the war and married Elizabeth Pyman in 1907. Gibson was a renowned golfer and had played in the Welsh team against Ireland at Royal Porthcawl in July 1914. He was serving as a captain with the Glamorgan Volunteer Artillery at the outbreak of war and on 11 August 1914 was granted the rank of temporary second lieutenant in the regular army, joining the 3rd South Lancs. He was posted to France, joining the 2nd South Lancs at Neuve Chapelle in the rank of captain and was killed during a German attack on his battalion's positions on 21 October. He is commemorated on the Le Touret Memorial.

German attacks continued throughout the following day but on a lesser scale and were again met with accurate fire from the British. The headquarters of the 1st SWB and 2nd Welsh set up their base in some ruins in Langemarck but, as Captain Rees of the 2nd Welsh noted, it was not pleasant there:

I saw a field gun shell strike the spire of the church just below the cross and send the cross 20 yards in the air. The church shortly afterwards caught fire and went up in a sheet of flame. A little later, Colonel Morland and Battalion H.Q. came to my Company H.Q. He had had two houses blown down over his head in succession in the village, and, as he remarked, it was safer in the front line.

Captain Athol Thomas Gibson, 2nd South Lancs, of Penarth, a Welsh golfing International.

The ruins of Langemarck Church. The ruins were completely flattened during the course of the war.

Battalion HQ of the 1st SWB was also having a similarly bad time in a neighbouring building when a salvo of German shells, or 'coal boxes' as the battalion war diarist wrote, came crashing through the air, flattening houses all around them and sending shards of window glass and pieces of furniture sky-high: 'A wonderfully awful sight in the night with the Church one glowing mass and showers of sparks coming up as some house fell in somewhere in the town.'

On 23 October the Germans attacked again in force against both the 1st and 7th divisions. The attack on the former was directed on the angle held by the 1st Coldstream Guards, 1st Gloucesters and 2nd Welsh from the village of Koekuit by the German 46th Reserve Division but it was again beaten off with accurate rifle and machine-gun fire. Captain Rees wrote:

At the corner of my hedge we had a machine gun. Colonel Morland and I stood by this gun for about an hour. We actually saw the Germans form up for attack and opened fire on their first line at 1,250 yards. From that time onwards we had every form of target from a company in mass, who tried to put a large haystack between us and them, but who formed on the wrong side of it, to a Battalion in fours near the edge of the Houthulst Forest. Sergeant Longdon, who was firing the gun, told me that evening that he reckoned he had killed a thousand Germans. I put it at 400 or 500 casualties. The enemy, who had not properly located us before the action began, started shelling and one shell nearly hit this machine gun, but fortunately caused only one casualty. By this time the attack had obviously been disposed of and with practically no loss to us. I never saw the Germans make a worse attack, or suffer heavier losses.

The 1st Division was relieved on the night of 23/24 October and moved back to billets in the area Ypres-Hooge-Zillebeke, ready for the next action. The men of the 2nd Welsh were not overly pleased with the results of this relief, as the *History of the Welsh Regiment* notes:

> The French Territorial is not a trained regular soldier. He fights well, as all Frenchmen do, but he is excitable and unmethodical, as all who have handed or taken over a trench line well know. On this occasion no sooner had the French relieved the Welsh than they began firing their rifles furiously, bringing down enemy artillery fire on Langemarck, through which our men had to pass. A great many unnecessary casualties were caused and 'C' Company had the terrible misfortune to have 39 men killed and wounded by one 8-inch shell.

Private Samuel Knight wrote of the bombardment:

> The shrapnel is shrieking through the lane. I can hear the groans of our wounded. One man drops helplessly into our dug-out. He extends an arm battered beyond description. We bandage it. His groans are terrible. A shell bursts very near us. The shrapnel pieces fall through our roof. A piece strikes me on the shoulder. Luckily its force is spent. I am all right. There is a heavy crash on my right. A shell has struck the barn. I hear loud wailings. The barn is ablaze. My comrades are being burnt. I hear intermittent bangs. The ammunition on their bodies is exploding. This continues for some time, a terrible death.

One of these men was an Australian from Melbourne: Private Robert Roland Jones (1118) is one of just three men of this group killed during the day to have a known grave and is buried in Perth Cemetery (China Wall) alongside Private Morris Evans (8136) of Llandovery.

During 24 and 25 October, the French 17th Division attacked alongside the British 2nd Division and carried the line forward almost 1,000 metres to Zonnebeke and the 2nd Division dug in at Broodseinde.

The Battle of Langemarck, which had been fought from 21 to 24 October, terminated the first part of the First Battle of Ypres, leaving the French holding the northern portion of the semicircle

Private Morris Evans of Llandovery, one of two brothers serving with the Welsh Regiment, who was killed by a shell at Langemarck.

A familiar sight during the Great War, an undamaged effigy of Christ on the Cross, in this case in the shell-damaged church at Fromelles.

round Ypres from the Ypres-Roulers road, while the British completed the southern portion, creating an arc in front of the city.

By now the 2nd RWF was also in action. On 19 October 19 Brigade had been issued orders to proceed to the area around the French village of Fromelles to fill a gap in the line between II and III Corps and left their billets at Vlamertinghe, reaching Laventie after a thirteen-hour march. At daybreak on the 20th the brigade relieved French troops on the outskirts of Fromelles, taking over hastily-dug trenches that offered little protection and thus required a lot of work by the already tired troops. This was still a peaceful area but Fromelles would, in less than two years' time, become infamous after a disastrous attack by the 5th Australian and 61st South Midland divisions. Frank Richards wrote in his classic book, *Old Soldiers Never Die*:

Little did we think when we were digging those trenches that we were digging our future homes; but they were the beginnings of the long stretch that soon went all the way from the North Sea to Switzerland and they were our homes for the next four years... We dug those trenches simply for fighting; they were breast-high with the front parapet on ground level and in each bay we stood shoulder to shoulder... Sandbags were unknown at this time.

By the morning of 23 October the 2nd RWF was hard at work digging new trenches around La Cordonnerie Farm. What would turn into a seemingly never-ending flow of casualties now began for the 2nd RWF during the battalion's first spell in the line at Fromelles, when Private Joseph Kynaston (9144) of B Company, a Dolgellau man, became the first member of the battalion killed in Flanders. Kynaston was the illegitimate son of Mary Kynaston and had served with the RWF since first enlisting in 1906. He was probably the first Welshman to be buried in Pont-du-Hem Military Cemetery, La Gorgue during the war.

The battalion lost three men killed on the following day, coming under attack from eleven lines of German infantry, who were beaten off by concentrated rifle fire. Further attacks continued throughout the day but all were repelled with few losses, although the next two days saw almost thirty more men killed while fighting off further German assaults. Twenty-nine of these men were buried together in a mass grave in Pont-du-Hem, although each now has his own headstone. Captain J.C. Dunn, the battalion medical officer, wrote of what he saw as a comedic moment during the burial of some of these men in his epic book *The War the Infantry Knew*:

> Another and very unpleasant incident was when we had, I think, 19 men to bury. A large grave had been dug and the first few chaps put in when the usual nightly attacks started. There was no cover where we were except the grave, so in we went – the quick and the dead together.

Lieutenant Loscombe Law Stable, killed in action on 26 October 1914.

Among those killed on the 26th was Lieutenant Loscombe Law Stable, who was buried next to a fellow officer, Lieutenant Ellis Robert Cunliffe Stone, who had been killed on the previous day. Stable died while bringing in a wounded man. He was born on 21 March 1886, the son of Daniel and Gertrude Stable, and was educated at Wells House School, Malvern and at Winchester before passing into Sandhurst. His Commanding Officer, Lieutenant Colonel Henry Delmé Radcliffe, wrote to his parents:

> About your gallant son, who was one of the subalterns in the battalion under my command: he was a most excellent soldier – fearless to a degree and always the most cheerful of companions and was therefore most popular with his

The graves of Lieutenants Loscombe Law Stable and Robert Ellis Cunliffe Stone in Pont-du-Hem Military Cemetery, La Gorgue.

brother officers and in his death is most deeply regretted by all ranks. He received his death wound, so it was reported to me, going to the assistance of one of the men who was wounded and lying outside of the trenches. This was just like him, as he was always a model of unselfishness and thoughtfulness for others.

He is buried in Pont du Hem Military Cemetery, La Gorgue and is also commemorated by a marble plaque in St Mary's Church, Llanbrynmair, Powys.

North of the BEF, the Belgians were under extreme pressure and, after much deliberating, the Belgian government decided that the only option to stem the Germans was to open the canal locks at Nieuport on 25 October 1914, flooding the ground east of the Yser Canal and effectively ending the German attacks against them. With no man's land now flooded, separating the Belgian and German armies, the situation, although far from ideal, secured the left (northern) flank of the allies.

While casualties continued for the 2nd RWF over the coming days, on 29 October another Welsh unit moved to France, the third Territorial battalion to go to France and the first Welsh Territorial unit there. The 1st/6th Battalion Welsh Regiment was a Glamorgan-based unit commanded by Lieutenant Colonel Lord Ninian Crichton-Stuart, a well-known member of the Welsh aristocracy and son of the Marquis of Bute. The battalion disembarked at Le Havre before moving to Calais, where it was put to work as Lines of Communications troops. On the same day the 1st/1st Brecknockshire Battalion, South Wales Borderers, another Territorial unit, embarked for service in India.

Corporal F.H. Hellings of B Company 1st/6th Welsh wrote to his parents in Swansea to describe his experiences during the battalion's move overseas in a letter that took up almost a third of a page of the 17 December issue of the *Cambrian Daily Leader*:

Our journey from Swansea was quite uneventful. On arriving at Southampton we immediately embarked and during the night sailed, arriving in Havre the following evening. It became necessary, however, to sleep aboard another night and on the morning of the 29th the work of unloading commenced.

The greater part of the transport liner's cargo was a batch of 500 horses, which our lads had to unload, together with our own transport wagons, machine guns and all the other necessary parts to an infantry battalion. Our next move was to a shed something similar to the one we inhabited for several months on the Swansea Docks. We passed the night here and the following morning cooked our breakfast in our canteens for the first time. These canteens are very useful, being made in three parts. The bottom portion is used for making your tea or coffee, a lid for this is used for a plate and the top cover comprises a frying pan with the handle folding inwards.

Men of the 1/6th Battalion, Welsh Regiment marching through Christchurch, Hampshire en route for embarkation for France.

After breakfast we marched to the station and entrained for an unknown destination somewhere near the firing line.

Our mode of transit was different to anything we had been used to, having to travel in cattle-vans, with about 30 men to each. This journey took us three days to accomplish and although it was impossible to obtain any sleep, we really enjoyed the experience.

October 29 also saw the opening of the Battle of Gheluvelt, a desperate action that saw two of the first members of the Welsh aristocracy fall during the war. Sadly these men were closely related.

Lieutenant the Honourable Alan George Sholto Douglas-Pennant was born on 11 June 1890, the eldest son and heir of the 3rd Baron Penrhyn of Penrhyn Castle, Llandegai, near Bangor, Caernarfonshire. He was educated at Eton before being commissioned in the Grenadier Guards in 1910 and had served as aide-de-camp to Lord Carmichael, the Governor of Bengal prior to the war. He had returned to England to rejoin the 1st Battalion, Grenadier Guards. Douglas-Pennant was killed in action on 29 October, aged 24, and is commemorated on the Ypres (Menin Gate) Memorial.

His uncle, Lieutenant the Honourable Charles Douglas-

Lieutenant the Honourable Charles Douglas-Pennant, son of George Sholto Gordon, 2nd Baron Penrhyn, and Gertrude Lady Penrhyn of Hall Place, West Meon, Hants. Douglas-Pennant had served in the Boer War. He was 37 years old when he was killed at Gheluvelt on 2? October 1914 and is buried in Perth Cemetery (China Wall).

CK W. H.	ALLAN W. E.	LYON G. T.	SIBLEY R.	FARR
D. J.	BABBAGE W. H. P.	McCABE J.	SPRING H. S.	FIELI
IGS S. C.	BARBER E.	McCLENNON W.	SWAINSON J.	FISHE
CK L. I. A.	BARE C. L.	MACDONALD A.	WILLIAMS G..M. M.	FITCH
ALE A. C.	BARKER W. E.	McDONALD J.	WINCHESTER J. H.	FITZ
EN F. H.	BARNDEN S. E.	McGIBBON R.	WOOD A. P.	FLET
EE T. H.		McINTOSH W. R.		FOLE
. L.				FORI

GRENADIER GUARDS

			FORS
MAJOR	**SECOND LIEUT.**	**SERJEANT**	FOSH
COLBY L. R. V.	WALTER S.	EDEN E. G.	FOX
		HURLEY H. L.	FRE
CAPTAIN	**COY. SJT. MAJOR**	MARSHALL I.	GAL
RENNIE G.	GARRARD E. J.	PARKER F. C..M. M.	GAR
	LITTLETON S.	SANDAY S.	GAR
LIEUTENANT		THOMAS W. J.	GAR
ANTROBUS E.	**COY. QMR. SERJT.**	WALTERS A.	GEO
COTTLE W. E. W.	RICHARDSON G. L.	WILLIAMS H..M. M.	GIBE
DOUGLAS-PENNANT	THOMPSON E. J.		GOD
HON. A. G. S.		**LANCE SERJEANT**	GOD
BLACKWOOD	**SERJEANT**	BINGHAM J. W.	GOD
LORD BASIL	AKERS G. F.	DAVIES H. R.	GOC
MILLER F. W. J. MacD.	BREWER A.	HEARN R. C.	GRE
WEBSTER G. V. G. A.	DIGBY J. H.	MARSHALL F. J.	GRIF
		WHITEHOUSE T. A.	

A section of the panel on the Ypres (Menin Gate) Memorial, showing officers of the Grenadier Guards killed at Ypres who have no known grave. The name of Lieutenant the Honourable Alan George Sholto Douglas-Pennant can be seen in the left hand column.

Pennant, of the 1st Battalion, Coldstream Guards, was killed in action on the same day. Another uncle, Captain George Henry Douglas-Pennant, of the 1st Battalion, Grenadier Guards, would be killed in 1915.

Charles Douglas-Pennant was born on 7 October 1877. He was educated at Eton and the Royal Military College, Sandhurst and in 1899 he joined the Coldstream Guards, serving in the Boer War. He was promoted to lieutenant in 1905 and in May 1911 joined the Reserve of Officers, being again gazetted to his old regiment, the 1st Grenadier Guards, at the outbreak of war. He was originally reported as missing on 29 October 1914, but was later confirmed as having been killed on the same day as his nephew. He was 37 years old and is buried in Perth Cemetery (China Wall). He married, in 1905, Lady Edith Anne Dawson, elder daughter of the 2nd Earl of Dartry. Douglas-Pennant is commemorated on the Roll of Honour in St Mary's Church, Newmarket and the Llandegai War Memorial near Bangor.

The day would also prove costly for the 1st RWF and for the 2nd Welsh. The 1st Division held the line from Polygon Wood to the Menin Road, with the 2nd Division on its left flank and the 7th on the right. The Germans had regrouped and planned to attack again to attempt to break through Ypres but the British were ready. The Germans attacked the British lines through thick fog at 5.30 am on the morning of the 29th and gained some ground, setting up machine-gun posts in Gheluvelt some 400 metres behind the British lines. A counter-attack was delivered by 3 Brigade, the 2nd Welsh along the Menin Road with the Queen's on their right and the 1st SWB on their left. During the heavy fighting that followed, the attack was beaten off, the 2nd Welsh losing nineteen men killed, while the 1st SWB lost just one.

Lance Corporal Barnard of the 2nd Welsh wrote of his experience during the day:

Company Quartermaster Sergeant John Burnett Cownie (7711), 2nd Welsh. Born in Edinburgh on 24 September 1886, Cownie had served with the battalion since 1902. He is the only member of the 2nd Welsh killed on 29 October to have a known burial and is buried in Divisional Collecting Post Cemetery and Extension, Ypres. The grave next but one is to an unknown soldier of the Welsh Regiment, quite probably one of the men killed that day.

At dawn on the 29th we heard that the Germans had broken through our lines, by using one of their favourite tricks, dressing their men in khaki taken off our dead. The Welsh had only just come in from the front line of fighting; therefore we were quite prepared for the advance and the 3rd Brigade were soon again in the thick of things. A company of the Welsh advanced with the Queen's, while the rest of the battalion went to the left towards Zonnebeke and Gheluvelt.

The fighting was very severe, as the Germans were in vastly larger numbers, but the orders were that they were to be driven back. So back they had to go, although their artillery and rifle fire was very heavy and we were losing many. When it became dark we had gained a kind of position in front of Gheluvelt. About fifty men now lined out, in the mangolds and mud, to keep the Germans back (they were mostly in a wood about 150 yards to our front), while the others hastily prepared a line of strong trenches. The usual rain came down; those who had a bit of biscuit or 'bully' had some consolation; the others just went without. Later some tea was brought round.

In front of us the Germans seemed rather busy. Towards dawn the R. E., under cover of a listening post of our men, lined our front with barbed wire. Those of us who were not occupying the trenches then went about a hundred yards to the rear, where there was a small embankment. We could not rest yet awhile, as we had to dig ourselves in, and, if possible, get a snack of something to eat. When it became light the Germans began to show us that they were in front and very close. They seemed to have concentrated all their artillery on the Welsh. First the shells searched the village and they were not long before they began to rake us out of our burrows. Somehow, they had got our range grand. Many of our people were hit, I myself catching one in the leg.

Further fighting to the south that day saw the loss of another well-known Welsh cricketer, Ralph Escott Hancock. He was born in Llandaff on 20 December 1887, the son of Frank Hancock, managing director of the Cardiff Brewing Company and a former Cardiff and Welsh International rugby player. Young Hancock was educated at Rugby School, where he showed a talent for cricket and horse-riding. He made his first-class debut for Somerset against South Africa in 1907, soon after leaving Rugby to enter the Royal Military College, Sandhurst. In the following year Hancock was commissioned in the 2nd Devonshires and service overseas interrupted his cricket career, before returning home in 1913 and marrying Mary Hamilton Broadmead, of Milverton, Somerset.

Hancock, now a lieutenant, played six more matches for Somerset after marrying, but following the outbreak of war embarked for France on 30 August 1914 to join the 1st Devonshires. In October the battalion, attached to the 3rd Division, moved to positions on the La Bassée Canal in support of the 1st Dorsets and captured Givenchy Ridge. Hancock soon showed his mettle and on 23 October carried out an act of gallantry that saw him awarded the DSO and subsequently mentioned in despatches. The citation of his DSO award was published in the *London Gazette* of 1 December 1914:

On 23rd October displayed conspicuous gallantry in leaving his trench under very heavy fire and going back some 60 yards over absolutely bare ground to pick up Corporal Warwick, who had fallen whilst coming up with a party of reinforcements. Lieutenant Hancock conveyed this Non-commissioned Officer to the cover of a haystack and then returned to his trench.

Hancock was killed in action less than a week later, on 29 October 1914, aged 26 and is commemorated on the Le Touret Memorial.

To the north the 1st RWF, already badly depleted in strength, had been at Veldhoek over the preceding days, rebuilding its strength with newly-arrived reinforcements. The 7th and 8th divisions had then moved south, relieving part of the Indian and III Corps on a line running south from Gheluvelt to Zandvoorde. The 1st RWF took up positions east-north-east of Zandvoorde on the night of 29/30 October.

Most of the 30th was spent by the men of the 1st Division digging in and improving the defences under sporadic German artillery fire. Meanwhile, at 6.45 am the Germans launched an artillery barrage against the 7th Division south of the Menin Road, following up just over an hour later with an infantry assault against the battered units holding the front line. The 1st RWF, a little over 400 strong, met the German advance with rifle fire but the 7th Cavalry Brigade on its right flank had suffered heavily and been forced to withdraw.

The first the 7th Division knew of this was when the 1st RWF came under enfilade fire and soon the battalion was cut off, fighting desperately to save themselves. Lieutenant Wodehouse of the 1st RWF wrote:

> We were holding a line about three-quarters of a mile long, A Company on the right, then B, D and C on the left. Battalion HQ was in a dugout about 600 yards to the rear. The trenches were not well sighted for field of fire. So far as I know, no-one was on our right: some 'Blues' were supposed to be there, but I did not see them. It was foggy in the early morning, so that the Germans could not shell us much, which was lucky, as they had two batteries on Zandvoorde Ridge. About 8 am the shelling increased and we saw large numbers of Germans advancing down a slope about 1,500 yards to our front. Also, I believe, large numbers were seen coming around our exposed right flank. The batteries on the ridge were now firing point-blank into our trenches, so that it was difficult to see what was happening and the rifle fire also increased from our right rear. No orders were received, so it was thought best to stay where we were and about midday the whole battalion was either killed, wounded, or taken prisoners.

The 1st RWF had suffered the loss of Lieutenant Colonel Henry Osbert Samuel Cadogan, Lieutenant Alfred Edwin Claude Toke Dooner, Second Lieutenant Rowland le Belward Egerton, Captain William Vincent (DCLI attached) and over ninety men killed, while almost all the rest were wounded, missing or had been taken prisoner. Captain Richard Vincent Barker had survived the action but was killed on the following day while attached to the brigade. The 1st RWF had been virtually

Lieutenant Colonel Henry Osbert Samuel Cadogan, commanding officer of the 1st RWF. Cadogan was the son of Reverend Edward and Alice Cadogan of Wicken, Northamptonshire. He was killed at Zandvoorde on 30 October 1914 and is buried in Hooge Crater Cemetery.

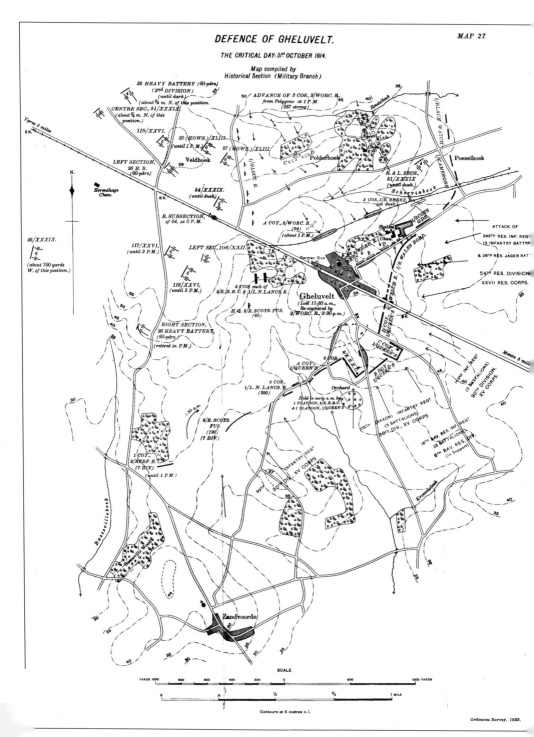

DEFENCE OF GHELUVELT.

THE CRITICAL DAY: 31ST OCTOBER 1914.

Map compiled by
Historical Section (Military Branch)

MAP 27.

35 HEAVY BATTERY (60-pdrs)
(2ND DIVISION)
(until dark)
(about ¾ m. N. of this position.)

CENTRE SEC. 51/XXXIX.
(about ¾ m. N. of this
position.)

118/XXVI.

30 (HOWS.)/XLIII.
(until 1 P.M.)

57 (HOWS.)/XLIII.

LEFT SECTION,
26 H. B.
(60-pdrs.)

Veldhoek

54/XXXIX.
(until dusk.)

B. SUBSECTION
of 54, at 3 P.M.

46/XXXIX.

6

(about 700 yards
W. of this position.)

117/XXVI.
(until 2 P.M.)

LEFT SEC. 106/XXII.

116/XXVI.
(until 2 P.M.)

2 COS. each of
2/K.R.R.C. & 1/L.N. LANCS.R.

H.Q. 2/R. SCOTS. FUS.
(60)

RIGHT SECTION,
26 HEAVY BATTERY
(60-pdrs.)
(retired in P.M.)

ADVANCE OF 3 COS. 2/WORC. R.
from Polygone at 1 P.M.
(357 strong)

Polderhoek

Poezelhoek

R. & L. SECS.
51/XXXIX.
(until dusk.)

2 COS. 1/R. BERKS.
(at dusk)

A COY. 2/WORC. R.
(94)
(about 1 P.M.)

German Gun
Regt.

Gheluvelt
(Lost 11·30 a.m.,
Re-captured by
2/WORC. R. 2·30 p.m.)

Stables
2/WORC. R. Chau.

ATTACK OF
245TH RES. INF. REGT.
(3 INFANTRY BATT.)
& 26TH RES. JAGER BAT.

54TH RES. DIVISION
XXVII RES. CORPS.

C COY.
1/QUEEN'S

A COY.
1/QUEEN'S

2 COS.
1/L. N. LANCS. R.
(250)

2 COS.
1/L. N. LANCS. R.

Orchard

B COY.
1/QUEEN'S

Held in early a.m. by
1 PLATOON, 2/K.R.R.C.
& 1 PLATOON, 1/QUEEN'S

2/R. SCOTS.
FUS.
(190)
(7 DIV)

INFANTRY REGT.
XV CORPS

1 COY.,
2/BEDF. R.
(7 DIV)
(until 1 P.M.)

Menin 5 miles

Zandvoorde

SCALE

YARDS 1000   800   600   400   200   0   500   1000 YARDS

0   ¼   ½   ¾   1 MILE

Contours at 5 metres v. i.

Ordnance Survey, 1923.

A map taken from the Official History, *showing the situation of the 1st SWB and 2nd Welsh north of the Menin Road, before Gheluvelt, on 31 October.*

annihilated with only just over ninety men left, temporarily attached to the Queen's, and over the coming weeks several parties of reinforcements joined to slowly rebuild the strength of the battalion.

For the men of the 1st Division their heaviest fighting would come on the following day.

October 31 saw one of the most famous Welsh actions of the war when the Germans launched a determined assault along the Menin Road, intended to capture Gheluvelt, smash their way through Ypres and drive the front towards the Channel coast. Early that morning the Germans launched a large-scale attack against a 12-mile front held by the British, from Messines up towards Polygon Wood. Their main effort was along both sides of the Menin Road and the gallant actions of the defenders have lived on in history.

The defence of the Gheluvelt area was entrusted to 3 Brigade, supported by two battalions of 2 Brigade (1st Loyal North Lancashire Regiment (LNL) and the 2nd King's Royal Rifle Corps (KRRC). The positions of the defenders can be seen on the map on page 86, from north to south: facing Polygon Wood the 1st Black Watch; the 1st Camerons; 1st Scots Guards; and 1st South Wales Borderers; 2nd Welsh astride the Menin Road; 1st Queen's; and the 2nd King's Royal Rifle Corps south of it.

The night of 30/31 October, prior to the main attack, had been disturbed by intermittent shelling and bursts of rifle fire, while incessant rain had turned the ground into a sea of thick mud that jammed the rifles of the men. The Germans had moved into their assaulting positions during the night and had dug in just over 100 metres in front of the 2nd Welsh. There was scarcely any ammunition left for the supporting artillery to cause any disruption to these German preparations, so the men in the front line knew they would be the only defence.

Shortly after 6 am the Germans, again shrouded in fog, made their attack on the 1st Division, which was beaten off everywhere except in an orchard 800 metres south of the Menin Road, where the Germans established themselves and proceeded to enfilade the 1st Queen's and extended their trenches towards the Menin Road. The fog cleared about two hours later and the Germans then launched an intense artillery bombardment of the British lines and all the front-line battalions suffered heavy casualties in the resulting cataclysm.

After just over an hour the German artillery moved on and German infantry attacked the weakened lines. Captain Marshall of the 2nd Welsh wrote:

Half-an-hour afterwards fire began to come from the direction of the wood on our left flank. We then found that the company which had dug in opposite to us was a machine gun Company with shields in front of their guns and their fire was so accurate and heavy that we soon lost a lot of men and found it impossible to fire over the parapet. We also found that there were only a dozen rifles that would fire, the remainder being either completely clogged up with clay or damaged by shell fire.

The situation was dire. Lieutenant Colonel Morland of the 2nd Welsh had been forced to withdraw the remnants of his battalion to Gheluvelt, where he convened with Lieutenant Colonel Leach of the 1st SWB, informing him that the 2nd Welsh had been overrun and that the Germans were streaming into Gheluvelt village from the south, cutting off the 1st Queen's. The 1st SWB then came under enfilade fire from the Menin Road before two of its companies became encircled and isolated. Some of the survivors of the 1st SWB were later interviewed in hospital at Hereford:

'It was at Ypres that we got knocked about,' said Private Summers. 'The battalion of 950, as it then was, could only muster some 225 and a couple of officers when the call was made afterwards.' This is how it happened. The Borderers were holding the Germans back, with the Welsh supporting on their flank. Apparently the Welsh received orders to retire at any rate, they withdrew before the eyes of the Borderers. The fighting was hot and the Borderers should also have retired and would thus have escaped the slaughter which followed. The men could only conjecture that their messenger met with a mishap and that in consequence the order was not delivered. Shells fell about the trenches in quick succession and under this protection the German infantry, thanks to the retirement of the Welsh, were able to creep behind some woods and partly envelop the Borderers. The battalion made a gallant stand against overwhelming odds, but their trenches were enfiladed and under the enemy's heavy crossfire the men at last sought whatever refuge they could find. Of those who were captured Private Perry managed to escape. One of the men had his major killed quite close to him in the trenches; another knew that his adjutant had fallen as he was making for one of the trenches. (*Western Mail.*)

The Borderers must have felt let down by their compatriots at the time, but did not know the full picture of the battle. The situation around the village must have resembled hell. Hundreds of bodies littered the battlefield, artillery fire was raining down all around the troops and the incessant machine-gun and rifle fire from the Germans continued to cause more casualties. Captain Rees of the 2nd Welsh wrote:

The shell fire around the barricade was very violent. Two shells burst in the house behind which I was sheltered, one cut the sign post neatly in half at the corner, another came through a wall about ten yards away and killed a man passing by. Eventually I got away with about a dozen men, four of whom were carrying Young in a mackintosh sheet and one man had a machine gun, of which the tripod had been blown to pieces and for which we had no ammunition. The stock of my rifle had been shot through in two places and the strap of my water bottle cut.

With the 2nd Welsh almost destroyed, Lieutenant Colonel Leach had sent for support: rallying the survivors of the 1st SWB and some Scots Guards, he counter-attacked the

Germans and after a brief hand-to-hand fight, the Germans fled. Gheluvelt was lost though and Leach stopped the advance of his men and decided to hold on to the position they had reached, just south of Nonne Bosschen, to prevent his men becoming isolated.

The front line of the 1st Division had been broken due to the overwhelming artillery fire and great numbers of German infantry, but isolated pockets of the 2nd Welsh and 1st SWB kept fighting throughout the day, slowing the German drive towards Ypres. An officer of the 1st Gloucesters who was at Gheluvelt wrote:

> Church, houses and windmill of Gheluvelt were reduced to ruins and the Welsh were practically wiped out where they stood and, soon after, dazed and broken men of this Regiment commenced to straggle back through Gheluvelt and Veldhoek. Whole companies were annihilated and the marvel is how anyone remained to help break the infantry attacks which were delivered again and again.

Lieutenant Colonel Morland had decided that the only way to recapture Gheluvelt was with a freshly-organized counter-attack but, while standing in a trench discussing the situation with Captains Moore and Rees, a shell burst nearby, killing Captain Waldo Alington Gwennap Moore and mortally wounding Morland, who died later that day. Captain Rees wrote of the latter:

Lieutenant Colonel Charles Bernard Morland, commanding officer of the 2nd Welsh. He was born in Montreal on 12 November 1866, the son of Thomas Morland. He had moved to England before 1871 and was brought up by his grandparents. Morland married Elma Alice Maud Abadam of Court Henry in 1894, a descendant of the Duke of Burgundy, and the couple had residences at Cilcennin and Llangyndeyrn. He was a long-serving soldier and had originally been commissioned in the Welsh Regiment in 1887. He died of wounds suffered at Gheluvelt on 31 October and is buried in Ypres Town Cemetery.

> I never saw him the slightest degree upset by anything that happened. He remained to the very end as cool and collected as if he was on parade at home. Moore also was a great loss and the Regiment lost one of its bravest officers when he was killed. Half-an-hour after I had got Colonel Morland carried off on a door, a message was brought me (as I now commanded the Welsh Regiment) which appointed Colonel Morland to command the 3rd Brigade. A shell had fallen on the Chateau at Hooge, mortally wounding General Lomax, commanding 1st Division. The command thereon devolved on General Landon, whose place Colonel Morland would have taken had he escaped. At this time (about 2 pm apparently), Corder and myself were the only two officers who had survived the fighting at Gheluvelt and we had about 25 men.

Brigadier General Fitzclarence, commanding 1 (Guards) Brigade, had witnessed the capture of Gheluvelt and had been instructed by Major General Lomax, commanding the 1st Division, to carry out a pre-arranged counter-attack from near Polderhoek Wood, south-east of the village. The only reserves left were the 2nd Worcesters, who were issued orders to recapture Gheluvelt.

By now, as already mentioned by Captain Rees, Major General Samuel Lomax, who had set up his HQ in Hooge Château, had been badly wounded when German shells crashed into the château. The disaster cost the 1st and 2nd division staff dearly, six officers being killed and a further two mortally wounded as well as Lomax.

At 1.45 pm the 2nd Worcesters sent their battalion scouts forward, followed by A Company. Advancing to about 500 metres of the village, the main body of the Worcesters then advanced, deploying in two lines 50 metres apart. The Worcesters drove forward under heavy artillery fire, capturing the northern side of the village and regaining almost 1,000 metres of ground. The men were surprised to find scattered remnants of the 1st SWB and 2nd Welsh still holding out and the gallantry of the Welshmen had surely been the deciding factor in the saving of Ypres that day.

The grave of Lieutenant Col. Charles Bernard Morland in Ypres Town Cemetery.

Instead it is the Worcestershire Regiment who laid claim to the saving of Ypres during the Battle of Gheluvelt, mainly due to the despatch of Sir John French, who named only the Worcesters in his report about the battle. The regiment has, quite rightly, celebrated the anniversary of Gheluvelt ever since, even having a park in its county town named in its honour, Gheluvelt Park. However, without the gallant stands by the 1st SWB and the 2nd Welsh, the Germans would not have been held up long enough for the counter-attack to have been so effectively delivered. In reality, none of these three battalions would have been able to save the situation alone and all three can proudly lay claim to the Battle of Gheluvelt being one of the greatest actions of the war.

Awards for gallantry were quite scarce during this early period of the war, but Captain Hubert Conway Rees of the 2nd Welsh received the Distinguished Service Order (DSO) for his handling of the remnants of the battalion and of the 1st Queen's during the fight.

During the day's fighting both the Welsh battalions had suffered considerable losses. Of the 1st SWB, Lieutenant Colonel Leach had been so badly wounded that he never returned to the battalion, although he was made Companion of the Order of St Michael and St George (CMG) for his services. Major William Lyttleton Lawrence, DSO, Captain Ian Bouverie Maxwell, Lieutenant Reginald Bracebridge Hadley and seventy-seven men had been killed; Captain Charles James Paterson had been mortally wounded, dying the following day. Only 224 men answered their names at roll-call

Major William Lyttleton Lawrence, DSO, second-in-command of the 1st SWB. He was born on 4 September 1873, the son of Arthur Garnons Lawrence and Edmundtina Lawrence (née Snead) of The Cedars, Chepstow. His father was originally from Carmarthen and William was well-known in the town, spending many of his holidays there visiting family. He was gazetted to the 2nd Battalion, South Wales Borderers in July 1893, becoming lieutenant in January 1896 and captain in September 1904 when he became adjutant of the battalion, and in December 1907 was appointed aide-de-camp to a divisional commander in India. He was posthumously awarded the Distinguished Service Order for his gallantry on 28 October. He has no known grave and is commemorated on the Ypres (Menin Gate) Memorial.

MAJOR W. L. LAWRENCE,
South Wales Borderers, awarded the D.S.O. after being killed.

that night. The 2nd Welsh had lost Lieutenant Colonel Charles Bernard Morland, the Adjutant, Captain Walter Hughes Ferrar, and Captain Waldo Alington Gwennap Moore killed and only three officers and fifty men answered roll-call. Fifty-six men had been killed on that day alone. Among the wounded was Private Samuel King, the 2nd Welsh diarist. One of the last entries in his diary concerned his escape from the battlefield:

I am bandaged. It is two miles to the nearest hospital. They are shelling the road that leads to it. I must adopt one of two courses. Either remain in the trench and die from loss of blood and exposure, or run the gauntlet of the road by crawling to the hospital. I choose the latter. I make my way along the gutter. Progress is very slow. I crawl over dead bodies, grinning carcases and felled trees. My crude bandage has become undone. My leg is fast becoming helpless. Will I ever reach the hospital? I make for a chalet. This is the field hospital. My wound is painted and dressed. I am placed on an ambulance wagon. We move off six miles down the line to the general hospital, a large reformatory school. Here I lie on straw and am given some food. My leg is absolutely useless to me.

Private Samuel Knight (8069), 2nd Welsh. The son of Jacob and Mary Knight (née Standing) of Stepney House, Cwmbwrla, Swansea, Knight survived his wounds and died in Swansea on 12 January 1978 at the age of 93.

King had been lucky. He had survived the retreat from Mons, the Battles of the Aisne and Marne and now Gheluvelt and by 1 November was safely in hospital at Rouen. He returned to St John's Hospital, Chester, where several pieces of shrapnel were removed from his leg and then returned home to Swansea on 23 December.

During the night of 31 October/1 November the remnants of the 2nd Welsh and 1st

A view of a reconstructed trench line within Sanctuary Wood.

Queen's dug in slightly to the north of the Menin Road, the strength of the battalion at the end of the day being 3 officers and about 50 men out of about 12 officers and 600 men on the previous night.

Elsewhere along the front line the fighting was nearly as heavy and the position just as perilous. To the south the situation was restored by a counter-attack of mixed companies from the Gordons, Northampton, Sussex and Oxford and Buckinghamshire Light Infantry, while further south the cavalry, backed by infantry, held on to the Wytschaete-Messines Ridge against heavy attacks, with the loss of part of Messines. It was here that the 1st Battalion, London Scottish became the first infantry Territorial unit to take part in the fighting.

By nightfall the British positions were the same as on the previous night, except that the 1st and 7th divisions had been forced back about a mile to a line running south from Polygon Wood to Klein Zillebeke and the French had taken over a section of the line south of the latter. The battered remnants of the 1st and 7th divisions remained in the line for several more days, the 1st SWB being one of the strongest battalions in the line here as a result of the previous fighting, with eight officers and 320 men in its ranks!

During the night of 1/2 November the remnants of 3 Brigade were relieved and moved into reserve in Sanctuary Wood, while the 1st Queen's moved into the rear area to rebuild. Over 50 reinforcements from the 3rd Welsh joined the 2nd Welsh at Sanctuary Wood on 2 November, making a total of 4 officers and 148 men, while the 1st SWB were put to work improving dugouts.

At 1.15 pm orders were received for 3 Brigade to assemble to repel a German attack south-west of Veldhoek. The battered remnants of 3 Brigade successfully attacked the Germans, driving them out of Herenthage Wood before digging in on its eastern edge, regaining much of the ground lost. Sergeant Edward Longdon (9874) of the 2nd Welsh was awarded the Distinguished Conduct Medal (DCM) for this action: 'For conspicuous gallantry and ability on 2nd November near Gheluvelt, when he served his machine gun until he was wounded and had become isolated. On two previous occasions he behaved with the greatest gallantry and resource in emergencies.' (*London Gazette*, 16 January 1915.)

The situation appeared to be less critical now as French reinforcements were streaming into the sector, but casualties continued at a steady rate over the coming days, the 2nd Welsh losing Lieutenant Geoffrey Dorman Partridge killed on the 3rd. On 4 November the Germans attacked, again under a thick fog, but were beaten off. Both the 1st SWB and 2nd Welsh then moved back into reserve, spending the coming days digging a new defensive line east of Hooge château. Time and again false reports of German attacks reached the men but by now the Battle of Gheluvelt was over.

Meanwhile the 2nd RWF were having a hard time of things at Fromelles, suffering daily casualties from sniping and shelling, although at a far lesser rate than their brother battalion, the 1st RWF. Each battalion in fact continued suffering a steady flow of casualties over the coming days, the 2nd Welsh losing thirty men killed on 6 and 7 November and the 1st RWF losing sixteen over the same two days, when 3 Brigade went forward in support of the 7th Cavalry Brigade to recover Zwarteleen, which had been lost. Sergeant Major Robert Evans (9071) of the 1st RWF was awarded the DCM for his gallantry here. The citation for the award reads as follows:

Lieutenant Geoffrey Dorman Partridge was born in Portsmouth on 24 December 1890 and educated at Bath College, at the United Services College, Windsor and at the Royal Military College, Sandhurst. He was commissioned in the Welsh Regiment in October 1911 and posted to the 2nd Battalion. Partridge was reported missing on 3 November and was subsequently presumed to have been killed in action on that date. He is commemorated on the Ypres (Menin Gate) Memorial. His brother, Captain Charles Burnett Partridge, RMLI was lost aboard HMS Good Hope *at the Battle of Coronel on 1 November 1914, just two days previously.*

For conspicuous gallantry and ability on the 7th November 1914, at Zillebeke, in continuing to lead his men in charge on the enemy's position when all the Officers and Senior Non-Commissioned Officers had been killed or wounded. The charge was successful, and, with the aid of another regiment, three maxim guns were captured. (*London Gazette*, 5 August 1915.)

One of several fine photographs from the Regimental Museum of the Royal Welsh in Brecon, depicting the 2nd Monmouths in breastwork trenches at Le Bizet.

On 6 November another Welsh battalion landed in Le Havre. The 1st/4th Battalion, Royal Welsh Fusiliers (4th RWF) was a Denbighshire-based Territorial battalion commanded by Lieutenant Colonel Frederick Charles France-Hayhurst. It was destined to join 3 Brigade, 1st Division on 7 December but for now it moved to Heuringhem, south of St Omer, for training in trench construction and attack following methods laid down in the newly-published *Infantry Training Manual.*

On the following day the 1st/2nd Battalion, Monmouthshire Regiment (2nd Mons) landed at Le Havre, entraining to join 12 Brigade, 4th Division at Le Bizet, just south of Ploegsteert. This was also a Territorial battalion recruited, as the name suggests, in Monmouthshire, and was commanded by Lieutenant Colonel Edward Boustead Cuthbertson (later Brigadier General).

While the two new Welsh units were beginning their first days in France, the Germans were preparing to launch another assault at Ypres. At 9 am on 11 November the Germans

Edward Boustead Cuthbertson was born on 13 June 1880 and educated at Marlborough. He was commissioned in the Argyll and Sutherland Highlanders from the Militia on 18 October 1899 and promoted to lieutenant on 3 July 1901, serving in the Boer War. In 1908 he served as equerry to Princess Beatrice, and became commanding officer of the 2nd Monmouths in 1911, taking the battalion to France. In May 1915 he was wounded and returned home, retiring as a brigadier general in 1922. He died on 13 May 1942.

attacked on a 9-mile front between Polygon Wood and Messines. The attack was heralded by the heaviest artillery barrage the British had yet faced and was again made under the cover of fog, but again was brought to a halt by rapid rifle fire from the British. Both the 1st SWB and 2nd Welsh were entrenched around Shrewsbury Forest and were part of the successful defence there; however, German gains were made north of the Menin Road, where the weakened British front was overrun by elements of the 2nd Guard Grenadiers, who secured the line up to Veldhoek Château. The German 2nd Guard Brigade then broke through the British 1 (Guards) Brigade south-west of Polygon Wood, creating a near 1,000-metre gap. The Germans then stormed through Nonne Bosschen Wood and briefly threatened the 2nd Division's gun line before a hastily-improvised counter-attack, containing a force made up mostly of military policemen (MPs) and stragglers under the command of Captain Charles Percy Graham of the 2nd Welsh, plugged the gap and forced the Germans out of Nonne Bosschen. Graham was awarded the DSO for his actions that day.

Lieutenant John Richards Homfray of the 1st SWB. Homfray was born on 18 October 1893, the son of Colonel Herbert Richards Homfray and Blanche Jessie Homfray of Penllyn Castle, Cowbridge. He was killed in action at Shrewsbury Forest on 11 November 1914 aged 21 and buried in Sanctuary Wood Cemetery.

The Battle of Nonne Bosschen was over by 13 November, the Germans suffering terrible casualties during their attempt to break through the Menin Road. The 2nd Welsh had lost Lieutenant Cecil Victor Powell Cornelius and fifteen men killed during the battle, while the 1st SWB had lost Lieutenant John Richard Homfray and twenty-one other ranks killed. Captain Rees wrote of an unusual event during the fighting in Sanctuary Wood:

> The wood was a snipers' paradise and continuous rile shooting went on with parties of Germans. Private John crawled out at dawn on 12th November and had a remarkable experience. He passed the enemy's advanced line and was

COLES A.
EARWAKER H. G.
GOITIA R. L., M. M.
SERVED AS JONES R.
JACQUES W.
JOHN G., D. C. M.
KIRKHAM E.
MORRIS G.
MORRIS M. R. D.
POTTS A.
PRING J.

Corporal Gwilym John's name on the Ypres (Menin Gate) Memorial. A native of Wilkes-Barre, Pennsylvania, John was originally afforded a proper burial but, as with so many other graves from this early period of the war, his grave was lost, hence his inclusion here.

examining their second line when he was captured by a party of six or seven Huns. Luckily a shrapnel shell burst overhead and the party scattered, he himself making good his escape and reaching the lines of the London Scottish away to our left. Here he was arrested as a spy and sent to Hooge, where he was released. During his absence a German sniper had done a great deal of damage. He severely wounded Captain Venables, also killing a corporal and a private and wounding Hewett and another private. John heard of this when he arrived and promptly went off and killed the German.

Lieutenant Cornelius was killed while attempting to rescue the wounded Captain Venables, who was mentioned by Rees in the passage above and was reported as having been posthumously awarded the DSO for his gallantry, although this award has not been traced. Private Gwilym John (985) was the sniper mentioned in the passage. He was born at Wilkes-Barre, Pennsylvania before returning to his parents' native Wales, joining the 2nd Welsh. When the 2nd Welsh were relieved on 14 November he had volunteered to cover the digging of a new trench that was required and collected six volunteers for the purpose. For his several acts of gallantry during the Battles of Gheluvelt and Nonne Bosschen he was recommended for the Victoria Cross. Unfortunately the award was downgraded to the Distinguished Conduct Medal. The citation reads: 'For gallantry and ability in obtaining most useful information as to the enemy's movements on two occasions under most difficult circumstances. Was captured by the enemy but escaped.'

He was killed at Kemmel less than two weeks later, on 25 November 1914. A report of his death in the 12 December 1914 edition of *Llais Llafur* contained the following comment from Lieutenant Trevor Rhys Allaway under the title 'King of Snipers Killed':

He was respected and admired by his officers, more than anyone I have ever heard. His deeds of gallantry are legion. When our commanding officer heard of his death he had a special grave dug for him. For myself, I should like to express my sincerest sympathies with his relatives in their loss. He was a man who can never be replaced.

John's grave was lost during the course of the war and he is now commemorated on the Ypres (Menin Gate) Memorial.

Friday, 13 November would see the death of the first Welsh airman during the course of the war. John Joseph Harrington was born in Newport, Monmouthshire on 24 February 1886, the son of John and Catherine Harrington of 6 King Street. He was educated at St Mary's Roman Catholic School in Newport and had served with the Royal Monmouth Royal Engineers (Militia) from 1905 until 1908, when he started working as an engineer for the British and Colonial Aeroplane Company at Filton, Bristol. He joined the RFC as an Air Mechanic 1st Class and embarked for France with the BEF on 12 August 1914. Harrington was killed in action on 13 November 1914 and was originally buried on a farm some 1,000 metres north of Zillebeke. His body was exhumed after the war and he was reinterred at Birr Cross Roads Cemetery.

From 15 November onwards the BEF began pulling out from the Ypres Salient, being relieved by the French, and took over a 21-mile front between Givenchy and Wytschaete, with I Corps being in reserve round Bailleul.

During the First Battle of Ypres, the British casualties totalled over 7,900 men killed, about 29,000 wounded and over 17,800 missing. The losses in officers had been so heavy that on 24 November orders were issued for all officers permitting them to wear the men's pattern web equipment instead of the Sam Browne belt and some officers began to remove their cuff rank badges in order to make them less distinguishable from their men.

The 1st RWF, with only eighty to ninety of its original strength left and the remainder made up of reinforcements, had moved into trenches at Cuinchy by 14 November and prepared to mount one of the first trench raids of the war. The weather was by now very cold and snow lay on the ground, making the digging of trenches all the more miserable. On the night of 24/25 November Captain Minshull Ford led a raiding party of fifteen men out into no man's land, where they were met with a terrific hail of fire that holed Ford's cap! The objective of the raid was to lay a charge of gun cotton in some farm buildings in which snipers had been operating, causing a great deal of trouble to the 1st RWF. The charge was successfully laid after the Germans beat a hasty retreat and the buildings were brought down.

Several officers joined the 1st RWF as reinforcements that month and most notable among them was a man whose post-war writings would prove to be classic reading for any Great War student: Second Lieutenant Siegfried Sassoon.

On 26 November a tragedy struck the Royal Navy when one of its *London*-class pre-dreadnought battleships, HMS *Bulwark*, suddenly exploded and blew apart while moored in the Medway Estuary, near Sheerness. *Bulwark* had a complement of 750 officers and men, of which only fourteen survived. Among the dead were sixteen Welsh sailors and Marines, all bar one of whom are commemorated on the Portsmouth Naval Memorial. The body of one of these Welshmen, Able Seaman George Henry Redman (PO/237084), the son of Catherine Redman of 27 Court Road, Barry Docks, was recovered from the sea and returned home for burial in his home town. Redman had served in the Royal Navy since 16 March 1908 and had only joined the crew of *Bulwark* in May 1914.

Siegfried Sassoon, one of the best-known of the Great War poets. Sassoon was awarded the Military Cross for a reckless act of gallantry following the death of his friend, David Cuthbert Thomas, at Fricourt in 1916, and wrote about him under the name Dick Tiltwood.

A subsequent court of enquiry established that a large number of 6-inch shells had been incorrectly stored in passageways connecting her magazines, enabling the explosion to tear through the ship, possibly after being triggered by the dropping of a shell. At the time this was the most catastrophic accidental loss in the history of the Royal Navy, which would only be exceeded by the loss of HMS *Vanguard* in 1917.

Back on the Western Front, for now at least, stagnant trench warfare had set in, although casualties continued to mount during the remainder of November and December, especially for the 1st SWB and 2nd Welsh, who would take part in one more major action before the year's end. The 2nd SWB, in China, saw its first action during November, while the 2nd Monmouths suffered their first man killed on 22 November, Private William Crowley (1684) of Pontypool. Crowley is buried in Le Touquet Railway Crossing Cemetery. The battalion remained in the Le Bizet trenches, south of Ploegsteert, for the remainder of the year, suffering twenty men and one officer killed. The officer, Second Lieutenant John Edward Paton, was just 19 years old when he was killed on 31 December, the son of John and Susan Paton of Waun Wern, Pontypool. He is buried in Calvaire (Essex) Military Cemetery.

On 3 December the 4th RWF moved to Bailleul to join 3 Brigade, 1st Division, finding itself in the same brigade as the 1st SWB and 2nd Welsh. The battalion's first few weeks were spent drilling, training and practising offensive movements around Bailleul.

Second Lieutenant John Edward Paton, the first officer of the 2nd Monmouthshire Regime killed in France. Paton i educated at Winchester College and had passed entrance examination fo Pembroke College, Cambridge. He instead i up a commission in the Monmouth Regiment an was killed at Le Bizet on December 1914, aged 1

Men of the 2nd Monmouths in the trenches at Le Bizet. South Wales Borderers Regimental Museum*)*

Another member of the Welsh aristocracy fell during December. The Honourable Henry Lyndhurst Bruce, eldest son of the 2nd Baron Aberdare, was killed in action on 14 December. Bruce was born on 25 May 1881 and was educated at Winchester and New College, Oxford. He had married an Edwardian pin-up girl, the actress Camille Clifford, in 1906, serving for many years in the 3rd (Militia) Battalion, Hampshire Regiment and subsequently in the Royal Scots, spending several months at the Royal Scots regimental depot training recruits.

Soon after the outbreak of war he was transferred to the 2nd Battalion, Royal Scots, joining them in France on 7 October and saw heavy fighting with the battalion during the next two months while acting as second-in-command.

He was killed near Wytschaete on 14 December while leading an attack on the enemy lines across very difficult ground. The first line of trenches had been taken but as he was climbing out of the captured position to lead the assault on the second line he fell, shot through the head. After his death a letter was received in London, in which Captain Bruce wrote:

> We had been heavily sniped for three days. I had one man killed, so I went for the sniper with a grenade. The first found the range, but was wide. The second landed just behind the trench and within five yards of the sniper. The sniping ceased entirely from that place and, as the grenades have a radius of about twenty yards, I think my friend was, to say the least, uncomfortable. In the afternoon we spotted smoke rising from behind a trench. My first grenade failed to burst, but my second landed about two yards behind a party.

The Honourable Henry Lyndhurst Bruce, eldest son of the 2nd Baron Aberdare. He was killed in action at Wytschaete on 14 December 1914 and is commemorated on the Ypres (Menin Gate) Memorial.

The first two members of the Monmouthshire Regiment to win gallantry awards during the war earned their Distinguished Conduct Medals during the 2nd Monmouths' time at Le Touquet. On 15 December Private Edwin Jones (1779) and Sergeant Albert Edward Pinchin (1599) rushed out into no man's land under heavy fire to rescue several wounded comrades. Pinchin was himself wounded in the attempt but remained with one wounded man, Private William Nicholls (210) of Llanddewi, Monmouth, until he died later that day before returning to the safety of the trenches. Nicholls is buried in Calvaire (Essex) Military Cemetery.

A view of some of the graves of men of the Monmouth Regiment buried in Calvaire (Essex) Cemetery, Belgium.

On 19 December the Indian Corps mounted an attack on the Givenchy front, but had to evacuate all the ground gained after coming under heavy artillery and trench mortar fire.

In retaliation, the Germans launched an assault against the Indians on the morning of 20 December, exploding ten mines below the Indian trenches and rushed the village. They also captured the front and support trenches on both sides and drove in a pocket 300 metres deep to the north of Givenchy in the direction of Festubert. The situation was serious, since if the gap to the north was not filled, the line might be rolled up on both flanks.

As a result, Sir Douglas Haig's I Corps was ordered to send a division to support the Indian Corps and he in turn ordered the 1st Division into action. At around 7 am on the 20th, gunfire booming in the distance, the 1st Division began its march from billets around Merville towards the battle area, reaching Béthune the following day, before marching through Gorre towards Givenchy in pouring rain.

While the 1st Division was on the march to its battle area, 20 December was the day that Wales lost its second airman killed during the war.

Wilfred Picton-Warlow was born at Laleston, Bridgend on 6 April 1884, the son of Colonel John and Eleanor Picton-Warlow (née Temple). He was a great-grand-nephew of Sir Thomas Picton, the Welsh general who was killed at the Battle of Waterloo. Picton-Warlow was educated at Clifton College and joined the Guernsey Militia before being commissioned in the Welsh Regiment in January 1903, becoming a captain in June 1913 after service in India and South Africa. He then volunteered to join the RFC later that year and trained as a pilot.

Picton-Warlow was among the first airmen in France after the outbreak of war. On 20 December he took off from St Omer to fly to Dover in his Blériot aircraft and was never seen again, presumably having crashed in the Channel. He was 30 years old and is commemorated on the Arras Flying Services Memorial.

By the time 3 Brigade reached the battle area on 21 December, the 1st Manchesters had recaptured Givenchy but had been driven back again and were clinging on to a small portion of the village.

1 (Guards) Brigade was ordered to retake Givenchy, attacking it from the north-west, while a French territorial division attacked it from the south. Meanwhile 3 Brigade was ordered to operate on the left of 1 (Guards) Brigade and to recapture the trenches between Givenchy and the hamlet of Rue de Cailloux by a frontal assault.

Orders were received to attack at 2.15 pm – the 2nd SWB on the left and the 1st Gloucesters on the right – with instructions to keep in touch with 1 (Guards) Brigade; the 2nd Welsh were in support at the Tuning Forks, half a mile west of Festubert, while the Munsters and 4th RWF were in reserve.

Captain Wilfred Picton-Warlow of Ewenny, Bridgend.

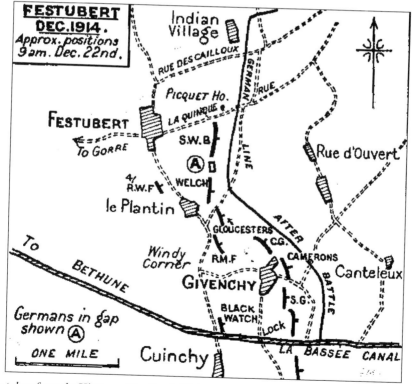

A map taken from the History of the South Wales Borderers *showing the dispositions of the 1st SWB and 2nd Welsh at Festubert.*

101

Just after 3 pm the two leading battalions left Festubert and Le Plantin respectively, but a gap immediately opened between them as the 1st Gloucesters veered away to the right to keep in touch with 1 (Guards) Brigade. Heavy German rifle and machine-gun fire began pouring into the attacking troops. As a result the 2nd Welsh were forced to fill the growing gap and support the 1st SWB and 1st Gloucesters. Captain Rees of the 2nd Welsh wrote:

> The advance was signalled by a hail of bullets, which swept across the dead flat marshy ground and came whistling down our road in undesirable numbers. I established my H.Q. behind a house, not far from where the road runs into Festubert. Here I was joined by General Butler, who directed me to despatch a platoon to the right to establish touch with the 1st Brigade, of whom nothing could be seen or heard. I sent Ridewood, who had that day been given a commission. They disappeared and nothing more was heard of them. He and his platoon came under a heavy fire at Le Plantin and he himself and most of his men were wounded. I only found this out the next day.

Within two hours of the opening assault, casualties had already been high among the attacking battalions and the men were desperately tired due to the sodden conditions underfoot. It was dark by now, yet the 1st SWB, 2nd Welsh and 1st Gloucesters working together reached a line of support trenches 800 metres east of Festubert, while the Germans retreated to the old British front line some 150 metres further back.

Many of the British troops had become isolated and with the darkness came disarray, although patrols sent out by each company during the night eventually found the locations of neighbouring troops and brought some organization into the line. Casualties for both Welsh battalions had been heavy: the 2nd Welsh had lost twelve men killed during the day, while the 1st SWB had suffered even worse, with thirty-nine men killed. More casualties would follow when the attack was renewed the following morning.

The 1st (Guards) Brigade had met with fierce opposition in Givenchy and had used up all of its reserves in its efforts to retake the village but it had been successful in its task, although a gap existed between it and the 1st Gloucesters. At 10.30 pm the 2nd Munsters were sent to bridge this gap but found the darkness too much of a hindrance and dug in 250 metres east of the road to Givenchy.

Several fine acts of gallantry were displayed by the men in the attack. Lieutenant Trevor Rhys Allaway of the 2nd Welsh was later awarded the Military Cross for his gallantry during the fighting,

Lieutenant Trevor Rhys Allaway of Llanbedr, Merioneth. Attached to the 2nd Welsh from the SWB, Allaway was awarded the Military Cross for his gallantry at Festubert on 21 to 22 December 1914. He was later accidentally killed by a bomb explosion on 29 June 1915.

while Corporal Jacob Edwards (8269) of the 1st SWB was awarded the Distinguished Conduct Medal for his gallantry during the night:

> Difficulties arose in getting necessary supplies to the men in the forward trenches and the only known communication trench being impassable, he, with another man, carried the rations over a fire-swept zone of 1,100 yards, after the ration party had been dispersed by heavy fire. He subsequently returned and took up ammunition to the same trenches.

Edwards was from the small village of Uffington in Shropshire, the son of Thomas and Sarah Edwards, and had served with the South Wales Borderers since enlisting at Brecon on 7 November 1903. He was a reservist who rejoined the colours on 5 August 1914 and served throughout the war. He died in Liverpool in 1958, aged 80.

Orders were given to renew the attack at 7 am the next day (22 October) and all the battalions involved rose to advance. Conditions were terrible on the muddy battlefield and, with their rifles jammed, the attack soon stalled, although the 1st SWB and 2nd Welsh managed to extend their lines, the latter closing the gap to the 1st Gloucesters in the process.

The 1st Munsters had made a gallant advance at 7 am and pushed further forward than any other of the 1st Division units involved, but with the loss of eleven officers, including their commanding officer and 200 other ranks, they were unable to hold on and had to be withdrawn. The battle dragged to an end in the Festubert marshland, the men exhausted. It had not been a failure, for the German offensive had been stopped and, although the Germans held onto the old British front line trenches, the assault of the 1st Division had regained their old support trenches, which were now consolidated into a new front. Festubert would become notorious, its marshy ground and high water table making trench-digging impossible and the line there became a series of outposts, known to the men as 'islands', fortified with sandbags, earth and whatever other material came to hand.

The casualties of the 2nd Welsh amounted to 3 officers and about 120 other ranks, including Lieutenant Geoffrey Montague Bradley, Second Lieutenant John Richard Baggalley Weeding and 28 men dead, while the 1st SWB had lost 7 officers and 223 men, including Second Lieutenant Ernest Haddon Owen and over 40 men dead. Due to the nature of the ground and subsequent fighting in the area, the majority of the dead have no known graves and are commemorated on the Le Touret Memorial, Richebourg-l'Avoué.

Both the battalions were mentioned in despatches for their efforts at Festubert, as were several individuals from each. Both remained in the line over the coming days and several attempts were made to drive the Germans out of a heavily-defended strongpoint.

The 4th RWF saw its first battle casualty here on 24 December when Private Elwy Hughes (7508), the 24-year-old son of Edward and Mary Hughes of 4 Adwy Lane, Llidiarth Fanny, Coedpoeth, was killed in the support trenches. He has no known grave and is also commemorated on the Le Touret Memorial.

The famous Christmas Truce was celebrated by men situated around Ploegsteert Wood some miles north and was reported by several Welshmen serving with other units in letters home. Rifleman Ernest Furneaux of the Rifle Brigade wrote home to his parents in Swansea:

I must tell you how I spent Christmas Day. Of course you would think under difficulties, but as luck would have it we were very happy. About five o'clock on Christmas Eve the Germans started lighting up Christmas trees in their trenches. We took no notice of them until they began to sing. Then we began to cheer them and to talk to one another as we are only about 80 yards apart. So by the light of their searchlight our officers went across halfway and their officers came to meet them. They shook hands and conversed for a while. It was agreed that we should have a day off and they would fire the first shot to start again. So from five o'clock on Christmas Eve until ten o'clock this morning (December 26th) neither side has fired, only walked about. Some of the Germans came across to us and we shook hands and had some chocolate and cigars from them. They seem pretty young, some of them. I had a nice dinner – made it myself – stew, potatoes, carrots, turnips and meat, which we had out of a garden nearby, and of course pudding.

John Powys Treloar, a banker at Pontypool prior to the war, wrote to his parents at Crickhowell School House to tell them of his Christmas experience, an annotated version of which was printed in the *Brecon and Radnor Express* of 7 January 1915:

Rifleman P.J. Treloar, Queen's Westminsters, in a letter to his parents, Mr and Mrs Joseph Treloar, School House, Crickhowell, states that about 6 o'clock in the evening of the 24th ult., the Germans started singing all sorts of patriotic songs and put lights all along their trenches. Our fellows replied by giving them some of their choice tunes and the Germans cheered vociferously. One or two of the latter seemed to speak English fairly well and yelled across greetings. By about 9.30 things became fairly quiet again and not a single shot was fired during the remainder of the night. When the morning broke on Christmas Day, the Germans were running about the top of their trenches and they also took a stroll around. There seemed to be a Most Remarkable Truce. During the morning 3 fellows and the writer of the letter went halfway between the trenches and had a yarn with two Germans, who were burying a dead comrade. He (the writer) managed to make himself understood. They exchanged cigarettes, shook hands and he returned with a little German ammunition and a button as a souvenir. Not a shot was fired up to the time they left on the morning of the 26th.

While units of the BEF situated north of the 1st Division celebrated a peaceful first Christmas of the war, the 2nd Welsh were ordered to make another attempt to capture a German strongpoint. On Christmas Day Lieutenant Hollingsworth, together with seventy men, was ordered to establish a post at the angle of the road about 300 metres to the left of the Welsh line and from there to attack the strongpoint. The party dashed across the open fields, losing four men killed and Lieutenant Hollingsworth wounded, but succeeded in securing a position in the communication trench about 120 metres from the enemy. Private George Church (8377) went ten times to and fro up the road on his bicycle under shellfire to deliver messages during the attack. For this and subsequent acts of gallantry he would later be awarded the DCM.

On 26 December the 2nd SWB moved back into the line alongside the 2nd Welsh. Several small actions occurred over the coming days but these two battalions, along with the 4th RWF in reserve, sat out the end of 1914 in squalid, uncomfortable positions. Captain Rees wrote:

The weather was atrocious and the condition of the actual trenches worse than anything I have seen. On one occasion it took me two hours to go along 150 yards of trench and return. In many places the mud and water was nearly waist deep and the men perched on mud islands.

It was a pretty miserable way to celebrate the New Year, but many men writing home to family and friends painted a warmer picture of life in an attempt to quell any anxieties they may have had. Private William Meredith of the 1st/4th RWF wrote to his parents at 28 Plasbennion, Ruabon:

Just a line to let you know I got your letter and Christmas card. I was very pleased to receive also the newspaper. We are in the trenches but we are quite well and take it all as a joke. We will not get any parcels until we get back to the Base. My brother-in-law, Private David Davies, of Ponkey, was taken ill on the way and is now in Hospital. My pals and myself are sticking it alright and you should hear the Germans shout for mercy when our boys set upon them. We get plenty of Quinine to keep the cold out. I hope you have had a merry Christmas and a Happy New Year as we enjoyed our Christmas alright in the trenches.

Private Ernest Edwards, a machine-gunner of the same battalion, wrote to a friend at Wrexham:

The parcel was A1 and we shall celebrate Christmas now. Kerry Lomas was very pleased at being remembered. You at home ought to be thankful you are English and not Belgians. It is a pity to see the women and children refugees all huddled up together, sleeping on straw, waiting to be sent to England. Some of them are so hungry they eat food we could not touch. One big town not far from us has been shelled to the ground by the German artillery. Our section is sleeping in a barn and while we were there two chaps began to make a row. The sergeant said: 'What is all the row about?' 'Evans has pinched half my straw,' replied Rolly. 'How do you know he has?' replied the sergeant, 'did you count them?' 'Yes,' said Rolly, 'I had two straws to start with and now I have only got one.' Our comrades keep us laughing for hours. All that I can say at present is that there is a war!

On a more downbeat note, a Reservist, Private Harry Ludlow of the 1st SWB, wrote to his minister at Brecon:

I cannot tell you much about the war, as we are not allowed to do so, but I can assure you we are having the best of the fighting. I am very sorry to tell you, but yesterday one of our companies was just going into the trenches, when one of the German 'coal-boxes' met them and did a lot of damage. I cannot tell you the number killed, as we do not know for certain yet, but I am positive of ten casualties. This war is terrible. It breaks one's heart in walking through the towns to see how they have been blown about. I am very thankful that this has not happened to England and sincerely hope that it never will. The boys are all doing well and are very happy, although they have an encasement of mud from feet to waist.

Chapter 7

The Raising of the 38th and 53rd (Welsh) Divisions

A s well as the Territorial units that had begun moving to France, three regular army divisions were on their way back to Britain from service around the Empire. These were the 27th and 28th divisions from India, which would subsequently move to France, and the 29th Division, which would in time head to Gallipoli. The rapid expansion of the army back in Britain, according to Kitchener's wishes, was now in full swing, with several service divisions being formed as well as other Territorial and Yeomanry divisions.

When the order for mobilization was issued on 5 August 1914, the 53rd (Welsh) Division, Territorial Force, was constituted as follows:

INFANTRY
THE CHESHIRE INFANTRY BRIGADE (Colonel E.A. COWANS)
4th Battalion, Cheshire Regiment
5th Battalion, Cheshire Regiment

A camp of units of the 53rd (Welsh) Division at Ammanford prior to the war.

6th Battalion, Cheshire Regiment
7th Battalion, Cheshire Regiment

THE NORTH WALES INFANTRY BRIGADE (Colonel F.C. LLOYD)
4th (Denbighshire) Battalion, Royal Welsh Fusiliers
5th (Flintshire) Battalion, Royal Welsh Fusiliers
6th (Caernarfonshire & Anglesey) Battalion, Royal Welsh Fusiliers
7th (Merioneth & Montgomery) Battalion, Royal Welsh Fusiliers

THE WELSH BORDER INFANTRY BRIGADE (Colonel J.J.F. HUME)
1st Battalion, Monmouthshire Regiment
2nd Battalion, Monmouthshire Regiment
3rd Battalion, Monmouthshire Regiment
1st Battalion, Herefordshire Regiment

THE SOUTH WALES INFANTRY BRIGADE
Brecknock Battalion South Wales Borderers
4th (Carmarthen) Battalion, Welsh Regiment
5th Battalion, Welsh Regiment
6th (Glamorgan) Battalion, Welsh Regiment
4th Battalion, Shropshire Light Infantry
7th (Cyclist) Battalion, Welsh Regiment was also within the Division

ARTILLERY
1ST WELSH (Howitzer) BRIGADE ROYAL FIELD ARTILLERY
1st Glamorgan Battery
2nd Glamorgan Battery
1st Welsh Ammunition Column

2ND WELSH BRIGADE ROYAL FIELD ARTILLERY
3rd Glamorgan Battery
4th Glamorgan Battery
Cardigan Battery
2nd Welsh Ammunition Column

CHESHIRE BRIGADE ROYAL FIELD ARTILLERY
1st Cheshire Battery
2nd Cheshire Battery
3rd Cheshire Battery
3rd Welsh Ammunition Column

4TH WELSH BRIGADE ROYAL FIELD ARTILLERY
1st Monmouthshire Battery

2nd Monmouthshire Battery
3rd Monmouthshire Battery
4th Welsh Ammunition Column
The Welsh Royal Garrison Artillery

ROYAL ENGINEERS
The Cheshire Field Company
The Welsh Field Company
The Welsh Division Telegraph Company

THE ROYAL ARMY SERVICE CORPS
The Divisional Headquarters Company
The Cheshire Brigade Company
The North Wales Brigade Company
The Welsh Border Brigade Company
THE ROYAL ARMY MEDICAL CORPS
The 1st, 2nd and 3rd Welsh Field Ambulances

On 3 August 1914 the infantry brigades, less the Herefords, who were due to go on army manoeuvres, were in camp when their training was cancelled and they were ordered back to their respective headquarters. The next day came the general order for mobilization (issued to them on the 5th) and the Territorial Force was embodied for war.

At the end of August 1914, the division concentrated in the neighbourhood of Bedford and Northampton and during the coming months battalion training continued, albeit constantly interrupted by trench-digging operations on the east coast. Within weeks of the outbreak of war the Welsh Division was ready, but much to the annoyance of its staff it was soon raided by the War Office and lost several battalions. The first to go was the Brecknock Battalion, South Wales Borderers, who left for overseas service in October, followed by the 6th Cheshires, the 2nd Monmouths, the 4th RWF, the 6th Welsh, the 4th KSLI, the 5th Cheshires, the 1st Monmouths and the 3rd Monmouths.

As a result of this the division lost part of its Welsh identity. To replace the aforementioned battalions, on 24 April 1915 four English home county battalions were transferred to the division.

The plethora of troops stationed in these two towns integrated well into the communities and were, in the main, fondly regarded by the locals. Some men even married local women, a happy occurrence that sometimes made headlines in the newspapers. One man, Sergeant Robert Roberts of the RWF, was brought before magistrates in Northampton accused of bigamy. He had married Florence Ada Crane but was already married and his first wife in Pwllheli, being dismayed to hear of his wedding, had quite correctly reported him to the police. Upon his arrest, Roberts admitted his guilt but stated that Miss Crane was fully aware that he was married!

The famed Welsh male voice choirs also helped make friends during these happy days. One issue of the *Bedford Times* reported:

> Lovers of good male voice singing should make the Howard Monument their Mecca. In our evening stroll after service last Sunday we happened upon a group of Welsh Terriers who were thoroughly enjoying themselves singing the hymns of the homeland in their native dialect. Davies, of Abercarn, Welsh Chaplain, led in this inspiring service, so different from the ordinary open-air service for which the square has been the venue. A number of ladies and gentlemen joined in the singing with evident enjoyment – presumably they are Welsh people living in the town and district – and the demeanour of the Bedfordshire section of the assembly was most respectful.

Towards the end of November the division was visited by the Chancellor, David Lloyd George, who attended a church parade officiated over by Reverend J.W. Wynne-Jones, the vicar of Caernarfon. Lloyd George, accompanied by his wife and daughter, had been paying a visit to his son Gwilym, an officer with the 6th RWF, who accompanied his father on a walk through his billets to meet a number of men from their home town of Criccieth. The parade was held at St Edmund's Church in Northampton and Reverend Wynne-Jones spoke at length about the loss of his son, Lieutenant Morys Wynne-Jones of the 36th Company, Royal Engineers, who had been killed at Ypres on 29 October.

On 3 July 1915 Major General Lindley, commanding the 53rd (Welsh) Division, received the order to prepare his division (less artillery) for service in the Mediterranean. The first battalions to move were the 5th and 6th Royal Welch Fusiliers, who entrained at Irchester during the night of 13/14 July for Devonport. Embarkation was completed on 19 July when the fleet of eight transport ships sailed. The story of the division will be told throughout the following chapters, but the new make-up of the infantry brigades within the division after final reorganization was as follows:

158 BRIGADE
5th Royal Welsh Fusiliers
6th Royal Welsh Regiment
7th Royal Welsh Regiment
1st Herefordshire Regiment

159 BRIGADE
4th Cheshire Regiment
7th Cheshire Regiment
4th Welsh Regiment
5th Welsh Regiment

160 BRIGADE
2nd/4th Battalion, (Queen's) Royal West Surrey Regiment

4th Battalion, Royal Sussex Regiment
2nd/4th Battalion, Royal West Kent Regiment
2nd/10th Battalion, Middlesex Regiment

In the meantime, following Lloyd George's call for the formation of a Welsh Army Corps, recruitment was well under way around the country. Early in the war it had been suggested that Wales should furnish another 36,000 of 38,000 men to form a new division. According to the 1911 census there were in Wales 315,075 men between the ages of 20 and 35 and 404,695 between the ages of 20 and 40. Conservative estimations showed that 15 per cent of this population had already enlisted, which still left a reserve of 268,823 men to draw upon under the age of 35 and 344,975 under the age of 40.

After consultation with the War Office and after being given permission by Lord Kitchener, the Welsh National Executive Committee was formed from leading personalities in Wales, proposing to raise the following units to make up a division: three brigades of infantry of four battalions each, consisting of 346 officers and 11,677 other ranks; two field and one signal company of Royal Engineers consisting of 14 officers and 600 other ranks; a Royal Army Medical Corps consisting of 51 officers and 650 other ranks and an Army Service Corps Detachment comprising 35 officers and 500 other ranks. That represented a total in all ranks of 13,873.

Recruitment for the new Welsh army began at once. The *Flintshire Observer* of 5 November reported:

NEW WELSH ARMY CORPS. Recruiting Begun. Important meetings in connection with the formation of the new Welsh Army Corps were held in Shrewsbury on Monday. Mr. D.A. Thomas presided at the Clothing and Equipment Committee and later the Earl of Plymouth presided at the Executive of the Welsh Army Corps, the attendance including General Mackinnon, Lord Dynevor and Sir Watkin Williams-Wynn. Recruiting for the new Welsh corps began on Tuesday and the first lot of recruits go to Rhyl. The scheme has the proviso that Colonel Evans will be able to keep what men he requires to maintain the three Welsh regiments at the strength the War Offices requires; and that the Welsh Committee should raise artillery, but no cavalry, except one or two squadrons. Later on it is proposed to use the artillery camp at Trawsfynydd (Merionethshire) and if the quarry-men and others of the district will make a special effort to form a company of artillery General Mackinnon promises that proper sheds will be erected for housing men during the winter. A national committee of county directors of the Welsh Territorial Force was formed to carry out the medical organisation of the Welsh Army Corps.

During another meeting of the committee at Shrewsbury in November it was announced that new technical units of the Royal Army Medical Corps, Royal Engineers, Army Service Corps and Royal Field Artillery would be formed for the new Welsh Division. A letter was read out stating that Mr Richard Marpole, the president of the Canadian Pacific Railway Company in Vancouver, had raised a number of Canadian men of Welsh heritage to serve in the new division. The announcement of the make-up of the division was also read out. (The battalion titles were later changed to numbers to conform with the expansion of their respective regiments but were the titles used during October 1914.)

Three infantry brigades would be created to form what was then entitled the First Division of the Welsh Army Corps. The original idea of forming a Welsh Army Corps was a romantic one and one that was unrealistic and, as a result, just the one division would be formed, initially numbered the 43rd (Welsh) Division. Local newspapers reported:

> The First Brigade, commanded by Colonel Owen Thomas and billeted at Llandudno, would consist of: North Wales Battalion of the Royal Welsh Fusiliers, now partially formed, under the command of Colonel Wynn Edwards; two Service Battalions of the Royal Welsh Fusiliers, to be formed; and the London Welsh Battalion, now partially formed.

> The Second Brigade, commanded by Colonel R.H.V. Dunn and billeted at Rhyl, would consist of: 1st Rhondda Battalion of the Welsh Regiment, under Col. Holloway; 2nd Rhondda Battalion of the Welsh Regiment, under the command of Sir Wm. Watts and now partially formed; Swansea Battalion Welsh Regiment, under the command of Col. Benson and now partially formed; and the Carmarthenshire Service Battalion, which is to be raised in command of Col. Scobie, C.B.

> The Third Brigade, commanded by Colonel Sir Ivor Philipps DSO and billeted at Colwyn Bay, would consist of: Monmouthshire Battalion of the South Wales Borderers, not yet formed; Service Battalion South Wales Borderers, not yet formed; Cardiff Service Battalion of the Welsh Regiment, under the command of Major Frank Gaskell, not yet formed; and the Service Battalion of the Welsh Regiment, to be raised in the county of Glamorgan and the command of which has been offered to Major C.J. Wilkie, secretary of the Glamorgan Territorial Force Association, who is now with the 9th Service Battalion of the Welsh Regiment at Salisbury.

According to this composition five battalions were to be recruited in the 41st area, three battalions in the 23rd area, three battalions in the 24th area and one battalion in London. A proposal to raise Welsh battalions in Liverpool and Manchester was also debated but was abandoned, although a large amount of recruiting for the new Welsh Division was carried out in the Bolton and Farnworth area of Manchester, especially for the 15th (Carmarthenshire) Battalion, Welsh Regiment (15th Welsh). The men were to be clad in Brethyn Llwyd, a native grey Welsh cloth that was produced in woollen mills in Carmarthenshire, Cardiganshire and North Wales.

With the composition of the new division agreed upon, recruiting began in earnest. Local recruiting committees were set up around the country and arrangements were put in place for the billeting of the men locally before they were despatched to join the battalions in North Wales. The Carmarthenshire County Committee was one such organization; presided over by Sir Stafford Howard, the committee worked tirelessly throughout the early stages of the war to recruit enough men to form the Carmarthen Battalion, the 15th Welsh. The Executive Committee, at Shrewsbury, decided to cede the powers of naming the commanding officers (COs) of the new battalions to the Lord Lieutenant of the relevant county in which the battalion was raised, but these new COs would have to be picked from a list of men thought suitable for such positions, which would be drafted by General Sir Henry Mackinnon of the War Office. The COs would then work with their Lord Lieutenant to pick their officers.

By the second week of December 1914 almost 10,000 men had volunteered to serve with the Welsh Division and were in training in North Wales. Another meeting was held in Shrewsbury on 2 November, chaired by Sir James Hills-Johnes VC GCB, at which it was decided to raise three Welsh Royal Army Medical Corps (RAMC) Field Ambulance units.

Recruiting in London for Welshmen was steaming ahead. The *Llangollen Advertiser* of 1 January 1915 stated:

A mixed group of men from the 38th (Welsh) Division Royal Army Medical Corps units.

LONDON WELSH BATTALION. The 1st Battalion of London Welsh now numbers between 1,100 and 1,200 men. It is intended to send another draft of recruits to North Wales next week and also a fine band of ex-army bandsmen that has been organised. With a view to raising a second battalion the committee, Major Ivor Bowen and the officers ask that Welshmen living in centres outside London and the Principality and who are desirous of joining the Welsh Army Corps, should get in touch with them at the headquarters, Gray's Inn, so that all Welshmen may be banded together.

While recruiting was the priority in Wales, work was in full swing at Kinmel and Bodelwyddan Parks to erect wooden hutments to house the large number of recruits due to arrive there. The North Wales Pals Battalion RWF had moved from Rhyl to Llandudno in the middle of November to join the First Brigade, while the Swansea and Carmarthenshire Battalion Welsh Regiment moved to their vacated billets at Rhyl. The north Wales coast was now bustling with thousands of fresh recruits from all parts of Wales and the men were made to feel very welcome by the townspeople of Rhyl, Llandudno and Colwyn Bay, although drunkenness was beginning to be a problem, leading to the imposition of limited opening hours in the local pubs. Members of the divisional artillery were billeted in west Wales around Aberystwyth but had not, as yet, been issued with field guns for training. Instead the men made good use of telegraph poles strapped to carts to practise their driving skills!

Also billeted at Conway during December was another newly-raised battalion: the Salford Pals Battalion of the Lancashire Fusiliers. Forty huts had been erected on Conway Morfa for the battalion, which arrived at Morfa military station. The Englishmen drilled and practised their shooting on the local range and carried out further training on the mountain and moorland to the south of the camping ground.

There was some concern among the townsfolk of Rhyl during December when it was discovered that the local police force was compiling a list of unmarried men in the town between the ages of 19 and 38. Flintshire Police were also carrying out the same exercise at the behest of the Flintshire County Council Recruiting Committee, but so far nothing like this was being carried out in Caernarfonshire or Denbighshire. This concern also spread to south Wales, where the Welsh Army Corps officials felt compelled to publicly declare that they had no intention of doing the same in Cardiff or Glamorgan.

Men continued to arrive in the training areas in north Wales throughout December. On Friday 11 December the 3rd Monmouths paraded in Abergavenny prior to entraining to join the Welsh Army Corps. However, the battalion would instead join 83 Brigade, 28th Division in France on 14 February 1915, ten months before the Welsh Division moved overseas.

Local newspapers were full of stories of men enlisting, publishing long lists of men from certain towns joining up and the mood around the country was so patriotic and positive that the call to form a battalion of Welsh Guards also started to become more vocal. One of the major campaigners was Henry Philipps of Picton Castle, Pembrokeshire. He tirelessly campaigned throughout the early months of the war for the War Office to form such a regiment, sending the following letter to all the major newspapers in Wales as well as touring Wales to give stirring speeches:

> Sir,
> At such a serious time in the history of our country and when recruits for the Army are so urgently needed, may I suggest, through the columns of your paper, that one or more battalions of Welsh Guards might be formed as soon as possible? I am certain that the patriotic feeling of Welshmen, especially in such a crisis, will readily respond and if supported by all lords-lieutenant and other influential people throughout the Principality of Wales, the movement would be rapidly and successfully carried through. Rightly or wrongly, I have for a long time been of the opinion that if a regiment of Welsh Guards could be raised it would be a popular move and would be supported by many and I don't think there could be a more suitable time than the present to carry this out, especially when we have daily evidence in the press of the splendid response that is being given to the call to arms in all parts of Wales. We all know that there are English, Scotch [sic] and Irish Guards: Why not Welsh?
> Yours truly,
> H. PHILIPPS.
> Picton Castle, Haverfordwest.

This campaigning carried on over the first winter of the war, until enough pressure had been placed on the War Office to cede to the demands of the campaigners and the Welsh Guards would eventually be established on 26 February 1915 by Royal Warrant of His Majesty King George V.

The battalions for the new Welsh army were almost fully formed by the end of 1914 and were attached to infantry brigades at first numbered the 128th, 129th and 130th brigades of the 43rd Division (1st Division Welsh Army Corps), although this was later changed to the 113th, 114th and 115th brigades of the 38th (Welsh) Division. According to the *History of the 38th (Welsh) Division*, the origins of each battalion were as follows.

128 Brigade (later 113 Brigade)

On 3 September the War Office sanctioned the raising of a North Wales Pals Battalion of the Royal Welsh Fusiliers and sixty-eight recruits joined and formed the nucleus of that battalion at Rhyl on 2 October, moving to Llandudno on 18 November. The battalion later became the 13th Battalion, Royal Welsh Fusiliers (13th RWF). Recruiting for the battalion was so brisk that sanction was obtained to create a 16th Battalion (16th RWF).

On 30 October Lieutenant Colonel Owen Thomas was appointed to command 128 Brigade and on 2 November commenced raising a Caernarfon and Anglesey Battalion at Llandudno that had its headquarters at Maenan House, Lloyd Street and became the 14th Battalion Royal Welsh Fusiliers (14th RWF).

The 15th Battalion, Royal Welsh Fusiliers (15th RWF) was inaugurated at a meeting of Welshmen in London on 16 September, presided over by Sir E. Vincent Evans and recruits began to pour in, but it was not until 29 October that the battalion was officially recognized as the London Welsh Battalion, with its HQ at the Inns of Court Hotel, Holborn. The battalion joined the brigade at Llandudno on 5 December.

129 Brigade (later 114 Brigade)

The 10th Battalion, Welsh Regiment (10th Welsh) was recruited in the Rhondda Valley and was formed on 1 October at Codford St Mary in Wiltshire as part of the 25th Division but on the 30th of that month the battalion was transferred to 129 Brigade of the 43rd Welsh Division at Rhyl and became the 10th Battalion (1st Rhondda), Welsh Regiment and numbered six officers and 800 other ranks.

The 13th Battalion, Welsh Regiment (13th Welsh) was recruited from the same district and formed at Sophia Gardens, Cardiff on 23 October, though the elements of the battalion had been forming prior to that date at the Depot Barracks, Cardiff and by that time the battalion was 500 strong. On 3 November the battalion moved to Prestatyn and on the 17th joined 129 Brigade at Rhyl, becoming the 13th Battalion (2nd Rhondda), Welsh Regiment.

The 14th Battalion, Welsh Regiment (14th Welsh) had its origin in the Swansea Cricket and Football Club, who formed a Club Training Corps on 13 August and turned part of the grounds into a rifle range. The Corps was subsequently adopted by the township, a subscription of £7,000 was raised for its maintenance and by the end of September 200 men had been enrolled and drill was in full swing on the Swansea Cricket Field. The battalion joined 129 Brigade at Rhyl on 1 December and became the 14th (Swansea Battalion), Welsh Regiment.

The formation of the 15th Battalion, Welsh Regiment (15th Welsh) bears a later date and the nucleus of the battalion was made at Rhyl by a draft of seventy-one men (mostly from Lancashire) from the 10th Welsh on 21 November. A draft of 350 joined the battalion on 23 January from Porthcawl, 250 further men were enlisted from the Bolton area and it was not until the end of February that the battalion was made up to full strength by men enlisted in Carmarthenshire. The battalion took its place in 129 Brigade as the 15th (Carmarthenshire Battalion), Welsh Regiment.

130 Brigade (later 115 Brigade)

The 10th Battalion, South Wales Borderers (10th SWB) commenced recruiting at Ebbw Vale and Cwm on 12 November and drew recruits from Tredegar, Abercarn, Crumlin, Pontnewydd, Newport, Blackwood and Abertillery; those recruits almost entirely consisted of Monmouthshire colliers and iron-workers. By 4 December the strength of the battalion was 320 and on 30 December it moved to Colwyn Bay nearly 600 strong to join 130 Brigade as the 10th Battalion (1st Gwent), South Wales Borderers.

The 11th Battalion, South Wales Borderers (11th SWB) was formed at Brecon Barracks on 5 December and on 9 January joined 130 Brigade at Old Colwyn only 100 strong. Recruiting was carried out in the Gwent district of Monmouthshire and

Breconshire and especially at Pengam; at first it was slow but later became so brisk that both the 10th and 11th battalions each sent a company to form part of the 13th Battalion. Some 100 recruits enlisted in Liverpool. The battalion was named the 11th Battalion (2nd Gwent), South Wales Borderers.

The 17th Battalion, Royal Welsh Fusiliers (17th RWF), along with the 18th and 19th battalions of that regiment, was originally formed on 2 February as part of 128 Brigade. The headquarters of the battalion was at Charlton Street, Llandudno and a recruiting depot was formed at Blaenau Ffestiniog. The battalion remained with this brigade until 14 July 1915, when it was transferred to 130 Brigade (by that time renumbered 115).

The 16th (Cardiff City) Battalion, Welsh Regiment (16th Welsh) commenced recruiting at Cardiff in November 1914 and owed its origin to the Cardiff City Council. The battalion was, however, actually formed at Porthcawl and moved from there to join 130 Brigade at Colwyn Bay on 31 December 1914, being at that time 500 strong. The battalion was authorized by the War Office to wear the Cardiff City coat of arms as their collar badge.

The 19th Battalion, Welsh Regiment (19th Welsh) was formed as the Divisional Pioneer Battalion at Colwyn Bay in February 1915 and the nucleus of the battalion was composed of drafts from infantry battalions of the division but the majority of the men were recruited direct from Glamorganshire, hence their title of the 'Glamorgan Pioneers'. In April drafts were received from the 123rd and 151st Field Companies, Royal Engineers (RE). The battalion was with Divisional Headquarters at Colwyn Bay until the move to Winchester. It is believed that the battalion was the first pioneer battalion to be enlisted as such.

On 29 April 1915, the number of the division was changed to the 38th and the brigades were renumbered 113th, 114th and 115th. The idea of forming a Welsh Army Corps was abandoned and the 38th Division became known as the Welsh Division, with its HQ at Colwyn Bay. By the end of October 1914 Sophia Gardens at Cardiff was crammed with several thousand recruits for the Welsh Division. These men were duly sorted out and sent to either Porthcawl (for men suitable for artillery, engineers or Army Service Corps duties), or to Prestatyn and Rhyl to join the Welsh Regiment infantry battalions there.

All recruits for the artillery remained at Porthcawl until the end of January 1915, before being sent to the Pwllheli area, where the batteries formed and trained. Thus by the end of February 1915 the entire 38th (Welsh) Division had been formed and was in north Wales.

Of all the other attached troops, one of the more interesting was the forming of a Royal Army Medical Corps unit, later the 130th Field Ambulance, which was created from members of the Order of St John of Jerusalem, many of whom had first-hand experience as first-aiders in the south Wales collieries. All the associated support troops also moved to north Wales.

The division also originally comprised four battalions of bantams (men who were under the minimum height for soldiering), of whom no mention has been made above:

they were the 18th and 19th Royal Welsh Fusiliers, the 12th South Wales Borderers and the 17th Welsh. These battalions were left behind in north Wales when the division moved to Winchester during August 1915 and later formed part of another division.

In September the division was inspected by Lieutenant General Sir Archibald Murray, who reported so favourably that the division was placed in Kitchener's fourth 100,000, though it really belonged to the fifth 100,000, and was warned to be ready to proceed to France around the end of November. The division was reviewed on Crawley Down on 29 November 1915 by Her Majesty the Queen, accompanied by Princess Mary. During the next few days, with the exception of the artillery, which remained behind to fire a course at Lark Hill, the units of the division marched to Southampton to embark for France and were railed to the neighbourhood of Rocquetoire, not far from St Omer, to assemble. The move was completed on 5 December 1915 and the division became part of XI Corps under the command of Sir Richard Haking, KCB, DSO. Towards the end of December the artillery of the division arrived and the whole division moved to St Venant, where it relieved the 46th (North Midland) Division in Corps reserve.

The future activities of the 38th (Welsh) Division will be integrated into the story of the *Welsh at War* at the appropriate time; however, its final make-up was as follows:

INFANTRY
113TH INFANTRY BRIGADE (Brigadier General Owen Thomas, M.P.)
13th (1st North Wales) Battalion, Royal Welsh Fusiliers
14th Battalion, Royal Welsh Fusiliers
15th (1st London Welsh) Battalion, Royal Welsh Fusiliers
16th Battalion, Royal Welsh Fusiliers
113th Machine-Gun Company
113th Light Trench Mortar Battery

114TH INFANTRY BRIGADE (Brigadier General R.H.V. Dunn)
10th (1st Rhondda) Battalion, the Welsh Regiment
13th (2nd Rhondda) Battalion, the Welsh Regiment
14th (Swansea) Battalion, the Welsh Regiment
15th (Carmarthenshire) Battalion, the Welsh Regiment
114th Machine-Gun Company
114th Light Trench Mortar Battery

115TH INFANTRY BRIGADE (Brigadier General H.J. Evans)
2nd Battalion Royal Welsh Fusiliers (joined 1918)
17th (2nd North Wales) Battalion, Royal Welsh Fusiliers
10th (1st Gwent) Battalion, South Wales Borderers
11th (2nd Gwent) Battalion, South Wales Borderers
16th (Cardiff City) Battalion, the Welsh Regiment
115th Machine-Gun Company

115th Light Trench Mortar Battery
Plus other attached infantry, including the Divisional Pioneers:
19th (Glamorgan Pioneer) Battalion, the Welsh Regiment
Divisional Cyclist Company
Machine-Gun Battalion
176th Machine-Gun Company
'D' Squadron, Royal Wiltshire Yeomanry

ARTILLERY
119th Brigade, R.F.A.
120th Brigade, R.F.A.
121st Brigade, R.F.A.
122nd Brigade, R.F.A.
38th Heavy Battery
Divisional Ammunition Column
(a) 'V' Trench Mortar Battery (Heavy)
(b) 'X' Trench Mortar Battery (Medium)
(c) 'Y' Trench Mortar Battery (Medium)
(d) 'Z' Trench Mortar Battery

ROYAL ENGINEERS
123rd Field Company, R.E.
124th Field Company, R.E.
151st Field Company, R.E.
Divisional Signal Company

ARMY SERVICE CORPS
Divisional Train (Nos. 330–333 Companies, A.S.C.)
235th Divisional Employment Company
38th Divisional Mechanical Transport Company

ROYAL ARMY MEDICAL CORPS
129th Field Ambulance
130th (St John) Field Ambulance
131st Field Ambulance
No. 5 Mobile Bacteriological Section
49th Mobile Veterinary Section

Welsh units also provided major elements of several other divisions:
13th (Western) Division. This division had one brigade, 40 Brigade, which comprised
three Welsh battalions: 8th Battalion, Royal Welsh Fusiliers; 4th Battalion, South Wales
Borderers; and 8th Battalion, Welsh Regiment.

19th (Western) Division. This division had one brigade, 58 Brigade, which comprised three Welsh battalions: 9th Battalion, Royal Welsh Fusiliers; 5th Battalion, South Wales Borderers; and 9th Battalion, Welsh Regiment.

22nd Division. This division had one brigade, 67 Brigade, which comprised four Welsh battalions: 11th Battalion, Royal Welsh Fusiliers; 7th Battalion, South Wales Borderers; 8th Battalion, South Wales Borderers; and 11th Battalion, Welsh Regiment.

40th (Bantam) Division. This division had one brigade, 119 Brigade, which comprised four Welsh battalions: 19th Battalion, Royal Welsh Fusiliers; 12th Battalion, South Wales Borderers; 17th Battalion, Welsh Regiment; and 18th Battalion, Welsh Regiment.

74th (Yeomanry) Division. This division had one brigade, 231 Brigade, which comprised three Welsh battalions: 24th Battalion, Royal Welsh Fusiliers; 25th Battalion, Royal Welsh Fusiliers; and 24th Battalion, Welsh Regiment.

While several divisions contained just one or two Welsh battalions, the Guards Division contained just one Welsh regiment: the 1st Battalion, Welsh Guards.

1st Division. This division contained two Welsh battalions: 1st Battalion, South Wales Borderers and 2nd Battalion, Welsh Regiment; the 1st/6th Battalion, Welsh Regiment later joined as Divisional Pioneers.

3rd Division. This division contained just one Welsh battalion: 10th Battalion, Royal Welsh Fusiliers.

7th Division. This division contained one Welsh battalion: 1st Battalion, Royal Welsh Fusiliers.

25th Division. This division contained just one Welsh battalion: 6th Battalion, South Wales Borderers.

28th Division. This division contained two Welsh battalions: 1st Battalion, Welsh Regiment and 23rd Battalion, Welsh Regiment.

29th Division. This division initially contained just one Welsh battalion: 2nd Battalion, South Wales Borderers, but the 1st/2nd Battalion, Monmouthshire Regiment later joined as Divisional Pioneers.

46th (North Midland) Division. This division contained just one Welsh battalion: 1st/1st Battalion, Monmouthshire Regiment, but also became famous when 137 Brigade, led by Welshman Sir John Vaughan Campbell of Golden Grove, Carmarthenshire, captured Riqueval Bridge, opening the way through the Hindenburg Line during the Advance to Victory in 1918.

Chapter 8

1915
The Escalation of the War
More Welsh Units Arrive

With the first year of the war having drawn to a close, the line of the Western Front had firmly formed and 1915 would prove to be a difficult year for the allies. As far as the Welsh units were concerned, many battalions would move to France during the year and the majority would see heavy fighting before the year was out.

At the end of 1914 the 1st Division (4th RWF, 1st SWB and 2nd Welsh) were still in the trenches at Festubert, miserable, wet and cold, the latter two having suffered such grievous casualties that their composition had been totally transformed by reinforcements. The 2nd RWF had meanwhile been enduring a torrid time in the Fromelles sector in very similar terrain, also wet, muddy and cold; while the 1st RWF had been having a relatively peaceful time, albeit also cold and muddy, rebuilding and training in the villages of Le Fayel and Montagne in Picardy after moving out of the battle area on 5 December, remaining here for over two months.

After spending the New Year in the line the 1st SWB moved into reserve on 4 January, followed by the 2nd Welsh four days later. On the same day the 2nd RWF moved to Bois Grenier and took up positions on the left flank of the 1st RWF. It was, by now, relatively peaceful and along the Western Front the men were kept busy digging and strengthening the defences. Lieutenant A.K. Richardson of the 1st RWF wrote of this period:

During December 1914 the 1st Battalion was holding the line between Touquet and La Boutillerie and, owing to the very wet state of the trenches, an order was issued that one platoon from each company was to go out of the line into a ruined farm about 150 yards to our rear and there the men were to be given a chance of cleaning themselves and resting. One platoon went out each day at 'stand-to' in the morning and returned at 'stand-to' at night. An old woman arrived at the farm one day, dug a safe out of a manure heap, placed it in a wheelbarrow and departed with her rescued savings in broad daylight and in full view of the enemy.

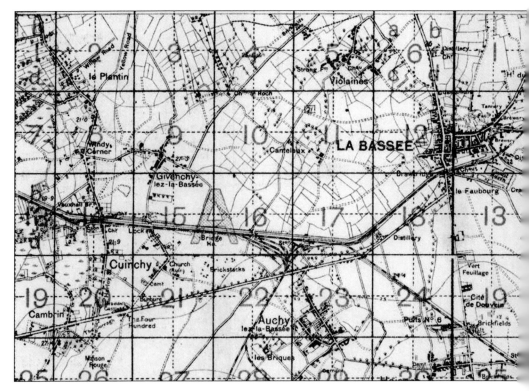

A section of trench map 36CN, showing Givenchy and the La Bassée Canal.

On 12 January 1915, the entire 3 Brigade was sent to hold the Givenchy subsector, which ran from the La Bassée Canal on the right, round the front of the village of Givenchy to a point about 150 metres to the north of it, where it bent back sharply for 500 metres towards Festubert. On the right were the 1st Munsters, then the 1st Gloucesters, while the 2nd Welsh, which had two platoons of the 4th RWF attached, held the village front. The 1st SWB were on the left.

The 1st Welsh, which had been in Chakrata, India under the command of Lieutenant Colonel Thomas Owen Marden at the start of the war, had been ordered home to England in November 1914 and landed at Plymouth just a few days before Christmas. The battalion set up camp in Hursley Park, near Winchester, spending the festive season in tented accommodation in a muddy field before marching to billets in West Downs School in Winchester. Reservists joined the battalion here to bring it up to full strength. The battalion was attached to 84 Brigade, 28th Division.

Just before going to France the 28th Division was inspected by King George V and Field Marshal Lord Kitchener. The regimental goat 'Billy', which had been presented to the 1st Welsh by King Edward VII, was refused permission to embark for France with the battalion and was sent back to Cardiff to become the 3rd Welsh mascot. On the night of 15/16 January the headmaster of West Downs School gave the battalion officers a champagne dinner to wish them luck and the following morning the 1st

Welsh marched to Southampton to embark aboard the SS *Cardiganshire*, disembarking at Le Havre on 18 January, where the men were billeted in cotton warehouses in the docks.

The men were each issued with a goatskin coat – which already smelt badly – and were fed and watered by lady volunteers who ran a canteen at the docks serving hot tea, coffee and cakes. On 19 January, the 1st Welsh entrained in horse trucks and detrained the next day at Hazebrouck, marching 7 miles to Merris, where the battalion went into comfortable billets. Back in England, one of the first known female Welsh casualties of the war occurred on that same day when Nurse Ellen Myfanwy Williams, the daughter of John and Elizabeth Williams, of 38 Feidr Fawr, Cardigan, died at West Bromwich after being taken ill while working for the Red Cross. The 26-year-old's body was brought home for burial in Cardigan Cemetery.

Being so near to two large French towns, Béthune and Armentières, the men began enjoying the odd rest day, relaxing in their capacious squares. Both towns were and still are built around such squares, surrounded by cafés and restaurants. It was during these early days of the war that the soldier gained a real thirst for *vin blanc* (white wine), *vin rouge* (red wine) and *oeuf et frites* (egg and chips).

Many of the British units at the front bore witness to, or were visited by, King George V on his first tour of the front. The first two weeks of January were relatively peaceful throughout, with the various war diaries of all the units mentioning little other than the hardships of the weather and the incessant digging. The only real item of note was the death of Taffy IV, the regimental goat of the 2nd Welsh, who died of heart

*Some officers of the 2nd Welsh at Givenchy 1915: Captain Aldworth along with Lieutenants Leycester and Betts. (*Welsh Regiment Museum*)*

Troops travelling aboard French railway trucks, famously labelled 40 Hommes, 8 Chevaux. *The trucks were, as the name suggests, horse trucks: smelly, cold and uncomfortable!*

Men of the 6th Welsh wearing their goatskin coats. These notoriously smelly coats provided an ideal breeding ground for lice and were never used after the first winter of the war. (Welsh Regiment Museum)

*The grave of Taffy IV, the regimental goat of the 2nd Welsh. He died on 20 January 1915 and is buried on the La Bassée Canal Bank. (*Welsh Regiment Museum*)*

failure at Béthune on 20 January. Taffy was afforded a burial on the banks of the La Bassée Canal, much to the disgust of the local residents!

The death of Taffy IV may have been on the minds of some of the men of the 2nd Welsh later that night, as Private Richard Morgan (11967) and Lance Corporal William Price (12942), both of C Company, got drunk and shot their Company Sergeant Major, Hughie Hayes. Hayes died in hospital at Béthune the following day. Morgan and Price were later tried for murder and sentenced to death.

Company Sergeant Major Hughie Job Hayes (5019) was the son of Edward and Mary Hayes of 31 Ashdown Road, Kingston upon Thames. He had entered the Duke of York's Royal Military School in 1892 and served during the Boer War. After eighteen years of service in the army and surviving the carnage at the Battle of the Aisne, Hughes had fallen victim to two soldiers who he knew well. He was 32 years old when he died on 21 January 1915 and is buried in Béthune Town Cemetery.

Among the steady stream of casualties suffered by the 1st RWF during January was Second Lieutenant John

The grave of murdered CSM Hughie Hayes of 2nd Welsh.

125

Trevor Rees, who was mortally wounded and died on 22 January. He is buried in Bois-Grenier Communal Cemetery. Rees was born in Penarth on 7 November 1893, the son of Dr John Hugh Rees and his wife Gwendoline. He was a pupil at the Cathedral School from April 1905 to July 1908 and then at Shrewsbury School until 1911, serving in the Officers' Training Corps. He was commissioned from the Artists' Rifles in the 1st RWF on 10 November 1914. One of his men wrote of his death:

> In losing Mr Rees the Regiment has lost one of the most daring and bravest officers it has ever had. He knew no such thing as fear… He made us all love him, by his daring bravery, cheerfulness and consideration for the sick and weak; and I myself have lost the best friend I have ever had in my six years of soldiering.

The first of thirteen Welsh international rugby players to fall during the war was lost at sea during this time. Charles Gerald Taylor was born at Ruabon on 8 May 1863, the son of Reverend Alfred and Annie Taylor. His father was headmaster of Ruabon Grammar School, where Charles was educated. He had played rugby for his home club before playing for the London Welsh and Blackheath. He gained nine Welsh caps during an international career that lasted from 1884 until 1887 and had also been Welsh pole-vaulting champion. Taylor joined the Royal Navy on 1 July 1885 as acting assistant engineer and during a successful career had risen to the rank of engineer captain by the outbreak of war. He was initially posted to the battlecruiser HMS *Queen Mary* and on 20 November 1914 was transferred to HMS *Tiger*. On 24 January 1915, *Tiger* was one of the vessels engaged in the Battle of Dogger Bank and was struck by shellfire from the German cruiser SMS *Blücher*. Taylor was killed during the engagement and his body was returned to Britain to be buried at Tavistock New Cemetery in Devon.

The grave of Second Lieutenant John Trevor Rees in Bois-Grenier Communal Cemetery.

Charles Gerald Taylor, the first Welsh rugby international killed during the Great War.

The relative peace was fated not to last. By 24 January the defenders of Givenchy were aware that a storm was brewing and preparations were put in place for a German attack. This turned out to be a wise precaution, for at 7.30 am on 25 January a heavy bombardment on the British lines heralded a strong attack on the village. At about 8.15

am the fire lifted and the German infantry attacked, breaking through a trench held by the 2nd Welsh. Captain Lord de Freyne led his C Company of the 1st SWB from reserve to prevent the enemy breakthrough, while Captain Salomon advanced with B Company. The 1st Gloucesters were fighting in the manner for which they were renowned, surrounded and firing to front and rear, while the 4th RWF also came into the action, several waves of Germans attacking them in their positions at Welsh and Scottish trenches alongside the 2nd Welsh.

The 2nd Welsh rallied and brought up machine guns to support their counter-attack, strengthened by B and C companies of the 1st SWB, one company of the 4th RWF and one company of the Black Watch. This combined attack did the trick: Second Lieutenant C.H. James (3rd Borderers, attached 2nd Welsh) found himself with fifteen men under Corporal W. Thomas (6406) about 40 metres from the main trench, charged with them straight across the open into the Germans and captured almost fifty prisoners, re-establishing the original line.

The Germans had attacked along the whole front of the village with 1,800 men in six lines and, except for the one breakthrough, were mown down by rifle fire. The breakthrough had occurred where the trench had been demolished by German artillery. To the south of the canal the enemy attacked Cuinchy and 1 Brigade and the French lost some trenches that were not recovered until February.

The 2nd Welsh were well-rewarded for their efforts. Lieutenant William George Hewett and Lieutenant Frederick Joseph Aglio Dibdin (3rd Sussex, attached) both won the Military Cross (MC) for the part they took in repelling the attack. (The decoration of the MC was introduced on 28 December 1914 for officers below the rank of major and for warrant officers. (Lieutenant Hewett was the first to win it in the 2nd Welsh and Second Lieutenant E.W. Bryan in the 1st Welsh.) Company Sergeant Major Thomas Herbert Scott, Corporal W. Thomas (6406), Corporal J. Finnigan (8953), Private L. Rogers (1946), Private G. Church (8377) and Private J. Burridge (8503) were all awarded the DCM and Lance Sergeant W. Harvey was mentioned in despatches for their gallant conduct in the action that cost the 2nd Welsh the following in casualties: Second Lieutenant Francis Henry Stanley Hawkesworth (3rd Borderers attached) and nineteen other ranks killed, and Second Lieutenants A.R.O. Peck and J.A.G. Leask (King's Own, attached) and thirty-eight other ranks wounded.

Captain Hugh Maxwell Broome Salmon, who was awarded the Distinguished Service Order for his gallant leadership of the counter-attack at Givenchy on 25 January 1915. Salmon is to the right, alongside his brother.

The 1st SWB was also well-rewarded. Captain Hugh Maxwell Broome Salmon was awarded the DSO 'For conspicuous courage at Givenchy on 25th January, 1915. Although wounded, he brought up men from the local Reserves under heavy fire on two occasions and remained throughout the day with his Company in action.'

Sergeant W. Wilcox (8836) and Corporal E.J. Williams (11338) were both awarded the DCM for re-mounting machine guns under heavy fire. Captain Lord de Freyne (Francis French) was mentioned in despatches. The battalion's losses were not heavy, with twenty-one men killed and Captain Salmon and Second Lieutenant Nisbet and forty men wounded.

Meanwhile the 4th RWF had suffered twelve men killed during the fighting, three of whom – Privates Edward Evans (7299), William Fail (5261) and John Griffiths (6843) – were from the village of Rhosllanerchrugog in Denbighshire.

The Givenchy sector now quietened down and some reshuffling of officers took place. Captain Hubert Charles Rees left the 2nd Welsh to return to Wales, joining the staff of the 38th (Welsh) Division, and Major Archer George Prothero joined the battalion from the 1st Welsh in order to

Lieutenant Frederick Joseph Aglio Dibdin of the 3rd Sussex attached to the 2nd Welsh. Dibdin was awarded the Military Cross for his gallant at Givenchy on 25 January 1915.

take command. The 1st SWB received a draft of ninety-two men on 26 January and another 240 reinforcements on 1 February, along with several officers, bringing the battalion up to full strength. The 2nd RWF had been fortunate enough to have had a quiet month, but by the end of January rising water levels in the Lys Valley meant that the men were constantly at work improving defences and erecting sandbag parapets. The incessant flooding of the trenches here made the soldiers stationed in the area think that German engineers had gained mastery of the ground and were diverting water into the British lines! The Germans were, of course, in the same predicament.

After the failure of the British and French local attacks in the middle of December 1914, the weather had become too poor for anything more than minor attacks. The German advance in 1914 had created a large salient between Reims and Amiens, threatening the communications of the French with their northern front. To counter this threat, General Joffre and Field Marshal Sir John French met to draw up plans for an offensive as soon as the weather improved and the British had brought in more troops. General Joffre realized that if the German salient could be pierced then their lines of communication would be open to attack, so he drew up a plan for an attack in March: the French Tenth Army was to capture the heights of Vimy Ridge and the British First Army Aubers Ridge.

To strengthen the French Tenth Army, Sir John French agreed to relieve the French divisions in front of Ypres as soon as British reinforcements became available.

Germans in a primitive trench in Flanders, early 1915.

Accordingly, early in February the 27th and 28th divisions (the latter containing the 1st Welsh) relieved the French 31st and 32nd divisions at Ypres. The 1st Canadian Division landed in France on 17 February and the 46th (North Midland) Division, the first complete Territorial Division to do so, landed on 27 February.

The 28th Division had been unlucky: it was posted to the infamous Hill 60 sector of Ypres; not the ideal place to begin its first tour of duty in the trenches. On 26 January the 1st Welsh was inspected by Sir Horace Smith-Dorrien, commanding Second Army, and two days later by the Commander-in-Chief, Sir John French. It had been notable that Merris, where the battalion was billeted, was as peaceful as Winchester but that peace would soon come to an end.

Senior officers and one NCO per company were attached to units of the 27th Division in the trenches but as that division was also newly-arrived, nothing was learned except not to show one's head above ground for more than a second in daylight and never twice in the same place or a sniper would put a bullet through it. No one in the 1st Welsh had any idea what was in store for them and the men enjoyed several days of peace, shopping and strolling through Bailleul when the opportunity arose.

The first experience of the 1st Welsh in the trenches was in front of Hill 60 during February. The battalion was sent by motor bus to Vlamertinghe, where it arrived in the dark, and the men set off on foot to Ypres, receiving rations in a field on the way. The column was met by French guides at Ypres and the men were astounded to see these men in their old pre-war blue overcoats and baggy red trousers. The Frenchmen led the 1st Welsh to some old brickyards in Zillebeke, just west of Hill 60, where the battalion HQ was set up in a kiln.

On 4 February the battalion relieved the Northumberland Fusiliers in the front line and found the trenches to be deep but not very protective due to their poorly-made parapets. In fact, during its first two forty-eight-hour tour here, twelve men were killed and thirty-seven wounded, several being shot through the parapet. (The battalion's first man killed in the trenches was Private David Richards (5948), the 39-year-old husband of Kate Richards, of Rose Cottage, Woodland Road, Upper Town, Loughor.) Conditions were dire and Lieutenant Colonel Marden wrote of this time:

> Sanitary conditions were bad and the French never bothered about their dead in those days. Many were built into the parapet and it was considered the correct thing to shake one hand which hung helplessly out of a traverse when passing the spot and to say 'Hello, Froggie'. The men hated digging through what they called 'cemeteries'.

Little is known of how much units such as the 1st Welsh were aware of happenings elsewhere, but on 11 February the first Welshman of the war was executed: his crime was quitting his post. Corporal George Henry Povey (10459) served with the 1st Battalion, Cheshire Regiment (1st Cheshires). He was born in Sealand in 1891, one of eight children of Dinah and Robert Povey. The family lived at 2 Davies Cottages, Hawarden. During the Christmas period Povey's battalion was holding trenches around Wulverghem. Hostilities resumed following the Christmas period and, in terrible conditions, men were regularly subjected to trench raids by the Germans, which led to a high level of fear among some of the men. Early in the morning of 28 January there was an alarm that the Germans were in the trench. The alarm proved to be false but several men still panicked, some of whom, including Povey, fled. Povey was sent back into the line, but charges were brought against him and four other men as follows: 'When on Active Service, leaving his post without orders from his superior officer'. The men, none of whom had a defending officer, were tried separately by a Field General Court Martial that was convened in Bailleul on 3 February. The other four men were each sentenced to ten years' penal servitude, while Povey received the death sentence. On 8

LEA S. W.
McCARTHY F., D
McGARRY J.
MOLYNEUX G. W
POVEY G.
POWNALL J. C.
ROBERTS A. S.
ROBERTS W. S.
SMITH W. L.

Corporal George Povey's name o. the Ypres (Menin Gate) Memorial Povey was the first Welshman to l executed during the Great War.

February, Field Marshal French confirmed the sentence and Povey was executed at St Jans-Cappel in the Ypres Salient at 7.45 am on 11 February 1915. No records of his burial have emerged and Povey is commemorated on the Ypres (Menin Gate) Memorial.

Two more Welshmen would follow him just four days later: Private Richard Morgan (11967) and Lance Corporal William Price (12942), both of the 2nd Welsh, who had shot their Company Sergeant Major Hughie Hayes while drunk, had been sentenced to death as mentioned above. On the morning of 15 February both men were executed by firing squad and were buried at Béthune Town Cemetery, near their victim.

The 1st Welsh marched back to hutments 7 miles west of Ypres on 11 February to rest, but on 14 February were ordered up to support 85 Brigade, which was suffering heavy casualties in taking over trenches around 'the Bluff'. The battalion reached the area but was not needed and marched back to camp. Lieutenant Colonel Morland, along with his company commanders and company sergeant majors, remained there to prepare for moving into the line the following day:

The grave of Private Richard Morgan (11967) of the 2nd Welsh at Béthune Town Cemetery. He was shot at dawn on 15 February 1915.

> It was a miserable, rainy, cold day and we arrived at Lankhof Château at dusk to find it crowded with officers from all sorts of units, including Belgian artillerists, who kindly gave us some tea, as of course we had nothing but iron rations on us... The cellar was so low that one could just sit upright and could not stand at all, but at any rate it was dry and warm, though airless. Having been informed of the horrors of the situation, we struggled back to the Château to hear that C.S.M. McCarthy, who had won the D.C.M. in the South African War and was one of our stoutest fighters, had been very badly wounded as he was leaving Y trench. He died the next day. 'Annie' Lloyd (Lieutenant Gerald Aylmer Lloyd), his Company Commander, said that he knew he would suffer the same fate when he took over Y trench and, sad to say, his premonition was right.

The grave of Lance Corporal William Price (12942) of the 2nd Welsh at Béthune Town Cemetery, shot at dawn on 15 February 1915.

That night the 1st Welsh relieved the 3rd Royal Fusiliers in the worst trenches it had yet seen. The march up to the line was bad enough, muddy and surrounded by dead bodies, but the trenches themselves were shocking:

> T trench (Major Hoggan), was on a sort of hillock (the

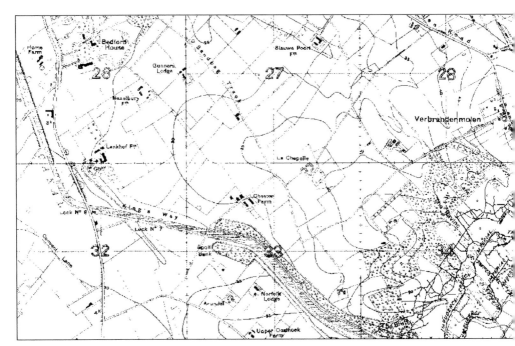

A section of trench map 28NW4 Zillebeke, showing the locations of Lankhof Farm and The Bluff (bottom left) and part of the Ypres-Comines Canal.

Bluff), but there was a good deal of dead ground in front and to the north of it. It was regularly and accurately shelled twice a day by the enemy. X trench was only a series of small dugouts under a bank with a 40-yard view. It protected T from small parties creeping in under the hillock. Y trench (Lieutenant G. Lloyd) was merely a ditch with a very weak parapet and under close fire (40 yards) of the very strong German line. There were also ruined houses in advance of both flanks which gave trouble. The trench was knee-deep in water and casualties always occurred when entering and leaving the trench. It was not properly supported by fire from either T or Z and was untenable. Z trench (Major Toke) had been strong once, but was now only partially held. It was subject to enfilade fire from one of the cottages. The parapets were not bulletproof and sandbags were shot down as soon as placed. B Company (Captain Montgomery) and the Grenadier platoons had better trenches on the south of the Canal.

The 1st Welsh had a torrid time at the Bluff. During the first forty-eight hours it lost twenty-eight men killed (including Captain Gerald Aylmer Lloyd and Lieutenants Reginald Thomas Buckingham Pope and Hilary Gresford Evan-Jones) and twenty-nine wounded (including Lieutenant Henry William Warren-Davis). The heavy number of casualties was caused by Z trench being situated in a wood with no field of fire. A section of the wood had been captured by the Germans, who then established bombers and snipers in it. Lieutenant Colonel Marden therefore requested permission to withdraw his men to a trench in the rear but it was a further two days before permission was given for this, hence the aforementioned casualties.

The deaths of the three officers mentioned above brings to light a mystery that has proved impossible to solve to this day. The three officers were buried next to each other within the grounds of Château Rosendal, a fine country house that was destroyed by gunfire early in the war. The site of the château is now enclosed within Bedford House Cemetery. Within Enclosure 3 of this immense cemetery, near to a part of the moat of the ruined château, lie two of these men: Captain Gerald Aylmer Lloyd and Lieutenant Reginald Thomas Buckingham Pope. Lieutenant Hilary Gresford Evan-Jones, who was buried alongside them, is not there. Instead he is commemorated on the Ypres (Menin Gate) Memorial to the missing.

Several contemporary sources prove that Evan-Jones was buried alongside his two fellow officers, so he should still be there; however, despite repeated attempts by the author to prove this to the CWGC, all efforts have hit a brick wall. Instead, buried either side are two other men: the first is Corporal John Stowe (10194), a Canadian who served with the 1st Welsh and was killed on 21 February 1914; the second grave is marked as 'Believed to Be' the grave of Private Daniel Farmer (10130), 1st Yorks and Lancs. It seems that the key to this mystery is the grave of Private Farmer but we shall probably never know.

One of the mysteries of the war. The graves of Corporal John Stowe, officers Captain Gerald Aylmer Lloyd and Lieutenant Reginald Thomas Buckingham Pope, all of the 1st Welsh, side by side in Bedford House Cemetery. Lieutenant Hilary Gresford Evan-Jones was buried alongside the two officers but is no longer there.

Lieutenant Hilary Gresford Evan-Jones was born on 22 January 1889, the son of the Reverend Richard Evan-Jones M.A., vicar of Llanllwchaiarn, Montgomery. He was educated at Charterhouse and at Hertford College, Oxford. He graduated in 1910 and on 5 October that year was commissioned in the 1st Welsh. Evan-Jones was to have been married to Nancy Bolton, the only daughter of Major W.N. Bolton, Commissioner of Kyrenia, but his leave was cancelled when the battalion was recalled to England. In one of his last letters home he wrote:

Lieutenant Hilary Gresford Evan-Jones, who was killed in action at the Bluff, near Hill 60, on 16 February 1915.

We have just finished our first eight days – divided between the supports and the firing line. I had the worst bit of trench to look after with my platoon and did all right, but had a good few casualties, considering the 96 hours I was actually up – two killed and nine wounded. I made two night expeditions by myself with some bombs, which I successfully dropped into the German trenches. During my first I met a German gentleman apparently at the same job as myself. My revolver accounted for him all right, as we were only two feet apart. The trenches are from 30 to 75 feet apart in most places and sometimes closer. We are now off on a four days' rest, which is absolutely ripping. It is splendid to get out of the noise and to get some proper food and sleep. I think, if anything, I am rather enjoying this. Cold feet are the worst part of the show, but my men are all such rippers, it makes up for lots. I hate having them hit, otherwise it is quite cheery. I had a sing-song in my trench the other evening, which did not please the Germans. I sat in a chair, which collapsed and I went straight to sleep where I lay. The strain is fairly big up there.

Letters to his father from Lieutenant Colonel Marden informed him that Evan-Jones had been buried with his two brother officers Lloyd and Pope in the gardens of the Château Rosendal, 3 miles south-east of Ypres. This is where the mystery of his being commemorated on the Ypres (Menin Gate) begins:

I regret most deeply having to inform you of the death on the 16th inst., in the trenches, of your gallant son Hilary. As far as we can ascertain, his death was instantaneous from a rifle bullet but many of his platoon were shot down at the same time and there was no one in the trench who could give accurate information as to what happened. He is a great loss to us as he was such a good soldier and so popular with all ranks. As you know, probably, he was selected to lead the Second Grenadier platoon and had behaved so gallantly during his former turn of duty in the trenches, where he kept the spirits of his whole platoon up by his energy and enterprise, that I brought his name especially to the notice of the Brigadier. He crept out of the trenches alone on several occasions and threw bombs into the enemy's trenches.

Captain Gerald Aylmer Lloyd was born on 17 April 1888, the son of Francis Aylmer Lloyd and Eugenie A. Lloyd of 75 Iverna Court, Kensington. He was educated at Cheltenham College and at the Royal Military College, Sandhurst before being commissioned in the 1st Welsh on 19 September 1908. His brother, Lieutenant Francis Charles Aylmer Lloyd, died of wounds on 8 October 1915.

Lieutenant Reginald Thomas Buckingham Pope was born on 29 July 1891, the son of Reginald Barrette Pope and Mary Richardson of 41 Sussex Square, Brighton. Educated at Brighton College, Rottingdean School and Bradfield College, he then entered Sandhurst before being commissioned in the 1st Welsh on 20 September 1911. Lieutenant Colonel Marden wrote to his brother:

Captain Gerald Aylmer Lloyd, killed in action at the Bluff, near Hill 60, on 16 February 1915.

> We had a most terrible time... Your brother thought he had seen a sniper and got up with a rifle to try and shoot him, when almost immediately he was hit right through the fore-head. He died at once without any suffering at all. When night fell I managed to get his body back and had him sent out of the trenches. He is buried at Château Rosendal, Ypres between Captain Lloyd and another officer.

Again, more fuel for the mystery of Evan-Jones' missing grave. Pope's older brother, Lieutenant Cyril Montagu Pope of the 2nd Worcesters, was mortally wounded at Polygon Wood on 24 October 1914 and died on the way back to the 22nd Field Hospital.

Lieutenant Reginald Thomas Buckingham Pope. He was killed in action at the Bluff, near Hill 60, on 16 February 1915.

The battalion was relieved on the night of 17/18 February and the following day Lieutenants B.T. Phillips, G. Brewis and C.E.N. Lomax, together with 126 men, were sent to hospital suffering from trench foot. On 19 February the battalion returned to the trenches but Marden decided to send in only one platoon, ordering it to dig new trenches along a new position south of the canal. This proved to be a lucky decision for the battalion, as on the following day a German attack annihilated the platoon, killing Lieutenant Cecil Henry Dundas and thirty-one men, the survivors being taken prisoner. If the whole battalion had gone into the line it might well have been wiped out.

In response, Brigadier General Wintour, commanding 84 Brigade, sent a combined force of the King's Own and of the 5th Royal Fusiliers to retake Y Trench under the orders of Lieutenant Colonel Marden, who also added a company from the 1st Welsh. The attackers advanced through the wood at dusk in three lines with fixed bayonets and were not spotted until they got within 30 metres of the enemy's trenches, which were masked by tall broken stumps and tangled undergrowth, but they were then met with heavy machine-gun and rifle fire and the attack faltered. Lieutenant Whitehorne of the 1st Welsh lost an arm and the casualties all round were very heavy. Another attack later that day also failed, suffering even greater casualties.

Lieutenant Cecil Henry Dundas, killed in action at the Bluff, near Hill 60, on 2(February 1915.

During its first spell in the trenches the 1st Welsh had suffered heavily: 71 men had been killed or died of wounds, 86 more had been wounded and 41 were missing, including Lieutenant Douglas and 37 other ranks taken prisoner.

The 1st Welsh were relieved on the night of 21/22 February by the 1st Lincolns of 5 Brigade. All the units of the 28th Division had suffered from high rates of casualties and also from trench foot during their first spell in the trenches. As a result, on 23 February the 1st Welsh marched 14 miles to Bailleul and went into billets in the town to enjoy some rest before moving into the Dranoutre sector. Out of the 26 officers and 993 other ranks that had gone into trenches at Hill 60 three weeks earlier, just 10 officers and 452 other ranks remained. A large number of reinforcement officers and men joined the battalion at Dranoutre. The line here was just a series of unconnected outposts that could only be approached by night, so each battalion was given the task of connecting these posts into a continuous trench. To help alleviate shortages of manpower, two additional battalions were attached to the 28th Division, one of which was the 1st Monmouths, which had landed in France on 13 February.

Chapter 9

The Raising of the Welsh Guards

Back in Wales, following much campaigning, especially by Henry Philipps of Picton Castle, agreement had finally been reached to create a new regiment, the Welsh Guards. Permission to raise the new regiment had originally been given by King George V on 6 February and Lord Kitchener was commanded to carry out the necessary work. The Royal Warrant to form the regiment was granted on 26 February. Kitchener duly summoned Major General Sir Francis Lloyd to his offices in London on 6 February and issued him with the orders to form the new regiment. Lloyd wrote of this moment in his foreword to the *History of the Welsh Guards* during September 1919:

> Accordingly, as I was commanding the London District, I was sent for by the Field-Marshal and ordered to raise a battalion immediately. On my asking Lord Kitchener how soon he expected this to be done, he replied, in his usual abrupt manner: 'In a week!' My answer was: 'They shall go on guard on St David's Day' – and they did!

The nucleus of the Welsh Guards was soon formed, with 300 Welshmen transferring from the Grenadier Guards and non-commissioned officers transferring from the Grenadier and Scots Guards after careful selection had been carried out. Command of

The original officers of the Welsh Guards.

the Welsh Guards was given to Lieutenant Colonel W. Murray Threipland, who began building up his team of officers and NCOs, a number of whom were brought in from both the Grenadier Guards and Scots Guards, while other well-known figures in Wales applied for commissions in the new regiment.

Although there were obviously calls for Welsh officers for the regiment, many were in fact English, some with Welsh surnames! The original officers of the Welsh Guards were as follows, by order of date of joining, complete with original units and rank allocated to them:

Major W. Murray-Threipland, Grenadier Guards, to Lieutenant Colonel, Commanding.

Captain G.C.D. Gordon, Scots Guards, to Major and Adjutant.

Superintending Clerk W.B. Dabell, Grenadier Guards, to Lieutenant and Quartermaster.

Captain the Hon. A.G.A. Hore-Ruthven, VC, Captain King's Dragoon Guards, to Major and second-in-command.

Lieutenant A.P. Palmer, DSO, to Captain of No. 4 Company.

G.W. Philipps.

Captain Durham L.I., Captain of No. 3 Company.

R.G.W. Williams-Bulkeley.

Lieutenant R. of O. Grenadier Guards, Captain of No. 2 Company.

Second Lieutenant O.T.D. Osmond Williams DSO, Scots Greys, Captain of Prince of Wales's Company.

Lieutenant J.H. Bradney, to Captain and second-in-command of Prince of Wales's Company.

Second Lieutenant Rhys Williams, Grenadier Guards, to Subaltern.

Lieutenant H.E. Allen, Royal Fusiliers, to Subaltern.

Lieutenant H.E. Wethered, Royal Artillery, to Subaltern.

Lieutenant Viscount Clive, Scots Guards, to Subaltern.

Second Lieutenant P.L.M. Battye, Grenadier Guards, to Subaltern.

Lieutenant W.H.L. Gough, Montgomeryshire Yeomanry, to Subaltern.

Captain R.W. Lewis, Glamorganshire Yeomanry, to Subaltern.

Captain J.J.P. Evans, Welsh Horse Yeomanry, to Subaltern.

Second Lieutenant the Earl of Lisburne, Scots Guards, to Subaltern.

Second Lieutenant K.G. Menzies, 2nd Life Guards, to Subaltern.

Second Lieutenant B.T.V. Hambrough, Welsh Regiment, to Subaltern.

Lieutenant J.A.D. Perrins, Seaforth Highlanders, to Subaltern.

Lieutenant H.T. Rice, East Riding Yeomanry, to Second Lieutenant.

Second Lieutenant G.C.H. Crawshay, Welsh Regiment, to Second Lieutenant.

Second Lieutenant H.A. Evan Thomas, Coldstream Guards, to Second Lieutenant.

Second Lieutenant W.A.F.L. Fox-Pitt, Cheshire Regiment, to Second Lieutenant.

Lieutenant the Hon. P.G.J.F. Howard, Leinster Regiment, to Second
  Lieutenant.
Second Lieutenant F.A.V. Copland-Griffiths, Rifle Brigade, to Second
  Lieutenant.
G.C.L. Insole, to Subaltern.
Second Lieutenant E.G. Mawby, Royal Fusiliers, to Second Lieutenant.
Second Lieutenant H.G. Sutton, London Regiment (T.F.), to Second
  Lieutenant.
R. Smith, to Second Lieutenant.

Although there were political movements to attempt to get the HQ of the new regiment situated in Wales, Sir Francis Lloyd stressed the importance of it being in London, as were the HQs of the other Guards regiments. A more pressing debate was about which emblem would be chosen as their cap badge. A large number of people pressed for the Prince of Wales's plumes to be adopted, but this was too close to that already in use by the Welsh Regiment; then the Welsh dragon was put forward, but again other units bore that emblem. Debate then centred around the secondary choices of either a daffodil or a leek. After many arguments the famous leek won the day:

> The long rivalry between the Leek and the Daffodil bids fair to end and victory secured by the former. Other nations have adopted their emblems once and for all, the English have their Rose, the Scotch their Thistle and the Irish their Shamrock. Why the Welsh should waver in their selection has been a mystery. Undoubtedly the Leek claims priority. Now that the King has sanctioned the Leek as the emblem for the Welsh Guards, there is a possibility that the Daffodil will rightly have to take a back seat. The motto of the Guards has also been well chosen, 'Cymru am Byth', together with the Red Dragon to complete the National colours. On Monday over 1,000 people watched the Welsh Guards as they marched from Wellington Barracks to Buckingham Palace, as the band played stirring Welsh songs, including *The Queen's Dream*, *Harlech* and *Land of my Fathers*. (*Carmarthen Journal*, 5 March 1915.)

At the behest of the king, the Welsh Guards duly mounted their first King's Guard at Buckingham Palace on 1 March 1915, St David's Day, a tremendous achievement, and recruitment then moved into full swing.

Sir Francis Lloyd inspected the new regiment at the White City on 24 March and was impressed by the 800 men standing proudly to attention. Within two more weeks the 1st Battalion, Welsh Guards was up to full complement and recruiting had begun for a 2nd Battalion.

While the Welsh Guards were readying for their move to France, the war was about to step up a gear, both on the Western Front and with the opening of the Gallipoli campaign.

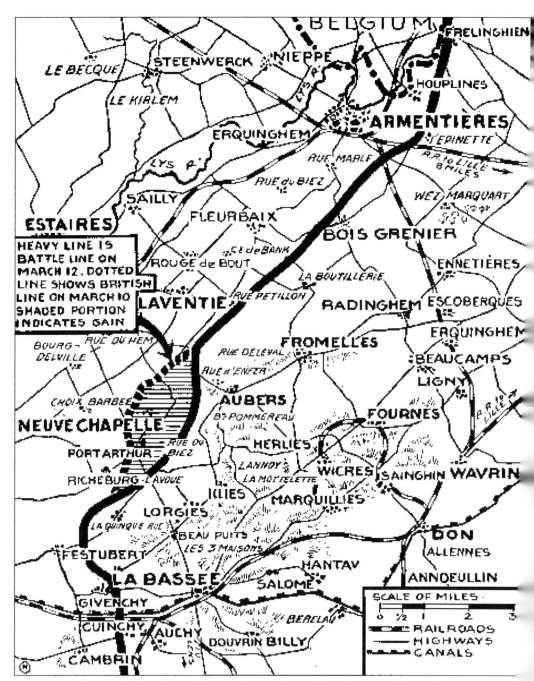

A map showing the British and German lines at Neuve Chapelle, 10 to 12 March 1915.

On the day that the Welsh Guards mounted their first guard, the Welsh units in France celebrated their first St David's at the front in the customary fashion. Captain J.C. Dunn of the 2nd RWF wrote:

A really lazy day with no parades, fatigues, or riding class. A few shells dropped rather close in the afternoon. The St David's Day Dinner was at Streaky Bacon Farm. Eighteen officers ate their leek; the Brigadier, the only guest, was the eighteenth. It was eaten to the roll of the Drum, but there was no Goat. The reported speech of the Junior Subaltern in replying to 'The Ladies', proposed by the Senior Subaltern, was a model of brevity and point. Turning at once to the General, he said, 'Talking of the ladies, what about a spot of leave, sir?' and sat down hurriedly.

Meanwhile the 4th RWF had borrowed a goat from a local farmer to carry out their customary dinner, gilding its horns before marching it around the table to a drum roll off a biscuit tin, during which time nine officers ate their leeks!

During St David's Day the 7th Division was relieved from the Le Touquet trenches by the 1st Canadian Division, which had recently arrived from Salisbury Plain after disembarking in England on 14 October 1914. This would be the first of five Canadian divisions to serve on the Western Front and contained a large number of Welshmen who had migrated to Canada. The 1st RWF moved into billets at Laventie on 5 March, where it received copies of the 7th Division's orders for a forthcoming offensive. The battalion moved back into the line two days later, suffering four men and eleven wounded by artillery fire on the 10th.

As a preliminary to a forthcoming attack on Aubers Ridge, on 10 March a combined assault by IV Corps and the Indian Corps captured the village of Neuve Chapelle. Heavy fighting continued on 11 and 12 March, but their gains were consolidated. Although none of the Welsh units were directly involved during this battle, on 24 March 3 Brigade was moved to Neuve Chapelle to relieve the Jullundur Brigade (Indian army) and the 1st SWB and 2nd Welsh took over trenches there. The intention had been that the 1st Division would be ready to pounce should the 2nd Division have attained its objectives but various delays and mishaps, notably the lack of artillery support, had held up the attacking forces and this second push did not materialize.

Another member of the Welsh aristocracy lost his life on the second day of the battle, on 11 March. The Honourable George Henry Douglas-Pennant was the son of George Sholto Gordon Douglas-Pennant, 2nd Baron Penrhyn, and Gertrude Lady Penrhyn, of Penrhyn Castle, Bangor, Caernarfonshire. He served in the Boer War and was aide-de-camp to Lieutenant General Sir Leslie Rundle from 1903 to 1907. Douglas-Pennant was in India at the outbreak of war and returned swiftly to England, being posted as captain to King's Company, 1st Grenadier Guards, in November 1914. He was leading King's Company in the battalion's charge at Neuve Chapelle when he fell to the ground, wounded by shrapnel. His men picked him up and carried him off and he uttered the words 'There's not much wrong with me...' before dying. He was buried in an orchard close by and a cross put over his grave to mark the spot. His grave was lost some time during the war and Douglas-Pennant, who was 38 years old, is commemorated on the Le Touret Memorial. His brother, the Honourable Charles Douglas-Pennant, had been killed on 29 October 1914.

The offensive at Neuve Chapelle saw increased activity to the north at Ypres and cost the life of a young officer of Welsh heritage who, along with his four younger brothers, became the inspiration for J.M. Barrie's most famous characters. George Llewelyn Davies was born on 20 July 1893, the son of Arthur Llewelyn Davies and Sylvia Davies, née du Maurier. He was the cousin of the novelist Daphne du Maurier. Barrie had befriended the family and became close to Sylvia and her sons just prior to the turn of the century, basing his characters Peter Pan and the Lost Boys on them. After the death of Arthur in 1907, Barrie became even closer to the family and upon Sylvia's premature death in 1910 he unofficially adopted the children.

Captain the Honourable George Henry Douglas-Pennant, 1st Grenadier Guards.

The eldest child, George Llewelyn Davies, was educated at Eton College, where he excelled at sports. He was then educated at Trinity College, Cambridge, where he followed in the footsteps of Barrie and his uncle, the actor Gerald du Maurier, joining the Amateur Dramatic Club. Following the outbreak of war, George and his brother Peter volunteered for the army and both brothers were commissioned in the 6th Battalion, King's Royal Rifle Corps on 15 August 1914. While Peter survived the war, and gained the award of the Military Cross whilst serving with the battalion, poor George had been attached to the 4th Battalion, Rifle Brigade and was shot in the head and killed while the battalion was at Ypres on 15 March 1916, aged 21. He is buried in Voormezeele Enclosure Cemetery No. 3. Just six days earlier his uncle, Guy du Maurier, had been killed at Kemmel.

Among several Welshmen killed while serving with non-Welsh units during the Battle of Neuve Chapelle was Captain Percy Standish Hore of the 52nd Sikhs. Hore was born at St Asaph on 10 August 1881, the son of Frederick Standish Hore and Harriet Susannah Hore (née Williams) and was educated at Wellington College. He was commissioned from the Militia in the SWB in January 1901 and during the Delhi Durbar of 1903 he acted as adjutant to the 1st SWB. In May 1904 he joined the Indian Army, being promoted to captain in January 1910. Hore was attached to the 59th (Scinde) Rifles, Indian Army during the early months of the war and was killed when the Germans counter-attacked at Port Arthur on 12 March 1915. He is buried at Le Touret Military Cemetery, Richebourg-l'Avoué. A letter written to his parents by a fellow officer stated:

Captain Percy Standish Hore, Indian army, of St Asaph.

His death was splendid and it gave me very great pleasure to see his services were recognised by a mention in despatches.

I have often talked to men, both of the 52nd and 59th, who were there when he was killed and you cannot imagine with what enthusiasm they speak of his gallantry and devotion to duty that fated day. In fact all through those last three days his example and gallantry did a very great deal towards keeping the regiment together and keeping up their spirits in a very trying situation. And so it was when he was in the 59th in the fighting near Givenchy in December. I think it was his work then, in a very similar and trying situation, that earned him his mention in despatches.

This German counter-attack failed but the British had been forced to expend almost all of their meagre supply of artillery shells, necessitating the postponement of the next phase of the offensive, and on 13 March the Battle of Neuve Chapelle ground to a halt. In three days of fighting the British had suffered 7,000 casualties, while the Indians had suffered a further 4,200. German losses were estimated at roughly 10,000 men.

In this sector, apart from the recent fighting, the troops were finding that the situation was relatively comfortable. Breastworks had been built instead of trenches and the defensive system was strong and relatively dry. Arrangements for the provision of bathing facilities and dry clothes for the men had also been made, so trench life was becoming more organized and slightly more bearable. Casualties for the 4th RWF, 1st SWB and 2nd Welsh continued during the coming days, although at a much slower pace. The 1st SWB unfortunately lost two officers to snipers: Lieutenant Hamilton Henry Travers, the son of Brigadier General Jonas Hamilton du Boulay Travers, CB CMG and Mrs Travers of Plas Emm, Criccieth, Caernarfonshire, was shot on 28 March and died at Béthune later that day, while Captain John Francis Bill, the son of Ronald Edward and Eugenie Lambert Bill, of 53 Uxbridge Road, Ealing, London was killed on 29 March. Travers is buried in Béthune Town Cemetery, while Bill was buried at Edward Road Cemetery No. 2 at Richebourg-l'Avoué. After the war the graves within this small cemetery, several of them of Welshmen who were killed during the fighting here in May 1915, were re-interred at Cabaret Rouge British Cemetery, Souchez. The latter's brother, Kenneth Bill, also fell.

Captain John Francis Bill, killed in action on 28 March 1915 by a sniper's bullet.

The 1st RWF, meanwhile, held trenches south of the village of Fauquissart and had also not been involved in the Battle of Neuve Chapelle. Casualties within the battalion had also been light but two officers were killed: Captain Charles Edmund Wood, the 30-year-old son of Edward John Wedge Wood and Lettice Wood of Meece House, Stone, Staffordshire, was killed by a sniper while directing rifle fire onto the enemy trenches on 11 March; Second Lieutenant Horace Frederick Parkes, the 25-year-old son of Harry C. and

K. Parkes, of Heatherbrae, The Avenue, Moordown, Bournemouth, was killed the following day while maintaining communications with 21 Brigade. Wood is buried in Fauquissart Military Cemetery, Laventie, while Parkes is commemorated on the Le Touret Memorial, Richebourg-l'Avoué. Thirteen other ranks were killed on 13 March following a bombardment on the German trenches that brought about a retaliatory bombardment by the Germans.

Casualties continued at a low rate throughout the remainder of March and the first weeks of April, but several Welsh units earmarked to be used for another forthcoming offensive whilst the month would see the first landings at Gallipoli and the first use of poison gas by the Germans during the Second Battle of Ypres.

Another member of the Welsh aristocracy was killed in action in Flanders on 13 April. Lieutenant William Glynne Charles Gladstone was the son of William Henry Gladstone and the Honourable Gertrude Gladstone of Hawarden Castle, Flintshire and was the grandson of the Right Honourable W.E. Gladstone, the former prime minister. Young Gladstone had been the Member of Parliament for Kilmarnock Burghs since 1911, but his sense of duty saw him take up a commission in the 1st RWF on 15 August 1914. He had joined the battalion in France on 15 March and was killed in action while attempting to locate a German sniper on Tuesday, 13 April. His body was, most unusually, brought back home and interred in St Deiniol's Churchyard at Hawarden on 23 April.

He is, reputedly, the last fallen British soldier to be allowed to be brought home for burial during the Great War.

Captain Charles Edmun Wood, born on 23 December 1884. Wood w educated at Harrow and Sandhurst before being commissioned in the 1st RWF on 8 January 1905 He was killed at Fauquissart on 11 Marc 1915.

Lieutenant William Glynne Charles Gladstone, MP of Hawarden, killed on 13 April 1915.

The funeral of William Glynne Charles Gladstone.

Chapter 10

The Second Battle of Ypres

O n 5 April the 1st Welsh was withdrawn from the Dranoutre area to rejoin the 28th Division at Ypres and two days later was reviewed by General Sir Horace Smith-Dorrien KCB, commanding the Second Army. The 4th RWF, 1st SWB and 2nd Welsh of the 1st Division were in the Neuve Chapelle area; the 1st RWF at Fauquissart; the 2nd RWF at Fromelles; the 2nd Monmouths at Le Bizet; the 2nd SWB were preparing for a seaborne invasion of Gallipoli; and, on 8 April, the 1st and 3rd Monmouths had arrived at Ypres by bus before marching to positions east of Polygon Wood to relieve French troops. Both battalions were attached to the 28th Division. During its first tour in the trenches the infantry of the 28th Division had suffered so severely from casualties and trench foot that they had been temporarily replaced by brigades from other divisions, but the rest of the 28th Division remained in their positions and by 14 April the infantry had rejoined and the 1st Welsh was in camp at Poperinghe.

Men of the 3rd Monmouths marching during manoeuvres at Bow Street, near Aberystwyth, in 1910.

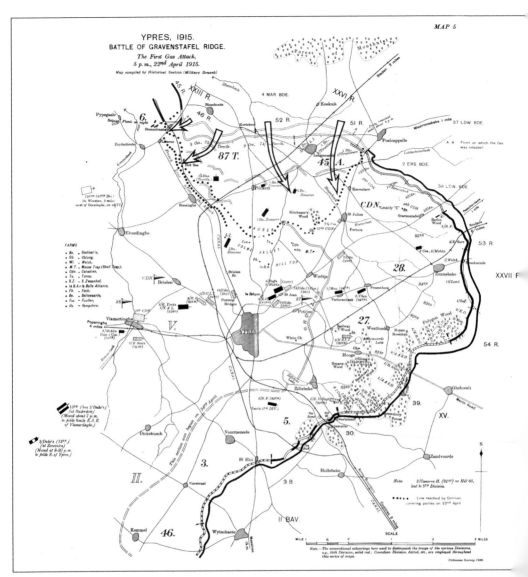

A map taken from the Official History *showing the disposition of troops in the Ypres Salient prior to the German gas attacks.*

On 15 April the 1st Canadian Division passed through the town and the units of the 28th Division entertained some of their units. The 7th Battalion, Canadian Infantry CEF (Canadian Expeditionary Force) was entertained by the 1st Welsh. The Canadians were on their way to take up positions in the salient at Gravenstafel, north-east of Ypres. On their right flank lay the 28th Division, while on the left flank were two French divisions, holding the line from a position south-west of Poelcapelle running west towards Steenstraat, where the line then ran northwards along the Yser Canal.

The Canadians were in position by mid-April and the scene was now set for the

Second Battle of Ypres. (The first Welshman to die on the Western Front while serving with the Canadians was Sergeant Algernon Venables Plunkett (51260), 16th Battalion, CEF of Rhyl who was killed on 19 April. The second was Sergeant Thomas Stanley Hubbard (29521) of the same battalion, of Wrexham, who lost his life on the 21st. Both these men are commemorated on the Menin Gate Memorial.)

The 28th Division had been allocated the Broodseinde sector of the Ypres Salient. As part of the movement into the line on 16 April the 1st Welsh marched to huts 1 mile west of Ypres. The town was under fire from heavy German artillery and its destruction was slowly beginning. On the following morning the 1st Welsh marched up to relieve the 5th Royal Fusiliers at Broodseinde, just beyond Zonnebeke, at the extreme point of the Ypres Salient. The men had just reached their positions when at 7 am a series of tremendous explosions was heard coming from the direction of the Frezenberg Ridge, followed by a roar of guns some distance to the south.

The explosions were from mines that had been laid by the British, including men of the Monmouths, under Hill 60 in February. The 28th Division had then handed over the sector to the 5th Division who had continued preparations to capture the position from the Germans. Hill 60 itself was a low mound of spoil that had been created by the digging of a cutting for the Ypres-Comines railway some years before the war. The hill formed a low rise on the crest of Ypres Ridge at the southern flank of the Ypres Salient and was named after the contour that marked its boundary and allowed the Germans a high platform with observation over Ypres and Zillebeke. The first Royal Engineer tunnelling companies had been formed by Sir John Norton Griffiths early in 1915 in order to counter German tunnelling in the Hill 60 sector. By 10 April these new companies had laid six mines beneath Hill 60 in order to smash the main German defences on the hill. The explosions heard by the 1st Welsh on 17 April were these mines being detonated, hurling men, earth and concrete skywards, obliterating the German strongpoints and opening up a crater some 21 metres deep. The attacking troops of the 5th Division then rushed the shattered Germans and by 12.30 pm had consolidated their gains on the hill.

A present-day view of Hill 60, showing some of the undulations in the ground of the shattered hill.

Fighting continued at Hill 60 over the coming weeks and its ownership changed hands again. The whole hill is now treated as a war grave as a consequence of the severity of the underground war – a place where hundreds of men disappeared forever.

Immediately upon taking up the line at Zonnebeke the 1st Welsh discovered a gaping hole of almost 150 metres in the front line that had been opened up following a bombardment by a large German *minenwerfer* (the *minenwerfer* or 'mine-launcher' was a devastating muzzle-loaded weapon that proved to be especially useful for trench warfare, capable of lobbing shells at a high trajectory into the allied trenches: 'The bomb weighed 220 pounds and made a crater eight or nine feet deep in the soft ground, while large jagged pieces, two feet and more long, flew for 100 yards all round, it was a terrifying weapon'). The Northumberland Fusiliers had regained some of the lost trench before handing the line over to the Welshmen during the night.

The 1st Welsh had A Company (Major Toke) on the left and D Company (Captain Torkington) on the right, with B and C companies in support in Zonnebeke. Both company commanders were warned of the presence of the Germans in the centre of the line, so Major Toke went out to verify the location of the *minenwerfer*, coming into contact with a German patrol in so doing. He managed to return safely, having found their positions in a fortified cellar. Torkington's company attacked the position but was forced to retire after suffering casualties, so Lieutenant Henry William Warren Davis was sent up with a party of bombers from B Company to support Torkington in the attempt to destroy the *minenwerfer*.

Lieutenant Henry William Warren Davis of the 1st Welsh, killed at Broodseinde on 18 April 1915.

Warren Davis and eight men were killed during the attack, while Captain Torkington, Lieutenants Newington and Herbert and Second Lieutenant Whitfield were wounded. Lieutenant Henry William Warren Davis was born on 27 December 1891, the son of Henry Warren Davis and Christobel Warren Davis of The Warren, St Ishmael's. He was educated at Malvern College before attending Sandhurst and was gazetted in the Welsh Regiment on 14 February 1912. He was killed while stooping to aid a wounded man during the assault. Warren Davis was 24 years old and was buried at Zonnebeke. His grave was lost during further fighting in the area, so he is commemorated by a Special Memorial within Bedford House Cemetery. The *History of the Welsh Regiment* records: 'Lieutenant Davis was a great loss – a fine sportsman and an excellent bomber and shot, he was developing into an invaluable sniping expert.' In *The Hungry One* by C.P. Clayton, he is noted as being called 'Crwt' among his fellow officers and was totally fearless, acting against orders when attempting to rescue wounded men in no man's land when he was killed. He is also commemorated in St Ishmael's Church, Pembrokeshire.

The 1st Welsh made another attempt to capture the *minenwerfer* that night; supported by an artillery bombardment, A and D companies made a bombing attack

The memorial to Lieutenant Henry William Warren Davis in St Ishmael's Church.

from both flanks but were beaten back again by machine-gun fire from the German line. Corporal Davies (9991) of A Company was awarded the Russian Order of St George 4th Class for gallantry during the attack, while Company Sergeant Major Weeks brought in the body of Lieutenant Warren Davis.

The trenches at Broodseinde were very close, sometimes just 7 metres apart, and the Germans had the advantage of holding the high ground. The salient also allowed the Germans to expose the British to enfilade fire.

In an attempt to divert German attention away from Hill 60, on 21 April the 1st Welsh was ordered to make a feint attack and bombed the Germans opposite. This tit-for-tat warfare was about to come to an abrupt end.

The fourth, fifth and sixth Welshmen executed during the war also met their deaths at this time. Gunner William Jones (62971) of 43 Battery, Royal Field Artillery had been sentenced to death for desertion. He was executed on 20 April 1915 and is buried in La Chapelle-d'Armentières Communal Cemetery.

Just two days later two men of the 1st RWF were executed for desertion: the unusually-named Private Major Penn (10958), of Stourbridge and his friend Private Albert Troughton (10853), of Foleshill, were sentenced to death for

The grave of Gunner William Jones (62971) of 43 Battery, Royal Field Artillery. Jones was shot at dawn on 20 April 1915 and is buried in La Chapelle d'Armentières Communal Cemetery. He was possibly not Welsh but there are no surviving service records to prove otherwise.

149

The graves of Privates Penn and Troughton 1st RWF at Estaires Communal Cemetery, shot for desertion on 22 April 1915.

desertion and both were executed at Mazingarbe, a village near Loos known by the troops as the slaughterhouse, on 22 April 1915. Both men were buried together in Estaires Communal Cemetery. Their deaths did not even merit a mention in the battalion War Diary, even though today the men are seen as victims of the barbarism of the war and were pardoned in 2006.

i) The Battle of Gravenstafel Ridge
At 5 am on 22 April, following an intense artillery bombardment, the Germans opened the valves of hundreds of cylinders containing about 160 tonnes of chlorine gas on the northern edge of the Ypres Salient. The gas drifted quietly across no man's land and hit the trenches of French colonial troops, who were terrified by this burning mist that crept up on them. The Frenchmen either died or fled, opening up a 4-mile gap in the line, allowing the Germans to advance and capture the villages of Langemarck and Pilckem, as well as threatening Steenstraat and Het Sas on the Yser Canal. The German attack heralded the opening of the Second Battle of Ypres and was the first time that poison gas was used on the Western Front.

With the Germans having pierced the salient and threatening to exploit their breakthrough, the situation became desperate. Fortunately the Germans had planned only a limited offensive and, without adequate reserves, were unable to exploit the gap. After advancing just over 3 kilometres they stopped and began digging in.

Canadian troops were able to defend their flank by using cloths soaked in urine to counter the effects of breathing in the gas and generally stood firm against the German

Germans attacking under a cloud of poison gas.

assault. The 13th CEF in particular was especially hard hit after being attacked from three sides.

At Kitcheners' Wood, the 10th CEF was ordered to counter-attack into the gap created by the gas attack and at around 11.46 pm advanced into the wood with the support of the 16th CEF, clearing it at a cost of over three-quarters of their men.

Among the Canadian casualties during the day were at least ten Welshmen, all (bar one) of whom have no known grave and are commemorated on the Menin Gate Memorial: Private Ithal Davies (20605), 10th CEF, of Pontypridd; Private Edwin John Davis (6320), 1st CEF, of Briton Ferry; Private Henry Edwards (29062), 16th CEF, of Wrexham; Sergeant Edward Gardiner (8631), 2nd CEF, of Rhyl; Private Arthur Henry Hoare (20225), 10th CEF, of Roath; Corporal Henry Clifford Lewis (27223), 15th CEF, of Penarth; Private Ernest John Palmer (6728), 1st CEF, of Barry Dock; Private Enoch Thomas (19925), 10th CEF, of Ruabon; Private David John Vincent (20829), 10th CEF, of Ebbw Vale; and Private John Gordon Wills (20836), 10th CEF, of Cardiff. The only man with a known grave is Private Arthur Henry Hoare (20225), 10th CEF, who is buried in Roeselare Communal Cemetery. He most probably died of wounds later that day as a prisoner of war.

In command of the 5th CEF during the battle was Lieutenant Colonel George Stuart Tuxford, a Welshman who had emigrated to Canada from Penmorfa, Caernarfonshire with his wife Jemima in 1890 to take up ranching at Moose Jaw. He had played football for Llandudno and later captained the Canadian football team. One of his men wounded during the attack was eventually sent to a Welsh hospital, where he recounted his experiences:

> I entered the first line trenches on Monday, 19th. The first two days there was hardly a shot fired. It was the Thursday, 22nd, they started very heavy shelling

The imposing memorial, known as Brooding Soldier, at Gravenstafel. The memorial was erected to mark the site of the first use of poison gas and to commemorate the Canadians killed in the battle.

Brigadier General George Stuart Tuxford, the Welsh-born commander the 5th (Western Cavalry) Battalion CEF and future commander of 3 Canadian Infantry Brigade.

of our trenches and used poisonous gases in the form of shells or bombs – l can't say for certain. They were terrible things, especially as you can't hear them coming. They explode with a zipp bang, zipp bang and you commence choking almost at once. The bombardment became heavier and heavier until about Saturday and the ground all a tremor – one continual earthquake. We were losing heavily on all sides; it was a terrible sight, but we stood it and continued holding on until Sunday. It was hell. Had our artillery been helping us our losses would have been considerably less, for they could have dropped shells near enough to their batteries which would have compelled the Germans to cease fire. It was shell fire that caused our losses. In spite of position and losses we stuck it and kept up a rapid fire when they attacked which amazed them. Our own colonel (Colonel Tuxford) was at the back of us walking up and down the trenches, a coat over one arm, a revolver in his other hand, encouraging us and shouting,

'Give 'em hell, boys, I know you can do it.' We did; we kept them back for hours until we were relieved. I got a wound last Sunday night, 25th, from a bursting shrapnel shell.

Tuxford himself had written home to his brother in Conway about the fighting, a resumé of which was published in the *North Wales Chronicle* of 14 May 1915:

In a recent letter home, Colonel Tuxford described how they had been in the thick of the fighting for eight days, during the last four of which they had had little food and drink and scarcely any sleep. He had lost a lot of officers and men, but personally came out unscratched, except that he was hit on the ankle by a shrapnel bullet, but it did not cause a wound. 'Just luck,' he declares, 'I seemed to bear a charmed life.' Of his brigade, only a quarter were left. 'But the Canadians are magnificent,' he says. He lost all his kit and had then only the clothes he stood in.

He later wrote an 'After Action Report on Second Ypres', which proved to be a very important document in the future development of command in the Canadian forces. He commanded his battalion in the Battle of Festubert until being invalided out of the line on 22 May and on 16 March 1916 returned to duty and was promoted to brigadier general. He was given command of 3 Canadian Infantry Brigade of the 1st Division; a command he held for over three years, becoming the longest-serving brigade commander in the Canadian Corps. During this time the 1st Division fought in the Battle of Mount Sorrel, the Somme, Arras, Ypres, the Second Battle of Arras and the Battle of the Hindenburg Line. Tuxford died in Canada on 4 February 1943.

Private Gerald Foulkes of Bagillt was also among the men recovering in Welsh hospitals after suffering gas poisoning, while another Welsh Canadian, Private Francis, who was in hospital at Bridgend, told one news reporter of his ordeal, also mentioning a story of Lord Kitchener that proved to be sadly prophetic:

It was at the time the South African War broke out. Private Francis was on the same boat, HMS *Iris*, as Lord Kitchener when he went to meet Lord Roberts at Gibraltar. Kitchener, after the voyage, told the captain that he did not mind being on a battlefield but he did not like being at sea.

In just over twelve months' time the old soldier would lose his life at sea.

The fighting and subsequent regaining of the line by the Canadians at Gravenstafel also gave rise to one of the most famous legends of the war, which has still to be proved fact or fiction. Many newspapers of the day reported the grisly discovery, one of which, the *Abergavenny Chronicle*, published a letter from a local soldier:

CRUCIFIED CANADIANS. Trooper Reeds, of the 2nd Lifeguards (Machine-gun Section) in the course of a letter written home to a friend, says: The

Canadians fought grandly and completely routed the enemy, capturing all they had lost and more besides. As they advanced they found two of their comrades nailed to doors, quite dead. I wonder what Dr Lyttelton will think of that! I expect he will say: 'Be kind to the Germans!' Yes, and like one of the Canadian officers said: 'I guess, sonny, we will!'

The incident is immortalized in folklore and film and also in the bronze memorial statue entitled 'Canada's Golgotha', which was sculpted and cast by the artist Francis Derwent Wood in 1918 and is held in the Canadian War Museum.

Canada's Golgotha, the statue immortalizing the myth of the crucified Canadian soldier at Ypres.

ii) The Battle of St Julien

On 24 April the Germans launched another attack in an attempt to obliterate the salient and another artillery bombardment was followed by yet another gas attack and this time the Canadians were the targets. The fighting was desperate and the Canadians were hampered by their Ross rifles which were jamming; nevertheless, they stood firm, despite heavy losses. In forty-eight hours 6,035 Canadians, one man in three, became casualties, of whom more than 2,000 died.

The 1st Welsh, along with the 1st and 3rd Monmouths, had been in the trenches at Broodseinde when the gas attack was launched. The 1st Welsh had been relieved the following night and had moved back to huts a mile north-west of Ypres. A road that had been quiet and peaceful on the way out to the trenches some days before now resembled hell, being littered with dead horses, mules and debris and most of the buildings alongside it destroyed:

No one seemed to know much about the gas attack, except that the French colonial troops had bolted and some were occasionally seen moving singly across country near the huts. Shelling went on spasmodically and some went near the billets, but no one took any notice of them and in the afternoon the officers played the sergeants at Rugby football. We were all looking forward to a real night's rest when the order came for the Battalion to move up to the Frezenberg ridge, in support of the 84th Brigade. We could not start for some time as the circular road was blocked by the 10th Brigade moving up into position to counter-attack at St Julien. (*History of the Welsh Regiment.*)

The 1st Monmouths, however, had remained in the line and during the day had seen heavy fighting, suffering ten men killed on 24 April. At dawn on 25 April 10 Brigade, commanded by Brigadier General Hull, attacked St Julien but, without adequate artillery cover, was beaten off and the troops were forced to dig in south of the village. The Germans attacked again that afternoon, so the 1st Welsh were moved up to Zonnebeke in case they were needed, taking up positions in ditches below Frezenberg Ridge, from which there was a splendid view over the battlefield.

Private Arthur Alexander Evans (1829), 1st Monmouths, of Newport, who was killed at Broodseinde on 24 April 1915.

Although heavy fighting continued, the 1st Welsh remained relatively untouched throughout the day, though the 1st Monmouths lost ten more men killed and saw a continual drain on their manpower over the coming days as 28 Brigade sat in its positions at Broodseinde while the main battle raged to the north.

A further sixteen Welsh Canadians were killed during the resulting fighting: two officers – Lieutenant Wilfred Cashel Brotherhood, 14th CEF, from Tintern and Lieutenant John Gibson Kenworthy, 16th CEF, from Tenby – and fourteen other ranks.

John Gibson Kenworthy was born on 27 August 1881, the son of John and Mary H. Kenworthy of Tenby. He had emigrated to Canada with his wife Iris after having served for ten years with the Lancashire Fusiliers. He enlisted at Valcartier on 7 September 1914 into the 16th CEF and, given his previous military experience, at once gained a commission as lieutenant with the battalion. On 24 April 1915 the Canadians were desperately clinging on to their positions at St Julien when Kenworthy was reported as missing, believed wounded in action. His body was never found, so he is commemorated on the Menin Gate. A brother, Donald, was killed

Private Joseph H. Jones (9), 8th CEF, of Stanley Road, Skewen. He was killed in action on 25 April 1915.

just weeks later, on 17 May, while serving as a captain with the 1st Somerset Light Infantry nearby.

In the following days, none of the Welsh units saw any real action and were only spectators as the Battle of St Julien raged on, but Corps HQ began preparing plans to withdraw its troops to a new and shorter line covering Ypres, which was to run from Hill 60, in front of Hooge and Frezenberg, round by the north end of the GHQ Line to join the French at Turco Farm. The withdrawal of some 2 miles was carried out successfully between 1 and 4 May.

By 2 May the 1st Welsh had taken up a line running from Mouse Trap Farm to the Wieltje-Fortuin Road and were on the left of 84 Brigade. Situated almost 400 metres in front was 10 Brigade, which was to withdraw through the Welsh on the night of 4/5 May.

The 3rd Monmouths were astride the Ypres to Zonnebeke Road at Frezenberg on the morning of 2 May when the Germans launched yet another gas attack. This time they were the victims of the gas, but luckily the wind shifted soon afterwards and the cloud blew back onto the German trenches. The 3rd Monmouths lost almost ninety men killed during the day, among them Lieutenants Alexander Evan Fraser, Charles Herbert George Martin and Second Lieutenant Henry William Terrent Reid. Following what

Lieutenant John Gibson Kenworth *Tenby who was killed in action on* *April 1915.*

appears to be a similar pattern so far during the war, all three of the officers killed during the attack have known graves, while the vast majority of their men do not and as a result are commemorated on the Menin Gate Memorial.

Lieutenant Alexander Evan Fraser was born on 29 July 1880, the son of James Campbell Fraser and Emily Fraser of Ingleside, Lynton, Devon. He was 34 years old when he was killed on 2 May 1915 and is buried in La Brique Military Cemetery No. 2.

Lieutenant Charles Herbert George Martin was born on 5 October 1882, the son of Edward Pritchard Martin and Margaret Martin of Dowlais. He was educated at Eton College and Magdalen College, Oxford. He then worked at the University of Glasgow and was commissioned in the Monmouthshire Regiment in 1912. Martin was 33 years old

Lieutenant Charles Herb *George Martin, of the 1s* *Monmouths, killed at* *Frezenberg on 2 May 19*

when he was killed on 2 May 1915 and is buried in Sanctuary Wood Cemetery.

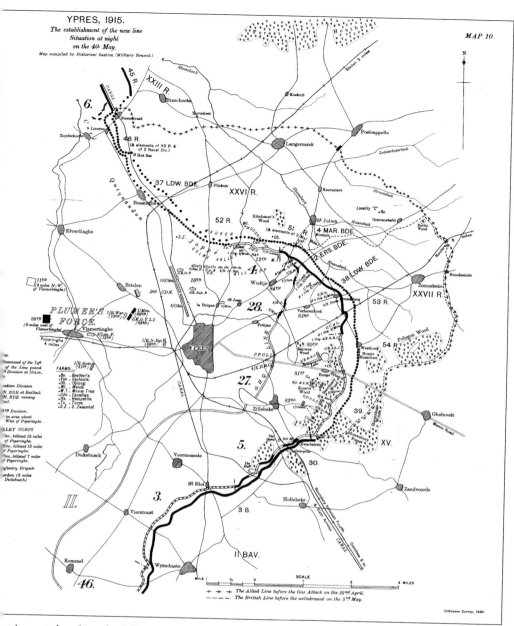

A map taken from the Official History, *showing dispositions of troops on 4 May 1915.*

Second Lieutenant Henry William Terrent Reed was the son of Lancelot George and Ellen Reed of Durham. He was an assistant master at Cheltenham College before the war. He was 30 years old when he was killed on 2 May 1915 and is buried in La Brique Military Cemetery No. 2, Ieper.

Also killed during the day were seven Welshmen serving with the 1st Dorsets, all south Walians.

On the night of 3/4 May the 1st Welsh began the digging of new support trenches and occupied them the next night but, being in low ground, they had flooded. On the night of 4/5 May 10 Brigade moved back as planned, leaving 84 Brigade in the front trenches with a single line of barbed wire in front to slow any German attacks. The 1st Welsh lost one officer, Lieutenant Vivian Bruford Llewellyn-Jones, and eight men killed during the day, while the 1st and 2nd Monmouths lost five between them.

By the morning of 5 May the line ran as follows: the 27th Division from Hill 60 to half a mile short of the Ypres-Roulers road; the 28th Division from there to Mouse Trap Farm and the 4th Division up to Turco Farm; 84 Brigade held its line from right to left with the Suffolks, 1st Monmouths, 12th London and the 1st Welsh.

When dawn broke on 5 May the Germans began shelling the front lines, not realizing that 10 Brigade had withdrawn and that they were now shelling no man's land. It wasn't until later that afternoon that German aircraft spotted the British had retreated and the artillery moved onto the new lines. Both the 2nd and 3rd Monmouths again suffered badly, losing Lieutenant Henry James Walters and nineteen more men killed, while the 1st Welsh lost twelve more men.

The Germans began their softening-up of the British lines again the following morning, their artillery fire being almost unanswered by the British due to the need for the bulk of the British artillery shells being reserved for the impending attack on Aubers Ridge. A further twenty-nine men of the 3rd Monmouths were killed during the day and six of the 1st Welsh. That night the 1st Welsh were relieved and moved back into support, while all three battalions of the Monmouths remained in the trenches.

After another artillery bombardment on the morning of 7 May the Germans attacked again. A company of the 1st Welsh, under Second Lieutenant Edward William Bryan, was sent back up to support the 5th Royal Fusiliers, while the 2nd Monmouths lost one officer, Captain Illtyd Edwin Maitland Watkins, and five men killed; the 3rd Monmouths lost four men. Watkins was born on 25 March 1890, the son of John Maitland Watkins, of Castle Parade House, Usk. He was educated at Downside School and at King's College, Cambridge, joining the Monmouthshire Regiment on 25 March 1909. He was 25 years old when he was killed at Frezenberg on 7 May 1915 and was buried on the battlefield at La Brique, St Jan by his men. His grave was lost at some point afterwards and Watkins is commemorated on the Ypres (Menin Gate) Memorial.

Captain Illtyd Edwin Maitland Watkins of th 2nd Monmouths, killed Frezenberg on 7 May 1915.

Second Lieutenant Edward William Bryan became the first officer of the 1st Welsh to be awarded the MC for his gallantry during the day:

For conspicuous gallantry and devotion to duty on 7th and 8th of May, 1915. His company dug a trench during the night of the 7th and held it all next day under such heavy shell fire that the trench became obliterated and two machine

Second Lieutenant Edward William Bryan winning his Military Cross, the first won by an officer of the 1st Welsh.

guns were buried. He not only kept his company in hand and cheerful, but rendered assistance to another regiment, and, on being relieved, refused to quit his position till the machine guns, one of which was 12 feet underground, were dug out. This work was done under heavy fire. (*London Gazette*, 23 July 1915.)

iii) The Battle of Frezenberg

The heaviest fighting so far as the 28th Division was concerned came on 8 May. Still holding on to their positions on the slopes of Frezenberg Ridge, the division was in a precarious position. The Germans had decided to make a determined drive to break through to Ypres and this would be the centre of their assault.

After putting down an intense bombardment onto the trenches held by 83 and 84 brigades, the Germans launched their infantry attack at 8.30 am but were driven back. As a result another artillery bombardment crashed down on the same trenches before the Germans renewed their attack, but despite heavy losses among the defenders the Germans were again driven off.

By around 10 am a third assault broke the front of 83 Brigade on either side of Frezenberg village and the Germans began exploiting their breakthrough. The defenders were by now extremely weakened, having been in more or less continuous action since 22 April and first the Suffolks and then the Cheshires were overwhelmed.

The 1st Monmouths then bore the brunt of the attack, fighting desperately until they in turn were overwhelmed, with battalion HQ cut off at the time.

Captain Harold Thorne Edwards of Newport, Monmouth, gathered a band of men together in a brave attempt to organize a defence but was surrounded. The Germans called on them to surrender but were met with the response 'Surrender be damned' as Edwards, armed with his pistol, attacked the surrounding Germans. The scene is commemorated in a painting in the entrance of Newport Civic Centre. Lieutenant Colonel Charles Lawson Robinson then gave the order for the survivors of the 1st Monmouths to pull back from the front line to form a flank against the German attacks from the right but he was shot through the neck and killed. It was only a stout resistance by the 5th Royal Fusiliers and a counter-attack by the 12th London (Rangers) that stemmed the pressure and the survivors of the 1st Monmouths pulled back to the support trenches. One of them, Private Rees Jones, wrote:

Captain Harold Thorne Edwards of the 1st Monmouths, the son of Thomas Stephen Edwards (solicitor) and of Alice Elizabeth Edwards, of 24 Stow Hill, Newport. On 8 May, Edwards was last seen alive surrounded by Germans and diving into them with his pistol, shouting: 'Surrender, be damned! Rapid fire boys.' He was shot dead and is buried in New Irish Farm Cemetery.

We were in the trenches for three weeks up to and preceding the 8th of May. On that morning, about 5.30, the enemy started shelling us and kept it up heavily until about 11 o'clock, when they came and charged our trenches in their thousands. A good many of our men were lying killed or wounded in the trenches to the right and left of where I was. I was shot in the face by a rifle bullet about 11 o'clock, when the word was passed up 'All for yourselves'. We then commenced to retire and four of us – Capt. Baker, his orderly, the telephonist and myself – were all together in that part of the trench and immediately retired down the communication trench and got out on the open ground at the back. I took shelter in a hole made by a Jack Johnson shell and on looking out I saw Capt. Baker lying on the ground a few yards away. He had been shot, I think, in the hip or lower part of the body and was quite unable to rise. I went to his assistance and dragged him about seven yards nearer the hole, when he told me to look after myself. I then went on to Ypres, which I reached safely and was attended to at the hospital. When I left Capt. Baker, the Germans were only about 60 yards away and were coming on swiftly, firing all the time.

The 3rd Monmouths had also suffered badly, so more troops were sent up from reserve to bolster the weakened defences. The 1st Monmouths had lost a total of seven officers: Lieutenant Colonel Charles Lawson Robinson, Major Edward Styant Williams, Captains Harold Thorne Edwards and Claude Wilfred Stanton, Lieutenant Edward

Stone Phillips (his brother Captain Leslie Phillips was killed at Frezenberg with the 1st Welsh), Second Lieutenants Henry Anthony Birrell-Anthony and William Victor Stewart, and 132 men killed. The 2nd Monmouths, who had not been so heavily involved, had lost twenty-one men killed, while the 3rd Monmouths had lost seven officers: Captains Robert Oswald Gardner and James Lancaster, Lieutenants Francis Neville Groves, Charles Sydney Reed and John Patson Worton, and Second Lieutenants William Lucius Palmer and Charles Malin Clifton Sorby, and forty-three men killed. The 1st Welsh had lost sixteen men killed. Two of the Monmouth battalions had been almost wiped out. On the spot where these brave men fell, about half a mile north of Wieltje, is a memorial stone erected by the parents of Henry Anthony Birrell-Anthony in memory of all the men of the battalion killed there.

The memorial stone at Wieltje to Lieutenant Henry Anthony Birrell-Anthony and the men of the 1st Monmouths who fell during the Battle of Frezenberg Ridge on 8 May 1915.

Lieutenant Colonel Charles Lawson Robinson, CO of the 1st Monmouths, was the son of Robert Robinson of Howlish Hall, Bishop Auckland. He had lived in south Wales for many years in his capacity as inspector of mines and had served with the 89th Company, Imperial Yeomanry in the Boer War. He was 45 years old when he was killed at Frezenberg on 8 May 1915 and is commemorated on the Ypres (Menin Gate) Memorial. He is also commemorated on a war memorial inside St John's Church, Maindee. The *Monmouth Guardian* of 21 May 1915 published a report about his death:

Private advices received on Wednesday stated that Colonel Robinson, the commanding officer of the 1st Battalion Monmouthshire Regiment, was killed at the front last Sunday. Col. Robinson, who was well known throughout the Rhymney Valley, was by profession a mining engineer, served as a volunteer in the South African war. Soon after his return to this country he was transferred from the mines inspectors' district in Durham to the South Western District and was a Government mines inspector under the late Mr J.B. Martin. Some years ago Col. Robinson was transferred to Scotland and became chief mines inspector for Scotland. He had not lived in Monmouthshire for several years. After he went to live in Scotland he still retained his association with the Monmouthshire Territorial Corps and it was from that circumstance that he went to the front as commanding officer of the 1st Battalion. He was an expert in the use of explosives and there is reason to believe that he directed some of the most important mining operations at the front during the last two months.

WALKER C. G.
WALKER R.
YOUNGS W. L.

YOUNG J. H.
YOUNG W. H.

COOMB
CREWE
CROSSL
CROSSL

MONMOUTHSHIRE REGIMENT

LIEUT. COLONEL	SERJEANT
ROBINSON C. L.	DAVIES A.
	DAVIES T. C.
MAJOR	EDWARDS S.
WILLIAMS O. M.	ELLWAY F. J.
	CARBUTT W.
CAPTAIN	HAILSTONE W.
GARDNER R. O.	HARVEY C. V.
LANCASTER J.	HEARDER K.
PERRY B. L.	JONES E. W.
STANTON C. W.	JONES R. C.
WATKINS I. E. M.	KILMINSTER H. W.
	MILES W. C.
LIEUTENANT	NASH W.
GROVES F. N.	PREWETT G.
MARTIN C. H. G.	PRITCHARD W.
PHILLIPS E. S.	RUCK S. R.
REED C. S.	SPENCER J. H.
WALTERS H. J.	TURNER W.
WORTON J. P.	WATERS W.
	WELLS J. J.
SECOND LIEUT.	WHITE A. I.
BIRRELL-ANTHONY H. A.	LANCE SERJEANT
ONIONS W.	JONES T.
PALMER W. L.	KEYSE W. M.
STEWART W. V.	MORGAN H.
TOWNSEND H. V.	SHAW J. E. W.
QMR. SERJEANT	CORPORAL
DIX A. J.	BROWN R. W.
	COUNSELL T. H.
COY. SJT. MAJOR	CURTIS T.
BOOTH W. J.	HANNEY G. S. P.
GARDNER H. J.	JAMES A. W.
GILL J. T.	JAMES T. D.
LIPPIETT G. H.	

50

DADE J
DALLIM
DANCE
DARKNE
DAVIES
DAVIES
DAVIES
DAVIES
DAVIES
DAVIES.
DAVIES
DAVIES
DAVIES
DAVIES
DAVIES
DAVIES
DAVIS A
DAVIS J.
DAWES V
DAWSON
DELAHAY
DICK W. .
DRUMMOI
DUCKHAM
DWYER T.
EAGER J. F
EDWARDS
EDWARDS
EVANS A.
EVANS A.
EVANS A. I
EVANS D. I
EVANS D. 2
EVANS E.
EVANS G.
EVANS I.

A section of Panel 50 on the Ypres (Menin Gate) Memorial, showing the names of many of the members of the regiment killed at Ypres. Lieutenant Colonel Charles Lawson Robinson's name is to the top left of the panel.

By the afternoon the remnants of the 5th Royal Fusiliers had been surrounded and the Germans had captured the village of Verlorenhoek, but they were thrown back following a counter-attack by the 2nd East Surrey. The retreating enemy ran through the cornfields across the front of the 1st Welsh and were mowed down by machine-gun and rifle fire, bringing some degree of revenge for the Welshmen.

During the following night of 10/11 May 10 Brigade was moved up to relieve 84 Brigade, which marched out via Ypres to camps at Herzeele, 8 miles west of Poperinghe, where it remained for ten days. Here the 1st Welsh received a draft of three officers and 215 men, mostly from the SWB. During the period between 17 April and 10 May the casualties suffered by the 1st Welsh had amounted to 2 officers and 80 men killed and 12 officers and 297 men wounded: a total of 14 officers and 377 other ranks.

The survivors of the 1st and 3rd Monmouths remained in the line and were merged temporarily to form a composite battalion. On 11 May they were again hit hard by a renewed German push towards Ypres, losing another forty-seven men killed.

The Battle of Frezenberg continued until 13 May, when an unsuccessful attack was made on the whole of the Ypres front held by the 27th Division, the Cavalry Force (which had relieved the 28th Division) and the 4th Division. The total casualties in the battle from 8 to 13 May amounted to 456 officers and nearly 9,000 men.

Among the final casualties of the Battle of Frezenberg was a young Welsh poet, a son of Lord St David's. Colwyn Erasmus Arnold Philipps was born on 11 December 1888, the son of John Philipps, the Right Honourable the 1st Viscount St David's and his wife Leonora Gerstenberg, of 3 Richmond Terrace, Whitehall, London and of Picton Castle, Pembrokeshire. He was educated at Eton and Sandhurst. At the age of 20 he received a commission in the Royal Horse Guards and on 30 July 1909 was promoted to lieutenant. By the outbreak of war Philipps had risen to the rank of captain. The Royal Horse Guards were attached to 7 Cavalry Brigade, 3rd Cavalry Division and landed at Zeebrugge at the beginning of October. The division fought in the defence of Antwerp before being sent to Ypres. Philipps was killed in action on 13 May 1915, aged 26, and is commemorated on the Menin Gate Memorial. In a letter sent to his bereaved parents by a brother officer, it was said: 'He fell in an attack on the German Trenches on Thursday, 13th. His end was worthy as his life, as he was the first man in the German trenches and killed five Germans before he was shot in the head at close quarters and instantly killed.'

Captain the Honourable Colwyn Erasmus Arnold Philipps, Royal Horse Guards.

His brother, Captain Roland Erasmus Philipps, MC, was killed on the Somme on 7 July 1916. During his short life, Colwyn Philipps had gained a strong reputation for his poetry and numbers among the war poets of the Great War. His poems were published by his family after his death, one of which was entitled *Release*:

There is a healing magic in the night,
The breeze blows cleaner than it did by day,
Forgot the fever of the fuller light,
And sorrow sinks insensibly away
As if some saint a cool white hand did lay
Upon the brow and calm the restless brain.
The moon looks down with pale unpassioned ray –
Sufficient for the hour is its pain.
Be still and feel the night that hides away earth's stain.
Be still and loose the sense of God in you,
Be still and send your soul into the all,
The vast distance where the stars shine blue,
No longer antlike on the earth to crawl.
Released from time and sense of great or small,
Float on the pinions of the Night-Queen's wings;
Soar till the swift inevitable fall
Will drag you back into all the world's small things;
Yet for an hour be one with all escaped things.

The 28th Division had suffered horrific casualties on 8 May: the survivors of the six battalions of 84 Brigade totalled only 1,400 men on 9 May and were made into two composite battalions. The 1st Monmouths and the 12th Londons were attached to the 1st Welsh and the 5th Fusiliers, the Cheshires and 1st Suffolks formed a battalion under Major R.T. Toke. On 14 May Lieutenant Colonel Marden was sent to take temporary command of 83 Brigade. The 1st Suffolks had lost all but one of its officers and 947 other ranks between 18 April and 8 May. The Germans had gained ground from the 28th Division but it had stood firm. The Princess Patricia's Canadian Light Infantry (PPCLI) of the Canadians, which contained a number of Welshmen in its ranks, had also made a gallant stand to the north, almost being wiped out.

Captain Julian Henry Francis Grenfell DSO, 1st (Royal) Dragoons, the nephew of a Swansea coppermaster.

The battle had also cost the life of another war poet with links to Wales, Captain Julian Henry Francis Grenfell DSO. Grenfell was born in St James's Square, London on 30 March 1888, the son of William Grenfell and Ethel Priscilla Fane (later Lord and Lady Desborough). He was a nephew of Pascoe St Leger Grenfell, copper merchant, of Merthyr House, Swansea and a cousin of Captain Francis Octavius Grenfell VC. He was educated at Eton and at Bailliol College, Oxford before gaining his commission in the 1st (Royal) Dragoons on 15 September 1909. Grenfell embarked for France on 7 October 1914 and had become known for his bravery, being mentioned in Sir John French's despatch of 17 February 1915 and was awarded the DSO for work carried out during a reconnaissance in no man's land. On 13 May he had been talking to a group of fellow officers of the 1st (Royal) Dragoons when he was struck by a splinter from a shell that exploded nearby. Badly wounded, Grenfell was evacuated to the military hospital at Boulogne, where he died on 26 May, aged 27. He is buried in Boulogne Eastern Cemetery. His most famous work was the war poem *Into Battle*, which he wrote while waiting to move up to the front line near Ypres. His brother, Second Lieutenant Gerald William Grenfell, was killed nearby by machine-gun fire on 30 July 1915.

> The thundering line of battle stands,
> And in the air Death moans and sings;
> But Day shall clasp him with strong hands,
> And Night shall fold him in soft wings. (*Into Battle*, Chapter 7.)

iv) The Battle of Bellewaarde Ridge

All the Welsh units at Ypres that had been involved in the Battle of Frezenberg had been severely damaged and were moved into reserve after being relieved. The 1st and 3rd Monmouths withdrew to billets at Vlamertinghe to recover and began absorbing replacements, while the 1st Welsh moved to farms near Herzeele until 22 May, when it moved back up to relieve the 1st Cavalry Brigade in trenches near Hooge. On that day the three Monmouth battalions were given orders to merge and on the following day the 1st and 3rd Monmouths marched to woods at Vlamertinghe.

As far as the Welsh units at Ypres were concerned, little had happened at the front in the meantime, except that the French had driven the Germans back across the Yser Canal and had reoccupied Steenstraat. During the night of 23/24 May the 1st Welsh were relieved from the line and were marching back to Vlamertinghe when the sound of artillery fire could be heard. The Germans had launched another gas attack on a 4-mile front from Hooge to Turco Farm, pounding the area with artillery before following up with an infantry assault. The British had managed to hold their lines but were eventually forced to withdraw, losing just over half a mile of depth to the salient.

All the units of 84 Brigade were hurriedly ordered to move back to the front line and assembled at Hellfire Corner, about half a mile east of Ypres. The battalions rested for a while in fields alongside the road while the situation was relayed to the officers. The British line had been broken for a distance of half a mile north of Wieltje and on both sides of Bellewaarde Lake, for a total distance of almost 2,000 metres. In an attempt to save the situation, at 11.30 am orders were received for 84 Brigade to counter-attack to restore the line. The brigade moved off, following the line of the railway west of Ypres, all the while under artillery fire. Lieutenant Colonel Marden, commanding the 1st Welsh, was wounded and Major R.H. Toke took command.

The plan was for 84 Brigade to attack on the left and 80 Brigade, 27th Division, on the right, supported by artillery fire, but 80 Brigade had been delayed, so the Cheshires took up their position and the assaulting troops advanced towards Wittepoort Farm, which stood on a slight rise above the rest of the country and was presumed to be where the main bulk of the German forces were.

At about 4 pm the first attacking battalion, the Northumberland Fusiliers, began advancing but were held up by wire and suffered large numbers of casualties. The 1st Welsh were then moved up by Major Toke and succeeded in crossing through the wire, following the small parties of the Northumberland Fusiliers who had got through and advanced across no man's land. The 1st Welsh crossed the Menin Road to attack but were brought to a halt, suffering Captain Leslie Phillips (whose brother had been killed with the Monmouths on 8 May) and a large number of men killed.

All the assaulting troops were suffering high numbers of casualties and the situation worsened when the Germans lay down effective artillery fire. Heavy fighting continued throughout the day. By around 7 pm 80 Brigade had arrived and was ordered to carry out a night assault: 84 Brigade was to be supported by the 2nd Battalion, King's Shropshire Light Infantry (2nd KSLI) of 80 Brigade in an attack north of the Menin Road, with the Suffolks advancing on Wittepoort Farm from the south. The remainder of 80 Brigade was to attack on the right of the Suffolks. The hour of the attack was fixed for 12.30 am on 25 May. The 2nd KSLI, together with one company of the 1st Welsh, were to storm Wittepoort Farm, while the remainder of the 1st Welsh, together with the few of the Northumberland Fusiliers and Cheshires who survived, were to attack Railway Wood.

The assault went ahead at 12.30 am as planned but was met with heavy machine-gun and rifle fire by the Germans, but the British reached their objectives and fierce hand-to-hand fighting ensued. The 1st Welsh drove through Railway Wood but suffered a large number of casualties and a platoon of the 2nd KSLI who moved up to support the Welsh was all but annihilated.

As dawn broke, the Welsh came under heavy fire from a German trench that had not been cleared and the British artillery opened up on the ridge, catching the British troops holding the edge of Railway Wood. The survivors crawled back across no man's land into a sunken road to the west of the wood. The attack had been carried out with great gallantry but had been in vain. The 1st Welsh had lost five more officers – Captains Leslie Phillips and Charles Coke Torkington, the Adjutant, Edmund Henry Herbert Westby, Lieutenant Charles Gordon Rumsey and Second Lieutenant Henry Angrave Cecil Topham – and 108 other ranks were killed during the Battle of Bellewaarde. A large number of the men were the former South Wales Borderers who had reinforced the battalion just days earlier.

The composite Monmouths battalion was lucky not to have been heavily involved in the attack at Railway Wood, suffering just eight men killed over the two days. It was relieved during the night of 25/26 May and moved back to billets in Vlamertinghe Woods, while the 1st Welsh was relieved by the 2nd Royal Scots. The Germans were as exhausted as the allies by now and the offensives at Aubers Ridge and in the Artois prevented them moving reinforcements to Ypres. A period of relative peace now fell upon the Ypres front.

No honours were awarded to either the 1st Welsh or the Monmouths for the action, except for the award of the Order of St Michael and St George and the Russian Order of St Vladimir, 4th Class with Swords, to Lieutenant Colonel Thomas Owen Marden. Reviewing 84 Brigade on 21 May, Sir John French said:

You have fought the Second battle of Ypres, which will rank among the most desperate and hardest fights of the war. You may have thought because you were not attacking that you were not helping to shorten the war. On the contrary, by your splendid endurance and bravery you have done a great deal to help the offensive further south… Your colours have

Captain Leslie Phillips of the 1st Welsh, killed at Bellewaarde on 24/25 May 1915. Phillips was the son of Edward and Elizabeth Phillips of Newport. His brother had been killed just weeks earlier. He was buried just south of the Menin Road but is today commemorated on the Ypres (Menin Gate) Memorial.

Second Lieutenant Henry Angrave Cecil Topham of the 1st Welsh, mortally wounded at Bellewaarde 24 May 1915. Topham was the son of John Henry and Dorothy Marian Topham of Morley Hall, Derby. He died of wounds on 25 May 1915 and is buried in Bailleul Communal Cemetery Extension.

many famous names emblazoned on them, but none will be more famous or well-deserved than that Second Battle of Ypres.

The 6th Welsh, as mentioned, had arrived in France on 30 October 1914, but instead of moving to the front had been retained on the lines of communication at Calais under Lieutenant Colonel Lord Ninian Crichton Stuart. On 30 May a disaster struck the battalion. A party of men from the battalion was travelling in a motor lorry when it was hit by another, sending it crashing into the canal. Six men were drowned in the tragedy: Private William Baird (2365) of Swansea, Bandsman Richard Thomas Harris (317) of Cwmbwrla, Private Thomas Edward Lewis (2426) of Cymmer, Private William Edward Lovett (2549) of Maesteg, Private Richard Pugh (2365) of Pennal, Merioneth and Private Francis Henry Richards (1751) of Neath. All six men are buried in Calais Southern Cemetery.

Lieutenant Thomas Owen Marden, 1st Welsh. He was mentioned in despatches and made commander of the Order of St Michael and St George and the Russian Order of St Vladimir, 4th Class with Swords, for his work commanding the battalion during the Second Battle of Ypres.

Richard Thomas Harris was the husband of Margaret J. Harris of 4 Bryn Terrace, Middle Road, Cwmbwrla, Swansea. He was 32 years of age and was a member of the 6th Welsh prior to the outbreak of the war. He had been employed at the Cwmbwrla Tinplate Works.

The rest of the men in the battalion were reported to have been in good spirits otherwise and were cheered to receive orders to move to Wizernes prior to joining

Private Richard Thomas Harris of the 6th Welsh, tragically drowned in an accident at Calais on 30 May 1915.

84 Brigade on 5 July, joining the 1st Welsh in the trenches at Kemmel, where the men were initiated into trench warfare beside their regular army compatriots.

A platoon of the 6th Welsh in France.

None of the Welsh units would see further action until the Battle of Loos later in the year. Meanwhile the 1st Welsh, rebuilt after their ordeals at Frezenberg, were holding positions at Ridge Wood, near Dickebusch. On 22 June the young Lieutenant Cadwallader John Coker was shot by a sniper while firing over the parapet. The son of Gould and Florence Coker of Lane End, Mayfield, Sussex, he was educated at Wellington College and Oriel College, Oxford before being commissioned in the 1st Welsh on 15 September 1914. Coker was a gallant officer who had already been wounded at Hooge but had still assisted several men who were wounded with him before going to the aid post himself. He was buried by his men in Ridge Wood Military Cemetery.

Lieutenant Cadwallader John Coker of 1st Welsh, killed by a sniper near St Eloi on 22 June 1915.

One of the first Welsh airmen to move to the Western Front was tragically killed during an accident on 7 July. Captain Arthur Henry Leslie Soames was the son of Frederick and Julia Soames, of Bryn Estyn, Wrexham. He had served with the 3rd Hussars prior to the war before transferring to the 3rd (King's Own) Hussars. In 1912 he gained his aviator's certificate flying a Vickers monoplane at the Vickers School, Brooklands. Soames flew over to France as part of the first RFC contingent early in the war and was mentioned in Lord French's despatches of 8 October 1914. He was among the first men to be awarded the Military Cross when his name was published in the New Year's Honours List of 31 December 1914 and was decorated by the king at Buckingham Palace. By February 1915 Soames was promoted to flight commander at the Central Flying School, Netheravon. He was tragically killed during an accident at Netheravon on 7 July 1915 when fragments of a new high-explosive bomb he was testing exploded and struck him from 90 metres away. Soames was 28 years old and was buried with full military honours in All Saints' Churchyard, Gresford.

Lieutenant Cadwallade John Coker's grave at Ridge Wood Military Cemetery.

The Soames family saw further tragedy during the war. Captain William Miles Kington DSO, of the 1st RWF, who was killed at Ypres on 20 October 1914, was a brother-in-law of the above, while a brother, Lieutenant William Noel Soames, died of heart disease while serving with the Cheshire Yeomanry on 19 May 1916. Three other brothers – Evelyn, Julian and Cecil – also served as officers during the war but survived, although Julian was badly wounded during the retreat at Mons and lost a leg after being wounded a second time, having been commissioned in the Royal Welsh Fusiliers on 24 July 1915.

As a break from the monotony of trench warfare, on 11 July the 1st and 6th Welsh played a rugby match, the 1st Welsh scraping a win by one try against a team that included several Swansea players. Nothing of note occurred until 8.45 pm on 3 August when the Germans blew a mine under the Welsh positions at Ridge Wood, burying sixteen men. Gallant work was carried out by Captain Egerton, Lieutenant Weber and Sergeants Reynolds and Price, who led a party of men who eventually pulled ten men out alive. The six men killed and presumably still buried there are Lance Corporal James Stanley David (30737) of Swansea, Privates Charles Louis Davies (11136) of Tufnell Park, London, Thomas Hopkins (13182) of Pontcanna, Cardiff, William James Evans (30738) of Pontarddulais, Francis Martin (33544) of Longton, Staffs and Albert Morgan (36045) of Beaufort, Breconshire.

Underground warfare proved to be a major danger to troops in the front line, especially in the Cuinchy and Ypres sectors. Both the 1st and 6th Welsh suffered from German mines blown in the St Eloi area over the coming months.

Lance Corporal James Stanley David (30737), 1st Welsh, the 23-year-old son of Walter and Elvira David of 76 Glanbrydan Avenue, Bryn Mill, Swansea. One of six men killed by a mine on 3 August 1915, he is commemorated on the Ypres (Menin Gate) Memorial. He had returned from a lucrative position in Argentina to enlist early in the war.

The 4th RWF, 1st SWB and 2nd Welsh, with the 1st Division, had moved into a quiet sector after the Battle of Aubers Ridge. The 2nd Welsh War Diary recorded the French-dug trenches as being 'almost works of art as well as nearly shell proof, since some were lined with steel girders.' The French sanitary arrangements were something else though, seemingly built with no regard for health or hygiene and were often a bone of contention among British troops moving into French areas.

Among a number of reinforcement officers who joined the 2nd Welsh was a young Lieutenant Robert Graves, an officer of the 3rd RWF who had embarked for France on 12 May 1915. Graves was an outspoken man who would prove to be a brave officer and was already a well-respected poet. He became one of the most well-known war poets, writing numerous poems and books both during the war and in later life. One of his books, *Good-bye to All That*, contained some scathing references to the 2nd Welsh, who felt compelled to mention it in their history of the regiment:

One of these, 2nd-Lieutenant R.R. Graves, subsequently wrote a book in which he criticised the peaceful attitude of the battalion at this period. Having just arrived in France he

Robert von Ranke Graves. As well as being one of the Great War poets, Graves forged a highly succesful literary career after the war, including such works as I, Claudius, *which was turned into a TV series and also adapted for theatre and radio.*

apparently did not realise the necessity for men, who had just come out of a disastrous and exhausting battle like Aubers, to recuperate their moral and physical forces. It is noteworthy that both the Regular Battalions of the Welsh were in France at the same time, which was not the case with many units and that their losses had been so heavy that their ranks, both commissioned and other, had to be filled from battalions which had been more fortunate in their casualty lists.

The 2nd RWF were in the trenches at Bois Grenier on 11 July when a group of men were playing about with a shell fuse that one of them had found. The fuse exploded, killing three men instantly and wounding two, while one man was also killed by a sniper. Privates Samuel Hand (9155), Albert Jones (10319) and Frederick Stait (9108) are buried in Bois-Grenier Communal Cemetery, while Privates William Bolton (9561) and Harold Matthews (11449) are buried in Erquinghem-Lys Churchyard Extension. Hand, Stait and Bolton were all Birmingham men. (Stait was probably the man listed as being killed by a sniper that day.)

To the north, at 7 pm on 19 July a large mine that had been dug by men of 175 Tunnelling Company RE, was blown beneath the German line at Hooge. The mine formed a crater almost 40 metres in diameter, which was rushed and consolidated by men of the 4th Middlesex.

In retaliation, on 30 July the Germans introduced a new terror weapon when they attacked positions held by the 14th (Light) Division at Hooge with *flammenwerfern* (flame-throwers). The division had been unfortunate as it had only taken up the line a week previously but incurred the full wrath of the German attack.

The 8th Rifle Brigade held the lip of the crater, with the 7th KRRC on their right, south of the Menin Road. At 3.15 am the men were awoken by a massive explosion. The Germans had blown up the ruins of Hooge Château stables and then attacked with *flammenwerfern*, sending huge jets of flame across no man's land onto the British positions. With the stench of petroleum in the air and fire raining down on them, both battalions then came under artillery, rifle and machine-gun fire that reached as far back as the ramparts of Ypres.

The shattered survivors attempted to defend the crater but were forced to withdraw, the Germans capturing and consolidating the old front line. To the left, 42 Brigade had not been attacked, while the 46th (North Midland) Division, to the right, managed to stand firm. Reinforcements were rushed up and the British established a new front line, attempting a counter-attack by the 6th DCLI of the 41st Division and the 9th KRRC of the 42nd at 2.45 pm. Some ground was regained but the Germans attacked again with *flammenwerfern* later in the night and were this time beaten off. The ground was not retaken by the British until 9 August, when the 6th Division made an assault.

During heavy fighting along the front that day at Givenchy, IV Corps suffered over 2,700 casualties; the 3rd Division, at Bellewaarde, lost over 3,500, while the 14th (Light) Division lost just under 2,500 men at Hooge. Among those killed were at least seventeen Welshmen: four officers and thirteen men.

One of the officers was the second Welsh international rugby player to be killed during the war, William Purdon Geen. He was born in Newport on 14 March 1891 and was educated at Haileybury College and Oxford. He played for Oxford in four varsity matches, from 1910 to 1913. He played rugby for Newport and Monmouthshire before gaining the first of his three Welsh caps against South Africa in 1912. In August 1914, Geen was commissioned in the King's Royal Rifle Corps and was sent to France in May 1915 to join their 9th Battalion. He was killed in action during the second *flammenwerfer* attack at Hooge on the night of 30/31 July 1915, aged 24, and is commemorated on the Menin Gate Memorial. His obituary was published in the *Glamorgan Gazette* of 13 August 1915, part of which reads as follows:

Second Lieutenant William Purdon Geen of Newport, the second Welsh international rugby player killed during the war.

Lieut. William Purdon Geen, of the King's Royal Rifles, who was 'missing' after the fighting on the last day of July, held high rank in Oxford and South Wales Rugby. In his day he was a dazzling left wing three-quarter back and his best Rugby was drawn from him when he had Ronald Poulton playing inside to him. No wing was ever better matched in physique, in style, in skill and in 'colour' than were these brilliant sons of Oxford – Willie Geen and Ronnie Poulton.

'LE CORPS
IT   SECOND LIEUT.
    FARMER H. C. McL.
    GEEN W. P.
    GIBB J. H.
    HABERSHON P. H.
    HAMILTON V. L.
    HARMON W. B.
    HAYCROFT F. A.

William Purdon Geen's name on the Ypres (Menin Gate) Memorial.

Among the other Welshmen killed were Lieutenant Colonel Charles Slingsby Chaplin of Ruabon, commanding officer of the 9th KRRC; Major John Jeffreys Bulkeley Jones-Parry of Edeyrn, second-in-command of the 6th DCLI; and Second Lieutenant the Honourable Gerald William Grenfell of the 8th Rifle Brigade, a war poet and brother of Captain the Honourable Julian Grenfell DSO, who had died of

Second Lieutenant the Honourable Gerald William Grenfell, of the 8th Rifle Brigade, a war poet.

wounds on 26 May 1915. The brothers were the sons of Lord Desborough and cousins of Field Marshal Francis Grenfell, Baron Grenfell of Kilvey, Glamorgan.

The other ranks killed were Lance Corporal Robert Parsons (10614), 6th DCLI, of Swansea; Sergeant Richard Maunder (A/689), 8th KRRC, of Abertysswg; Lance Corporal Frederick Linley Jagger (S/7663), 9th Rifle Brigade, of Cardiff; Rifleman Harry Bonney (S/1032) of Barry; Rifleman David Connelly (R/5824), 9th KRRC, of Bridgend; Rifleman Arthur Edward Gaisford (S/182), 8th Rifle Brigade, of Barry; Rifleman Gwilym Griffiths (S/1596), 8th Rifle Brigade, of Trealaw; Rifleman Thomas Hartrey (S/1028), 8th Rifle Brigade, of Llancarfan; Private Ralph Frederick Jones (16330), 6th Somerset Light Infantry, of Abergavenny; Rifleman Ivor Morgan (S/3206), 8th Rifle Brigade, of Blaengwynfi; Rifleman Walter Sinfield (S/1016), 8th Rifle Brigade, of Barry; Rifleman Thomas John Smout (S/3207), 8th Rifle Brigade, of Glyncorrwg; and Sapper George Galbraith (7307) of No. 2 Siege Company Royal Anglesey Royal Engineers. Most of these men are commemorated on the Menin Gate.

Charles Slingsby Chaplin was born in Norfolk Square, Hyde Park on 31 May 1863, the son of Clifford and Rosa Chaplin. He was educated at Eton and Pembroke College, Oxford before joining the City of London Regiment from the Militia in 1885. He subsequently transferred to the Green Jackets before being gazetted captain in the King's Royal Rifle Corps in 1894, serving in India and during the Boer War, where he was mentioned in despatches. He married Gwladys Hamilton Creek of Erbistock House, Ruabon, in 1905. On 19 August 1914 he was given command of the 9th KRRC and had become a well-respected commander among his men before being shot in the head and killed at Hooge on 30 July. Chaplin has no known grave and is commemorated alongside many of his men on the Menin Gate. His son, Major Patrick Slingsby Chaplin, was killed with the 2nd KRRC in North Africa on 1 June 1942. Both father and son are commemorated on the same war memorial at Erbistock, near Overton.

While the battered Welsh units on the Western Front rebuilt following severe losses at Ypres and Neuve Chapelle, new units were readying to move overseas, both to France and to Gallipoli, where that campaign had also stagnated into trench warfare.

On 13 June the 13th (Western) Division sailed from Devonport for service at Gallipoli. Among its units were the 8th RWF, commanded by Lieutenant Colonel Archibald Hay, the 4th SWB, commanded by Lieutenant Colonel Franklin Macaulay Gillespie, and the 8th Welsh, commanded by Lieutenant Colonel John Arthur Bald.

Between 14 and 19 July the 53rd (Welsh) Division sailed from Devonport for service at Gallipoli. Among its units were the 5th RWF, commanded by Lieutenant Colonel Basil Edwin Philips, the 6th RWF, commanded by Lieutenant Colonel Thomas W. Jones, the 7th RWF, commanded by Lieutenant Colonel Thomas Hubert Harker, the 4th Welsh, commanded by Lieutenant Colonel William Bramwell Jones and the 5th Welsh, commanded by Lieutenant Colonel Morgan Morgan.

Between 16 and 21 July the 19th (Western) Division moved to France. Among its battalions were the 9th RWF, commanded by Lieutenant Colonel Henry John Madocks, the 5th SWB (Pioneers), commanded by Lieutenant Colonel Courtney Vor Trower and the 9th Welsh, commanded by Lieutenant Colonel Charles Henry Young. After training in the Calais area, the division marched by stages to the Laventie area for trench initiation, where it came under the orders of the Indian Corps.

While the division was moving to France, some of the few surviving original members of the 1st SWB returned home to Wales on some well-earned leave. The *Glamorgan Gazette* of 23 July 1915 reported on their arrival:

THE ORIGINAL BORDERERS WIPED OUT WITH THE EXCEPTION OF 14. All that are said to be left of the original 1st Battalion South Wales Borderers who went out to the front with the first body of the Expeditionary Force on August 4th are fourteen, all the others having been wounded, killed, captured or sick. Of that small band of survivors on the active list, seven came home on leave last week and from an account of their experiences by one of them, Private William Roberts, Rhallt, Welshpool, the gallant fourteen seem to have borne charmed lives. They have come scatheless through no less than six bayonet charges, in which there was the fiercest hand-to-hand fighting and Private Roberts states that he himself was buried under trenches blown up by the German artillery on four occasions. He and the other thirteen also survived two gas attacks. 'Our hardest bit of work,' he says, 'was one day last December. We made a forced march from Zonnebecke to Festubert, a distance of 28 miles, carrying our full kit, between 7 pm and 9 o'clock the following morning and in the afternoon we charged and carried three lines of German trenches.' None of the officers who went out with the regiment in August are now in it. Among the fourteen survivors in the rank and file are Private Bennett, another Welshpool man, Privates Knott and Stevens, South Wales men; Private Ireman and Wingfield, two Lincoln policemen; Privates Norman and Leech, two London men; and Private Jones, a Bristol man.

It is time to leave France for now and concentrate on the arrival of the 13th (Western) and then the 53rd (Welsh) divisions in Gallipoli.

Chapter 11

Gallipoli:
The Landings

While the war was raging in Flanders, another theatre of operations had burst into action: Gallipoli.

On 12 March the 2nd SWB, under Lieutenant Colonel Hugh Gilbert Casson, a Boer War veteran, was in camp at Rugby with 87 Brigade, 29th Division and was inspected by King George V. Four days later, on 16 March, the division began to entrain at Rugby for Avonmouth and that night the 2nd SWB began to embark aboard the SS *Canada*. At 5 pm the following day the convoy left Avonmouth, passing through the Straits of Gibraltar on the 21st and arriving at Malta on 24 March. After disembarking a number of sick men, the convoy steamed for Alexandria two days later, arriving on the 29th and the 2nd SWB disembarked that evening, the men marching to Mex Camp, where a strict training regime began. The battalion remained here until 8 April.

Gallipoli (Gelibolu) is a small town on the Dardanelles Peninsula, guarding the Dardanelles Straits. The straits are the gateway to the Black Sea, a vitally important route that the allies hoped to capture to open up supply routes to Russia and to force Turkey out of the war. The Germans had delivered a crushing blow to Russia at Tannenberg at the start of the war and had been driving eastwards. Turkey had entered the war on their side, threatening Russia from the Caucasus, so Russia had appealed to the allies for help. Gaining control of the Dardanelles would re-establish communications with Russia and release shipping locked in the Black Sea by Turkey.

The plan was initially to force the passage of the Dardanelles using a combined fleet of British and French warships, but foolishly on 19 February both navies had begun shelling strategic positions along the coast in order to soften up the Turkish defences prior to the main attack, thus alerting the Turks to their intent. As a result, during the first months of 1915 the Turks began strengthening their defences with heavy guns and searchlights and laid minefields in the narrow straits.

On 18 March the main attack was launched. The fleet, comprising eighteen battleships with supporting cruisers and destroyers, entered the straits and began shelling the Turkish forts. The French battleship *Bouvet* was sunk by a mine, causing it to capsize with her crew of over 600 still aboard and the allied minesweepers retreated under heavy fire. Sustaining heavy casualties, the fleet began to turn in the narrow channel but, unbeknown to them, the Turks had laid a strip of mines in the

The battleship HMS Queen Elizabeth *leaving Mudros.*

turning area. As a result HMS *Irresistible* and HMS *Inflexible* wandered into the minefield and suffered critical damage. HMS *Ocean* was despatched to rescue the *Irresistible* but was also damaged by an explosion and both ships eventually sank. HMS *Ocean* had been attached to the Reserve Fleet at Pembroke Dock at the outbreak of war and her loss was reported in the local newspapers, which were especially proud of the conduct of one officer from Haverfordwest:

> Admirable Conduct of a Naval Officer. TO RECEIVE THE DISTINGUISHED SERVICE CROSS. Sub-Lieutenant (now Acting-Lieutenant) STEPHEN AUGUSTUS BAYFORD, R.N.R., H.M.S. *Majestic*. Midshipman JAMES CHARLES WOOLJIER PRICE, H.M.S. *Ocean*. These officers were both in command of picket boats on the night of 13th-14th March. When the *Ocean*'s boat lay helpless, having been struck in the boiler-room by a shell, the *Majestic* took her in tow, under heavy fire, the conduct of these two young officers being altogether admirable, as was their handling of their boats. Midshipman Price is the eldest son of Mr Charles Price, brother of Mr Herbert J.E. Price, of this town and we offer the gallant young officer our warmest congratulations on the distinction his courageous behaviour has elicited. (*Haverfordwest and Milford Haven Telegraph*, 18 August 1915.)

The French battleships *Suffren* and *Gaulois* were also damaged, so Rear Admiral John de Robeck, commanding the fleet, sounded the general recall to save what remained of his force.

The Turkish gun batteries had almost run out of ammunition, but de Robeck was not to know that and the attack was heralded as a great triumph by the Turks. The British came to the conclusion that they could not force their way through the Dardanelles unless troops were first sent to occupy the Gallipoli Peninsula in force to silence the Turkish guns so, following an idea put forward by Winston Churchill, planning for the landing of troops on Gallipoli commenced. Command of the campaign was given to General Sir Ian Hamilton.

The 2nd SWB sailed from Alexandria on 9 April and arrived at the Greek island of Lemnos the following day. Assembling there within Mudros harbour was a vast invasion fleet comprising 78,000 men. The Australian Imperial Force (AIF) and New Zealand Expeditionary Force (NZEF) had been encamped in Egypt undergoing training prior to being sent to France, but were despatched to Mudros instead after being formed into the Australian and New Zealand Army Corps (ANZAC) under the command of Lieutenant General William Birdwood. The British 29th Division, the Royal Naval Division and the French Oriental Expeditionary Corps joined the ANZACs under Hamilton's command. The operation would be complicated by the limited forces available, the rugged terrain of the peninsula and the small number of suitable landing beaches as well as severe logistical difficulties, but a landing was planned for 25 April.

Warships assembling in Mudros Harbour, Lemnos during April 1915.

As well as the Welshmen in the 2nd SWB, among the ANZAC forces were many men of Welsh heritage. For example, one ANZAC unit, the 4th Battalion, Australian Imperial Force (4th AIF) was commanded by a Welshman, Lieutenant Colonel John Astley Onslow-Thompson, of Pontyates, and contained at least four other Welshmen in the battalion: the author's great-grandfather, Private David Thomas John (244); Sergeant Robert Watson (189), the nephew of the Bishop of St David's; Private Stephen Ebenezer Havard (2281) of Johnstown, Pembrokeshire; and Private Philip Owen (1167) of Brynamman, while the 3rd Battalion had a young officer of Welsh descent, Second Lieutenant Owen Glendower Howell-Price, in its ranks; a man who would later become its commanding officer and be awarded the DSO.

The 4th Battalion, AIF parading at Mena Camp, Giza, under the shadow of the pyramids. The battalion was commanded by a Welshman, Lieutenant Colonel Astley John Onslow Thompson, and contained a number of other Welshmen in its ranks.

Stationed at Mudros Harbour were the battleships HMS *Queen Elizabeth*, *Triumph*, *London*, *Prince of Wales* and *Ark Royal*, along with various destroyers and troopships. The men spent the coming days practising disembarking from pinnaces and rushing the beaches of Lemnos. A Turkish torpedo boat, the *Timur Hissar*, entered the harbour on 16 April and caused chaos by firing three torpedoes at the troopship *Manitou*. Around sixty of the troops on deck hurriedly rushed into a lifeboat but in the confusion a rope was jerked, causing a davit to break off and crash into the lifeboat, resulting in fifty men being drowned. The 2nd SWB reported the loss of two men of the battalion drowned in the mêlée on 16 April: Lance Corporal Frost and Private Henry Hogg (9983). Frost was later discovered alive and well in hospital in Malta after being rescued by a tug, while Hogg's body was never recovered.

By 23 April all training was complete and the 2nd SWB left Mudros aboard the Cunard liner RMS *Alaunia*; the following day the battalion received orders to transfer aboard the battleship HMS *Cornwallis*. By 5 am on 25 April the invasion fleet was in position off the Gallipoli coast and the men began disembarking onto the lighters and pinnaces that would take them ashore.

The plan drawn up for the invasion by Sir Ian Hamilton and his staff was relatively simple. The allies planned for the ANZACs to land near Gaba Tepe on the western coast, about 15 miles north of Cape Helles, and advance across the peninsula, cutting off the Turkish troops at Kilitbahir, while the 29th Division would land on several beaches around Cape Helles and advance upon the forts at Kilitbahir. The men would then capture the Ottoman forts and artillery batteries so that the naval force could

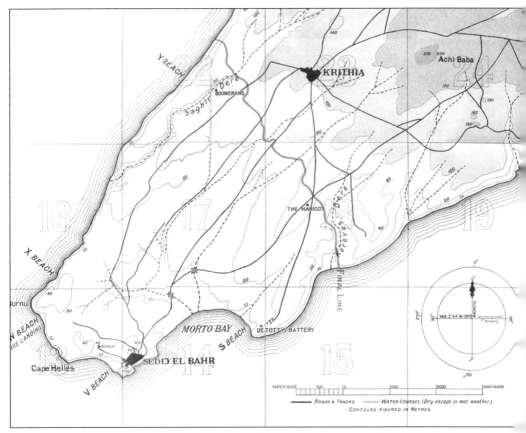

A map showing the landing beaches around Cape Helles, 25 April 1915.

advance through the straits towards Constantinople. The French were to make a diversionary landing at Kum Kale on the Asian shore before re-embarking to hold the eastern area of the Helles sector. There was also a planned diversion that would be carried out by the Royal Naval Division at Bulair.

The invasion force was covered by a heavy naval barrage while being rowed ashore. The ANZACs landed in a small cove, later known as Anzac Cove, early on the morning of 25 April but came under heavy fire from Turkish positions overlooking the beaches. The main force of the Royal Naval Division took part in a mock landing to the north of the peninsula off Bulair, the narrowest point, intended to draw Turkish reinforcements away from the main landings. The Helles landing was made by the 29th Division with elements of the Royal Naval Division, under the command of Major General Aylmer Hunter-Weston. The division landed on five beaches in an arc about the tip of the peninsula, named from east to west as S, V, W, X and Y Beaches. Three companies of the 2nd SWB had been allocated the task of landing at S Beach and capturing De Tott's Battery, while its remaining company was attached to Plymouth Battalion, Royal Marine Light Infantry, of the Royal Naval Division and was despatched to Y Beach.

At Y Beach, during the first engagement around the village of Krithia (the First Battle of Krithia), the allies were able to land unopposed and advance inland, but with no orders to exploit the situation the force was ordered back to Y Beach while the Turks brought their reserves up to prevent another breakthrough.

The main landings were made at V Beach, beneath the old Sedd el Bahr fortress, and at W Beach, a short distance to the west on the other side of the Helles headland. The covering force from the Royal Munster Fusiliers and Hampshires landed from a converted collier, the SS *River Clyde*, which was run aground beneath the fortress so that the troops could disembark via ramps to the shore, but the men were met with withering machine-gun fire. The Royal Dublin Fusiliers landed at V Beach from open boats, while the Lancashire Fusiliers landed at W Beach.

The 2nd SWB began their journey through Morto Bay under cover of mist from HMS *Cornwallis* to S Beach, landing at around 7.30 am. Shells burst in the water all around them but the boats reached the shore without loss; B and C companies landed on the beach, while D Company under Major Margesson landed on rocks beneath De Tott's battery.

While the men from the first two companies were fully loaded with packs, those of Margesson's command were wearing lightweight uniforms, shorts and minimal baggage in order to scale the rocks to take their objectives. Lieutenant Robert Philip Behrens became the first officer of the battalion killed at Gallipoli, being shot while still at sea. Major Margesson himself was shot in the chest and killed while directing

A scene of one of the Gallipoli beaches during the campaign.

Lieutenant Robert Philip Behrens was born at Chorlton, Lancashire, on 4 December 1893, the son of George Benjamin Behrens and Helen Elizabeth Behrens. Helen was the daughter of John Morgan Davies, of Froodvale, Llanwrda and the sister of Oswyn St Leger Davies, of Vron Yw, Denbighshire. Robert was educated at Cordwalles, Maidenhead and had gained a commission in the 2nd SWB. He was killed during the landings at S Beach on 25 April 1915 and was buried from HMS Cornwallis *that same day. Behrens was 21 years old and is commemorated on the Helles Memorial.*

fire to support B and C companies, while Captain Roland Gaskell Palmer was killed while commanding A Company at Y Beach.

Major Edward Cunninghame Margesson, at 43 years old, was one of the oldest and most experienced officers in the 2nd SWB. He was first commissioned in the SWB in 1891 and had seen considerable foreign service. Captain Roland Gaskell Palmer, aged 38, was the only son of Herbert and Emily Palmer of 16 Ovington Square, Chelsea and had been commissioned in the SWB in 1897, serving in the Boer War of 1899–1902.

By 8 am the battalion was well-established ashore after having attained its objective of capturing De Tott's battery though it then came under shell fire from inland Turkish guns. HMS *Cornwallis* retaliated quickly and the sky was soon filled with the sound of massive naval shells flying overhead. A detachment of Royal Marines from *Cornwallis* had gone ashore with the 2nd SWB to aid them in reaching their objectives and it must have been an eerie feeling for them to have their own ship firing over them.

The Turkish response was strong all along the coast. Out of ammunition and left with nothing but bayonets to meet the attackers on the slopes leading up from the beach to the heights of Chunuk Bair, the Turkish 57th Infantry Regiment received orders from Mustafa Kemal, commanding the 19th Division: 'I do not order you to fight, I order you to die. In the time which passes until we die, other troops and commanders can come forward and take our places.' The regiment was all but destroyed.

At W Beach, later known as Lancashire Landing, the Lancashire Fusiliers were able to overwhelm the defences despite the loss of 600 men. The battalions that landed at V Beach suffered about 70 per cent casualties from machine-gun and sustained artillery fire. Six awards of the Victoria Cross were made among the Lancashires at W Beach, while a further six Victoria Crosses were awarded among the infantry and sailors at V Beach and another three were awarded the following day. Among these awards was the first to a Welshman at Gallipoli.

Able Seaman William Charles Williams was born in Stanton Lacy, Shropshire on 15 September 1880, the son of William and Elizabeth Williams. The family moved to Chepstow and Williams was raised there from the age of 7. He joined the Royal Navy in 1895 and was promoted to boy, first class in 1896, seaman in 1898 and able seaman

The battleship HMS Cornwallis *firing a salvo at Turkish positions at Gallipoli.*

in 1901. He was commended for his bravery when serving aboard HMS *Terrible* in the Naval Brigade off South Africa during the Boer War and in China during the Boxer Rising.

He left the regular service in 1910, joining the Royal Naval Reserve, and worked in the police force and in a steel works in Newport but he was mobilized in August

Able Seaman William Charles Williams VC, of Chepstow.

1914, rejoining the Royal Navy and early in 1915 was posted aboard the converted steamship HMS *River Clyde*, which had been adapted for use as a landing ship for the invasion of the Gallipoli Peninsula.

By 11 April the *River Clyde* was in Mudros harbour, where she took aboard some 2,000 men of 86 Brigade, 29th Division. On the morning of 25 April she sailed to take part in the landing at Cape Helles under the command of Commander Edward Unwin and beached at V Beach beneath the Sedd el Bahr Castle, on the tip of the Gallipoli Peninsula. Three gallant attempts to land from her by the men of the Munsters, Royal Dublins and Hampshires all ended in failure and it was nightfall before the men tried again.

Williams became one of six men from the *River Clyde* to win the Victoria Cross during the day. The *London Gazette* of 16 August 1915 reads: 'The King has been graciously pleased to approve of the grant of the Victoria Cross to the undermentioned Officers and men for the conspicuous acts of bravery mentioned in the foregoing despatch.' The despatch stated:

> As the 'River Clyde' grounded, the lighters which were to form the bridge to the shore were run out ahead of the collier, but unfortunately they failed to reach their proper stations and a gap was left between two lighters over which it was impossible for men to cross; some attempted to land by jumping from the lighter which was in position into the sea and wading ashore; this method proved too costly, the lighter being soon heaped with dead and the disembarkation was ordered to cease.
>
> The troops in the 'River Clyde' were protected from rifle and machine-gun fire and were in comparative safety.
>
> Commander Unwin, seeing how things were going, left the 'River Clyde' and, standing up to his waist in water under a very heavy fire, got the lighters into position; he was assisted in this work by Midshipman G.L. Drewry, R.N.R., of H.M.S. 'Hussar'; Midshipman W. St A. Malleson, R.N., of H.M.S. 'Cornwallis'; Able Seaman W.C. Williams, O.N. 186774 (R.F.R. B.3766) and Seaman R.N.R. George McKenzie Samson, O.N. 2408A, both of H.M.S. 'Hussar'.

The 34-year-old from Chepstow has no known grave and is commemorated on the Portsmouth Naval Memorial. He had become the first posthumous Royal Naval winner of the Victoria Cross. There are two memorials to him in Chepstow: a painting of the event by Charles Dixon hangs in St Mary's Church, and a naval gun from the German submarine *UB-91*, presented by King George V, stands in the town's main square beside the war memorial. In Shropshire, a memorial plaque is affixed to the parish war memorial in the churchyard at Stanton Lacy. His Victoria Cross is held in the Lord Ashcroft collection and is sometimes displayed at the Imperial War Museum.

Back on S Beach the 2nd SWB were holding on to their gains, sustaining heavy casualties from snipers from the direction of Hill 236. Lieutenant Colonel Casson

The naval gun presented to Chepstow by King George V in honour of Seaman William Charles Williams.

therefore decided to secure their positions against any impending counter-attack. D Company and a platoon of C held De Tott's, three platoons of B and one of C formed the front line along a ridge facing north, the remainder being in support nearer the beach, while a field hospital was set up in some trees below De Tott's.

No counter-attack materialized but the remainder of the 29th Division was held up and as a result the 2nd SWB were ordered to hold their positions. By the end of the first day of the Gallipoli campaign, according to the War Diary, the battalion had lost at S Beach Major Margesson and Lieutenant Behrens and twelve men killed; Captains Dudley Graham Johnson and Gerald Hailey Birkett and Lieutenant W.J. Chamberlain and forty men wounded, with six other ranks missing. At Y Beach, where A Company had landed, Captain Palmer, along with 17 other ranks, had been killed, 42 had been wounded and 9 more were missing. In reality, casualty figures were hard to work out at the time due to the confusion that arose during the fighting and in fact only sixteen men of the battalion are officially listed as being killed on the 25th.

During the night there were several heavy bursts of fire from Turkish positions along a ridge some 800 metres away, but the main problems of dwindling ammunition and supplies were averted when two pinnaces arrived from *Cornwallis*, towing boats crammed with supplies.

Meanwhile the ANZACs had begun landing at around 4.30 am and were advancing up the cliffs overlooking Anzac Cove. Lieutenant Colonel Onslow Thompson of the 4th AIF had led his men ashore at midday and immediately moved them to support the troops that had landed earlier. The 4th AIF moved to positions at 400 Plateau, filling

Landing supplies on the Gallipoli beaches.

a gap to the side of the 8th AIF, and stemmed a Turkish counter-attack. On the following morning Thompson received unconfirmed orders to carry out a general advance and at 3 pm that day led his men forward, veering to the left flank with half the battalion while Major MacNaughton took the remainder. Thompson's men became isolated in a clearing known as the Daisy Patch and begun suffering heavy casualties. Charles Bean, the Australian historian, later wrote: 'So, led by two of the bravest and most highly trained officers in the force, without the vaguest instruction or any idea as to an objective, the 4th – the one whole and intact battalion in the 1st Division – went blindly on to Lone Pine...in a brave but useless advance.'

In this dire situation Thompson ordered a retreat, leading his men back across 400 Plateau under heavy rifle and machine-gun fire. However, he did not make it to safety; instead he fell dead among dozens of his men, the victim of one of the many errors with which the war was strewn.

Thompson was not the first Welshman killed at Gallipoli while serving with the ANZACs. That dubious honour goes to at least eight men killed during the first day: Private Charles Bale (479),

Lieutenant Colonel Astley John Onslow Thompson, commander of the 4th Battalion, Australian Imperial Force. Thompson was from the mining village of Pontyates in Carmarthenshire and had emigrated to Australia many years before the war, where he managed the Camden Park Estate near Sydney. Thompson's body was recovered from the battlefield after his death on 26 April and he was buried in the wall of a trench. His grave was later reinterred in 4th Battalion Parade Ground Cemetery.

184

7th Battalion, AIF of Newport, Monmouthshire; Private Arthur Clifford Bowen (6/1018), Canterbury Regiment, NZEF of Gelligaer; Private Fothergill William Swinfen Cottrell (288), 11th Battalion, AIF of Caerau; Private Rhys Emlyn Griffiths (428), 7th Battalion, AIF of Llanelli; Sergeant James Muncaster Lovatt (303), 9th Battalion, AIF of Betws-y-Coed; Private George William Moss (1164), 9th Battalion, AIF of Pontypool; Private John Elias Roberts (984), 6th Battalion, AIF of Bethesda; and Private Humphrey Williams (1121), 12th Battalion, AIF of Newborough.

Cottrell's death perfectly illustrates the chaos surrounding the landings. His battalion landed as part of the first wave at around 4.30 am under heavy rifle and machine-gun fire before attacking the Turkish trenches and driving the defenders back, occupying trenches about three-quarters of a mile beyond the beach. Cottrell was 22 years old when he was killed during the landings and is also commemorated on the Lone Pine Memorial. His parents received varying reports of their son's death. Early interviews with surviving members of his battalion reported that he had been wounded and hospitalized at Alexandria, while another man stated that he had seen him in England some months after. A court of enquiry was held in France on 10 April 1916 and it was only during the course of that enquiry that Cottrell was officially recorded as missing, presumed killed on 25 April 1915.

The 1st Battalion, Border Regiment, also part of 87 Brigade, had landed at X Beach under the command of Major Charles Davies Vaughan DSO. Vaughan was born on 22 August 1868, the son of Captain Herbert Vaughan and Julia Vaughan, of Brynog, Felinfach. He had served in the South African War of 1899–1902 and had been awarded the DSO for his gallantry there. At the outbreak of the Great War he was in Burma with the 1st Battalion, Border Regiment. He had married Dorothy Jean Ashby at Maymyo, Burma, on 14 August 1914 and she returned to her home at Crabtree Cottage, Wanborough, Guildford, Surrey, while Vaughan returned with his battalion to England, landing at Avonmouth on 10 January 1915. He was 47 years old when he was killed at X Beach and is buried at Pink Farm Cemetery, Helles. He is also commemorated on a memorial at St Michael's Church, Ystrad. His brother, Philip, died later in the war. (Another Welshman killed in Vaughan's battalion during the landings was Private Joseph Edward Williams (6280) of Rhyl.)

Of all the Welshmen killed during the day, the first was most probably Able Seaman Arthur James Taylor (J/7878) of Cardiff. Taylor had joined the Royal Navy on 9 June 1911 and by 5 June 1914 was serving aboard the battleship HMS *Queen*. He had been among a large number of sailors allocated to a 'picket list', taking the ANZACs ashore aboard small craft called pinnaces. He was killed when his pinnace was struck by a Turkish shell while bringing troops to Anzac Cove during the early hours.

A very well-known Welshman was killed during the second day of the campaign: Lieutenant Colonel Charles Hotham Montagu Doughty-Wylie, VC, CB, CMG. Doughty-Wylie was born on 23 July 1868 at Theburton Hall, Theburton, Leiston, Suffolk, the son of Henry M. Doughty and Edith Doughty (née Cameron). He married Lilian Oimara Wylie on 1 June 1904 and the couple bought a house at Bangor Teifi, Cardiganshire.

A view of the Lone Pine Memorial, Gallipoli. The memorial bears the names of 4,900 Australian and New Zealand servicemen who died in the Anzac area – the New Zealanders prior to the fighting in August 1915 – whose graves are not known. Others named on the memorial died at sea and were buried in Gallipoli waters.

After passing out from Sandhurst in 1889, he was commissioned in the Royal Welsh Fusiliers and served around the Empire in India, Crete and Afghanistan, before fighting in the Boer War, the Boxer Rebellion and in Somaliland. He then became British Consul in Turkey, leading a party of Ottoman troops to quell a massacre at Mersina and was awarded the Order of the Medjidie by the Ottoman government.

After the outbreak of the Great War he was attached to General Sir Ian Hamilton's headquarters staff, which was preparing for the landings at Gallipoli, due to his in-depth knowledge of 'all things Turkish'. Following the landings at Cape Helles on 25 April 1915, several senior officers had been killed, so on 26 April Doughty-Wylie organized and led an attack against the village and fort at Sedd el Bahr. Although successful, Doughty-Wylie and his second-in-command were both killed at the moment of victory. He was 46 years old and was buried close to where he was killed.

Lieutenant Colonel Charles Hotham Montagu Doughty-Wylie VC, CB, CMG, killed Sedd el Bahr on 26 April 1915.

His grave is today the one solitary Commonwealth war grave on the Gallipoli Peninsula. He was posthumously awarded the Victoria Cross for his actions. The citation was published in the *London Gazette* of 23 June 1915 and reads as follows:

On 26th April 1915 subsequent to a landing having been effected on the beach at a point on the Gallipoli Peninsula, during which both Brigadier-General and Brigade Major had been killed, Lieutenant-Colonel Doughty-Wylie and Captain Walford organised and led an attack through and on both sides of the village of

Sedd el Bahr on the old castle at the top of the hill inland. The enemy's position was very strongly held and entrenched and defended with concealed machine-guns and pom-poms. It was mainly due to the initiative, skill and great gallantry of these two officers that the attack was a complete success. Both were killed in the moment of victory.

The isolated grave of Lieutenant Colonel Charles Hotham Montagu Doughty-Wylie VC, CB, CMG.

His lover – the writer, traveller, spy and archaeologist Gertrude Bell, who would become one of the chief architects of the campaign in Mesopotamia – reputedly visited his grave while the Gallipoli campaign was still in full swing.

Meanwhile, the 2nd SWB had survived the first night at Gallipoli but the Turkish defences were still firm. The men continued work on improving their defences while fighting continued from the other beaches and the battalion lost another twenty men killed during the day, one of whom was Lance Corporal Charles James Foley (10629), one of the men awarded the Distinguished Conduct Medal at Tsingtao. Also killed that day was a Canadian member of the battalion, Lance Corporal Charles Henry Abbott (10657) of Winnipeg.

Among the awards received by officers and men of the 2nd SWB for the Gallipoli landings, the following three men were awarded the DCM for their gallantry during the day:

Private Herbert Clent (18651):

During the operations following the landing, Private Clent, accompanied by two other men, went out beyond the most advanced position to the assistance of four wounded men and remained out under a very heavy fire until he was able to bring them into safety. He then at once rejoined the firing line. He has on all occasions given a fine example of bravery and devotion to duty.

Private Percy Hendy (9929):

During the operations following the landing, Private Hendy, accompanied by two other men, went out beyond the most advanced position to the assistance of four wounded men and remained out under a very heavy fire, until he was able to bring them into safety. He then at once rejoined the firing line. He has on all occasions given a fine example of bravery and devotion to duty.

Lance Corporal Alfred Richard Spinks (9121):

During the operations following the landing, Private Spinks, accompanied by two other men, went out beyond the most advanced position and remained out, under a very heavy fire, attending four wounded men until he was able to bring them into safety. He then at once rejoined the firing line. He has on all occasions given a fine example of bravery and devotion to duty.

The 2nd SWB were firmly established at De Tott's by the end of the day, but the commanders of the allied forces seemed unaware of their success and no further orders reached the battalion until the afternoon of 27 April. Lieutenant Colonel Casson was informed that French troops would relieve the battalion, which was to march across the peninsula to rejoin the remainder of 87 Brigade. It was almost 7 pm before the first French troops arrived and it was at some time after midnight that Casson marched the battalion off towards X Beach, arriving there at around 5.30 am on 28 April.

The battalion was tired but relatively unscathed compared to the other units within the brigade, so Casson was ordered to get his men ready for an attack against Achi

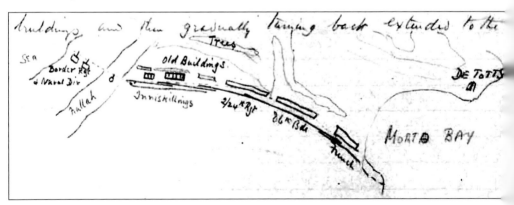

Map showing the positions of the 29th Division at Gallipoli on 28 April 1915. The 2/SWB are shown as 2/24th – originally the regiment was the 24th of Foot. (Battalion War Diary)

Baba by 8 am. The brigade was to advance north-east astride Gully Ravine, with 88 Brigade on its right ordered to attack Krithia. The attack began as planned but as the sun rose higher the heat and the poor terrain began to slow the men.

The Turks, by now reinforced by a fresh division, began putting up a stout fight, the rugged terrain within Gully Ravine giving them ideal defensive positions, and the attack began to wither. At around 1 pm the Turks counter-attacked against the Border Regiment and only a timely salvo from the guns of HMS *Queen Elizabeth*, anchored offshore, saved the situation. By now the attack had petered out; the exhausted troops had no more to give and the last reinforcements had been brought in at 2.30 pm to counter a Turkish attack. By dusk only the 2nd SWB were holding on to their gains, the remnants of both 86 and 87 brigade having been forced to retire due to the French failure to advance. The battalion had lost a further 12 men killed, 29 missing and 86 wounded during the day. As night fell upon the parched and tired men, the heavens opened and the first night in Gully Ravine became one of suffering as conditions changed to soaking wet and cold.

The landings had initially given some hope of success, but the failure by the allied commanders to exploit any successful gains had, unknown to them, doomed the future of the campaign. Apart from a few limited advances inland by small groups of men, most troops stayed on or close to the beaches, so the allied attack lost momentum and the Turks had time to bring up reinforcements. The failure to capture Achi Baba on 28 April marked the end of the first stage of the Gallipoli campaign and the situation settled into a stalemate.

The mood was now gloomy throughout the peninsula but news was relayed to the men that an Australian submarine, HMAS *AE2* under the command of an Irishman, Lieutenant Commander Henry Stoker, had succeeded in getting through the straits on

An atmospheric photograph of some simple whitewashed wooden crosses overlooking the sea.

the night of 24/25 April and had torpedoed a large Turkish gunboat. This news raised the morale of the troops ashore, especially the ANZACs, and is believed to have contributed to the decision to keep the men ashore to continue the campaign instead of conceding defeat and withdrawing them to safety.

The remainder of April proved uneventful for the 2nd SWB but at around 10 pm on 1 May the position in front of 87 and 88 brigades was attacked by masses of Turks shouting 'Allah! Allah!'. Furious fighting continued overnight and the men later commentated on the noise of the Turkish attack: 'The noise was deafening, they yelled and shouted like madmen, but above all the cry of "Allah" could be heard.' The British pushed the line forward on the following morning, advancing across ground covered with Turkish dead, but with little artillery support and the men being exhausted, they withdrew to their original positions in the afternoon. The 2nd SWB were relieved and moved to the beach, where the men could at last get some sleep.

A further attempt to break out of Gully Ravine was attempted, with the intention of taking the town of Krithia. On 6 May an attack took place by 88 and 125 brigades from a line running from Gully Ravine to the sea but it made little progress. A further attempt was made on 7 May by 88 and 125 brigades, with 87 Brigade in reserve. Lieutenant Colonel Casson had been sent to command a brigade of the Royal Naval Division so Captain Greenway took command of the 2nd SWB. His orders were to push through the attacking brigade should a breakthrough be made and advance towards Krithia. The Borderers advanced up Gully Ravine and relieved some territorial troops in the front line and overnight advanced and dug a new fire trench from the sea to the gully, with a communication trench back to the original line. On the following morning the New Zealand Brigade and the 2nd Australian Brigade arrived after being moved from Anzac to support the attack on Krithia and 87 Brigade was ordered to support their attack.

An inadequate artillery bombardment opened up at 5.30 pm on 8 May and ten minutes later the attack began. Heavy fire then opened up on the attackers and the effort failed about 100 metres from the Turkish trenches. Twenty-eight men from the 2nd SWB had been killed.

With the Gallipoli campaign already having stalled, the British began planning to send reinforcements to the area to prepare for an attempt to break the stalemate. The 2nd SWB would remain, for the time being, the only Welsh unit ashore, holding on to its positions in Gully Ravine.

The Gallipoli campaign was not all about fighting on land, however. Even after the failure of the initial naval expedition into the Dardanelles Straits, the Royal Navy and the French maintained a powerful presence offshore, the mighty battleships using their powerful naval guns to strike Turkish targets ashore.

However, this was not an easy or safe task. Many ships became casualties to the incursions of German submarines, Turkish torpedo boats and mine-layers during the campaign. Of these, HMS *Inflexible* had been mined and damaged on 18 March; HMS *Irresistible* and HMS *Ocean* were mined and sunk on 18 March; HMS *Goliath* was torpedoed and sunk on 13 May; HMS *Triumph* was torpedoed and sunk off Anzac

The Canopus-*class battleship HMS* Goliath, *sunk off the Gallipoli coast on 13 May 1915.*

Cove on 25 May; HMS *Majestic* was torpedoed and sunk off Cape Helles on 27 May; the destroyer HMS *Louis* ran aground during a gale and was destroyed by shellfire on 31 October; while the submarines *E7*, *E15*, *E20* and *AE2* were also sunk. The French lost their battleship *Bouvet* on 18 March, the battleship *Masséna* in November, and four submarines.

Of interest to the role played by Wales in the war was the loss of the battleship HMS *Goliath* on 13 May.

Upon the outbreak of the Great War, many reservists were recalled for active service and joined ships in the reserve fleets. HMS *Goliath* was classed as a first-class battleship of the *Canopus*-class and was laid down at Chatham Dockyard on 4 January 1897. She was launched on 23 March 1898 and commissioned at Chatham on 27 March 1900. Designed for the China station, she had a narrow draught to enable her to use the Suez Canal. She remained there until 1903 and in 1904 went into commissioned reserve at Portsmouth. In May 1905 she joined the Mediterranean Fleet, transferring to the Channel Fleet in December and remaining there until March 1907. She was then commissioned in April 1909 at Sheerness for the 4th Fleet (Nore Reserve).

HMS *Goliath* was mothballed in 1913 and joined the 3rd Fleet (Pembroke Reserve) at Pembroke Dock, to be brought out in August 1914 to join the battle squadron operating from Devonport. Her complement was drawn up from the Royal Naval Reserve on 2 August 1914 and included a large number of Welsh personnel, mainly from the towns of Milford Haven and Pembroke Dock.

She was despatched in September 1914 to the East Indies for escort duties, operating against the German light cruiser *Königsberg* in November (Rufigi River,

East Africa). In April 1915 she was transferred to the Dardanelles to support the landings at X and Y Beaches at Cape Helles. She was damaged on 25 April and 2 May and was finally sunk while at anchor in Morto Bay on 13 May by three torpedoes fired by the Turkish torpedo boat *Muâvenet-i Millîye*, with the loss of 570 of her crew. At least thirty-eight of these men were Welsh.

One of the men was Private Thomas George Parry (PLY/15060), Royal Marine Light Infantry. Parry was born on 12 November 1891, the son of Arthur Rees Parry and Margaret Parry, of Thomas Street, Llanelli. He had enlisted into the Royal Marines during 1909 and had seen service around the world prior to the outbreak of war. He was posted aboard *Goliath* following her recommissioning. He was 23 years old when he died during her sinking on 13 May and is commemorated on the Plymouth Naval Memorial, Devon.

Private Thomas George Parry (PLY/15060) of the Royal Marine Light Infantry. He was killed during the sinking of HM Goliath *in Morto Bay on 13 M. 1915.*

The 2nd SWB were involved in several more attempts to dislodge the Turks from their positions to the east of Gully Ravine throughout May and especially June, when the Turks launched several attacks of their own. From 11 to 16 June Second Lieutenant Michael Spartali and eleven men were killed, while between 17 to 27 June four officers – Lieutenant John Jordan, Second Lieutenants Hugh Lancelot Cass, Barham Ivor Lewis Jones and Cubitt Noel Rundle – and twenty-nine men fell.

Another large attack was planned for 28 June: 87 Brigade was to lead, the 2nd SWB starting the attack west of Gully Ravine, while the Border Regiment would attack to the east and the KOSB and Inniskillings would then advance through them.

At 9 am on 28 June an artillery bombardment opened up and the attacking troops rose from their trenches and advanced. The 2nd SWB managed to capture their objectives despite heavy losses and the supporting battalions then advanced. The western attack proved successful, the troops reaching a point later called Fusiliers Bluff, but the eastern attack was not so fortunate.

The 2nd SWB had suffered Lieutenant Wrinch Joseph Charles Budd and thirty-six men killed, Lieutenant John Frank Bradley mortally wounded, and Captains Habershon and Williams, Lieutenant Ffrench and Second Lieutenant Nicholas and 160 men wounded, many of whom died over the coming days. Lieutenant Rupert Charles Inglis of Glangwye, Builth Wells, a man who had become renowned for his gallantry, also died on 29 June of wounds suffered earlier in the month.

Lieutenant Rupe Charles Inglis of 2nd SWB. A nati of Builth Wells, . died of wounds 29 June 1915.

His brother, Harold John Inglis, also served with the 2nd SWB and was awarded the Military Cross for the action, later being recommended for the VC but awarded the DSO:

Second-Lieutenant Harold John Inglis, 3rd Battalion, the South Wales Borderers (attached 2nd Battalion). For conspicuous gallantry on the 10th and 11th June, 1915, during operations south-west of Krithia. He and his brother (Lieut. R.C. Inglis, of the same battalion) made a gallant attempt to capture an enemy's sap, distant about 90 yards. Crawling over the open ground with their men, they reached the sap, which was about five feet deep, increasing to seven or eight feet, down which the party had to proceed in single file. The party were checked in the deepest part of the sap by machine gun fire and bombs and had to retire. Second-Lieutenant H.J. Inglis then made a second attempt and again seized the sap-head. Advancing along the sap, he was wounded and was eventually forced to retire by very heavy rifle fire. He showed great skill and gallantry in a difficult position. Lieut. R.C. Inglis was wounded and has since died of his wounds.

One of many casualties during the coming months of stalemate was a former Aberystwyth Town footballer. Captain Edward Dickinson was born at Burnley in 1886, the son of Dr David Dickinson and Jane Dickinson. He had played football for Aberystwyth while studying at the university and was science master at Darlington Technical College prior to the war. He enlisted into the Durham Light Infantry at the outbreak of war and on 24 October 1914 was commissioned in the 11th Battalion, Yorkshire Regiment (the Green Howards). In November he was promoted lieutenant and on 29 December 1914 was gazetted as captain. He left England on 25 May 1915 for the Dardanelles with reinforcements for the 1st Battalion, Royal Dublin Fusiliers, who had suffered so badly during the *River Clyde* landings, and arrived at Cape Helles on 14 June 1915. Dickinson was killed at Gallipoli on 28 June 1915 aged 29 and is commemorated on the Helles Memorial.

Captain Edward Dickinson, the former Aberystwyth footballer.

There was more to come for the Welsh soldiers here, but for now the main focus of attention becomes the Western Front and a maritime tragedy. Men continued to fall at Gallipoli over the coming months, but it was not until August that any major attacks would occur.

Chapter 12

The Sinking of the *Lusitania*

The month of May would see a tragedy on a scale not seen since the sinking of the RMS *Titanic* on 15 April 1912. In February 1915 the German government announced a campaign of unrestricted warfare. This meant that any ships carrying goods to and from Britain were in danger of attack from U-boats. This broke an international military agreement that any passenger-carrying ships were to be stopped and searched for any goods of military value before their destruction rather than risk any civilian lives.

On 1 May 1915 the Cunard liner RMS *Lusitania* left New York for Liverpool via Queenstown, Ireland. Aboard her were 1,257 passengers and 650 crewmen. At 1.20 pm on 7 May, as the *Lusitania* rounded the southern Irish coast heading back to Liverpool, the German submarine *U-20* surfaced to recharge her batteries. Spotting the *Lusitania*, her Captain Schweiger ordered the firing of a single torpedo at the helpless liner. The torpedo struck the *Lusitania*, setting off a second larger internal explosion. Sinking rapidly and listing badly, only six out of forty-eight lifeboats were launched successfully and within just eighteen minutes the *Lusitania* had disappeared.

Of the 1,907 passengers and crew on board, around 1,200 lives were lost despite valiant rescue attempts by local lifeboatmen and fishermen and the arrival of some Royal Navy destroyers. Among the dead were over 100 American citizens, causing an outcry in the press on both sides of the Atlantic. In the days following the disaster, huge efforts were made to recover bodies floating in the Irish Sea and many that had washed up on the coast. Many of these were buried in Queenstown (now named Cobh), while some were returned to their families for burial.

Among the people on board were at least forty Welsh passengers and crew, including several entire families, a male voice choir known as the Gwent Glee Singers and also many people with Welsh connections. They – and details of what became of them – are listed below.

Henry Adams, aged 58, was born at Tenby on 13 May 1856, the son of William Adams and Susannah Adams (née Gunstone). He was a successful businessman prior to the war and had married an American, Annie Elizabeth McNutt, in 1915. The couple had booked to return to Britain aboard the RMS *Lusitania* four weeks after their marriage. Adams and his wife had boarded a lifeboat but a wave swept Adams overboard and he was drowned. A casualty list from Cunard shows that his body was found but he does not appear on the burial register of the *Lusitania* victims. He is, in fact, buried along with his first wife in St Mary's Churchyard, Tenby.

THE SYRACUSE HERALD. EXTRA

PRICE TWO CENTS   VOL. 29, NO. 11,885.   SYRACUSE, N. Y., FRIDAY EVENING, MAY 7, 1915.   ON SALE EVERYWHERE IN SYRACUSE AT OR BEFORE 5 P. M.

THE LUSITANIA SINKS

The Lusitania, British Liner Torpedoed To-day by German Submarine.

GREAT WASTE IN PRINTING, SAYS WITNESS IN LIBEL TRIAL

Home, Testifying for Roosevelt, Charges Extravagance.

PROTEST BY IVINS

Barnes Counsel Tries to Bar Testimony—May Be Stricken Out, But It Will Leave Bad Effect on Jury

Big Cunard Liner Goes Down After Submarine Attack.

HAS 1,400 PASSENGERS

Fate of Those Aboard Liner Unknown, But It Is Believed Most of Them Were Saved by the Ship's Boats.

Believe Ship Was Afloat for More Than 12 Hours

News Strikes Washington Officials Like a Bomb

SAY SHIP WAS BEACHED

TRAWLER DON BLOWN UP

SENT CALL FOR HELP

FLEW AMERICAN FLAG

First Class Passengers Aboard

THE LUSITANIA

First News From Queenstown

MRS. SARAH LANSING DIES

'The Lusitania Sinks'. Outraged headlines in an American newspaper, the Syracuse Herald, on 7 May 1915.

Edward Booth-Jones, aged 38, of Colwyn Bay was an antiques dealer with shops in St Anne's Square, Manchester, Chester and Bond Street, London. He sold his chain of shops to move to America with his family to set up a new business. The family was returning to Wales to visit relatives when they were all lost during the sinking of the

The commemorative headstone to Henry Adams at Tenby.

Henry Adams, the Tenby businessman drowned while escaping from the stricken Lusitania.

Lusitania. His wife Millichamp was 25 years old and their daughter Ailsa was 8 years old, while their son Percival was aged just 4. The bodies of Millichamp and Ailsa, who was found dressed in a green velvet dress, lace-up boots and a blue jersey, were recovered from the sea and buried together in Queenstown.

Musician Edwin Carr-Jones, aged 37, of Barmouth was a member of the *Lusitania*'s band, which was midway through playing the *Blue Danube* waltz when the torpedo first struck. His body was not recovered.

Paul Crompton, aged 44, of Barry, Glamorgan, was travelling with his wife and six children from their home in Pennsylvania to visit family in Wales. He was the grandson of Lord Romilly of Barry. The whole family of eight was lost: his wife Gladys Mary, aged 38, and their six children: Stephen, aged 14; Alberta, aged 13; Katherine; Paul, aged 9; John, aged 6; and Peter, aged just 9 months. Gladys was the elder daughter of Major General G. Salis Schwabe CB and Mrs Salis and the granddaughter of Sir William Milbourne James of Swansea.

Annie Crosby of Bagillt was a nurse who had emigrated to Vancouver in 1910, along with her sister Ellen. Both sisters were returning to Wales to visit their mother at The Cottage, Voelgron, Bagillt, when they were drowned in the sinking.

Annie Davies, aged 52, of Gowerton was returning to Wales to visit her daughter,

Mrs J. Lewis Phillips, at Greenfield Villas, Llanelli. Her body was identified by members of her family and buried at Queenstown.

Fred Davies, aged 37, was a member of the *Lusitania*'s crew and was the son of Ivor and Mary Ann Davies of 13 Jeffrey Street, Newport, Monmouthshire. He was drowned.

George F. Davies, aged 43, was the conductor of the Gwent Glee Singers and was drowned.

John Davies, aged 62, was a member of the crew; the son of John and Ann Davies of Dylynog, Denbighshire. He was drowned.

Robert H. Duncan, 3rd Engineer, of Porthmadog, was the brother-in-law of David Jones of 18 Snowdon Street, Porthmadog. He was rescued after being in the water for over two hours.

Alexander Hubert Ferrier of Bangor was the brother of Mr E.L. Ferrier of Montrose, Bangor. He was an Irishman and had been a fruit farmer in British Columbia but was returning to Britain with his wife and child to take up a commission in the army. His wife, Elizabeth Mary, was rescued but Alexander and their young daughter Sheila, who was just 18 months old, were drowned. Elizabeth identified the recovered body of her daughter who was buried in a mass grave in Queenstown.

Margaret Elizabeth Foulkes (née Hughes), aged 42, a stewardess aboard the *Lusitania*, was the daughter of John and Jane Hughes of Sandycroft. She was drowned.

Richard Gaul, aged 35, a greaser aboard the *Lusitania*, was the son of James and Sarah Gaul of Swansea. He was drowned.

Christopher William Griffiths, aged 32, had been one of many Welsh ex-pats who had settled in Winnipeg and was returning to Wales to visit his family. He was rescued.

George Edward Harries, aged 30, of Pembroke, was a waiter aboard the *Lusitania* and drowned. He is commemorated on the Tower Hill Memorial, London.

William Spencer Hill, aged 29, of Llangattock, was the conductor of the Gwent Glee Singers. He carried out a series of fund-raising concerts around Wales after being rescued and returning home safely.

John Bernard Stoughton Holborne, aged 43, of Holyhead, was the cousin of Mr H.H. Williams JP DL of Trearddur and Trecastell, Anglesey. His family was from Holyhead but Holborne lived in Edinburgh, where he was a well-known university lecturer. He was rescued from the water and later purchased the Scottish isle of Foula.

David Taraulais Hopkins from Fforestfach, Swansea, was a renowned baritone who was returning to Fforestfach after a tour of North America with the Gwent Glee Singers. He was drowned.

Thomas Owen Hughes, aged 41, was the son of John and Ellen Hughes of Ffrith, Treuddyn. He worked for Cunard as a storekeeper aboard the *Lusitania*. As a merchant mariner he is commemorated on the Tower Hill Memorial, London. He lived with his wife Alice Hughes at 78 Northgate Street, Chester.

Henry St Giles Humphreys, aged 29, was the son of Reverend

The Welsh baritone, David John Hopkins, of Fforestfach, Swansea.

Henry James Humphreys and Sydney Humphreys (née Williams) of Llangan Rectory. Although Welsh-born, he was a nationalized American who had gone to California in 1913. He was returning to enlist and was one of three brothers who lost their lives during the war.

Alfred Jones, aged 36, a night-watchman aboard the *Lusitania*, was the son of Mary Ellen Jones of Wrexham. He was drowned.

Evan Jones, aged 59, was the son of John and Joyse Jones of Cwmhowel, Llansawel. He had emigrated to America in 1883 to escape a paternity lawsuit and settled at Ottumwa, Iowa where he worked as a coal miner and became a naturalized American citizen in 1896. After almost thirty years living in the town, Jones decided to sell up and return to Llansawel, where his family and illegitimate daughter still lived to see out the rest of his life. His death triggered an international lawsuit when his siblings fought a bitter battle over his substantial estate with his daughter.

Frederick Robert Jones, aged 30, was born in Portland Street, Aberystwyth, in 1885 and was the only son of Peter Jones JP. He was educated at Alexander Road School and Aberystwyth County School before serving an engineering apprenticeship in Green's Foundry, Aberystwyth and took up employment at Metcalfe's engineering works in Manchester and the Great Western Railway works in Swindon. To progress his career he left for Canada in March 1912 and was employed in construction work on the Canadian Northern and Canadian Pacific railways. Realizing the urgent need for his engineering skills for the war effort, he made the decision in 1915 to return home on the first available vessel and offer his experience to the booming armaments industry. He was drowned.

Frederick Robert Jones of Aberystwyth.

Isaac Talbot Jones was a baritone with the Gwent Glee Singers and was drowned in the sinking.

Mary Elizabeth Jones, aged 43, was born in Llanfairfechan in 1872, the youngest daughter of Richard and Grace Jones of Church Cottage, Llanfairfechan. She had worked as a stewardess for Cunard for many years and had moved to 95 Brynland Avenue, Bristol. She survived the sinking but after two hours in the water she had lost her strength and slipped into the depths. Her body was later recovered and buried at Queenstown. A brass plaque in her memory was erected at Llanfairfechan Church in August 1916.

William Gwynne Jones, aged 24, of Blaina, was a member of the Gwent Glee Singers. He found an overturned lifeboat and used it to rescue William Spencer Hill.

Owen Ladd, aged 33, was born at St Dogmaels in 1882, the son of William and Phoebe Ladd. His parents later moved to The Mount, Eglwyswrw, while he moved to Pentre, Rhondda, where his brother John resided. Ladd had gone to Canada prior to the war and lived at 218 Carlton Street, Winnipeg, Manitoba, where he worked as a jeweller and had acted as secretary for a touring Welsh choir. His elder brother, David James Ladd, was already living in Winnipeg with his wife, Allie Dee Ladd. By 1915 he had decided to go home to live with his parents at Eglwyswrw and sailed from New York aboard the *Lusitania* on 1 May 1915. He was drowned in the sinking.

Owen Ladd (right) with his brother, David James Ladd.

Frank William Lancaster, aged 50, was from Swansea. He had travelled widely, running a rubber plantation in Ceylon before travelling to Canada. He was returning aboard the *Lusitania* with the intention of settling down in Swansea where his brother, Doctor le Cronier Lancaster, practised but was drowned in the sinking.

Idwal Lewis, 3rd Officer, was the son of John Lewis JP of Belle Vue, Porthmadog. He spent over four hours in the water and was almost exhausted when he was spotted and rescued.

Lady Margaret Haig Mackworth, aged 32, was the daughter of David Alfred Thomas and had travelled with her father from a visit to his Pennsylvania coal mines. She toured Wales on her return, giving speeches relating to her experiences during the sinking. She died in London on 20 July 1958, aged 75.

Charles Martin, aged 31, was the son of Isaiah Martin of Berry Street, Conway. He was returning from Pittsburgh to visit his family but was drowned in the sinking.

Walter McLean, aged 38, was a member of Salem Chapel, Porthmadog and was returning to Wales to visit his mother at Gwynle, Garth. He worked in Canada and France as a representative of the T. Faton Company. He was drowned in the sinking.

Lady Margaret Haig Mackworth, daughter of Lord Rhondda, who also survived the sinking of the Lusitania.

Dewi Michael, aged 38, was one of the members of the Gwent Glee Choir and was saved from the sea. He was interviewed after returning home: 'I shall never forget my experiences; it was so awful and so terrible. It will ever be indelibly impressed on my memory. What I saw and what I heard will ever be amongst the most vivid re-collections of my life.' The choir had intended to sail home on the SS *Transylvania* but the *Lusitania* was ready to go and, being a faster steamer, the choir thought it would be nice to get home early.

James Osborne, aged 30, a fireman aboard the *Lusitania*, was the son of James and Catherine Osborne of Swansea. He was drowned.

Cecilia Owens, aged 36, was from Swansea. She was rescued but lost her twin sons, Reginald and Ronald, aged 8, as well as her brother Alfred Smith, her sister-in-law Elizabeth Smith and her nephew Hubert. She returned to her husband in America afterwards but returned to Swansea after the war, dying there on 20 July 1966 aged 87.

Owen Owens, aged 65, an able seaman aboard the *Lusitania*, was the son of Owen and Mary Owens, of Holyhead. He was drowned.

Charles Edwin Paynter, aged 63, was the son of William Cox Paynter, of Tyddyndai, Amlwch. He was a timber broker and occasionally worked for the Mersey Docks and Harbour Board and was returning from a business trip to America with his daughter Irene, who was saved. His body was recovered from the sea and he was buried in Bidston Churchyard, Cheshire. Irene lived in the village of Syresham for the rest of her life.

Polly Phillips, a stewardess aboard the *Lusitania*, was from Swansea and was the sister of Harry Phillips, of 149 Bryn Road, Swansea. She was rescued from the sea and returned to Glasgow where she lived with her sister Fanny, another Cunard stewardess.

Thomas Pringle from Wales, a first-class waiter aboard the *Lusitania*, was saved. Pringle was a Welshmen who had worked for Cunard for several years. During the *Lusitania*'s final voyage he was serving as orderly to the ship's medical officer. Pringle was a well-known visitor to Llangollen and his many friends there were relieved to hear of his being saved.

Arnold Rhys-Evans, aged 23, was from Cardiff and was private secretary to David Alfred Thomas (see below). He had accompanied him and his daughter, Lady Mackworth, on a visit to their Pennsylvania coal mines and was rescued from the sea.

Alfred F. Smith, aged 34, was the husband of Elizabeth and father of Hubert and Helen Smith and was originally from Swansea. Only his 6-year-old daughter, Helen, was saved, living a long life before dying in Swansea on 8 April 1993, aged 84. His wife Elizabeth was 34 years old, while Hubert was just 6 months of age.

Alfred and Elizabeth Smith of Swansea and their daughter Helen. Helen and her aunt Cecilia were the only survivors from the seven family members travelling on board the Lusitania.

David Alfred Thomas, the Welsh coal magnate, who survived the sinking of the Lusitania. *Thomas later became Lord Rhondda.*

The grave of David Thomas at Carvan Chapelyard, near Whitland. His son Ernest and his wife Mary Hannah, both victims of the Lusitania *sinking, are commemorated on the weed-covered kerbstones.*

David Alfred Thomas, aged 59, was a well-known Cardiff coal magnate and a close political adviser to David Lloyd George. He had been visiting his coal mines in Pennsylvania along with his personal secretary and daughter, Lady Mackworth. He returned to America later that year to discuss munitions contracts. He was later elevated to the peerage and became Lord Rhondda.

Ernest Thomas, aged 33, was a builder, the son of David and Ann Thomas, of 16 St John Street, Whitland. He had emigrated to Canada with his wife Mary Hannah and lived at 318 Notre Dame, Winnipeg. The couple were returning to Wales to visit his parents at Whitland when they were both drowned in the sinking. His body was recovered and buried at Queenstown, while Mary's body was not recovered.

George Henry Thomas, aged 21, an assistant officer's steward aboard the *Lusitania*, was the son of George Henry and Jessie Lavinia Thomas of St Thomas Green, Haverfordwest. He was drowned.

Thomas J. Williams, aged 32, from Wales was rescued.

William Williams, master-at-arms, of Porthmadog, was the grandson of William Williams, butcher, of Tremadoc. He was rescued.

The wireless operator aboard the *Lusitania* was a Welshman who had a lucky escape. Arthur Wilkins was the son of Elizabeth Griffiths, of the Brown's Hotel, Laugharne and had served aboard the *Lusitania* since her launch. He was at Liverpool, due to sail on the *Lusitania* to New York prior to her disastrous return voyage, when at short notice he was posted to another ship due to a member of staff being taken ill.

On Wednesday 12 May the SS *Kyleford* arrived at Barry Docks and the captain went ashore to inform the port authorities that he had picked up two bodies from the sea while steaming past the Irish coast. One body was that of a marine fireman wearing a lifebelt, while the other was that of a well-dressed lady. The bodies were brought to Barry Town Mortuary to await an inquest. A week later the woman was identified as Catherine Dietrich Willey, a 57-year-old American from Lake Forest, Chicago. Her body was embalmed and shipped to the US for burial. Mrs Willey was en route to France to work for the Red Cross.

Over 240 survivors were shipped from Dublin to Holyhead aboard the SS *Greenore*, where huge crowds, including anxious families of the victims, had gathered to greet them.

The sinking of a passenger liner full of civilians drew an angry response around the world. It ultimately helped to bring America into the war on the side of the allies and was a massive propaganda coup for recruitment into the British armed forces. As well as committing mass murder of civilians, the Germans had made an error of judgement, similar if nowhere near the same scale as to that of the Japanese attack on Pearl Harbor in December 1941.

Mrs Catherine Dietrich Willey, an American who was on her way to France to work as a Red Cross volunteer. Her body was recovered off the Irish coast and taken to Barry Dock where she was identified a week later.

While widespread condemnation of the atrocity filled the newspaper columns around the country, smaller articles showed the public that the conflict was still raging in Gallipoli and in Flanders.

Chapter 13

The Battles of Aubers Ridge and Festubert

On the Western Front, the French Commander-in-Chief, General Joffre, had asked Sir John French for the support of the British for a French offensive into the Douai Plain around late April or early May 1915. The French objectives were to capture the heights at Notre Dame de Lorette and Vimy Ridge. The British First Army was further north, between La Bassée and Ypres and it was decided that they would attack in the southern half of their front line, near the village of Laventie. Their objective was a length of higher ground known as Aubers Ridge, comprising the villages of Aubers, Fromelles and Le Maisnil. This was near the same area that had been unsuccessfully attacked in the Battle of Neuve Chapelle, so this time the Royal Engineers had been put to work tunnelling beneath the German positions to lay mines.

However, the Germans had also learned a lesson from Neuve Chapelle and had strengthened their defences, erecting machine-gun posts and fortifying their lines with multiple rows of barbed wire and two lines of breastworks. These were supported by concrete emplacements or pill-boxes, many of which still litter the land today.

The offensive was planned to begin on 9 May and would involve an assault by the 1st Division and the Meerut Division on a 2,000-metre frontage from Chocolat Menier Corner, north-east of Festubert, to the Port Arthur crossroads, south of Neuve Chapelle, coupled with an attack by the 8th Division north-east of Neuve Chapelle. The 2nd and Lahore divisions would support the main attack, which was to push towards the line Rue du Marais-Lorgies-La Cliqueterie Farm, where it would meet the 8th Division driving southward. The 1st Division planned to use 2 and 3 brigades, the latter on the left, next to the Meerut Division. The 1st Munsters and the 2nd Welsh were the attacking battalions, with the 1st SWB and 1st Gloucesters in support.

The British were confident of success and Company Sergeant Major Joshua and Sergeant Mack of the 2nd Welsh noted how the men went up to the trenches singing 'in anticipation of a real successful fight with the Boche, instead of the dreary nerve-racking atmosphere of the trenches.' However, the number of artillery pieces was limited and shells were in short supply, so their use had been rationed and this misplaced confidence among the British would soon be tested.

As the men got into their attack positions the 2nd Welsh split into four: C Company (Captain Hore) on the right; B Company (Captain Aldworth) on the left; with D Company (Captain Furber) and A Company (Captain Campbell) in support. The 1st

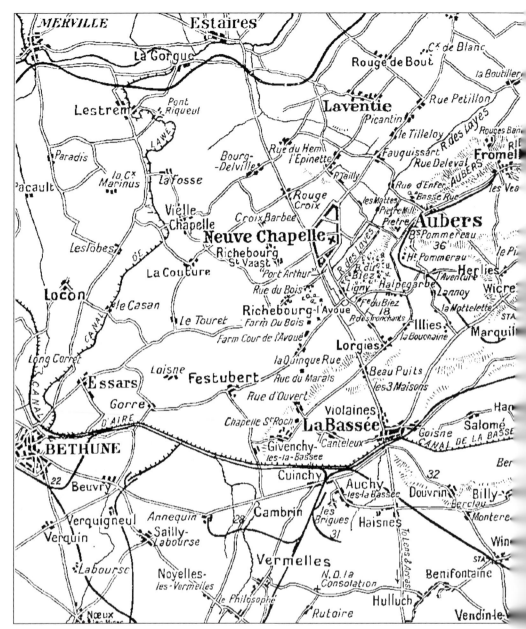

Map showing the Aubers Ridge and area.

SWB were behind the Welsh, the 1st Gloucesters behind the 1st Munsters and the 4th RWF were to mop up. Lieutenant Cripps of the 2nd Welsh wrote:

On the Welsh front there was a distance of about 150 yards between the opposing lines. About 20 yards in front of our parapet was an old trench half full of water; about 25 yards further on ran a stream, some three yards across and two feet to four feet deep with banks about two feet above the water level; then about 80 yards further came the German wire, behind which the raised enemy parapet was clearly visible. During the night the Royal Engineers had placed duckboard bridges, made of new unpainted wood, across the stream. Two platoons per Company in the first wave were to cross the stream and lie down, awaiting the other two platoons, which were to follow after the interval of a minute. The reserve companies were to advance across the open and occupy the front line trenches vacated by the leading companies.

At 5 am the bombardment opened up, the field guns began laying down fire in an attempt to cut the wire, while the howitzers bombarded the enemy breastworks and the heavy guns fired on enemy battery positions behind the lines. Forty minutes later the men attacked. Lieutenant Cripps continued:

> The shooting of the field guns was very erratic and many casualties occurred from short rounds. Dawn broke – a fine sunny morning and looking across no man's land the white bridges showed up very plainly. Few shells appeared to be going anywhere near the German wire or parapet and the tops of the bayonets of the Germans, crouching behind their parapet, could be clearly seen. As the first wave mounted the parapet it was met with a hail of bullets and many men fell back, dead or wounded, into the trench. At the end of a minute I blew my whistle and the second wave went over the top. There were no troops visible – every man was down and there were heaps of dead and wounded by every bridge.

The 4th RWF were waiting behind their breastworks for their first taste of battle while the first lines of men were cut down. When the battalion rose from its line to attack it was met by such a volume of fire that it never reached the front line. The CO, Lieutenant Colonel Frederick Charles France-Hayhurst, Captain Eric Evans, Lieutenant Brian Croom-Johnson, Second Lieutenant John Turner Clough Hazeldene, Lieutenant M. Perne (RAMC attached) and eleven other men were killed, while total casualties amounted to sixty-five men killed or wounded.

The 1st Munsters managed to get some men across no man's land into the enemy trench but they were never seen again. All along the front of I Corps the attack had failed and a heavy bombardment had to be put down to enable the survivors to withdraw.

The 1st SWB and the 1st Gloucesters then moved into position to relieve the 2nd Welsh and 1st Munsters and delivered another attack at 4 pm but that also met with failure,

Lieutenant Colonel Frederick Charles France-Hayhurst, commanding officer of the 4th RWF, killed at Aubers Ridge on 9 May 1915. He was the son of Colonel Charles Hosken France-Hayhurst, of Bostock Hall, Middlewich, Cheshire.

while the 4th RWF, now under the command of Major Meares and planning to attack at the same time, were instead told to stand firm before being withdrawn from the line that night, moving to Harisoires. The 2nd Welsh were also withdrawn to billets in Hinges, while the 1st SWB moved out at midnight and marched to billets in Hingette.

All the units involved had suffered terrible casualties. The 1st SWB had lost Captains Robert Woodward and Arthur Reginald French (Lord de Freyne); his brother, Lieutenant George Philip French; Lieutenants Alfred Clulow Fitzgerald Garnett-Botfield, Martin Viner Pollock and Noel Price James Turner; Second Lieutenants Edward Phillips Jackson and Alan Langlands; and fifty-six other ranks killed. Altogether its ranks had been thinned by ten officers and 224 men.

Arthur Reginald French (Lord de Freyne) was the son of Arthur French, 4th Baron de Freyne and Marie, Lady de Freyne, and was the husband of Lady Annabel de Freyne of 1 Green Street, Park Lane, London. He was educated at Sandhurst prior to being commissioned in the Royal Fusiliers, but resigned his commission in 1905 to become a private with the United States army, joining the 1st Battalion, 8th Infantry. He served in the Philippines until his father's death in 1913 and bought out his American enlistment to return to London, becoming the 5th Baron de Freyne.

Captain Arthur Reginald French (Lord de Freyne) the 1st SWB, killed on 9 May 1915.

Both Lord de Freyne and his brother, George Philip French, took up commissions in the 1st SWB and both were killed during the Battle of Aubers Ridge on 9 May. The brothers were originally buried together in Edward Road Cemetery No. 2, but their graves were relocated to Cabaret-Rouge British Cemetery, Souchez in 1925 and both men now lie in Plot XXVII, Row A, Grave 5.

Lieutenant Alfred Clulow Fitzgerald Garnett-Botfield was born at Bishop's Castle on 16 June 1892, the son of William Egerton Garnett-Botfield of Decker Hill, Shifnal. He was educated at Eton and Trinity College, Cambridge before being commissioned in the Rifle Brigade on 15 August 1914. After training at Sheerness he was posted to the 1st SWB in France on 22 January 1915. He was 22 years old when he was killed on 9 May. Captain A.C. Lloyd wrote to his mother after his death:

Lieutenant Alfred Clulov Fitzgerald Garnett-Botfi of the 1st SWB, killed on May 1915 aged 22.

> Your very gallant son fell in action on the 9th (Sunday). His platoon was ordered out to an advanced trench under protection of our artillery fire. The order was given to advance from there and though heavy Maxim gun fire was coming from the German lines, he at once and without any hesitation gave the command, 'Prepare to Advance.' I was

myself hit and just saw him leap out of the trench, only to fall at once, instantaneously killed. I have recommended him for his gallant conduct and only hope that an official recognition of his qualities as a soldier will receive due mention... A more efficient subaltern than your son could not be found, always ready for any work however hazardous and always most cheerful. The men all loved him and would follow him anywhere, as they always knew he could lead them.

Major Reddie wrote:

On the 9th an assault in the early morning had been attempted on the enemy's trenches. This was unsuccessful, so another was made in the afternoon, when our battalion were detailed to carry it out in one part of the line. Your son's platoon during the artillery bombardment had to crawl along an old trench in front of the breastwork in order to get nearer the enemy's lines. This they had to do under heavy fire, but succeeded so far. When the time came for the assault your son jumped up to lead his men and was shot at once before he got any distance. Several attempts were made at night to recover his body, but owing to the enemy's fire it was found impossible to do so before we were relieved at midnight but it is still hoped to do so and we had arranged to bury all the officers in an orchard near a place called Windy Corner... His body was afterwards recovered and buried on the 10th in the evening by being carried across our trench on one of the bridges used for the ditch about 100 yards on the left of the cinder track. The ditch between our line and the German line is the most permanent guide. This ditch, about 4 feet deep and 16 feet wide, runs parallel to our line, then at right angles to this into the German. The spot would be about 250 yards to our left of this junction and 40 yards from this point back in the direction of the Rue du Bois.

Garnett-Botfield's grave was subsequently lost and as a result he is commemorated on the Le Touret Memorial, Richebourg-l'Avoué.

Lieutenant Noel Price James Turner was born on 7 December 1878, the son of the Reverend John James and Harriette Augusta Turner of Pentreheylin, Llanymynech, Montgomeryshire. He was educated at Charterhouse and Keble College, Oxford and had served during the Boer War with the Montgomeryshire Yeomanry. Turner married Minnie Beck at Guilsfield near Welshpool on 25 September 1902 and the couple lived at Sylfaen Hall, Welshpool. He was commissioned in the South Wales Borderers on 4 September 1914 and was attached to the 2nd Welsh until joining the 1st SWB in March 1915.

Lieutenant Alfred Clulow Fitzgerald Garnett-Botfield's name on the Le Touret Memorial.

Lieutenant Noel Price James Turner, 1st SWB, of Sylfaen Hall, Welshpool. He died at Béthune of wounds suffered that same day, on 9 May 1915.

The grave of Lieutenant Noel Price James Turner at Béthune Town Cemetery.

Turner died in hospital at Béthune on 9 May after being severely wounded earlier that day and is buried in Béthune Town Cemetery.

The 2nd Welsh had suffered considerable losses, losing six officers: Lieutenants Hugh Gerald Annerley Corder, George Robert Murray Crofts, Frank Irving Pascoe Wells and Kenneth Herbert Clayton Woodroffe, and Second Lieutenants John William Betts and James Trevor Crawley Vincent. Eighty-three men were also killed during their attack on 9 May. Five more officers and 154 other ranks were wounded and thirty-two men were missing. Company Sergeant Major William 'Spud' Murphy (9011), one of the dead, had been a renowned rugby player, having played for Newport, Cardiff and the army. (Woodroffe's brother Sydney Clayton Woodroffe was awarded the Victoria Cross at Hooge on 30 July 1915 and was killed in the process. His medals are in the Lord Ashcroft collection.)

Second Lieutenant James Trevor Crawley Vincent was the son of the former Welsh rugby international, Sir Hugh Corbet Vincent, and Lady Bronwen Adelaide Vincent of Bronwydd, Bangor and the grandson of the Reverend James Crawley Vincent, vicar of Caernarfon. He was educated at Oswestry and Rugby schools and at Bangor University College. He was just 19 years old when he was killed near Richebourg-l'Avoué on 9 May and is buried in St Vaast Post Military Cemetery.

Lieutenant Kenneth Herbert Clayton Woodroffe of the 2nd Welsh, killed on 9 May 1915. He is commemorated on the Le Touret Memorial. Woodroffe was the son of Henry L. and Clara Woodroffe of Thorpewood, Branksome Avenue, Bournemouth. His brothers Sydney and Leslie also fell. Sydney was awarded the VC.

Second Lieutenant James Trevor Crawley Vincent, 2nd Welsh, killed on 9 May 1915.

The memorial and original grave marker to Second Lieutenant James Trevor Crawley Vincent, 2nd Welsh, in Bangor Cathedral.

The grave of Second Lieutenant James Trevor Crawley Vincent, 2nd Welsh.

A memorial to him and his original wooden grave marker are displayed in Bangor Cathedral, while his replacement Portland headstone bears the inscription: 'May Light Perpetual Shine Upon Him.'

Many acts of gallantry were performed by the men of all these battalions during the battle. While many men of the 4th RWF, 1st SWB and 2nd Welsh were mentioned in despatches for the battle, among the awards given to members of the 2nd Welsh, Captain Thomas Preston Aldworth gained the DSO and Second Lieutenants Brian Morgan Dunn and Bertram Upton Sinclair Cripps the MC, while Corporals Thomas George Earl (18587) and James Northey (9563) were awarded the DCM.

Among the many brave deeds carried out by men of the 1st SWB, Private David Doyle (15389) was awarded the DCM for standing in a flooded ditch for over an hour holding a wounded man before bringing him in to safety when darkness closed in, and Lieutenant Alexander Charles Masters was wounded while risking his life to save a badly-wounded man. Masters went on to gain the DSO and MC later in the war.

The failure of the attack was due to the strength of the German defences and the inadequacy of the artillery barrage, which failed to cut the wire or to break down the enemy positions. The Germans had constructed impressive breastworks, 6ft high with a parados (parapets to protect the back of the breastworks), with dugouts and machine-gun emplacements that were impervious to all but the heaviest artillery.

On the right the French Tenth Army made an advance in its centre of just over 2 miles on a frontage of 4 miles but accomplished little elsewhere. The French had more guns than the British and their assault took place after six days of bombardment that demoralized the enemy and destroyed much of their defences.

Learning from the experience at Aubers Ridge, Sir Douglas Haig now ordered three days' continuous bombardment with heavy guns and, in spite of a large number of defective fuses, the enemy's defences were sufficiently damaged to make another assault viable.

It was now the turn of the 7th Division, including the 1st RWF. The division had been in support of the 8th Division during its attack on Aubers Ridge and was intended to be used to exploit any breakthrough made by the 8th Division. The 8th Division had initially made gains before German artillery began taking a heavy toll on the men and was forced to pull back. As a result, the 1st RWF were not called upon to move out of their assembly trenches and on the night of 10/11 May marched back to billets in Essars.

After four days at Essars, on the morning of 15 May the 1st RWF marched back via Le Touret and Rue de l'Épinette to take up positions in the front-line trenches at Rue Cailloux. The First Army was given the task of capturing the German defences: one division holding the line from Rue-du-Bois to Chocolat Menier Corner and a second division, 550 metres north, was to capture the German trenches to the left of Festubert village.

At 10 am that day all the attacking battalions were in position: on the left, the 2nd Division had 6 Brigade and 5 Brigade in front, with 4th (Guards) Brigade in reserve.

The artillery lifted beyond the German trenches at 11.30 am and the infantry began to advance. The line running from Rue-du-Bois to Ferme du Bois was attained by 6 Brigade with few casualties and the men began to consolidate their gains. On the left, between them and Port Arthur, 5 Brigade hit a sterner defence but some men of the 2nd Inniskillings reached the German front line and were reinforced. The Gharwal Brigade of the Meerut Division, which had advanced to conform with 5 Brigade, was cut down in no man's land.

The 1st RWF spent the night in the trenches, having received orders to attack the German front line and then to move east to take their first and second line trenches. At 12.45 am on 16 May the 2nd Division ordered a further bombardment to coincide with the attack to be carried out by the 7th Division. The support battalions of 6 Brigade, 2nd Division failed to leave their trenches due to heavy crossfire from the area between the two divisional attacks that had not been suppressed by the bombardment. The support battalions of the Gharwal Brigade also attempted to move forward but were cut down by machine guns.

At 2.45 am the British bombardment on the 7th Division front intensified, opening gaps in the German breastworks and at 3.10 am the first platoons of 20 Brigade (2nd Scots Guards and 2nd Borderers) left their trenches to close up with the Germans before the barrage lifted. Heavy casualties were suffered by both when they advanced too far and got caught in their own bombardment. Many of these men were buried in a mass grave near Rue-du-Bois.

At 3.15 am, even though the 2nd Division had failed to advance, the 7th Division attack began. On the right 22 Brigade attacked across Duke's Road towards the School House and the Northern Breastwork, with 2nd Queen's and 1st RWF in the first wave. The 1st RWF advanced in four waves, each of its companies in two lines, and scaled the parapets of the German breastworks. The battalion suffered heavy casualties from shelling and machine-gun fire. Among the first to fall was the CO, Lieutenant Colonel Richard Edward Philip Gabbett, who was shot dead as soon as he raised himself from the trench. Major G.F. Dickson, the second-in-command, took over but soon fell wounded, while the battalion kept up the attack in a cloud of green lyddite fumes, taking the first and second German lines. The battalion medical officer, Lieutenant Kelsey Fry, a close friend of Siegfried Sassoon, was shot through the elbow as he attended to a wounded man but bravely remained on duty on the battlefield.

Suffering heavy casualties, Captain Stockwell, who had now taken command, collected a number of Scots Guards to bolster his troops and began advancing the remnants of his command towards La Quinque Rue.

In the meantime, at around 3.45 am, 22 Brigade moved forward, reaching the German lines and working their way through the trenches using grenades. Two hours later Douglas Haig altered his plans and directed the Sirhind Brigade to move to support the 2nd Division. By 6 am the main objectives of the attack had been attained and by 6.30 am the 1st RWF had joined up with the 2nd Royal Warwicks, 2nd Scots Guards and the Queen's near the orchard. A German counter-attack was then repulsed but the men now came under intense German artillery fire.

Heavy fighting continued throughout the day and, as night closed in at 7.30 pm, the 1st RWF were ordered to withdraw to La Quinque Rue, forced out by lack of support from 20 Brigade on their left and by heavy German shelling. The battalion had suffered terrible casualties during the day. The War Diary stated that Lieutenant Colonel Richard Edward Philip Gabbett, Captain Stanley Jones, Lieutenants Robert Hermann Ackerley and Rowland Edmund Naylor, Second Lieutenants Harold Gerome Lynch and John Torrington Morris had been killed. Second Lieutenants John Brown Savage MC, and Henry Laidley Garland Edwards died of wounds. Captain Herbert Stonehouse Coles and Second Lieutenant Leonard Jones were missing (both were later confirmed dead), and nine other officers had been wounded. In addition, 118 other ranks were posted as having been killed, 271 wounded, 164 missing, and 6 wounded and missing. This made a total of almost 600 casualties out of the original strength of 25 officers and 806 other ranks! The men killed actually amounted to 212 other ranks once the missing had been properly accounted for over the following days.

Lieutenant Henry Laidley Garland Edwards was born in Carmarthen in 1886, the son of the Reverend Alfred George Edwards, the vicar of St Peter's Church, and of Mary Lindley Edwards. In 1889 his father was appointed Bishop of St Asaph and in 1920 became the first Archbishop of Wales. Edwards was educated at Eton before studying law at New College, Oxford and worked in South America before being commissioned in the Royal Welsh Fusiliers in March 1915, along with one Robert von Ranke Graves. The 30-year-old is buried in Brown's Road Military Cemetery, Festubert.

Lieutenant Arthur Kenneth Richardson of the 1st RWF wrote a detailed letter to his parents about the action, a copy of which is in the battalion War Diary:

My dear Mother and Father, we have just had the most awful battle and thank God I have come through unscathed. Then came the time, the whole of our line with one leap were over the parapet and on towards the German lines. It was a sad spectacle owing to fearful rifle and machine gun fire mowing our poor fellows over, not to speak of high explosive and shrapnel shells... We arrived in the 2nd Line; on our way across we met the 1st prisoner. My fellows wanted to bayonet him, but I managed to keep them back. We went down a communication trench filled with dead Germans and our fellows (Queen's). When I got some way down I was told that I could bomb the 3rd Line from the end but on arrival found it too great a range, so went back into 2nd Line, where I met Major Kirkpatrick on whom the command of Queen's had fallen... He told me that Stockwell with a handful of men were on the extreme left of the line with no support. I at once packed off there, on arrival I found Stockwell with Warmsley, who appeared to be the sole survivors of the Regt.

The battle continued over the coming days, with the 1st Canadian Division being brought in to support the attacks.

Under cover of darkness on the following night the bodies of some of the fallen officers were collected from the battlefield and buried. The bodies of Herbert Stonehouse Coles, Leonard Jones and Robert Hermann Ackerley could not be found, although Ackerley's body was recovered on the night of 18/19 May when the men were bringing in the bodies of over 110 other ranks.

Twelve men were buried in-between the German first and second lines, while the remainder were buried in a long mass grave along with Ackerley. Coles and Jones are the only officers of the 1st RWF killed that day not to have a known grave and are commemorated on the Le Touret Memorial. Lieutenant Colonel Richard Edward Philip Gabbett, the 47-year-old son of Wyndham Gabbett, of Mount Rivers, Newport, Limerick is buried in Guards Cemetery, Windy Corner, Cuinchy.

Robert Hermann Ackerley was the 23-year-old son of Richard and Eliza Helen Ackerley, of Quisisana, Llandrindod Wells, Radnorshire, and was educated at

The grave of Lieutenant Colonel Richard Edward Philip Gabbett at Guards Cemetery, Windy Corner, Cuinchy.

Pont-du-Hem Military Cemetery, La Gorgue.

Eton. When the graves registration workers carried out their post-war clearances of the battlefields, the mass grave of these men of the 1st RWF was discovered in map reference SH.36.S.20.d.95.65. Two large wooden crosses marked the graves, but the only identifiable remains were of Ackerley, Corporal Samson Edwin Rowley (9714) of Lilleshall and Private Richard James Jones (5708) of Northop, Flint. The bodies were all exhumed and reinterred in Pont-du-Hem Military Cemetery, La Gorgue. The cemetery was used to concentrate burials from smaller cemeteries in the area after the war and as a result has many unknown graves. Nonetheless, just three men identified from over 100 burials is a tragedy. The remainder are commemorated on the Le Touret Memorial.

Lieutenant Robert Hermann Ackerley of Llandrindod Wells, killed at Festubert on 16 May 1915.

Company Sergeant Major Frederick Barter (3942) of the 1st RWF became the first man from Cardiff and the first Royal Welsh Fusilier to win the Victoria Cross during the war. Barter was born in Cardiff on 17 January 1891, the son of Samuel Barter. He enlisted in the RWF on 4 December 1908 and by the outbreak of war was a Special Reservist, working at the Cardiff Gaslight and Coke Company. He rejoined the 1st RWF with the rank of company sergeant major and embarked for France with the battalion. Barter was one of many men of the 1st RWF who performed gallant deeds during the battalion's destruction at Festubert on 16 May but his gallantry was seen to have been conspicuous, leading to him being awarded the Victoria Cross. The citation for his award was published in the *London Gazette* of 26 June 1915:

Company Sergeant Major Frederick Barter of the 1st RWF, awarded the Victoria Cross for his actions at Festubert.

213

On 16 May 1915 at Festubert, France, Company Sergeant-Major Barter, when in the first line of German trenches, called for volunteers to enable him to extend our line and with the eight men who responded, he attacked the German position with bombs, capturing three German officers, 102 men and 500 yards of their trenches. He subsequently found and cut 11 of the enemy's mine leads situated about 20 yards apart.

Barter returned to Wales the following month to be invested with his award by King George V. The *Flintshire Observer* of 27 July noted:

WELSH V.C. HONOURED, Company-Sergeant-Major Barter, of the Royal Welch Fusiliers, who was decorated with the Victoria Cross by the King last week, paid a visit on Thursday to Wrexham, the headquarters of his regiment. He was given an ovation by the townspeople, two bands and an immense crowd of people meeting him at the station and escorting him through the streets of the town. He was cheered to the echo and on entering the ballroom of the Imperial Hotel, the subscribers to a public testimonial gave him a cordial greeting. The Mayor of Wrexham, on behalf of the subscribers, presented Sergeant-Major Barter with a silver casket containing £35 and said that his brilliant feat showed that the same spirit animated the British soldier to-day as in the days of old (cheers). Sergeant-Major Barter, in returning thanks, said that he only did what any other soldier would have done. He saw present many wounded soldiers who were with him at Festubert and he was sure that had the opportunity occurred they would have done as he did.

He was commissioned as an officer on 26 August 1915, ending the war as a captain and being awarded the Military Cross in 1918. The citation in the *London Gazette* of 26 July 1918 reads:

For conspicuous gallantry and devotion to duty when ordered to make a flank attack. He led his two platoons up a precipitous hill and turned the enemy's flank. Then, placing one platoon with two Lewis guns to command the enemy's line of retreat, he gallantly led an attack with the other platoon from the rear and flank, killing or capturing practically the whole garrison.

Curiously Barter was rescued by an Indian rifleman, Karanbahadur Rana at El Kefr, Palestine, on 10 April 1918; an action that resulted in the rifleman being awarded the Victoria Cross for saving Barter's life. He served with the Home Guard as a major during the Second World War. He died on 15 May 1952 and is commemorated at Bournemouth Crematorium. Barter's medals are displayed at the Royal Welsh Fusiliers Museum, Caernarfon.

The battalion was well rewarded for its efforts. As well as Barter's Victoria Cross, other men were rewarded. Among them, Second Lieutenant John Brown Savage was awarded the Military Cross: 'For conspicuous gallantry at Festubert, on May 16th, 1915, when, as Acting Adjutant of his battalion, he displayed the greatest bravery in cheering his men forward although severely wounded near the German parapet. At Neuve Chapelle also he displayed marked ability and courage.' (*London Gazette*, 23 July 1915.)

The following were awarded the DCM:

Private Isaac Allen (9969): 'For conspicuous gallantry on the 16th May 1915, at Festubert, when, in company with a Sergeant-Major and two other men he volunteered to assist in bombing down German trenches, 500 yards of which they captured together with 102 prisoners, including three officers.' (*London Gazette*, 5 August 1915.)

Private George Brooks (6210): 'For gallant conduct and ability on the 16th May 1915, at Festubert, when in charge of a machine gun, which he worked with great accuracy under a very heavy fire, putting a German machine gun out of action. Subsequently he was able to bring his gun out of action under a heavy shell fire.' (*London Gazette*, 5 August 1915.)

Sergeant John Butler (9935): 'For conspicuous gallantry and devotion to duty on the 16th May 1915, at Festubert. Although wounded before the assault was made, he advanced with his machine gun, brought it into action and continued to fire it though he was again wounded. He showed the greatest courage and resource throughout the operations.' (*London Gazette*, 5 August 1915.)

Sergeant Merton Capelen (10927): 'For conspicuous gallantry on the 16th May 1915, at Festubert, when, although wounded in the face early in the action, he continued to lead his men under heavy fire, remaining with his Company until the evening.' (*London Gazette*, 5 August 1915. His brother Bert would be killed later in the war.)

Private William Chilwell (10710): 'For conspicuous gallantry on the 16th May 1915, at Festubert, when he was the first to volunteer on four separate occasions for duty of the greatest danger. Later in the same day he volunteered to attack a house 70 yards away, two other volunteers with him being killed. He gave a fine example of courage and devotion to duty.' (*London Gazette*, 5 August 1915.)

Lance Corporal James Frederick Condrey (8280): 'For great bravery and devotion to duty on the 16th–18th May 1915, at Festubert, when acting as stretcher-bearer. While bringing in wounded under a heavy fire he was himself wounded and although he could no longer carry in men he continued to go out and dress the wounded under fire until exhausted.' (*London Gazette*, 5 August 1915.)

Lance Corporal William John Welsh (6258): 'For gallant conduct and great bravery on the 16th to 18th May 1915, at Festubert as a stretcher-bearer. He brought in a large number of wounded single-handed, having previously bandaged many serious cases.' (*London Gazette*, 5 August 1915.)

For the 1st RWF the Battle of Festubert was over. At 7.45 pm on 17 May the remnants of the battalion marched to billets in Oblinghem and the following day moved further back to Ecquedecques, via Chocques and Lillers where the battalion was paraded and addressed by the GOC 22 Brigade. Drafts of reinforcements then began arriving to rebuild the battalion.

Festubert had been an expensive gamble but several localized successes had been overshadowed by the shell shortage that had again blighted the attack. The British (and Canadians) suffered over 16,000 casualties while the French lost 102,000, against German losses of 50,000. On 15 May 1915 an article appeared in *The Times*, written by military correspondent Colonel Charles à Court Repington based on information given to him by the Commander-in-Chief, Sir John French. The latter also sent copies of all correspondence between him and the government on the question of the supply of ammunition to the MPs David Lloyd George, Arthur Balfour and Bonar Law. The scandal that erupted as the public read about men losing their lives unnecessarily as a result of the shortages proved to be the downfall of the Liberal government under Herbert Asquith and led to the formation of a coalition government and the appointment of Lloyd George as the first Minister of Munitions and a reduction in the power of Lord Kitchener. The politics also undermined the reputation of Sir John French and would contribute to his removal later in the year.

No major operations took place during the summer apart from some minor actions at Bellewaarde Ridge and Hooge to straighten out the salient that had been left following the end of the Second Battle of Ypres. Other Welsh units would once again be among the combatants.

Chapter 14

Gallipoli:
Sari Bair and the Landings at Suvla

(See Map on page 237)

Since the 2nd SWB had landed at S Beach on 25 April the Gallipoli campaign had stagnated into the attritional trench warfare that it was supposed to have overcome if the breakthrough into the Black Sea had been a success. The troops on the peninsula had not managed to break out from their landing places and by August, almost four months into the campaign, most of the forces were still in their original positions, even after several large-scale battles, notably at Krithia and Anzac Cove. The 2nd SWB had suffered a continual drain on manpower, especially following heavy fighting in Turkey Trench at the top of Gully Ravine on 28 June, when Lieutenant Wrinch Joseph Charles Budd and thirty-seven men had been killed.

General Sir Ian Hamilton, GOC Mediterranean Force, set out a new plan to secure the Sari Bair Range and capture high ground on Hill 971 and Chunuk Bair. To carry out this plan, Hamilton's original 5 divisions had been increased to 15, while the 6 original Ottoman divisions had grown to 16.

The allies planned to land two fresh infantry divisions from IX Corps at Suvla Bay, 5 miles north of Anzac, followed by an advance on Sari Bair from the north-west. At

Dugouts on the Gallipoli Peninsula.

Anzac an attack would be made against the Sari Bair range, with the 3rd Light Horse Brigade attacking Baby 700 in tandem with a New Zealand attack on Chunuk Bair. Hill 971 would be attacked by a combined force drawn from the Gurkhas of the 29th Indian Brigade and the 4th Australian Infantry Brigade.

To support the offensive, the 13th Division had moved from Mudros and landed at Cape Helles between 6 and 16 July, relieving the 29th Division. The 4th SWB landed at V Beach at 4.30 pm on 15 July and, together with the 8th RWF, marched to take up the front line at Gully Ravine on 16 July. The 4th SWB suffered its first casualty at Gallipoli after occupying the front-line trenches the following day, 17 July, when Private William O'Brien (12659), the husband of Mary O'Brien (née Cavill), of 1 Barrack Hill, Newport, was shot by a sniper and killed. The redoubtable Regimental Sergeant Major George Halford (13852) was also badly wounded during the battalion's first time in the line, dying in hospital at Alexandria on 12 August 1915. Halford had played a key part in the training of the battalion and his death was seen as a serious loss by the CO, Lieutenant Colonel F.M. Gillespie.

Lieutenant Wrinch Joseph Charles Budd of 2nd SWB killed at Gallipoli on 28 June 1915. Budd was the son of Edward and Mary Budd, of 84 Melrose Aven Norbury and had served during the Boer War. He i commemorated on the Helles Memorial.

The 4th SWB had a formidable rugby team, having played several matches just prior to embarking for service in Gallipoli. Among its team members were the former Llanelli RFC players Llewellyn Davies, Ike Lewis, Steve Reynolds and John Williams.

The rugby team of the 4th SWB in June 1915, just prior to embarking for service at Gallipoli.

Also among the Welsh troops to move to Gallipoli was No. 5 Siege Company, Royal Monmouth Royal Engineers, a former Militia unit with a proud history, raised in the county town of Monmouth. The company's specialist skills were to be employed in the erection of landing stages, piers, pontoon bridges and in the sinking of wells to water the tremendous number of troops and animals moving to the harsh, arid peninsula.

The company had moved to Egypt in June 1915 and was initially put to work on the Suez Canal defences. On 2 July it embarked from Port Said for Alexandria and on the following day embarked aboard the SS *Mercian* for Mudros, where the men were put to work in building piers. On 18 July the company received orders to proceed to Gallipoli and at 11 pm on 19 July landed at Lancashire Landing, Cape Helles. The strength of the company on landing was 205 officers and men, who were immediately split into detachments and put to work on several projects: making dugouts at Baker's Gully, creating a reservoir west of Lancashire Landing, sinking wells and installing water pumps, working on a sunken ship off Lancashire Landing, and setting up a traction engine repair shop and a carpenters' shop. Within the first week of landing, two officers and ten men were invalided to hospital after falling ill.

With reports of an impending Turkish counter-attack, the 29th Division also returned from Mudros, 86 and 87 brigades landing on 21 July at Gully Beach. The 2nd SWB had benefited from drafts of several officers and 199 men during its brief rest period.

The 8th RWF suffered their first casualty on 20 July when Private Bertram Slater (16046) of Ogmore Vale died of wounds suffered earlier in the day. The conditions were terrible for these newly-arrived men. Lieutenant S. Powell of the 8th RWF wrote:

> Got to the trenches about 5 yesterday afternoon after a very trying, dusty march up. We settled down fairly comfortably. Food and water are rather scarce, especially the latter and I am beginning to realise what real thirst is when you can't quench it, or have only one water-bottle to last the day.

On 30 July the 8th RWF, together with the rest of the division, marched down to V Beach to embark from a pier next to the beached *River Clyde* and returned to Mudros, as did the 4th SWB. The battalions remained at Mudros until 4 August, when they sailed for Anzac and landed at 9 pm while Anzac Cove was under shellfire. The men bivouacked in the shelter of White Gully. The 8th Welsh, by now the Pioneer Battalion of the 13th Division, landed on the following day.

During 1 August the Royal Monmouths lost their first two men killed on the peninsula: Lance Corporal Bertram William Mincher (7117) of Wolverhampton and Sapper Hubert John Edwin Hold (7112) of Wellington, Somerset were killed by Turkish shellfire while working at Cape Helles. Both men are buried in Lancashire Landing Cemetery. The loss of two comrades did not deter the company from continuing their work and by 6 August, as well as continuing with their other works, they had also built over 400 trench-scaling ladders in preparation for the forthcoming offensive.

Meanwhile the landing at Suvla Bay took place on the night of 6/7 August and came up against little opposition but, with limited objectives and unimaginative thinking from the commanders, no advance was made. The Turks then rushed troops up to occupy the Anafarta Hills, preventing the British from penetrating inland, thereby reducing the Suvla Front to static trench warfare.

The offensive was preceded on the evening of 6 August by diversions at Cape Helles and Anzac. At Helles, a diversion at Krithia Vineyard became a costly stalemate, while at Anzac a partially successful attack on the Turkish trenches at Lone Pine on 6 August, led by the 1st Australian Infantry Brigade, captured the main enemy trench line in an attempt to draw Turkish attention away from the main assaults at Chunuk Bair and Hill 971.

The battle was a historic moment in the history of the AIF and one of the most famous battles of the Gallipoli campaign. The Turks were located in deeply-dug trench positions that had been covered with pine logs and no man's land stretched for 150 metres across an open plateau. Several hours before the assault, three mines were detonated in front of the Turkish positions in order to give the advancing troops some cover. The artillery bombardment began at 4.30 pm, with the fire of the artillery batteries supplemented by fire from the heavy cruiser HMS *Bacchante,* which was anchored offshore. Most of the Turks were able to shelter from the fire by retreating into tunnels and when the fire halted, were able to get quickly back into their positions in the fire trench.

At 5.30 pm whistles blew all along the Australian line and the 2nd Battalion charged across no man's land, nicknamed the Daisy Patch by the troops, towards the Turks, followed by the 3rd and 4th battalions, while the 1st Battalion remained at Brown's Dip in reserve. When the Australians reached the trenches they were shocked to find the roofs of pine logs and were forced to cut their way through them before diving down into the trenches and attacking the Turks. It was a brutal affair as the men fought hand-to-hand using rifles, bayonets, knives and spades as weapons. Some Australians continued forwards and attacked the Turkish support positions but all were killed or captured. After severe fighting the front-line trench was taken and the 1st Battalion moved forward under heavy Turkish shellfire to reinforce its sister battalions.

At 7.30 pm the Turks counter-attacked with hand grenades and began attempting to bomb the Australians out of the trenches. Heavy fighting continued throughout the night, with the Australians using dead bodies to block communication trenches to delay the Turkish attacks. Throughout the night the Turks rushed reinforcements up to Lone Pine and over the next three days the Australians managed to beat off several counter-attacks after being reinforced themselves by the 2nd and 3rd infantry brigades. With ammunition running out, fifty Australians were put to work making improvised hand grenades from empty ration tins in an attempt to keep the troops supplied with munitions to keep the Turks at bay.

The Turkish counter-attack was called off on the afternoon of 9 August and the fighting subsided the following day, allowing the Australians to consolidate their gains.

Lone Pine had been the fiercest battle fought by the Australians and had resulted in the capture of 150 metres of ground along a 330-metre front, at the cost of over 2,227 Australians killed or wounded. The Turks had suffered as many as 7,000 casualties. Seven Australians were awarded the Victoria Cross for the battle. At least sixteen Welsh Australians were killed during the Battle of Lone Pine: Private William James Bates (2264), 4th Battalion, of Cardiff; Private Owen John Ellis (1937), 7th Battalion, of Caernarfon; Private David John Evans (546), 16th Battalion, of Corwen; Private Neville Gordon Gwynne Evans (1737), 2nd Battalion, of Cardiff; Private John Foster (1357), 3rd Battalion, of Colwyn Bay; Private David Thomas Francis (2137), 15th Battalion, of Hengoed; Trooper Mansell David Griffiths (621), 8th Light Horse, of Bridgend; Private Stephen Ebenezer Havard (2261), 4th Battalion, of Llanelli; Private Benjamin Davies John (2153), 11th Battalion, of Templeton; Lance Corporal Alfred John McClusky (450), 10th Light Horse, of Cardiff; Private John Owens (559), 3rd Battalion, of Holyhead; Private Percy Price (2211), 10th Battalion, of Boughrood; Private Allen Johnson Pritchard (902), 11th Battalion, of Crumlin; Private Frederick William Renshaw (2069), 1st Battalion, of Wrexham; Private Charles Henry Terry (1061), 1st Battalion, of Cardiff; and Sergeant David John Williams (1225), 16th Battalion, of Portmadoc.

Sir Ian Hamilton wrote of the assault in his despatches:

Two lines left their trenches simultaneously and were closely followed up by a third. The rush across the open was a regular race against death, which came in the shape of a hail of shell and rifle bullets from front and from either flank. But the Australians had firmly resolved to reach the enemy's trenches and in this determination they became for the moment invincible. The barbed wire entanglement was reached and was surmounted. Then came a terrible moment, when it seemed as though it would be physically impossible to penetrate into the trenches. The overhead cover of stout pine beams resisted all individual efforts to move it and the loopholes continued to spit fire. Groups of our men then bodily lifted up the beams and individual soldiers leaped down into the semi-darkened galleries amongst the Turks... The hand-to-hand fighting in the semi-obscurity of the trenches was prolonged and very bitterly contested. In one corner eight Turks and six Australians were found lying as they had bayoneted one another. To make room for the fighting men the dead were ranged in rows on either side of the gangway. After the first violence of the counter-attacks had abated, 1,000 corpses, our own and Turkish, were dragged out from the trenches.

Captain Charles Bean, the Australian historian, wrote: 'I watched those cheery, laughing, faithful boys go out over the parapet across the shrivelled fire-swept slope and into that cauldron which was a hell for the next three days.'

The 13th Division was part of the force allotted to General Godley to attack the positions along the Sari Bair Ridge and its two high points, Chunuk Bair on the south and Koja Chemen Tepe on the north. The ground was formed of steep, winding ravines that were overgrown with dense scrub and provided ideal defensive positions for the Turks.

The divisional troops set off in darkness late on 6 August, the 4th SWB leading the left covering column towards Aghyl Dere and by dawn of 7 August the right covering column, including the 8th RWF, had reached Rhododendron Spur on the southern shoulder of Chunuk Bair, about 400 metres from the summit. All the while the men could hear heavy fire coming from the direction of Lone Pine. The left covering column reached No. 3 Post at about 9.25 pm and advanced, meeting the Turks in a trench across Aghyl Dere. The enemy fled following a powerful attack and the hill was captured. The men of the 4th SWB began to dig into their captured positions at Damakjelik Bair. Communications were then established with the 4th Australian Brigade on their left.

On 7 August 34 Brigade landed at Suvla under heavy fire from Hill 10, Lala Baba and Ghazi Baba. The latter was captured after dawn but Hill 10 held out. 32 Brigade landed at C Beach, the 6th Yorks, supported by the 9th West Yorks, rushed Lala Baba shortly after midnight and advanced north towards Hill 10, where heavy fighting was going on. At 5.30 am a combined attack was made on Hill 10, which was finally captured. The assault on Chocolate and W Hills that had been planned to go ahead at that time was delayed, as the troops had suffered heavy casualties and were waiting for reinforcements.

33 Brigade landed at B Beach, relieving 32 Brigade on Lala Baba, sending a battalion to dig in from the Salt Lake to the sea to cover the landing places and two battalions north to Hill 10. Just before dawn the transports containing the 10th Division arrived in Suvla Bay and were landed at B Beach under heavy shrapnel fire, suffering heavy casualties. An attack up the steep rocky ground to Kiretch Tepe, which was strongly held by the Turks, was immediately carried out and by sunset had almost gained the summit.

All appeared to be going well and at 3.30 am the 8th RWF marched from Russell's Top to Monash Gully, ready to attack. Preceded by a naval bombardment, the 3rd Australian Light Horse launched their disastrous assault at Laing's Nek against Baby 700 at 4.30 am, intending to cut off the Turks in a pincer movement, with the New Zealanders attacking from the rear of Baby 700. The attack by the Light Horsemen was an unmitigated disaster. The New Zealanders were not in place and the artillery barrage had not damaged the Turkish defences and two waves of Australians were mown down by machine-gun fire. The attack should never have taken place.

Unfortunately for the men of the 8th RWF, at just after 5 am an incorrect message reached the CO that the Australian attack had been successful. A and B companies of the 8th RWF were already moving from the head of Monash Valley, between Russell's Top and Pope's Hill, against the Chessboard Trenches to support the Light Horse. A Company were topping the ridge when they were attacked with bombs and a machine gun from a trench on the very crest and the company began suffering heavy casualties. B Company had also reached the top of the ridge on their side, but also came under heavy fire and lost the leading platoon. At this point a staff officer arrived to say that the Australians had in fact failed to take the Nek and no further advance was to be made by the battalion. The two companies remained under cover in the gully until the evening, when they returned to Russell's Top. On 9 August the 8th RWF moved back

The grave of Sergeant William Botting Williams at Shrapnel Valley Cemetery.

Sergeant William Botting Williams (11910) of 8th RWF. He was the son of Thomas and Mary Ann Williams of High Street, Ammanford. Williams had worked at Ammanford Colliery and was one of the first to enlist at Ammanford in August 1914. He was killed in action on 7 August 1915, aged 21, and is buried at Shrapnel Valley Cemetery, Gallipoli.

to Bridges Road in Army Corps Reserve. Seventeen men had been killed and fifty wounded for nothing.

Among the men killed was Sergeant William Botting Williams (11910). Williams was the son of Thomas and Mary Ann Williams, of High Street, Ammanford. He worked at Ammanford Colliery and before that had served for a time in the Metropolitan Police Force before becoming one of the first men from Ammanford to enlist in August 1914. He is buried in Shrapnel Valley Cemetery, Gallipoli.

The 4th SWB lost 20 men killed during the first day and over 60 wounded and another 15 men killed on 8 August, mostly by artillery fire. Their worst casualties would, however, be suffered on 9 August. During the night of 8/9 August the battalion moved to the right to take the place of the 5th Wiltshires, who had been moved to Sari Bair.

At dawn on 9 August the Turks mounted a desperate counter-attack against the 4th SWB. Captain Kitchin sent forward two platoons, No. 11 under Lieutenant Miller and No. 12 under Second Lieutenant Cooper, who advanced under heavy fire to reinforce pickets held further forward by the battalion that were under severe pressure.

The fighting was brutal and bloody, mostly carried out at close quarters, and the battalion suffered a terrible number of casualties. Among them Second Lieutenant Leonard Gosse Cooper, a highly-regarded young officer, was killed and Lieutenant Miller severely wounded. Thirty-nine men from the 4th SWB were killed on 9 August alone. A further forty-eight men of the 4th SWB would be killed in the next three days.

Leonard Gosse Cooper was born on 15 June 1892, the youngest of three sons of Walter Percy and Emily Frances Cooper, of Ambleside, Abergavenny. Educated at Llandovery College between 1903 and 1910, Cooper played as a forward for the School XV. He had distinguished himself at Llandovery and gained a Classical Scholarship at Jesus College, Oxford. While at Oxford he was awarded the Goldsmith's Exhibition and First-Class Honours in Classical Moderations in 1914. The senior examiner at Oxford expressed the view that he ought to devote himself to research in the Classics, but at the outbreak of war in 1914 he applied for a commission in the army and on 29 August 1914 was gazetted temporary second lieutenant in the 4th SWB. His commanding officer described him as 'an officer of great ability and promise, who will be severely missed.' Cooper was 23 years old. He was reported to have been buried in 29th Field Ambulance Cemetery but his grave was lost and he is commemorated on the Helles Memorial.

Second Lieutenant Leonard Gosse Cooper, 4th SWB.

Lieutenant Colonel Franklin Macaulay Gillespie was killed while directing the fire of a machine gun and the battalion spent the remainder of the day under severe pressure, with its well-respected CO dead. Gillespie was born at Colchester on 19 August 1872, the son of Lieutenant Colonel Franklin Gillespie and Harriet Eliza Phyllis Gillespie. He was educated at Dover College and Sandhurst before being commissioned in the South Wales Borderers on 25 July 1891. He married Agnes Rose, the daughter of Sir Pryce Pryce-Jones, at Newtown, Montgomery on 27 July 1905. He had seen active service in West Africa and during the Boer War and on 19 August 1914 was given command of the 4th SWB. Gillespie was also reported as having been buried in 29th Field Ambulance Cemetery but, like Cooper's, his grave was lost and he is commemorated on the Helles Memorial.

Lieutenant Colonel Franklin Macaulay Gillespie, 4th SWB.

Prior to this, at B Beach, Brigadier General Hill, commanding three battalions of 31 Brigade and two battalions of 30 Brigade, was ordered to report to Major General Hammersley, commanding 11th Division, who instructed him to co-operate in the attack on Chocolate Hill from Hill 10 under the orders of Brigadier General, 34 Brigade. The attack commenced at 3 pm, the men raked by fire from Chocolate Hill,

British infantry landed at Suvla Bay crossing the Salt Lake.

but the mixed force of Irish and English battalions stormed the hill and captured it at about 5.30 pm. Later, the 5th Irish Fusiliers advanced and gained a footing on Green Hill.

After night had fallen, the troops on Chocolate and Green Hills began consolidating their gains. The results of the Suvla operation of 7 August had been disappointing, but the casualties had not been excessive and the scene was set for a further attack the next morning in conjunction with the ANZAC troops, now ready to assault the summit of Sari Bair.

The 8th Welsh had marched to the mouth of Chailak Dere by 7.20 am on 7 August and took up positions in reserve. Lieutenant Colonel J.A. Bald took a platoon forward to reconnoitre for an attack the next day and was severely wounded, so Major Yates took his place. At 5 pm the remainder of the battalion moved up to join the advanced platoon. The 8th Welsh suffered their first Gallipoli casualty during the day when Private Oswald Morris (13847), the 20-year-old son of William and Gertrude Morris of Leominster and a miner at Trebanos, was killed. The battalion did not go into action until the following day.

Before dawn on 8 August the summit of the ridge was heavily bombarded by monitors, cruisers and artillery. At 4.15 am the right column assaulted, the Wellington Regiment leading, the 7th Gloucesters in close support and behind them the 8th Welsh and the Auckland Mounted Rifles. The Wellington Regiment crossed Apex Ridge in the dark, dashed across the intervening 400 metres and reached the Turkish trench at the summit with few casualties. The 7th Gloucesters followed, spreading to both flanks, but the Turks became wise to the situation and began pouring fire into the attackers.

The 8th Welsh then moved forward, with A and D companies in the first line and B and C in the second line, at fifty paces distance and interval. As the men crossed Apex Ridge and attempted to deploy they came under heavy fire. The sun had risen and the men were now in full view. Major Yates and a small party reached a point some 300 metres from the right of the Wellingtons, but the Welshmen were falling fast and the advance of the remainder of the 8th Welsh stalled. As the day wore on, the casualties rose.

The 7th Gloucesters had lost all their officers and all their senior NCOs and their survivors met up with the remnants of the 8th Welsh. The Turks attacked throughout the day; the Wellington Regiment had to give way slightly, but the Auckland Rifles managed to get forward in support. Relief came at night when the Otago Battalion moved forward under cover of darkness. The remnants of the 8th Welsh were withdrawn to the shelter of the gully in reserve and at 8 am on the following day, 9 August, the battalion mustered only five officers and 274 other ranks: Captains Denis Digges La Touche, Charles Percy Gwyer and William Arthur Harding; Lieutenants John Nicholas Lewis and John Child Morris; Second Lieutenants Arthur Ewart Jones, Sydney Everard Jones and John Charles Marson and 151 other ranks had been killed. Captain William John Howells, a teacher at St David's College, Lampeter, was wounded in the fighting and died the next day aboard the hospital ship HMHS *Valdivia*. He was buried at sea that day and is commemorated on the Helles Memorial.

Captain Charles Percy Gwy 8th Welsh, killed on 8 Augus 1915 and commemorated or the Helles Memorial. He wa the son of Charles James Po Gwyer, of Egwood, Titley, Herefordshire. His brother Cyril also fell.

At least nine of the New Zealanders killed at Chunuk Bair fighting alongside the 8th Welsh were of Welsh birth: Private Frank Gilderoy Batters (8/900), Otago Regiment, of Prestatyn; Trooper Arthur John Farr (13/185), Auckland Mounted Rifles, of Usk; Private Malcolm Fraser (10/252), Wellington Regiment, of Cardiff; Corporal Ralph Giles (12/1637), Auckland Regiment, of Risca; Trooper Harry Compton Jones (13/557), Auckland Mounted Rifles, of Newport, Monmouthshire; Private Thomas Bertram Spencer Jones (10/826), Wellington Regiment, of Newport, Monmouthshire; Private Richard John Russell (10/2306), Wellington Regiment, of Holyhead; Private Edgar Sewell (10/1978), Wellington Regiment, of Newport, Monmouthshire; and Private Arthur Studley (10/168), Wellington Regiment, of Overton. All these men are commemorated on the Chunuk Bair (New Zealand) Memorial.

Captain William John Howei 8th Welsh, of Brook Cottage, Laugharne. Howells, was a schoolteacher at St David's College, Lampeter and a for student of Aberystwyth University. He died of woun on 10 August 1915.

The father of the 9th Baron Langford was killed here on 10 August. Geoffrey Seymour Rowley-Conwy was born on 14 September 1877, the third son of Conwy Grenville Hercules Rowley-Conwy JP DL of Bodrhyddan, Flintshire. The Conwys have been associated with the area around Rhuddlan Castle for at least 600 years, when Sir Henry Conwy was constable of Rhuddlan Castle. Rowley-Conwy was educated at Llandovery College between 1889 and 1896 and played rugby at wing for the 2nd XV before entering Exeter College, Oxford. In 1911 he married Bertha Gabrielle Cochran, daughter of Captain Alexander Cochran RN (Retired), of Ashkirk House, Ashkirk, Selkirkshire. They had two children: Geoffrey Alexander, born 8 March 1912 (Colonel the Lord Langford OBE DL) and Rosemary Marian, born 6 June 1915. Rowley-Conwy had been commissioned in the Loyal North Lancashire Regiment in 1901. In 1912 he was promoted to captain and by the time he landed with the 6th Loyal North Lancs on Gallipoli in

Major Geoffrey Seymour Rowley-Conwy, 6th Loyal North Lancashire Regiment.

July 1915 he was a major. The battalion was attached to 38 Brigade, 13th (Western) Division.

On the night of 9/10 August 1915, the 6th Loyals and the 5th Wiltshires replaced the New Zealand troops who had been fighting for the Pinnacle. The senior general staff officer, 13th (Western) Division, advised Major Rowley-Conwy's battalion to dig in on the reverse slope of their intended position of attack, fearing that they might be shelled off the forward slope. However, to dig in on the reverse slope was not possible due to its rocky terrain and an angle of 45 degrees, therefore only a few observation posts were dug. The main positions were taken up on flatter ground, known as The Farm. The opposing Turkish commander, Mustapha Kemal, assembled two extra brigades on the east side of the position and just before dawn on 10 August the Turks swept over the crest of the position in fifteen lines, overwhelming the British defences. In the confusion that followed, Rowley-Conwy was reported missing, only to be confirmed later as killed. He was 37 years old and is commemorated on the Helles Memorial.

Meanwhile, at Suvla the 10th and 11th divisions were attacking: 34 Brigade was to land at A Beach, capture Hill 10, despatch a battalion to capture Ghazi Baba and hold Suvla Point as a flank guard and then advance to the attack of Chocolate and W Hills; 32 Brigade was to land at C Beach, seize Lala Baba and then move north to Hill 10, advancing in support of 34 Brigade to attack Chocolate and W Hills; 33 Brigade was to land at B Beach, relieve 32 Brigade at Lala Baba and another battalion was to cover B Beach and connect up with the ANZACs, while the remaining two battalions were to go to Hill 10 as a reserve to 32 and 34 brigades.

As we have seen, the ANZAC operation had not gone to plan and at Suvla on 8 August the situation for the allies remained relatively unexploited, although Scimitar Hill was taken. Surprised by the inertia at Suvla, Sir Ian Hamilton came ashore from Imbros to enquire the reason. The answer given was exhaustion, lack of water and

British troops after landing at Suvla Bay.

confusion of units, although he was informed that an attack would be made on the morning of 9 August. Realizing that time was precious, Hamilton ordered a night advance to be made to secure the Tekke Tepe heights before Turkish reinforcements arrived. Organization was, however, too slow and Turkish reinforcements had been rushed into the area, recapturing Scimitar Hill and Tekke Tepe and were advancing towards Sulajik.

These important positions had been lost and the situation became critical. In order to relieve the shattered 11th Division, Sir Ian Hamilton sent for part of his reserve, the 53rd (Welsh) Division, which was on board transports in Mudros Harbour. HQ of the 53rd (Welsh) Division began landing at Suvla Bay at 7 pm on 8 August. HQ was set up on the beach and received orders to send two brigades to the 11th Division; however, only one battalion had so far landed, so the order could not yet be followed. From early morning, however, the battalions, as they landed at C Beach, were sent to the front line and the situation soon became confused.

No maps had been issued to any battalions of the division. They had no artillery, no signals company, were not trained or ready for warfare in this type of terrain and the men had not set foot on land for three weeks.

Among the first to land were the 5th Welsh at about 6 pm on 8 August. It was still light enough to see and the battalion was shelled while getting ashore. Battalions were then despatched singly or in pairs to the different brigades then in action: at 6.30 am the 2nd/4th Queen's of 160 Brigade were sent to 33 Brigade, where they reinforced the left of the attack and got on to Scimitar Hill, only to be driven back by the burning scrub that had been set alight by the shelling. The fire, spreading over the whole face of the hill in a mass of flame, killed the many wounded British and Turkish soldiers lying there. The 4th Sussex of 160 Brigade left the shore at around 11 am to join the Queen's. The fighting round Scimitar Hill had been very fierce; it ceased at noon and the attack had failed.

Meanwhile, battalions of 159 Brigade had been despatched to fill the gap between the battalions of 34 Brigade: the 4th Cheshires and 5th Welsh were ordered to Hill 10 to report to Brigadier General Sitwell, commanding 34 Brigade. Moving north from Lala Baba, they came under long-range shelling and arrived at Hill 10 at about 8.30 am. The battalions, led by the 5th Welsh under Major Dowdeswell, then advanced across the open plain.

The whereabouts of 34 Brigade were unknown and the officers of 159 Brigade had been told that they were 'somewhere in the scrub'. By now the fighting at Scimitar Hill had died down and men were wandering about freely across the open. The left half of the 5th Welsh lost touch with its two leading companies when they entered the scrub, so Captain Matthias had to go back to bring them up before moving forward to occupy an old Turkish trench. The remainder of the 5th Welsh and the 4th Cheshires were distributed between the right of 34 Brigade and the left of 30 Brigade at Sulajik.

The 4th Welsh did not complete its disembarkation until after daylight on 9 August and had suffered some casualties from shellfire but, at 11 am, together with the 5th Cheshires, were sent to report to Brigadier General Sitwell, commanding 34 Brigade, who had now left Hill 10 and whose headquarters were again described as 'somewhere in the bush'!

The three territorial battalions of the Royal Welsh Fusiliers – 5th RWF, 6th RWF and 7th RWF – disembarked on C Beach, Lala Baba, early in the morning of the 9th and remained there in bivouacs throughout the day. Orders for attack were issued that evening and 159 Brigade would commence its advance at 6 am on the 10th.

Private Tommy Owen, 7th RWF, of Snowdon View, Barmouth later wrote home to his parents of his experience during the landing:

I shall never forget that Sunday evening, August 8th, for that was the date of our landing. Our Navy was at it bombarding the adjacent hills (up which some of our troops were advancing), with terrible results. It was quite exciting watching this bombardment from the safety of our transport, which had anchored just inside the bay, not many yards from the shore. Every now and then lighters would pass our boat conveying wounded from the beach to the comfortable-looking hospital boats close by. Little did we think that before long some of us fellows would be taken from shore in that way.

Well, we were taken ashore from our transport in lighters. Never shall I forget my journey ashore in our lighter. There were about 200 of us below deck almost choked to death, as we were packed together like sardines. And this wasn't very comfortable with our heavy equipment which we carried. We landed safely and were ordered to take a few hours' sleep with our equipment on in case of emergency. There was a heavy bombardment going on and not very far off our troops were beating the Turks back. Airplanes were at it dropping star shells down, in fact, it was quite a sight to watch in the dark. I don't know how long the battle lasted for it wasn't long before I dropped off to welcome sleep, thankful, at any rate, that we were lucky enough to land without opposition...

We were marched off next morning about 4 a.m. and were brigaded on top a small hill. Then the Turks spotted us and they shelled us like mad for a good two hours. We were at breakfast at the time, so we had a new item on the menu that morning. Well we came off very lightly considering; our battalion having only twelve casualties, killed and wounded, although we were shelled every now and again all day after this, it was surprising how soon one got used to dodging shells. Towards evening we were moved off under the crest of a hill for cover. This was the hill Lala Baba which you may have read of. It was here that our brigade had to await orders for our advance.

Brigadier General Cowans decided to establish his headquarters at Anafarta Ova Farm, holding most of the 4th Welsh in reserve, while the 5th Cheshires moved up into the scrub and disappeared, as had the 5th Welsh and 4th Cheshires. Most of the night was spent by staff officers trying to locate troops and get them organized but with little success. It had been a hard day for these new troops, who had disembarked carrying just their packs and 200 rounds of ammunition and had had nothing to eat except for bully beef and biscuits and precious little water to drink.

Sir Ian Hamilton decided to renew the attack on the morning of 10 August with nine battalions of the 53rd (Welsh) Division, under the orders of Major General Lindley, the divisional commander. The six battalions that were scattered around Sulajik were to be withdrawn and concentrated, together with the three battalions of the RWF of 158 Brigade that had not been used on 9 August and were still at Lala Baba.

The attack to be delivered by 158 and 159 brigades was from Sulajik against the ridge to the south-east of Abrikja, on Scimitar Hill. The Cheshires and Welsh of 159 Brigade were to open the attack and gain the first ridge and 158 Brigade was to pass through them and capture the final objective under support of naval guns and the 11th Division artillery.

Orders for the attack reached 159 Brigade HQ after midnight. All its battalions were in the bush, where no communications could be had with 158 Brigade and, as a result, the 7th Cheshires and 4th Welsh attacked with no covering fire and the troops were met with terrific fire. Captains Hugh Mortimer Green, Alfred Hayward Howard and Lieutenant Allan Whitlock Nicholl Roderick were soon killed; however, Green's Company managed to seize a ruined house on a knoll and held on for a time before being counter-attacked and driven back. When day broke the two companies of the 5th Welsh found themselves in advance of the line and were attacked by the Turks. They had also been mistaken as Turks by the machine-gun teams of the 4th Welsh and as a result were forced to pull back to a trench line held by the 8th Northumberland Fusiliers and 11th Manchesters. The combined force rallied and drove the Turks back.

Meanwhile, 158 Brigade had failed to appear. Its troops had set out in the dark from Lala Baba across the Salt Lake and came under fire. The brigade then charged up a hill from the direction the fire was coming and ended up missing contact with 159 Brigade. An officer of the 53rd Division watched 158 Brigade advance:

The troops of the 53rd Division set off about 6 am across the Salt Lake. The Turkish shrapnel and rifle fire poured upon them as they advanced and only increased at the foot of Scimitar Hill. To watch parties of them attempting to steal up sheltered portions of the hill was a piteous sight. The cover was much reduced because the ground was now black with burning and most of the bushes gone. Many fell on all sides. The corner of a small wheat field near Abrikja was fringed with dead who looked like a company of men lying down in the shade. One saw many deeds of courage among officers and men.

The three battalions of 158 Brigade had left the beach at around 4.45 am, the 5th RWF leading, and headed across the bed of the dried Salt Lake, opening into artillery formation under shrapnel fire that caused some casualties. Once the brigade had got beyond the Salt Lake, the battalions deployed. Kenneth Taylor of the 5th RWF said: 'The hill, or rather ridge, in front of us had a gradual rise at first, which was covered with trees, hedges, bushes and oak scrub about waist-high. It was practically impossible to keep any sort of formation or keep touch and we were soon split up and rather disorganised.'

A similar tale was told by all three battalions. Lieutenant Colonel Jeff Reveley, commanding the 7th RWF, said:

It was apparently not known that the 159th Brigade had had to retire on the right, so that we were surprised at coming under rifle fire directly we reached the east side of Salt Lake, which we crossed under shrapnel fire from the hills in front. Under the shrapnel fire the battalion was opened out into artillery formation, remained very steady and suffered few casualties, the shrapnel appearing to burst too high up. The heavy rifle fire from the direction of Hill 50 drew our line, which was now extended in that direction, resulting in the swing to the right taking place too soon, so that our whole line was too much to the right – the 6th Royal Welch Fusiliers, who should have been on my left, being on my right. Messages were sent to the various companies of my battalion to work across more to the left and by the early afternoon they were facing south-east on a line running north-east from Sulajik.

The 5th RWF had passed through troops of 159 Brigade, who were mostly entrenched behind hedges, and had reached about 200 metres from the enemy by around 11.30 am when fire was opened up on them. Other troops of the brigade joined up with them: Lieutenant Colonel B.E. Philips of the 5th RWF was joined by Lieutenant Colonel T.W. Jones of the 6th RWF and an assault was ordered.

The situation had become exceedingly chaotic. The 5th RWF believed that they were to be in the centre with the 7th RWF on their right and the 6th RWF on their left; the 7th RWF believed they were in the centre, with the 5th RWF on their right! Utter confusion reigned among the scrubland, with parties of men scattered around: no one really knew the dispositions of any of the men and separate groups fought their own private battles.

Private Tommy Owen, 7th RWF, continued his tale of the advance in his letter:

> First we advanced across a mile of Salt Lake, the Turks shelling us like mad. Our Navy behind us in the Bay covered our advance by bombarding them in turn. In all we had about 3 miles to advance in short rushes and our chaps were falling like peas from their machine guns and snipers. Our company being the leading company suffered mostly and we lost all our officers very soon. Poor Lieutenant Buckley was the first to fall and we, Barmouth boys, missed him terribly as he was the most popular and best loved of all the officers. This was the 10th August and I shall never forget that day, although I wouldn't have missed it for worlds. It was the next day that I got hurt as fetching water a Lyddite shell burst knocked me unconscious, partly burying me and temporarily blinding me. I was taken to Malta and was there for three weeks in two hospitals. I arrived in England a fortnight ago, with a batch of New Zealanders and Australians.

Edmund Maurice Buckley was born on 1 December 1886, the son of Sir Edmund and Lady Sarah Mysie Buckley of Newtown and of 2 Marine Parade, Barmouth. His father was a former Member of Parliament, who had inherited the Dinas Mawddy Estate before becoming involved in the Hendre Ddu Slate and Slab Company. Buckley was educated at Cheltenham College and entered Manchester University in 1904 to study engineering. He left the university in 1907 and continued his studies while working as a draughtsman with Humber Works Limited at Beeston and Coventry, where he played rugby for Coventry Rugby Club.

Second Lieutenant Edmund Maurice Buckley 7th RWF, of Barmouth.

Buckley joined the Public Schools Battalion as a private at the outbreak of war and on 21 September 1914 was commissioned in the 7th RWF. He was mortally wounded during the advance on Scimitar Hill on 10 August and died in a field hospital two days later. He is buried in Lancashire Landing Cemetery.

Lieutenant Colonel Philips, CO of the 5th RWF, was killed on the top of the ridge and the same confusion existed there as on the immediate front. Officers took it upon themselves to begin to gather up their scattered groups of men and attempt to gain some control over the situation.

Later in the day the order was given for the whole line to advance at 5 pm, but Brigadier General Cowans realized that this was an impossibility; so he despatched the 5th Welsh under Major Dowdeswell to take command of all the troops he could find from the trenches to the left of Anafarta Farm and to seize a copse some 300 metres distant. The party dashed across the open ground but came under heavy fire and only about twenty men reached the copse. Dowdeswell led the remnants of his force back to safety during the night. By the end of the day no gains had been made but hundreds of men lay dead and dying on the ground.

On 10 August the 53rd (Welsh) Division had suffered significant casualties. Among its Welsh battalions it had lost the following:

5th RWF: its CO, Lieutenant Colonel Basil Edwin Philips; Second Lieutenants John Henry Frederick Leland, Robert Menzies Mocatta, Fitz Herbert Paget Synnott, Robert Clare Walton and twenty-eight men killed.

6th RWF: Major Wheller, Captain Arthur Charles Davies, Lieutenant Gwilym Rhys Jones, Second Lieutenant Philip Walter Jowett Bagnall and eight men killed.

7th RWF: Captain Edward Wynne Lloyd-Jones, Lieutenant Andrew Gordon Reed, Second Lieutenants Edmund Maurice Buckley, Russell Hafrenydd Jones, Bertram Baker Silcock and forty-seven men killed.

4th Welsh: Captains Hugh Mortimer Green and Alfred Hayward Howard; Lieutenant Allan Whitlock Nicholl Roderick and fifty-one men killed. Roderick was one of three brothers from the town of Burry Port, all officers, who were killed during the course of the war. Green's brother Cyril Mortimer Green was killed at Beersheba later in the war on 6 November 1917.

Captain Hugh Mortimer Green, 4th Welsh, of Aberystwyth, killed on 10 August 1915.

5th Welsh: Captains Rees Tudor Evans and Douglas Parker Robathan; Lieutenants Richard Stanley Evans, William David Russell Evans and Harry Edgar Osborne; Second Lieutenants Arthur John Allan Britton, Francis William Morgan Dunn, Oswald Coke Winstanley and twenty-one men killed.

On the next day, 11 August, 158 and 159 brigades were ordered to take over the divisional front and dig themselves in. 159 Brigade advanced towards Aghyl to join up with the 10th Division but came under fire and failed to advance beyond Anafarta Ova. Sir Ian Hamilton then brought up the 54th (East Anglian) Division in a last-ditch attempt to reach the Ejelmer Bay-Kayak Tepe Ridge to the left of the 53rd Division, using 163 Brigade of 54th Division but it too came under fire, sustaining heavy casualties. It was during this advance that the famous story of the lost E Company of the 5th Battalion, Norfolk Regiment occurred. Lieutenant Colonel Sir Horace Proctor-Beauchamp, with sixteen officers and 250 other ranks, mostly recruited from the king's Sandringham Estate, advanced into the scrub and were never heard of again. The story was turned into a film starring David Jason, entitled *All the King's Men*.

Meanwhile the 4th SWB, severely depleted in strength, received orders to attack

Kabak Kuyu on the afternoon of 11 August. The attack started at 7 pm, led by Second Lieutenant Aveling Francis Bell and Second Lieutenant Donald Arthur Addams-Williams with an advance party of 120 men but they came under machine-gun fire at once. Despite heavy casualties, the small force reached their objectives and digging parties then went forward to join them to begin to entrench. The battalion then beat off a counter-attack but its losses had been severe: Bell and Addams-Williams killed, Lieutenant Bury wounded and sixteen men killed. Reinforcements from Mudros arrived that night to join the battalion.

Second Lieutenant Donald Arthur Addams-Williams was born on 28 April 1896, the son of the Reverend Herbert and Grace Addams-Williams, of Llangibby Rectory, Monmouthshire. He was educated at Winton House, Winchester and at Marlborough College, joining the Public Schools Battalion, Royal Fusiliers after the declaration of war. He was commissioned in the 4th SWB on 18 November 1914 and was killed in action at Kabak Kuyu on 13 August 1915, aged just 19. His men attempted to recover his body several times but to no avail. Three months later a party of men from the Northamptonshire Regiment came across his body and buried him in 7th Field Ambulance Cemetery. Addams-Williams is commemorated on the village war memorial at Llangibby as well as on a fine marble plaque within St Cybi's Church, Holyhead.

Second Lieutenant Donald Arthur Addams Williams of the 4th SW

Captain A.W. Hooper, a friend of Addams-Williams, wrote to his mother to tell her of her son's death:

> May I offer my deepest sympathy in the loss you have sustained. Major Sir Lennox Napier was killed two days after your son. I am the only officer left out of the five who came out with the company and was in hospital wounded when Arthur was killed, hence I am somewhat handicapped, but I have spoken to Arthur's platoon sergeant several times about the sad incident and he has given me several little details about it.
>
> A covering party was sent forward to clear the enemy away from some wells from whence they had been sniping our troops for three or four days. This party was also to act

The memorial to Second Lieutenant Donald Arthur Addams-Williams in St Cybi's Church, Llangibby.

as a screen to keep the enemy from advancing or firing while the remainder of our battalion went forward and dug themselves in in an advanced position. Arthur, with his platoon, commanded a portion of this covering party. There were more of the enemy found near the wells than was anticipated and our covering party lost rather heavily. However, they nobly did their work and kept the enemy back while the new trenches were being dug.

Arthur was absolutely fearless and always very cheerful in the trenches. He took his men forward and had not advanced far before he was hit, he went on and presently was hit a second time.

However, though twice wounded, he continued to command his platoon, encouraging all of the men and showing them a noble example by his own heroism and disregard for self. A little time afterwards, while still advancing, he was wounded a third time. He turned completely round and must have died within a few seconds. His sergeant knelt by him as he died and has told me since that his death was a grand one to see.

The sergeant had to leave him to take charge of the platoon and when the covering party retired his body was not seen. Several times Sergeant Worthington (his platoon sergeant) volunteered to go forward and look for it; but the Turks were now holding the ground in very strong numbers and it would have meant a further sacrifice of life to send a search party out. Therefore, his body and those of two other officers who died the same evening were never recovered.

His death meant a great loss to his men, who thought so highly of him and to the whole company and also to myself, who found him an ever cheerful and lovable friend. The several parcels which have arrived for him have been distributed as you wished and the men appreciate the articles very, very much and wish me to thank you. We are still having rather a rough time of it. The weather has suddenly turned rather cold, and we were not prepared for the change.

Killed later in the day was Major Sir William Lennox Napier of Newtown, the pre-war CO of the 7th RWF who had retired in 1912. He volunteered to serve during the war and joined the 4th SWB in the rank of major, serving with his son Joseph. Napier was the son of Sir Joseph Napier, 2nd Baronet, and Maria, Lady Napier and was the husband of Mabel, Lady Napier, of 5 Harley Gardens, Fulham Road, London. He was 47 years old when he was killed by a sniper on 13 August and is buried in 7th Field Ambulance Cemetery. His son was taken prisoner at Gallipoli and survived the war, becoming Sir Joseph William Lennox Napier and was interviewed about his wartime experiences for the Imperial War Museum in 1984.

On 13 August HM Transport Ship *Royal Edward* left Alexandria for Mudros, carrying 1,367 officers and men who had been despatched from England as reinforcements for the 29th Division, a large number of whom were men of the 2nd SWB. During the morning the *Royal Edward* passed the British hospital ship *Soudan*, which was bringing sick and wounded men to Alexandria and was spotted by the German submarine *UB-14* some 6 miles off the island of Kandeloussa. Two torpedoes were fired at the *Royal Edward*, which sank within six minutes. The ship's captain managed to send out an SOS call and the *Soudan* returned, rescuing about 440 men. Two French destroyers and some trawlers rescued another 221. Casualty figures vary but fifty-seven of the men lost were men destined to join the 2nd SWB, while seven of her crew were Welshmen. The Borderers are commemorated on the Helles Memorial, while the seamen are commemorated on the Tower Hill Memorial. Among the men was Private Philip Evans (24938), the 23-year-old son of Philip and Maria Evans, of Mountain Cottage, Pentyrch.

Private Philip Evans (24938) of the 2nd SWB, lo aboard HM Transport Ship Royal Edward on 13 Augus 1915.

The 10th Division made one last attempt on 15 August to advance along the Kiretch Tepe Ridge with 30 and 31 brigades but met with heavy losses; the line stabilized on 17 August and trench warfare resumed. In five days the 53rd Division had lost 123 officers and 2,182 other ranks.

The Suvla landings had been a failure. This was not due to any failing by the men but largely of those in higher command, who had doomed the enterprise due to lack of initiative to make the most of the opportunities that had occurred on the first day and through lack of communication that turned the campaign into chaos. The fighting of 6 to 15 August had left the allied lines insufficiently advanced to secure Suvla Bay, so Sir Ian Hamilton decided on one more attempt to secure Scimitar and W Hills and also Hill 60 on the Anzac Front.

The 2nd SWB had, in the meantime, been in reserve before being sent back into the front line near Border Barricade from 12 to 16 August and were unaware of the loss of their comrades. The men were kept busy digging new saps and were continuously under fire; they were transferred to Suvla Bay early on 17 August and were attached to the 53rd (Welsh) Division. The reasoning behind this was to train the inexperienced territorials in the art of warfare, but by this time the division had tasted its first battle and the majority of the Borderers were reinforcements with little, if any, experience themselves.

On the evening of 19 August the 2nd SWB were relieved and moved to Chocolate Hill in preparation for a fresh offensive.

At 2.30 pm on 21 August the artillery bombardment opened up in front of 87 Brigade, backed up by naval artillery. The brigade had been detailed to attack Scimitar Hill, while 86 Brigade would attack W Hill on the right. The SWB was ordered to follow up the attack, although its machine-gun companies went with the first wave. The 11th (Northern) Division attacked on the right and the freshly-landed Yeomanry Division, with 5,000 men, was in reserve.

The artillery support was dire: even the naval bombardment did little damage due to the ships being unsighted and when the Inniskillings advanced they suffered terrible

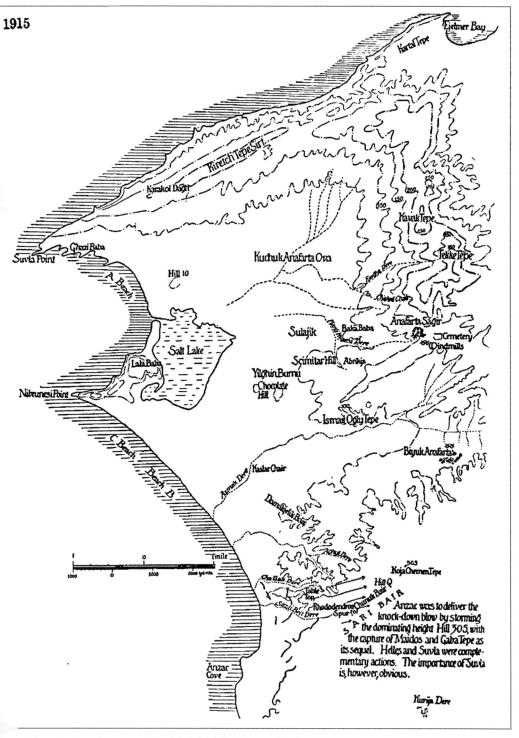

Map showing the area of the 53rd (Welsh) Division landings.

casualties. The crest of Scimitar Hill was reached in spite of this but they were forced back under withering fire.

The Border Regiment reinforced the attack but, with heavy fire from their left and 86 Brigade failing to make its objectives, the advance was halted. The 2nd SWB were then thrown into the attack but Major Going, now in command, found that chaos reigned among the troops in front. He began to reorganize the line, placing the Yeomanry in the centre, Borderers on the right and the 2nd SWB on the left and ordered the Inniskillings back to the support trenches.

Without support, the men were then ordered to withdraw and under cover of darkness the remnants of 87 Brigade returned. The 2nd SWB had suffered heavily again: three officers – Lieutenants Vincent McShane, Hugh George Nevile and Second Lieutenant Percy Edmund Burrell – and fifty other ranks had been killed. Together with the wounded and missing, the battalion had suffered 300 casualties. Regimental Sergeant Major Henry Westlake (4961) was awarded the DCM: 'On the 21st August at Suvla Bay he displayed great courage and resource in organising the water, ammunition and tool parties under fire.'

The 4th SWB had also been in action again at Kabak Kuyu, assisting an attack by battalions of the Australian and New Zealand infantry at Hill 60 (Kalajik Aghala) and suffered more casualties after being sent in to support the attack. The following three men of the battalion were awarded the DCM for their efforts there:

Private Matthew Beary (13102): 'For conspicuous gallantry on the 21st-22nd August 1915, near Sari Bair (Gallipoli Peninsula). Although untrained, he acted with skill and bravery as a bomb thrower, keeping the enemy at a distance and causing him considerable loss.' The regimental history mentions Beary as being 'a fine specimen of the Irishman turned Welsh miner'.

Corporal William John Gronow (13925): 'For conspicuous gallantry on the 21st-22nd August 1915, near Sari Bair (Gallipoli Peninsula). Although untrained, he acted with skill and bravery as a bomb thrower, keeping the enemy at a distance and causing him considerable loss.'

Sergeant William Myles (13113): 'For conspicuous gallantry and consistent good work from the 6th to the 21st August 1915, at Suvla, when he invariably exhibited great bravery and resource in the performance of his duties.'

The fighting at Hill 60 was merciless and the 4th SWB suffered another 7 officers and 102 men killed and missing and 11 officers and 286 men wounded. Fresh troops were brought up and fighting went on continuously until 27 August, when it ceased, leaving the Australians in possession of the hill.

Among the casualties was a 32-year-old Welshman. Lance Corporal George Watts (408) was born on 4 February 1883, the son of John and Esther Watts of The Lakes, Laugharne. On 31 May 1902 he enlisted at Devonport in the Royal Navy, signing up for twelve years, serving for over five years on active service and for six years on the reserve. By 1914 he was working as a miner in Australia and on 28 September 1914

enlisted in Townsville in the 15th AIF. He had landed with the battalion at Anzac Cove on 25 April, and apart from being hospitalized twice, he remained on the peninsula. During the fight for Hill 60 a detachment from A Company of the 15th AIF was sent to reinforce the unsuccessful attempt by the 13th AIF to take the position. Watts was wounded during the fighting and taken to the 16th Casualty Clearing Station on 27 August 1915 to be treated for a gunshot wound to his left arm. He was ferried aboard the hospital ship *Huntsgreen*, where he died of his wounds on 30 August 1915 and was buried at sea. He is commemorated alongside 4,931 comrades on the Lone Pine Memorial, Gallipoli.

It is now time to look at another theatre of war, Aden, before returning to the Western Front, where the BEF was preparing for a major attack at Loos in support of a French offensive to the north of Arras.

Chapter 15

The Aden Protectorate

The 1st/1st Brecknockshire [sic] Battalion, South Wales Borderers (Brecknocks) reached its war station at Pembroke Dock on 5 August 1914 and after two months on coastal defence duties at Dale and Milford was selected for overseas service. The battalion entrained from Neyland for Southampton on 29 October, embarked aboard the SS *Dilwara* and arrived in the Protectorate of Aden on 25 November 1914 to serve as the garrison, relieving the 1st Battalion, Lancashire Fusiliers, who returned to England to join the 29th Division. The battalion was commanded by Lieutenant Colonel Joseph Henry Russell Bailey (Lord Glanusk). There had been encounters with Turkish forces in the Yemen even before the Brecknocks arrived. Yemen bordered Aden and was garrisoned by Turks, threatening the security of the Protectorate. If the men on Gallipoli thought the climate was bad, then Aden was something else.

People at home were always immensely proud and supportive of the men serving overseas. Over the Christmas of 1914 a rugby match was played at Ystalyfera to raise funds for cigarettes for the Brecknocks. The *Cambrian Daily Leader* reported:

A view of the SWB 1907 summer camp at Porthcawl.

A Rugby benefit match was played at Ystalyfera on Christmas afternoon between teams selected by Mr. D.M. Evans, of Ystalyfera and Mr Dai Morgan, of Pontardawe. Howell Lewis, of Swansea and Lieut Hoskings, of Oxford University turned out for the home team. In the first half there was little to choose between the teams. Considering the state of the ground and the fact that all the boys were out of training, the exhibition was a good one, Pontardawe the first to score, D. Jenkins going over with a try. Fred Vaughan failed to convert. Just before the sounding of the final whistle the homesters made a dangerous rush and carried the ball over the visitors' line, with the result that Tom Morgan touched down. The kick at goal failed. The proceeds will be devoted to the purchase of cigarettes and tobacco for the Swansea Valley boys with the Breconshire Territorials now stationed in Aden.

The boys themselves also saw football as a means to escape the drudgery of life in Aden. The Reverend D. Saunders Jones, vicar of St David's, Brecon, received a letter from his son, who was a member of the Brecknocks:

Football is played every evening. One half of the Battalion played the R.G.A. yesterday and lost by 2-1. We had Ernie Green in goal; Dai Davies and Fred Phillips backs; J. Williams (Swansea Town), Bufton and Tim Williams half-backs; and Hoddinott, Steers, Monty Green, Larry Webb and Walter Williams (Builth Road) forwards. They played very well, considering that there was no grass about and the ground very hard and very fast.

Two battalions of Indian infantry had by now joined the Brecknocks. During the coming months the Brecknocks performed their duties under arduous conditions, with the men struggling in the heat. By June 1915 the Turks had become overconfident due to the lack of any incursions by the British into Yemen and they moved forward to reoccupy fortifications at Sheikh Saad. The Turks then began to shell the island of Perim, so troops in Aden were organized into the Aden Movable Company and ordered to prepare to join with local troops.

Some 400 men of the Brecknocks were allocated to the column, the remainder staying in Aden. A small artillery column was created to join it and on 3 July the force moved out to Sheikh Othman. Many men collapsed on the march, which was carried out during the full heat of the day, but by 7.30 pm the column had completed its 6-mile advance.

The march on the following day was even more arduous: 19 miles over difficult terrain to Lahej. Men and camels struggled in the heat and a large number of men fell down on the way, forcing the column to halt at midday. Firing began from the direction of Lahej, so the advanced guard, the 109th Indian Infantry and the artillery moved ahead. The column eventually reached Lahej later in the day but the men were utterly exhausted.

Thirteen men of the Brecknocks died of heat exhaustion on 4 July and two more were killed by Arabs who attacked Lahej that night. A further two men – Privates W. Lewis (2287) and H.J. Plevey (2114) – were captured and remained prisoners for the rest of the war.

Private Glynne Lougher Yorath (2201), from Cardiff, wrote a series of letters home from Aden, chronicling his experiences:

> Before we left England we were often told that life was unbearable in Aden and that it only rained here once every seven years or so. It is true that the thermometer stands comparatively high all the year round – it registers 75 and 78 degrees in the evenings at present – but we are able to drill and march with ease and shoot every day until noon... We found a well – but to our disappointment found it empty – so we decided to push on to another well which was about a mile further back and hold it until the guns fell back. We never found that well. We got off the track and were hopelessly lost in the desert without water, though we had dry bread, but we were afraid to eat it, as it would intensify thirst. We wandered about until about 12 o'clock and then we could go no further and decided to get a couple of hours' sleep and then search for water again. We could go another day without food, but we could not have lived another 24 hours without water. I fell asleep sucking the brass end of a cartridge. This was some relief. At 3 o'clock in the morning we pushed on and just as we had about chucked up the sponge came across an Arab hut, where we could get water. It was the filthiest stuff imaginable, but never in my life have I enjoyed a drink as I did that one. We filled our water bottles and after questioning the Arab found that we had wandered in a semi-circle and were about 10 miles from Shaik Othman, which we made for.

Yorath was commissioned on 20 November 1915 after being recommended for a commission by Lord Glanusk, was posted to the 12th SWB and was killed at Cambrai on 23 November 1917.

With the battalion now unfit for any further service, it was despatched to India on 5 August on being relieved by the 5th Buffs. By the end of August a number of men who had suffered badly in the heat of Aden returned home. The *Cambrian Daily Leader* of 25 August 1915 reported:

> About twenty members of the Breconshire Territorials arrived on Tuesday at the Albany Road Military Hospital, Cardiff, invalided from Aden, where they had been doing garrison duty since last October. In conversation with the men, they made it abundantly

Company Sergeant Major George Edward Best of the Brecknocks, invalided home i August 1915.

Aden - St. Point
The landing stage & S. S. Persia

A pre-war postcard of Aden harbour.

The Brecknock Battalion, SWB prior to embarking for Aden.

clear that they never want to see Aden again. 'The heat was enough to kill a cast-iron man, declared a member of the Ystradgynlais Company and there were very few of the battalion who did not spend part of the time in hospital. It is a fine place for reducing weight, I can tell you.'

The announcement of the dedication of the war memorial to the members of the Brecknocks who died on active service in Aden.

Before leaving Aden Lord Glanusk commissioned the creation of a brass memorial plaque to the members of his battalion that had fallen during their time in Aden. The plaque was unveiled in the Garrison Church at Aden.

A local newspaper reported on the battalion after its arrival in Mhow:

Relating some of his experiences, one of the men told a reporter that at Aden, to which the battalion first went at the end of October of last year, the heat was terribly trying and there was a good deal of sickness. They are now in a cooler climate, surrounded by green trees and grass, which remind them of home. The beneficial results of the removal soon became apparent in the improvement in the men's physical condition and they are now thoroughly fit. The conditions at their present station are very favourable for training on a large scale.

The battalion remained in its station at Mhow for the duration of the war, returning home in March 1919.

Chapter 16

The Prelude to the Battle of Loos

While the Welsh battalions on Gallipoli were facing perhaps their hardest fighting of the war, their counterparts on the Western Front were enjoying one of their quieter periods (relatively speaking, as casualties from 'trench wastage' continued on an almost daily basis). During the summer more Welsh units arrived at the front.

The 19th (Western) Division was inspected at Salisbury Plain by King George V on 23 June 1915. Advance parties left for France on 11 July and the main body crossed the English Channel between 16 and 21 July, moving to the point of assembly at Tilques, near St Omer. The division then moved to the area between Hazebrouck and St Omer for training.

The Welsh units within the 19th (Western) Division were: the 9th Battalion, Royal Welsh Fusiliers (9th RWF), under Lieutenant Colonel Henry John Madocks; 5th Battalion, South Wales Borderers (5th SWB), under Lieutenant Colonel Courtney Vor Trower; and the 9th Battalion, Welsh Regiment (9th Welsh), under Lieutenant Colonel Charles Henry Young. Both the 9th RWF and 9th Welsh were in 58 Brigade; the 5th SWB was converted into the Pioneer Battalion for the division.

A platoon of the 9th Welsh at Salisbury Plain just prior to embarkation for France.

By 27 July the division had moved to a new billeting area round Merville in Corps Reserve and the various brigades took it in turns to go into the trenches with either the Meerut or Lahore divisions to gain experience of the conditions and to learn the geography of the front line.

On 1 August the Indian Corps held the line from Port Arthur on the La Bassée Road to the Fauquissart Road, the Lahore Division on the right and Meerut Division on the left, a sunken road being the dividing line between the two divisions. A month was to pass before the 19th Division held a sector of the front line on its own.

The 2nd RWF, still with 19 Brigade, was in the same sector between Fauquissart and a location known as Red Lamp Salient, with the Lahore Division on its right. The nearest village, Laventie, was just behind the lines and was still relatively untouched by the war, offering the men decent billets and the officers a hotel and a restaurant. The town of Estaires was 5 miles further back, a larger town with more amenities that was used by the troops for their rest periods. On 17 August the brigade marched from the Fauquissart sector to Béthune to take the place of the 4 (Guards) Brigade in the 2nd Division, which was transferred to the newly-formed Guards Division, in the 2nd Division.

Béthune was another town well-loved by the soldier. Its typical Flemish centre consisted of a number of shops, restaurants and hotels situated around a large square and there was more than enough entertainment there for the men, funds permitting.

The square and belfry of Béthune, a sight familiar to any of the soldiers who served in the sector during the early stages of the war.

The Welsh Guards' first parade at Buckingham Palace.

Visiting Béthune today, the centre of the town has been rebuilt in much the same style as it was during 1915. The famous belfry still dominates the square and the officers who once frequented the Café du Globe and the Hôtel de France would recognize the town even today.

The reason that 19 Brigade was transferred to the 2nd Division was that permission had been given to form a Guards Division, which is why the 4 (Guards) Brigade had been transferred. Between March and June the Welsh Guards had been training at Esher, returning to Wellington Barracks at the end of the month and taking up duties as the Guards Battalion in the West End of London. On 3 August the battalion paraded in the gardens of Buckingham Palace and were presented with the King's Colour, which were consecrated by the Bishop of St Asaph.

On 7 August the king became colonel-in-chief of the regiment, a great honour for the newly-formed unit. In the early hours of 17 August the Welsh Guards left Waterloo Station for Southampton and then sailed to France, arriving at Le Havre at 7 am on 18 August to join 3 (Guards) Brigade of the newly-formed Guards Division.

While the Welsh Guards remained in Le Havre, the 5th SWB became the first Welsh unit in the 19th Division to suffer the death of a man in France. Company Sergeant Major James Maurice Keen (14104) was the husband of Sarah Ann Keen of 6 Inkerman Terrace, Tredegar. He died at Le Havre on 16 August and is buried in Ste. Marie Cemetery. He was 45 years old. The battalion had by that time left to gain instruction in pioneer work in the trenches, setting up HQ in a château in Gorre. The training involved setting up wire entanglements, revetting and improving trenches and communication trenches, the repair of defensive posts and receiving instruction from the sappers of the Indian Corps. Carpenters were engaged in making frames for the trenches, while other companies were busy on the roads.

58 Brigade was attached for instruction to the Dehradun Brigade and the 9th Welsh began its first tour of instruction in the trenches on 17 August. The 9th RWF began its tour at Neuve Église on 20 August. The 9th Welsh suffered its first two casualties on 22 August, when Captain George Owen Green and Private William Morris (14740) were killed. On the following day the 9th RWF suffered their first casualty when Second Lieutenant Richard Nixon Thomas died of wounds at Merville. He is buried in Merville Communal Cemetery. Thomas was born in Sydney in 1896, the son of David Brown Thomas and Elizabeth Maud Thomas. By 1911 the family had moved to England.

Captain George Owen Green was the son of James George Green and Jane Green of Panteg, Llanbadarn Road, Aberystwyth and the grandson of Alderman George Green, a mining engineer. Educated at Llandovery College from 1889 to 1895, he had married Elizabeth Ann Bevan and they went to British Columbia, where Green worked as an engineer in the gold mines. He also went to Canada to inspect mining property. He had held mining appointments as far afield as Russia and South America prior to the war. The family then returned to Aberystwyth, where Green was prominent in many local societies, including the golf club and St David's Lodge of Freemasons. Sadly, Mrs Green died in childbirth soon after arriving back home. At the end of 1914, Green applied for a commission in the army and was duly commissioned in the 9th Welsh. He was in charge of a working party near Laventie when he was killed by a German Sniper on

Captain George Owen Green, 9th Welsh, of Aberystwyth, one of the first two men of the battalion killed in France on 22 August 1915.

248

The grave of Captain George Owen Green at Rue-du-Bacquerot No. 1 Military Cemetery, Laventie.

23 August 1915 and is buried at Rue-du-Bacquerot No. 1 Military Cemetery, Laventie. He was 36 years old.

Private William Morris (14740) was born in 1897, the son of David and Ellen Morris of East Lodge, St Ishmaels. He enlisted at Milford in the 9th Welsh. Morris was wounded at Laventie and died later that day, on 23 August 1915. He was 19 years old and is buried at Merville Communal Cemetery.

On 22 August the 19th Division was told that by the end of the month it was to relieve troops of the 2nd and 7th divisions in the front line. The line ran from Grenadier Road communication trench, just north of Givenchy, to Farm Corner, near Festubert, and was to be divided into two sections: 58 Brigade was to take over the right and 57 Brigade the left; 56 Brigade was to be in Army Reserve in the Les Lobes-Lawe Canal-Lez Choquaux-La Tombe Willot area. Three battalions of each front-line brigade were to hold the front line with, one in support, the dividing line between brigades being a point where the Orchard support trench ran into the fire trench on the southern side of the Orchard Apex.

The division began to take over the line on the 28th; 57 Brigade relieving 22 Brigade of the 7th Division at night. The 10th Warwicks took over the right in the orchard, 10th Worcesters the centre and 8th Gloucesters the left, with the North Staffords being in reserve. During the day a tragic accident occured during bombing instruction at Gorre, killing two men and wounding a third, all of the 5th SWB. The dead men were Captain Trevor Edward Lewis of Tynant, Taff's Well and Private Raymond Dart (14058), the son of John and Annie Powell, of 3 Somerset Street, Pontnewydd. Both men are buried in Merville Communal Cemetery.

Early in September 87 Brigade moved to La Croix Marmeuse to begin its first proper tour of the trenches. On 30 August the 9th RWF took over the trenches south of Festubert to begin its first tour, while on 4 September the 9th Welsh took over some wet and muddy trenches from the 9th Cheshires to the north-west of Givenchy to begin its first proper tour of duty. The division was now seen as trained and ready for operations. Two weeks after arriving, a member of the 9th Welsh, Private Charles Evans, wrote home to his parents in Milford Haven to let them know how life in France was:

Private Raymond Dart (14058) of the 5th SWB, mortally wounded while grenade-training at Gorre or 28 August 1915.

Just a few lines to let you know that we are all right. We have had a rough time. One night last week the Germans tried to gas us, but it was not strong enough. It was like a thick fog coming over to our trenches. We have been in the trenches nearly a fortnight and we don't know when we are coming out for a rest. We caught a German in our barbed wire one night. He had a knife and a bomb. He was going to chuck the bomb over and then cut our chaps' throats, but the Welsh chaps were too cute for him and he was shot. He was the first German I have seen since I have been in France. We had a couple of Jack Johnsons on Wednesday and we had about 20 casualties and 5 buried and 20 wounded belonging to the Cheshires. The Germans were asking us when are we going to march to Berlin and we asked them 'When is the Kaiser coming to London?' I think I have told you all this time. CHARLIE.

The 4th RWF was transferred from the 1st Division on 1 September and joined the 47th (2nd London) Division as the Pioneer Battalion, initially working under the Royal Engineers. It would remain with the division for the rest of the war.

Meanwhile, the 22nd Division arrived in France in early September. Attached to 67 Brigade of the division were four more Welsh battalions landed between 5 and 6 September: the 11th RWF under the command of Lieutenant Colonel George William David Bowen; the 7th SWB under the command of Lieutenant Colonel James Grimwood; the 8th SWB under the command of Lieutenant Colonel William Dennistoun Sword; and the 11th Welsh (Cardiff Pals) under the command of Lieutenant Colonel Francis Russell Parkinson. The units concentrated around the town of Flesselles, north of Amiens and the River Somme. The weather was fine and the countryside there had barely been blighted by war. The 11th Welsh moved to billets in Suzanne and were attached to the 1st Devons at Maricourt for instruction in trench duties.

All four of these units suffered their first casualties of the war here. On 16 September Private Evan Douglas Davies (19010) of the 7th SWB, a Bedwellty man, was killed. He is buried in Aveluy Communal Cemetery Extension. On 18 September two men of the 8th SWB were killed during a German attack on their trenches: Sergeant John Watkins (16050) of Newport and Corporal Robert Davies (16526) of Abercarn. Both men are buried in Hangard Communal Cemetery Extension. Also on 18 September, Private David Rosser (14566) of the 11th RWF, a Tylorstown man, was killed. He is buried in Carnoy Military Cemetery. The 8th SWB lost two more men on 20 September, while on 21 September the 7th SWB lost another man killed and the 8th SWB lost another two. Also on 21 September, Lance Corporal Alfred Johnson (15334) of the 11th Welsh was killed by a shell that hit his dugout, becoming the battalion's first casualty in France. Johnson was the son of Isaac and Selina Johnson of 27 Tylcha Wen Crescent, Tonyrefail and was born in Malmesbury, Wiltshire. The 24-year-old is buried in Assevillers New British Cemetery.

Lance Corporal Alfred Johnson (15334), the first member of the 11th Welsh (Cardiff Pals) to be killed in France.

The division was only in France for a short time, as on 26 October it began to move out from the Somme for service in Salonika. In the meantime the 11th RWF would lose three more men killed in France: Private Arthur Way (24865) of Treharris died of wounds on 23 September; Private Herbert William Johnson (14573) of Liverpool died on 5 October; and Private John Eden (14091) of Widnes died of wounds on 19 October. The 11th Welsh lost two more men killed in France: Private William Hall Webster Coutts (15105) of Splott was accidentally killed while training on a Lewis gun on 9 October and Private Emlyn Pryce Matthews (14176) of Cardiff was shot by a sniper on 15 October. Matthews has no known grave, so is possibly one of the two unknown Welshmen buried in Assevillers.

Sergeant John Watkins (16050) of Newport, one of the first two men of the 8th SWB killed in France.

When the 22nd Division sailed for Salonika from Marseilles on 30 October, Lieutenant Colonel Parkinson, the man who had raised the 11th Welsh, was not among them. He was deemed as being too old for

The grave of Lance Corporal Alfred Johnson at Assevillers. There are two graves to unknown soldiers of the Welsh Regiment buried in the cemetery.

service there and he was replaced as CO by Lieutenant Colonel Albert Victor Cowley.

Also to arrive during September was the 25th Division, containing two more Welsh battalions: the 10th RWF, commanded by Lieutenant Colonel William Randall Hamilton Beresford-Ash, landed on 27 September; and the 6th SWB, the Pioneer Battalion to the division, commanded by Lieutenant Colonel Edward Vincent Osborne Hewett, landed on 25 September. The division moved via Chocques to the Le Sart area, where it concentrated before moving to the Armentières sector for trench familiarization.

Going back to the 19th Division, which was still in the trenches near Givenchy, the middle of September was spent in readying itself for the forthcoming Battle of Loos. During its last tour before the battle, the 9th Welsh lost Second Lieutenant Treharne and Private William Hart (38168) killed and Lieutenant Durtnall, the signalling officer, wounded. Private William Hart (38168) was the son of Joseph and Eliza Hart, of 45 Hoy Street, Canning Town, London. He lived at Hendre Eynon, St David's prior to the war, working as a farm

One of two graves to unknown members of the Welsh Regiment buried in Assevillers New British Cemetery, Somme.

labourer. He was wounded by shellfire on 21 September and died the following day, aged 19. Hart is buried in Brown's Road Military Cemetery, Festubert. Second Lieutenant Leslie Llewellyn Treharne was the son of Edward Treharne, JP (a surgeon) and Margaret Louisa Treharne, of Cadoxton. His father had played rugby for Pontypridd and Wales. Treharne was also wounded on the 21st and died on 24 September, aged 23. He is buried in Chocques Military Cemetery.

The second wife of Lord St David's, Elizabeth Frances Philipps, lost the first of two brothers during September. Second Lieutenant Edward Hugh Hastings Rawdon-Hastings was born on 31 August 1895, the younger son of the Honourable Paulyn Francis Cuthbert Rawdon-Hastings and Lady Maud Rawdon-Hastings, of 14 Stafford

The memorial plaque to the Rawdon-Hastings brothers in Roch Church, Pembrokeshire.

Mansions, Buckingham Gate, London. He was educated at Eton and Oxford before being commissioned in the 2nd Black Watch from Sandhurst in 1914. He joined the battalion in France in the summer of 1915, which was attached to the Bareilly Brigade, Meerut Division, having spent several years in India. He contracted enteric fever and was invalided to No. 14 Stationary Hospital at Wimereux, where he died on 15 September 1915, aged 20. Rawdon-Hastings is buried in Wimereux Communal Cemetery. He had been awarded the King George V Coronation Medal while acting as page to his uncle, the Earl of Loudoun.

Second Lieutenant Edward Hugh Hastings Rawdon-Hastings, 2nd Black Watch.

Chapter 17

The Battle of Loos

B y the end of the summer of 1915 the great losses suffered by the allies on the Western Front, together with equally large losses suffered by Russia and the diversion of large numbers of troops and much-needed munitions to Gallipoli had proved to the British (and everyone else) that artillery was the key to winning the war. As a result of the debacle at Neuve Chapelle and Festubert the might of British industry increased its efforts to get more artillery pieces and shells out to France.

A new army, the Third, was formed on 15 July, commanded by General Sir Charles Monro. It took over 22 miles of front from Hébuterne to Chaulnes, straddling the Somme.

General Joffre, the French commander-in-chief, planned to attack the Germans in the Champagne region and to cut off the Noyon Salient and pressed the British to co-operate with him by launching an attack against the Loos to Givenchy front. The French objected to this proposal due to the unsuitability of the ground, being marshy and well-defended, and that the loss of so many seasoned and experienced troops meant that the new divisions in France were not yet ready to undertake such a plan.

The French appealed to the British government to pursue their plans and in the end Lord Kitchener overruled Sir John French, ordering him to support the French to the utmost of his power. French reluctantly agreed to attack to the north of the French Tenth Army, which was to launch a major assault in the area of Vimy Ridge.

During the summer of 1915 the French had obtained a footing on the Vimy Ridge but had failed to completely capture it, so planned for a renewed offensive there on a 12-mile front.

The area to their left, between Liéven, Lens and Loos, was a large coal-mining area and was deemed unsuitable for an attack, so was not included in the plan. North of there, from Loos to Givenchy, the British were to attack on a 6-mile front with six divisions supported by 114 heavy guns. XI Corps was to be held in reserve and five cavalry divisions were standing by to exploit any gains. Sir Douglas Haig's First Army had responsibility for the attack and drew up two plans:

(1) An attack without gas by the 47th and 15th divisions on Loos and Hill 70; and by the 9th Division on the Hohenzollern Redoubt and Fosse 8; and the development of this first phase, if successful.

(2) An attack on the whole front by six divisions, employing gas and smoke, the two outer divisions forming defensive flanks while the remaining four

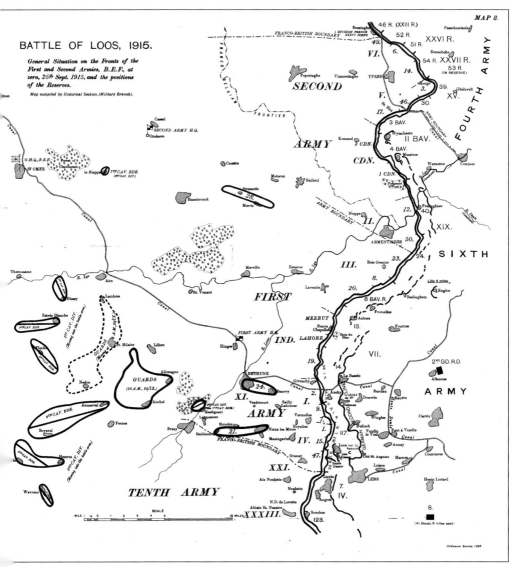

A map taken from the Official History *showing the dispositions of the attacking troops at the Battle of Loos on 25 September 1915.*

rushed the German second system and established themselves on the Haute Deûle Canal 4 miles distant. The Indian Corps north of Givenchy and two divisions of the Second Army, near Bellewaarde Lake, were to make subsidiary attacks to tie the enemy down.

The main French offensive was to be in the Champagne region, using a force of thirty-four divisions and eight cavalry divisions, attacking along a 22-mile front.

255

In the meantime the Germans, realizing the probability of attack, had constructed a second defensive system to the rear of their front line and had also constructed a number of concrete emplacements, as well as utilizing the chalky ground of the area to construct deep dugouts. Their front lines were well-protected by deep fields of barbed wire that were swept by machine guns.

Haig decided to precede the attack with a heavy continuous artillery barrage, followed by the release of poison gas from 5,500 cylinders that had been brought up into the front-line trenches by 24 September. Two newly arrived divisions, the 21st and 24th, were moved to the immediate rear in readiness to exploit any success, while the attacking units would comprise the following from the First Army: IV Corps – 47th, 15th and 1st divisions (Double Crassier to Vermelles to Hulluch Road); I Corps – 7th, 9th and 2nd divisions (Latter Road to Givenchy).

The 1st Division, as we know, contained the 1st SWB and 2nd Welsh; the 2nd Division, the 2nd RWF; the 7th Division, the 1st RWF; and the 47th Division, the 4th RWF. The 19th Division, containing the 9th RWF, 5th SWB and 9th Welsh, was to make a diversionary attack near Givenchy alongside the Indian Corps.

All the troops in the front line were fascinated by the arrangements for delivering the gas. The cylinders were dug into the face of the parapet and each was connected by either a rubber or flexible copper tube to a pipe that was buried in the parapet with the nozzle protruding from it. The gas was released by turning a screw and upon exiting the pipes formed a cloud which, it was hoped, would blow across no man's land into the German trenches, wind permitting of course. Special gas companies were formed within the Royal Engineers to handle and deliver the gas. The decision regarding whether or not to use the gas fell to Sir Douglas Haig, whose judgement relied on accurate weather forecasting from a meteorologist who was stationed at HQ. It was not until 3 am on the actual day of battle, 25 September, that the order was given to release gas at 5.50 am and to assault on the whole front at 6.30 am.

As planned, the Royal Engineers released the gas, but in several places along the line the wind changed direction and the gas blew back into the British trenches. At 6.30 am, all along the line the troops arose and began their slow walk across no man's land.

The 47th Division was to seize Loos and the Double Crassier and form a defensive flank facing south. The town of Loos was captured but the division failed to advance far enough along the Double Crassier – two spoil heaps – beyond Loos. The divisional pioneers, the 4th RWF, lost just one man killed during the day: Private Robert Thomas Hughes (7284), of Mill Bank, Llanrhaeadr, Denbigh. His CO wrote to his mother:

4th Royal Welch Fusiliers, Brit. Exp. Force, France, 1st Oct., 1915. Mrs Hughes, I write as the officer commanding B Company of this Battalion to sympathise very sincerely with you in the loss of your son, 7284 Private R.T. Hughes. I was with your son in action and always found him a very good soldier and was, in fact, very proud of him; besides which, he was always popular with his friends in his Platoon and Company. I was quite close to him when he was killed and I

A view of the devastated town of Loos after the battle.

can assure you that death was absolutely instantaneous. He died a soldier's death in action – the noblest and best death and as such everybody will reverence him. His loss is greatly felt by me and by all the officers in the Company and the Colonel commanding the Battalion has also requested me to express to you his sympathy. Again saying how deeply sorry and grieved I am, I remain, yours very sincerely, H.G. PICTON-DAVIES, O.C. 'B' Company. R.W.F.

The 15th (Scottish) Division rushed across the enemy first system into Loos, where the men began hunting down isolated groups of Germans in cellars and dugouts. Casualties had been heavy during the capture of the town, but the Scots chased the enemy over the top of Hill 70 and captured the redoubt there. Seeing the Germans running back into Cité St Elie, their second line of defence, the advance continued down the slopes of the hill only to be held up against the uncut wire of the Second Line. The Scots had advanced over 2 miles and had successfully captured a very strong defensive position and began digging in on the summit of Hill 70.

The 1st Division had taken over the line between the La Bassée Canal and Loos and was to capture the southern portion of Hulluch and trenches to the south and join up with the 15th Division. 1 and 2 Brigades were sent up into the attack, 3 Brigade (1st SWB and 2nd Welsh) being in reserve, ready to exploit a breakthrough. While the 1 Brigade attack was partially successful, advancing over 500 metres to the Lens to La Bassée Road, the brigade suffered heavy casualties and did not have enough manpower to attack Hulluch. Meanwhile, 2 Brigade had been held up by the Germans at Lone Tree, suffering from the effects of the gas that had blown back onto them and being stopped by barbed wire that had remained uncut from the artillery barrage. Fire was also poured into 2 Brigade from Bois Carré, a small copse that had been captured by 1 Brigade that morning. The 1st Black Watch were forced to deploy to assist 2 Brigade, thus further weakening the 15th Division.

Due to this failure, the Scots, still on Hill 70, were exposed to enfilade fire from the German Second Line to the north, and by the failure of the left of the 47th Division to occupy the end of the Double Crassier; thus it was also exposed to enfilade fire from the south. The Germans then attacked Hill 70 with fresh reinforcements at 1 pm, recapturing the hill.

With the 15th Division in trouble, the GOC 1st Division told 2 Brigade to collect what men it could and move south through the 15th Division area to outflank the enemy from that direction, while 3 Brigade was moved to support 1 Brigade during a renewed attack on Hulluch.

3 Brigade moved off with the 2nd Munsters, only 250 strong, on the right, the 2nd Welsh to their left and the 1st SWB in support. The trenches were, however, choked with wounded men, so 3 Brigade began moving over open ground.

The 1st SWB and 2nd Welsh had left their reserve positions at Philosophe at 3.30 am, moving through some old French trenches just in front of Vermelles. By now it had begun to rain and the Welshmen witnessed the gas blowing back over the front-line troops. The Munsters left Le Rutoire farm at around 10.45 am and moved up through communication trenches to La Haie Copse. No news of the battle was received by the remainder of 3 Brigade until about 11 am, when the 2nd Welsh moved forward, passing large numbers of wounded and gassed men en route to cross the German trenches north of La Haie Copse. The 1st SWB then received orders to follow, crossing no man's land before sheltering in the support trench east of La Haie.

The Welshmen then received news that the enemy were still holding on to their trenches between La Haie and Lone Tree and that 1 Brigade had managed to enter Hulluch, but were being pushed out due to lack of men. The 2nd Welsh moved off in extended order to reinforce 1 Brigade – A and D companies leading, B and C in support – and crossed the German front line to the north of the Vermelles to Hulluch Road. During the advance, the 2nd Welsh came under shell and machine-gun fire from Bois Carré, the support companies suffering some 150 casualties.

No sign was seen of the Munsters, so Lieutenant Colonel Prothero pushed the battalion on towards the German third line, Gun Trench, that was almost 1,000 metres behind their first line. The battalion then came under heavy fire from Hulluch and took heavy casualties. With the odds against him, Prothero ordered the survivors to wheel right towards the south of Hulluch and the right of 1 Brigade, bringing the battalion up against the rear of the Germans, and a fierce struggle broke out. Corporal William Morris (14582) of

Corporal William Archibald Morris (14582) of Carmarthen. Heralded for his display of courage at Loos, Morris was later awarded the DCM. He died at the 1st Southern Military Hospital, Birmingham on 2 May 1918 and is buried in St David's churchyard, Carmarthen.

258

Carmarthen was notably gallant in 'coolly walking about, receiving three bullets through his clothing and equipment'.

After a gallant fight, at 2.30 pm five officers and 160 Germans surrendered to C Company, which sent No. 12 Platoon to escort them to Noeux-les-Mines. Prothero then detached one company to get in the rear of Lone Tree Redoubt and then to the Lens to La Bassée Road, where the 2nd Welsh made contact with the 1st SWB. Meanwhile, 400 men of the 157 Regiment, 117th Infantry Division surrendered to the British. 2 Brigade was now able to move forward and gained touch with the 15th Division at Bois Hugo.

The *Official History, 1915 Volume 2* mentioned the part played by the 2nd Welsh: 'The leading of the 2nd Welsh after it had broken through and arrived in rear of the enemy trenches near Lone Tree, which resulted in the surrender of Ritter's force and enabled the 2nd Brigade to advance, was an exhibition of initiative only too rare on 25th September.'

The 1st SWB had not been heavily involved during the advance, losing just three men killed on the first day of the battle. Meanwhile, to the north, at Givenchy the 19th Division had suffered a disaster. 5 Brigade of the 2nd Division at Givenchy was to create a diversion just north of the La Bassée Canal. Its assault was carried out half an hour before the main assault after only ten minutes' discharge of gas and smoke and caught the Germans by surprise. The brigade got into the German lines and pushed forward to the German reserve trenches, where they were caught by machine-gun and rifle fire.

This short-lived success signalled the launching of the attack by the 9th RWF and 9th Welsh of 58 Brigade, who rose from their trenches to advance. Both battalions were mown down by machine-gun fire in no man's land and suffered terrible casualties.

The 9th RWF lost seven officers: Lieutenant Colonel Henry John Madocks; Major Charles Annesley Acton; Captains Lewis Stephen Hogg, Basil William Edmond Hoyle and Edward Geoffrey Payne; Lieutenant Charles Fleming Jelinger Symons; and Second Lieutenant Reginald Joseph Williams. In addition, 100 other ranks were killed, 4 officers and 129 men were wounded and 85 missing.

The 9th Welsh lost four officers: Captain William Montagu Hughes-Hughes; Second Lieutenants Charles John Randles Dawkins, Meredyth Owen and Douglas Jonathan Rogers Wilson – and 75 men killed, plus another 9 officers and 150 men wounded, several of whom died over the coming days.

One of the men of the battalion who died of wounds suffered at Loos was the young Lieutenant William Henry Kenrick Owen. He was born on 12 December 1893, the son of William Pierce Owen (a solicitor) and Ethel Owen, of Bodowen, Aberystwyth. He was educated at Aberystwyth

Lieutenant William Henry Kenrick Owen, of Aberystwyth, mortally wounded at Loos.

Grammar School and Shrewsbury School before being admitted to Clare College, Cambridge on 11 October 1913. On 15 August 1914 he applied for a commission in the army and joined the 9th Welsh. He was the battalion's Scouting Officer in the 9th Welsh and would have been one of the first out of the trenches when the whistles blew for the battalion to make its charge. He was badly wounded and was evacuated to the Military Hospital at Rouen, where he died on 1 October 1915, aged 21. He is buried at St Sever Cemetery, Rouen.

The commander of a Royal Artillery unit that witnessed the futile attack sent the following letter to Lieutenant Colonel Young of the 9th Welsh:

> May I be allowed to offer you my very real and sincere sympathy on the losses sustained by your Regiment... If ever a Regiment had won a VC pendant to their regimental crest, it is yours, for they knew what they were in for and went forward without demur. The regrettable losses and behaviour of the men at all events show the nature of the Kitchener regiments and if all are imbued with the same spirit as your command the ultimate issue of the war cannot be in doubt.

Private William Newell (306913), a former railway porter from Arthog, was serving at Loos with the 59th Field Ambulance, Royal Army Medical Corps. He wrote home on the night of 26 September to inform his father of his experiences during the opening day of the battle:

> Very severe fighting took place early yesterday morning and a large number of cases were attended in this field hospital in 14 hours. Yesterday I went for a few hours' sleep at 10 pm and was called again at 2 am this morning. I have just turned in now, but may be up again at any moment. This is our real work which we have looked forward to long since and I am very proud to say that everyone has and is doing splendid work.
>
> The 9th Welsh, 9th Cheshires and 9th R.W.F. have suffered terribly and practically all our patients are from these regiments. Two fellows whom I knew personally were among them. One a Corporal named Thomas who in civil life was booking clerk at Llandudno and the other Corporal Walter Thomas Pugh, who used to work for Messrs Lloyd and Williams, Barmouth and used to go to Garth regularly. Pugh was slightly cut by shrapnel over the left eye, but poor Thomas was badly wounded. It would really be too horrible for me to describe the suffering and wounds our fellow countrymen are bearing for the old country's sake and I can assure you these horrible sights will never in my whole career be forgotten.
>
> So far our division has been very lucky as regards casualties, considering the firing our fellows have been under. It appears several of the Welsh were between the German trenches and ours, lying wounded all day, so last night several fellows volunteered to fetch them in when it was dark, but as soon as our fellows attempted it the Germans opened a cruel fire upon them, so many

poor chaps (who could possibly recover if brought in) must suffer a lingering death. Until we are relieved from this action I cannot write but very little but will write when we are enjoying a rest.

During the assault by I Corps, the ground over which the 7th and 9th divisions and the right brigade of the 2nd Division had to advance was a flat, bare expanse that contained three strongly-defended and important German posts: the Quarries, Fosse 8 (which incorporated the Hohenzollern Redoubt) and the fortified village of Auchy. Behind the second line were the villages of Hulluch, Cité St Elie and Haisnes.

The 7th Division's orders had stated that their attack was not planned to capture any particular locality but to break down the enemy's defensive system and 'shake free from the present indecisive trench warfare'. Four objectives were given: the enemy's first-line trenches; the Quarries; Cité St Elie; and the Haute-Deûle Canal crossings at Wingles and Meurchin, with the high ground east of it. The 1st RWF would be in the rear, with the South Staffs attacking on the right and the Royal Warwicks on the left, and was to advance behind the two covering the left flank of the brigade.

At 6.30 am the leading brigades of the 7th Division advanced under a cloud of gas and smoke. With their gas helmets proving to be useless, the men removed them and many were gassed. Shrapnel fire burst overhead and as the men poured through the gaps in the wire they became easy pickings for the German machine-gun teams. Upon reaching the Lens Road, near the Vermelles to Hulluch crossroads, 20 Brigade was held up. Meanwhile 22 Brigade had crossed almost 500 metres over no man's land before becoming caught up in the barbed wire. On the left, 26 Brigade of the 9th Division attacked the Hohenzollern Redoubt and with great courage captured the heavily-fortified Hohenzollern Redoubt and Fosse 8 and got into Pekin Trench in the German Second Line just west of Haisnes, before being forced back. The gas had also blown back over the 9th Division and caused such casualties that not enough men survived to capture Madagascar Trench, the portion of the German front line opposite the Hohenzollern Redoubt; and as a result the 9th Division was forced to form a defensive flank instead of attacking the German Second Line.

Upon advancing at 6.30 am the 1st RWF came under heavy fire from the Hohenzollern Redoubt and from Big Willie Trench, so Captain Kearsley, leading the battalion, swung some men around to deal with this fire. He was badly wounded in the attempt. By now the 1st RWF had become tangled up with troops from the South Staffs and Royal Warwicks and it was not until the Queen's moved forward from the reserve at 8.30 am that the brigade advanced over the Quarries, a great chalk excavation on the crest line, 100 metres wide and 6 metres deep, honeycombed with dugouts, before being brought to a halt in front of Cité St Elie. The survivors withdrew to the Quarries to dig in. A further attack on Cité St Elie was carried out by 21 Brigade, but despite the extra manpower, the Germans held on to the village. By 7.30 pm the 7th Division was ordered to hold on to the positions it had gained. The 1st RWF had lost four officers: Captain Guy William Stuart Morgan, Lieutenants Henry John Francis Brunt, John Owen Iles and Walter Ibbe James; and ninety-seven men killed on the first day. Eleven officers and 264 men had been wounded, while 135 men were missing.

The 2nd Division (2nd RWF) had a day of disaster when attacking towards Auchy. 19 and 6 brigades on the right had to attack on the immediate left of the 9th Division along the La Bassée Canal, over an area strongly defended by the Germans, who had made strongpoints from brick stacks, embankments and cottages. The Germans had withdrawn from their front line trenches prior to the attack, so no man's land was wide and the Germans escaped the worst of the artillery bombardment. The attack of 19 Brigade was carried out by the 1st Middlesex and 2nd Argyll and Sutherland Highlanders, with the 2nd RWF in support. Their final objective was the far side of Auchy. The wind was blowing back over the British lines and a Royal Engineer officer declined to open the gas cylinders for this reason but was ordered to do so. As a result these two battalions of 19 Brigade rose from their trenches to advance through clouds of gas and smoke and were cut down by the Germans.

Lieutenant John Owen Iles, 1st RWF. Born on 18 May 1893, he was the son of Joh. Cyril Iles and Enid Agnes Machell Iles of Redhill, Farnham, Surrey. Educated Rugby and Caius College, Cambridge, Iles was killed Loos on 25 September 1915

Unknowingly, the 2nd RWF began to advance but soon found the ground littered with dead and wounded men and the gas was still drifting over no man's land. As they advanced they began to come under heavy fire and the men were forced to the ground. At 9 am a despatch runner brought forward orders to stand fast prior to relaunching the attack at 11 am, so the survivors crawled back to their trenches. Captain Samson was seen to fall wounded just outside the front-line wire. Lieutenant Harrison MacDonald Blair wrote:

> The Battalion attack was a forlorn hope. About 8 o'clock the officers blew their whistles and we went over, B Company on our left. I saw no shells bursting over the German trenches, so, the morning being bright and sunny, the German riflemen and machine-gunners took their toll of us undisturbed. We may have gone 40 yards and then the line just fell down. Samson was killed; Goldsmith and I were badly wounded; the casualties among the men were heavy.
>
> I was out of the picture with a wounded pelvis. A less wounded man near me wanted to carry me in, but I told him we would both be shot; however, he started to get up and was wounded again immediately. I crawled back slowly and was laid in the bottom of the trench, where I was nearly suffocated with gas before the Doctor came and had me moved to a narrow communication trench. I lay there for five hours. No stretcher could be used, even if one had been available. Eventually I was carried down slung on my putties between two rifles. It was an exceedingly painful journey. Once clear of the trench the medical arrangements were very good.

Captain Arthur Legge Samson, 2nd RWF. Samson was born on 1 June 1882 at Oxford Terrace, Paddington and was educated at Eton and Merton College, Oxford. He was known for being obsessed with cleanliness. He was awarded the Military Cross on 23 June 1915 before being mortally wounded on 25 September 1915 in the Battle of Loos. Frank Richards and Robert Graves referred to his gallantry, 'hit in seventeen places knuckles in mouth to stop himself crying out'. Samson's body was recovered for burial in Cambrin churchyard.

Frank Richards alleges in his book, *Old Soldiers Never Die*, that Blair was drunk during the attack. If so, he cannot be blamed for taking to alcohol to blur the horrors around him!

The signal to carry out the second attack never came. The 2nd RWF had lost two officers – Captains John Arthur Childe-Freeman MC and Arthur Legge Samson, MC – and thirty-six men killed. Lieutenant Colonel Williams and Major Clegg-Hill were wounded. Five officers and seventy-one men had been wounded.

The operations at Loos had been a partial success: those on the right and the centre had captured most of their objectives, while the left flank had failed in its attack. The three diversionary attacks that had been carried out at Neuve Chapelle, Bois Grenier and Bellewaarde were moderately successful, with numbers of Germans being captured. The French Tenth Army, which attacked on the right of the British gained little ground. The French broke through in the Champagne region and captured 14,000 prisoners, but had suffered heavy casualties and their offensive continued.

Sir John French had kept XI Corps, incorporating the Guards, 21st and 24th divisions, under his command in reserve. He was sceptical about the battle and did not want to place the reserves in the line; however, after negotiations with Douglas Haig, he agreed to move the 21st and 24th divisions on the line running from Noeux-les-Mines to Beuvry, about 5 miles behind the British front, on the morning of 25 September. Due to the

The grave of Captain Arthur Legge Samson at Cambrin Churchyard Extension.

conditions, the 21st and 24th divisions reached the battle area too late in the day to make any difference and, arriving during the night, were tired, wet and cold. The failure was caused by Sir John French's cautious approach in denying Douglas Haig the use of the reserves without his permission. The Guards Division, along with the Welsh Guards, remained in reserve, for now at least.

The Germans had now been allowed time enough to move their reserves into the line and, as a result, intermittent fighting continued throughout the first night of the battle, with the Germans launching counter-attacks along the line. By 2 am on 26 September the leading brigade of the 21st Division (63 Brigade) had relieved 2 Brigade, 1st Division at Chalk Pit Wood after a treacherous 3-mile march over strange shell-holed and wire-covered ground. No. 64 Brigade remained in reserve. The leading brigade of the 24th Division (72 Brigade) reached the Lens to La Bassée Road about the same time, but could not dig into the hard chalk and had to withdraw about half a mile to Alley 4, the old German communication trench, with 71 Brigade in support close behind. All these 'fresh' troops were wet, cold and tired.

Two of the German counter-attacks, from the direction of Hill 70, were repulsed. Another was carried out against the 1st SWB. As the Germans advanced through cover of darkness one of their men called out: 'Don't shoot; we are the Welsh!' The Borderers were not fooled and cut the Germans down with rapid rifle fire. When dawn broke on the 26th the Borderers collected from the German dead a large number of pickelhaubes (spiked helmets) as souvenirs, almost one for each man! Although the 1st SWB held firm, the Germans had regained the Quarries and Fosse Alley and the British held onto Fosse 8, which was occupied by 73 Brigade, 24th Division.

Following the results of the first day's fighting, it became apparent to Haig that an assault against the German second line from Hill 70 to Cité St Elie on the following day would be essential for future progress. The Germans were back in control of Hill 70 and were able to enfilade any attack to the north of it, so it had to be captured. As a result, at 9 am on 26 September the 15th Division, supported by one brigade from the 21st Division attacked the hill. Although initially successful, the Scots were driven off the hill by a determined counter-attack. The Germans then launched an attack from Bois Hugo and Chalet Wood, hitting 63 Brigade, 21st Division which, during the night, had taken over the trenches from 2 Brigade. The troops put up a brave fight but sustained heavy losses and were forced to withdraw towards Loos. Troops were rushed into the line in an attempt to stem the German flood; such heavy losses were suffered that the 21st Division attack was called off due to a lack of manpower.

While the 21st Division was heavily involved in a desperate defence, the 1st SWB, 2nd Welsh and the 1st Black Watch of 3 Brigade watched their comrades from their positions at Alley 4. Reports were sent back to HQ of what was happening, so the 3 Brigade attack was called off. The message did not reach the 2nd Welsh, as their telephone had been knocked out by a shell, and at 11 am the Welsh left their trenches and advanced. Unbeknown to the Welsh, a large number of Germans from Hulluch had joined in the counter-attack of the Germans from Bois Hugo and were across the Lens to La Bassée Road. The battalion War Diary says:

We immediately came under heavy fire, both rifle, machine gun and shell fire and began to lose men freely. To our horror we saw that no one else was coming on our left and that we were entirely on our own. We also fully realised that we were assaulting a place which had, no doubt, been strongly fortified during the night and which had not been bombarded. We reached the Hulluch-Lens Road, having lost about 100 men. Here the enemy defending the road surrendered. We

264

were now in the predicament of being entirely unsupported and only about 300 strong, with a perfectly impossible place to take in front of us. Just at this moment, 11.15 a.m., we saw a marvellous sight. Line upon line of men in extended order came over the crest of the hill behind us and advanced down the Hulluch-Lens Road and then up towards the German line of trenches on the crest of the rise. All the Germans who had advanced to attack us, on seeing these men advance, turned round and ran as hard as they could up the hill throwing away their arms and equipment and finally disappeared through their barbed wire and into their trench. Two of our Companies, 'B' and 'C', joined up with the advance of the troops on our right.

The 24th Division sent 72 Brigade into the battle from Alley 4 at 11 am and the brigade reached the positions of the 2nd Welsh after a 1,000-metre march across open land. The men were continually under fire from Hill 70 and Bois Hugo on their right and Hulluch on their left and after being reinforced by two battalions of 71 Brigade, reached the German Second Line, only to be halted by uncut wire. Meanwhile two companies of the 2nd Welsh, supported by part of the 11th Essex, attacked and captured trenches south of Hulluch.

Victory was within reach of the British, but the 21st and 24th divisions had suffered heavily and, with no further reinforcements, began to withdraw under a murderous crossfire. A small number of men of the 2nd Welsh, under the command of Company Sergeant Major Frederick O'Donald Collins (7745) and Sergeant Arthur Adams (8959) had bravely attacked Hulluch but were forced to withdraw also. Both Adams and Collins were awarded the DCM for their actions throughout the battle.

The attack on Hulluch by the 1st Black Watch and 1st SWB was also repulsed due to the 2nd Welsh having gone early and both battalions had suffered severe casualties before Lieutenant Colonel Gwynn of the 1st SWB ordered a halt to the attack. Second Lieutenant Louis Desormaeux Saunders and twenty-three men were killed and almost 100 more in total wounded, including Second Lieutenants Drury, Simmonds and A.E. Morgan; and H.G.F. Forster-Morris, who later died.

Second Lieutenant Louis Desormaeux Saunders, 1st SWB, the son of Cornelius D. Saunders and Ann (Haskell) Saunders. He was killed at Loos on 26 September 1915.

Second Lieutenant Herbert Gloyne Forster Forster-Morris was the only son of Reverend Herbert Forster-Morris, of Callington Rectory, Cornwall. Educated at Exeter and Sandhurst, he was commissioned in the 1st SWB on 15 July 1915. He was wounded at Hulluch on 27 September and died at No. 3 General Hospital on 10 October 1915, aged 19. He is buried in Le Tréport Military Cemetery.

The only chance for a breakthrough had fallen on the 2nd Welsh, of which now only seven officers and 180 other ranks survived. A fine act of humanity was witnessed during the afternoon by Company Sergeant Major Joshua of the 2nd Welsh:

> About 2 pm the Germans sent out a great many stretcher-bearers and R.A.M.C. men who worked the whole afternoon, binding up our wounded and sending all who could walk or crawl back to us. There were plenty of shells falling about, but, although they apparently lost some men, these Germans never stopped their good work.

Lieutenant Colonel Archer George Prothero of the 2nd Welsh, taken prisoner at Loos.

At around 3.30 pm a catastrophe occurred following the misunderstanding of an order that was sent out for all troops to hold firm in the old German trenches running between Loos and Hulluch. The mistake came when some battalion commanders thought they were being ordered to withdraw from the front trenches, leaving Hill 70 open. The Germans spotted the gap and advanced from Bois Hugo along the Lens to La Bassée Road and cut off and captured a large number of British troops: around eighteen officers and 500 men, including Lieutenant Colonel Prothero of the 2nd Welsh.

Meanwhile the 2nd Division had failed in an attempt to retake the Quarries and the Germans launched an artillery bombardment on the troops holding the Dump and Fosse 8 before recapturing them and almost retaking the Hohenzollern Redoubt.

It was now the turn of the Welsh Guards to make their entrance into the fray. During the night of 26/27 September the Guards Division moved up to relieve the 21st and 24th divisions, stabilizing the line from Loos to the right of the 1st Division in

Lieutenant Colonel Murray-Threipland.

Gun Trench. At 12.30 pm Lieutenant Colonel Murray-Threipland received orders that the 3 Guards Brigade would march to Loos in the following order: 4th Grenadier Guards, 1st Welsh Guards, 2nd Scots Guards and 1st Grenadier Guards, and was to capture the Chalk Pit and Fosse 14 before launching an attack on Hill 70 with the aim of recapturing it. The attack was to be made by the 4th Grenadier Guards, with the Welsh Guards in support at Loos.

Marching up to the line from the battered village of Vermelles must have been a harrowing experience for the untried Welsh Guards as streams of weary and wounded men filed past in the opposite direction. At 2.30 pm Threipland marched the Welsh Guards off to Loos. The *History of the Welsh Guards* gives the marching order, which contains some legendary names:

A view through the ruined streets of Loos, towards Tower Bridge.

The order of march was the Prince of Wales's Company, with Osmond Williams, Mawby, Geoffrey Crawshay, Smith and Philip Howard; No. 2 with Dick Bulkeley, Rupert Lewis, Keith Menzies and Copland Griffiths; No. 3 with George Philipps, Harry Rice, Randolph and Sutton; No. 4 with Palmer, Claud Insole, Basil Hambrough and Evan Thomas. Humphrey Dene was sent as liaison officer between the battalion and the brigade and Jim Jack Evans was with headquarters as scouting officer and general utility. The rest were left behind with the transport, or near it.

In front, upon marching over the crest in the road to Loos, the 4th Grenadier Guards came under heavy artillery fire, the Welsh Guards witnessing the sight of their fellow guardsmen marching through the puffs of smoke and fountains of dirt before moving through the firestorm themselves into Loos. Threipland ordered his men to occupy an old German trench before heading off to find the brigadier, who had set up his HQ in the village.

Threipland soon returned, with orders to move his battalion into the main street of the village to await orders. The Germans then began shelling the area with gas shells, so the men were forced to don their gas helmets, making life even more uncomfortable.

Orders were then received to move forward to the point held by the 4th Grenadier Guards and to advance from there and capture Hill 70. Threipland made the following arrangements: the Prince of Wales's Company would advance on the right, with the Grenadiers on the left. No. 2 Company Welsh Guards would support the Prince of Wales's and No. 3 the Grenadiers; the marker was a group of trees on the skyline. It was now about 6.20 pm and fifteen minutes later the Guardsmen began their attack on Hill 70.

Two trenches were soon captured but with darkness falling swiftly what was already a hard task began to get even harder. No. 2 Company had been held up by German trenches along a bank at the top of the hill and needed reinforcements. The situation regarding the other attackers was at the time unclear, but the Germans held tight onto their positions. While some of the attackers dug into their positions on the slope of the hill, many had reached the summit but came under murderous fire when they were illuminated by star-shells. The survivors desperately dug themselves into shell-holes to escape the devastating fire. The men eventually reorganized themselves and moved to the positions below the crest of the hill.

Casualties had been severe and the situation at Hill 70 was dire. Threipland had received no news of the Prince of Wales's Company, so he held back a company of the Coldstream Guards that had reported to help in the consolidation of the positions until the 2nd Scots Guards arrived. Late in the night two companies of the 2nd Scots Guards and the remainder of the 4th Grenadier Guards arrived and relieved the Welsh Guards.

Captains Osmond Traharn Deudraeth Osmond-Williams DSO and Arthur Percy Palmer DSO; Lieutenant Arthur Bertram Randolph; Second Lieutenants Edwin George Mawby, Ralph W. Smith and Hubert Joselin Sutton and forty-eight men had been killed. Palmer had been awarded the DSO during the Boer War. Osmond-Williams was the son of Sir Osmond and Lady Williams, of Penrhyndeudraeth, Merioneth and the husband of Lady Gladys Williams of 2 The Lawn, St Leonards-on-Sea. He had served with the 19th Hussars and Royal Scots Greys and was an obvious candidate to serve with the Welsh Guards upon its formation after having been awarded the DSO at Messines in 1914 for his role in leading the 12th Lancers in

Captain Osmond Traharn Deudraeth Osmond-Willi. DSO.

a counter-attack. Osmond-Williams was a renowned golfer and often played at the Royal St David's Golf Club at Harlech. He was mortally wounded while rescuing a wounded man and died later on 27 September. He is buried in Lapugnoy Military Cemetery. One of his fellow officers wrote to his wife:

> Never has a death caused more regret in this war and never has a 'field' funeral had such an attendance. Four generals, all the officers and 70 or 80 men attended. He could have had no greater compliment, as funerals here are so common that half-a-dozen intimate friends is a fair tribute to the dead man. I don't suppose there was a single officer or man more universally known or admired.

The relieving troops found that the positions below the crest of the hill were untenable, so dug into German trenches some way back while the Welsh Guards withdrew to Loos

The beautifully-located Lapugnoy Military Cemetery.

under fire. The battalion stayed in support until 7 pm on 29 October, when they marched back to Vermelles and on the 30th to Sailly-Labourse.

Although the Guardsmen had gallantly failed in their efforts to capture Hill 70, they had re-established the line in front of it and the 47th Division had recaptured Chalk Pit Copse, south of Loos. The British reserves were now exhausted, so Sir John French called on the French to take over the right of the line in order to enable the British to reorganize before continuing the offensive. On the 28th the 1st SWB were relieved and moved back to Noeux-les-Mines and on the 30th the 2nd Welsh were relieved by the Irish Guards and joined 1st SWB, with Lieutenant Hewett assuming command.

Lance Corporal Ivor Emmanuel (275), one of several men from the small town of Kidwelly who fell during the Battle of Loos.

Among the many honours awarded to the Welsh Guards for their first foray into battle was the DSO to Captain Sir Rhys Williams:

For conspicuous gallantry and great determination on the night of 27th-28th September, 1915, during the attack on 'Hill 70'. Captain Williams was in command of the Welsh Guards Machine Guns and performed very effective work until wounded. He then obtained a dressing for his wound and returned to the guns, which he continued to control until midnight, having had to lie on his back for the purpose owing to the nature of his injuries. (*London Gazette*, 2 November 1915.)

Rhys Williams was the son of Judge Gwilym Williams and Emma Eleanor Williams and later became a prominent politician, residing at Miskin Manor.

The DCM was awarded to Sergeant George C. Grant (48) of Altrincham:

Captain Sir Rhys Williams DSO Welsh Guards, one of the heroe of Loos and later a respected politician and MP.

For conspicuous gallantry on 27th/28th September, 1915, at Hill 70 and also at Loos. In addition to carrying messages under heavy artillery fire Private Grant made two attempts to bring ammunition forward to the firing line under heavy and continuous fire. In the first attempt he failed, but, volunteering again, he succeeded in the second attempt, thus enabling the men in the firing line to keep off the Germans, who were entrenched close in front of them. Later he attempted to carry in a wounded Officer, but a stretcher-bearer having been shot he was forced to fall back. He went forward again with assistance and this time was successful. In carrying a wounded man (Osmond-Williams) on his back towards the Dressing Station, on 28th September, he was himself seriously wounded. (*London Gazette*, 16 November 1915.)

Privates C.H. Witts, S.T. Harvard, F. Perry and W. Bateman became legends within the Welsh Guards during the fight for Hill 70:

These men succeeded in getting very close to the enemy line in the charge and jumped into a hole in which were built two shelters. In one shelter was a dead German officer and in the other two live German soldiers. They could not get back for three days and as a German sap from the main enemy line was only a few yards away and was occupied, it was not quite clear to them whether they were to consider the two German privates their prisoners or their jailers. However, they did get away and brought the two Germans with them, also the papers from the dead officer. (*History of the Welsh Guards.*)

Wales also gained its fifth Victoria Cross of the war during the diversionary attacks on Hooge. Rupert Price Hallowes was born in Redhill, Surrey, the son of Frederick Blackwood and Mary Ann Taylor Hallowes, and was educated at Haileybury College. In 1900 he joined the 20th Middlesex (Artists) Volunteer Rifle Corps and was commissioned in the Artists Rifles on 26 October 1909. He resigned his commission in April the following year when he moved to Wales to work for Robert Byass and Co. and was appointed assistant manager of the Mansel Tinplate Works in Aberavon, where his brother William Brabazon Hallowes was the manager. His mother also lived in the town and Hallowes quickly threw himself into local life, becoming assistant secretary of the Boy Scouts.

He rejoined the Artists Rifles in August 1914, arrived in France on 29 December 1914 and on 5 April 1915 was commissioned in the 4th Battalion, The Duke of Cambridge's Own (Middlesex Regiment). He was awarded the Military Cross for his actions at Hooge on 19 July 1915:

> During an enemy attack down a communications trench there was a shortage of bombs. He climbed out of the trench exposing himself to fire at the enemy and hitting several of them. He also assisted in constructing a block, dug out a communications trench under heavy shell fire and rebuilt a parapet that had been blown in. Throughout the night he assisted in keeping touch and supplying bombs. (*London Gazette*, 6 September 1915.)

*Second Lieutenant Rupert Price Hallowes VC MC, of Port Talbot, the third Welsh Victoria Cross winner of the Great War. (*National Army Museum NAM. 1993-04-140-2*)

Two months later Hallowes was awarded a posthumous VC following another series of actions at Hooge that occurred between 25 and 30 September 1915. According to the citation in the *London Gazette* of 16 November 1915:

> Second Lieutenant Hallowes displayed throughout these days the greatest bravery and untiring energy and set a magnificent example to his men during four heavy and prolonged bombardments. On more than one occasion he climbed up on the parapet, utterly regardless of danger, in order to put fresh heart into his men. He made daring reconnaissances of the German positions in our lines. When the supply of bombs was running short he went back under very heavy shellfire and brought up a fresh supply. Even after he was mortally wounded he continued to cheer those around him and to inspire them with fresh courage.

Hallowes died of his wounds on 30 September 1915 aged 34 and was buried at Bedford House Cemetery. He is commemorated on several memorials at Port Talbot, most notably at Neath Port Talbot Hospital.

While many towns and villages in Wales suffered the loss of their young men during the Battle of Loos, the small town of Kidwelly was especially hard hit by the tragedy suffered by the 19th Division, all men of the 9th Welsh: Privates Morgan Morgan and John Tucker were killed, Tom Lewis, Volin Jones, Charlie Peck and Sid Busst were wounded and Sam Evans fell into a 'Jack Johnson' hole and broke his arm. The town of Llanelli lost fifteen men killed on 25 September: nine were from the 9th RWF and

9th Welsh. Of the more than 500 Welshmen killed during the first day of the battle, 132 served with other units, including 20 with the Devonshires, 22 with the 5th KSLI, killed during the diversionary attack at Ypres, and 23 with Scottish regiments.

There were also many conspicuous acts of gallantry performed by individuals. Below are details of some of the many awards of the DCM given to other Welsh troops at Loos.

> Private Alfred Brooks (5778) of the 2nd RWF: 'For conspicuous gallantry on the 26th September 1915, at Cambrin, when he went over the parapet, in truer daylight, to look for a wounded man, whom he found 30 yards in front of our trenches and 130 yards from the German line. As the man was too badly wounded to bring in, Private Brooks dug him in with his entrenching tool and then returned for food and water, which he took out to him, being the whole time under heavy rifle fire from the enemy's trenches. The wounded man was brought in safely after dark.' (*London Gazette*, 16 November 1915.)

> Private Frank Pearce (10777) of the 1st RWF: 'For conspicuous bravery from the 25th to 29th September 1915, near Hulluch. Private Pearce, one of the regimental stretcher bearers, with great heroism and regardless of all personal danger, brought in wounded men throughout the day and night under heavy and continuous fire, carrying many of them on his back. His bravery and devotion to duty were beyond all praise.' (*London Gazette*, 16 November 1915.)

> Private George Pullen (7691) of the 4th RWF: 'For conspicuous gallantry on the 25th of September 1915, at Loos, when, on his own initiative, he successfully carried a telephone wire to the German trenches and in returning brought in some prisoners. Later he assisted to bring in a wounded man under very heavy shell fire. He was ultimately wounded when close to the trenches.' (*London Gazette*, 16 November 1915. Pullen was a miner from 8 Birchfield Terrace, Acrefair, Ruabon and was just 20 years old when he gained his award.)

> Lance Sergeant John Williams (13456) of the 9th RWF: 'For conspicuous bravery and devotion to duty on the 25th September 1915, near Festubert, when, although badly wounded himself – one hand was hanging by two threads only and he was also wounded in the shoulder – he assisted to bandage all the wounded near him, refusing to receive any assistance from the stretcher-bearers. While bandaging the wounded he found time to encourage and cheer on the rest of his Company as they passed him. Finally he walked down the communication trench to the First Aid Post without assistance.' (*London Gazette*, 16 November 1915.)

Lance Sergeant John Williams (13456) of 9th RWF, awarded the DCM for gallantry at Loos.

Private Richard James Fawcett (33129) of the 9th Welsh: 'For conspicuous gallantry on the 25th September 1915, near Festubert. During the advance on the enemy's trenches, when part of his company had become isolated, he volunteered to carry a message back across the open to our lines a distance of over 200 yards, swept by cross-fire from rifles and machine-guns. He successfully delivered his message and rejoined his company, later crossing the same ground again with another message.' (*London Gazette*, 16 November 1915.)

Private Richard John Fawcett (33129) of the 9th Welsh, awarded the DCM for gallantry at Loos.

Corporal Edward George Sheldrake (16965) of the 9th Welsh: 'For conspicuous gallantry and resource on the 25th September 1915, near Festubert. During the advance on the enemy's trenches, although twice wounded he continued to advance and by his coolness and bravery gave great encouragement to the men with him. Afterwards he rendered great assistance in collecting and bringing back the remainder of his company, at the same time contributing greatly to cover the retirement of two machine-guns. He was under a very heavy and continuous fire the whole time.' (*London Gazette*, 16 November 1915. Sheldrake worked at the Ocean Colliery, Blaengarw, prior to the war and was a much-respected local man.)

Of course, these were not the only acts of gallantry carried out by Welshmen during the day and many officers and men were mentioned in despatches and gained other awards, while many other Welshmen in the other units involved also gained gallantry awards during the period, one such won at the diversionary attack at Bellewaarde.

Lieutenant Gilbert France Watson was the nephew of the Bishop of St David's, John Owen. He served with the 1st Welsh Field Company, Royal Engineers, a Territorial unit, but had been posted to the 3rd Division. Watson was awarded the Distinguished Service Order for his gallantry:

For conspicuous gallantry and determination near Hooge. On the night of 24th-25th September, 1915, he made an excellent reconnaissance of the enemy's wire and on the 25th crawled out with two men and successfully cut it before the assault. During the assault, with a party of 12 sappers and 25 infantry, he dug 80 yards of a communication trench in two hours under very heavy fire, by which nearly three quarters of his men became casualties. He then reported for instructions and took the remains of his party into the captured positions in order to consolidate them. When retirement was ordered he got back to our original trenches with one sergeant, who was killed almost at once, and three or four men, and, finding the trenches unoccupied, he collected about 25 men of the

4th Battalion Gordon Highlanders and held on until relieved by another battalion after dark. Second Lieutenant Watson set a fine example of bravery and devotion to duty. (*London Gazette*, 7 December 1915.)

Both of Watson's cousins – Lieutenants Andrew Geraint Joseph Owen and John Peredur Owen (the bishop's sons) – were awarded the Military Cross during the war, the latter while serving with the RWF at Loos. Two of his brothers fell: Sergeant Robert Watson was killed while serving with the Australians at Gallipoli and Lieutenant Joseph Longstaff Watson was killed with the Canadians at Ypres in 1917. Watson later became a brigadier general and was Director of Manpower Planning at the War Office during the Second World War.

The Battle of Loos was not yet over, however. The British had lost all the tactical points they had gained on 25 September, with the exception of the Hohenzollern Redoubt. The French were about to take over the line on the south up to and including Hill 70, so the British efforts now turned to recapturing the Quarries and Fosse 8 with the intention of then resuming the offensive between Hulluch and Hill 70.

The 28th Division, containing the 1st Welsh and 6th Welsh, was now brought into the line, reaching Vermelles by the end of September in readiness to move up into positions near the Hohenzollern Redoubt. The redoubt was a closed, heart-shaped entrenchment, with a front face about 300 metres long. It was situated on a rise of ground some 400 metres in front of the Dump, the Corons and Fosse 8 and was connected to the trenches that guarded these strongpoints by two trenches called Big Willie to the south and Little Willie to the north. When the Germans recaptured Fosse 8 on 27 September they had failed to take the redoubt, but in the severe fighting from 28 to 30 September had recaptured much of the ground, with only three-quarters of the western face of the redoubt and Big Willie remaining in British hands.

At around 9.30 am on 1 October, 84 Brigade relieved 85 Brigade in the trenches, the 6th Welsh taking over the old British front line opposite the redoubt and Little Willie, with the Cheshires on their right. Their front extended from Central Boyau (a trench) to a long sap that had been run out to within 40 metres of Little Willie. The ground had been battered by the heavy fighting that had taken place there and all the communication trenches leading up to the redoubt and to the old British front line had been smashed out of all recognition. There had been no time to bury the dead, who lay all around.

At 3 pm the 1st Welsh moved up from Vermelles to take over the trenches of the 6th Welsh, ordered to deliver a night attack over the open on Little Willie and on the portion of the redoubt that was held by the Germans. The 6th Welsh were to move back into support trenches and then to return to the British front line when the 1st Welsh had gone over.

The 1st Welsh were to attack on a 400-metre front for a distance of about 300 metres at 8 pm; however, due to the condition of the trenches, the battalion did not reach their positions until dark and did not have time to familiarize themselves with the ground to be attacked. The War Diary of the 1st Welsh says:

Precisely at 8 pm the 1st Welsh crept over the parapet like one man. The second in command (Major A.H. Hobbs) and the O.C. Welsh (Lieutenant Colonel G.P. Hoggan) in the centre of the line. So silently was the advance carried out that the Regiment was within 100 yards of the enemy before being discovered. Then from both flanks machine guns spurted flame and the whole length of the opposing trench opened rapid lire. The C.O.'s voice rang out, 'Forward 41st. Get at 'em, Welsh.' In 20 seconds there were 250 men and a proportion of officers on the ground. The remainder were in the enemy trenches bayoneting those in the trench and firing at the retreating Prussian Guards.

Although the 1st Welsh had taken a heavy toll on the Germans, they had become cut off from their own lines and could not be resupplied. Bombers from the battalion were fighting a fierce battle against German bombers in the trenches and it was only by the use of these that the Welsh could maintain their positions. The bomb then in use was the cricket ball variety, the fuse of which could only be ignited by striking it on a piece of special matchbox material stitched onto the cuff of the tunic; however, the weather was poor and the bombers struggled to light their bombs. With supplies dwindling, volunteers were called for to go over open ground and fetch more bombs, returning with a fresh supply and with reinforcements of an officer and fifty-nine men. However, the Welsh trenches were now overcrowded and the Germans began to shell the Welshmen with a *minenwerfer*.

The situation was desperate, so the 6th Welsh began sapping forwards towards the 1st Welsh, while some of the 1st Welsh began sapping back towards their comrades. The Germans also began shelling the diggers and men were also being targeted by sniper fire. Company Sergeant Major George Mudford (7804) won the DCM for his gallantry during the night:

> For conspicuous gallantry and devotion to duty on the night of October 1st-2nd. After the trench known as 'Little Willie' had been captured, Company Sergeant-Major Mudford volunteered to go back to our trench, 300 yards behind, for reinforcements and to bring up bombs and ammunition. This he successfully did on nine occasions under very heavy shell and rifle fire. Owing to his gallantry and resource the garrison were able to hold the trench. (*London Gazette*, 16 November 1915.)

Lance Corporal Charles Evans (7018) was also awarded the DCM:

> For great bravery and devotion to duty on October 2nd, near Vermelles. In the early morning Lance-Corporal Evans went out in front of our parapet and brought in with great difficulty a man who was severely wounded, passing over 200 yards under heavy shell and rifle fire. Later he went out again on his own initiative and carefully searched the ground between the trenches for wounded. (*London Gazette*, 16 November 1915.)

At about 2.30 pm the Germans attacked in force and threw everything at the Welsh, whose survivors were forced back into the newly-dug communication trench. The 6th Welsh, holding the Germans back with rifle and machine-gun fire, suffered the loss of their bombing officer, Second Lieutenant Donald Burnie, the son of a former MP for Swansea. The CO, Lieutenant Colonel Lord Ninian Crichton-Stuart, hurriedly improvised a burial service for the young officer and read the commitment during the midst of the fighting. Soon afterwards the gallant Lord Ninian, who had bravely led his men from the front throughout the action, was killed, shot through the head while peering over the parapet. His men conveyed his body back to safety and laid it in a pine coffin before transporting it to Béthune.

After an hour of intense fighting, at around 3.30 pm the 1st Welsh began to withdraw to the old British line and the 6th Welsh held the communication trench named New Trench. A counter-attack that night by the survivors, supported by the 1st Suffolks and 2nd Cheshires, to recapture Little Willie met with no success and, on 3 October, the 1st Welsh and 6th Welsh were relieved and went back to rest billets. Losses among the two battalions had been severe.

The 1st Welsh had suffered the loss of six officers – Major Arthur Harold Hobbs, Captain James Lionel East Warren, Second Lieutenants Griffith Davies, Thomas John Carlyle Davies, Ruthven Pomfret Hore and Percy Paris Pope – and 125 men killed, plus 8 officers and 245 men wounded.

Thomas John Carlyle Davies was the son of John Benjamin and Agnes Esther Davies, of the London and Provincial Bank, Main Street, Pembroke. Educated at Llandovery College from 1911 to 1914, he was the college captain of rugby and an

*Second Lieutenant Thomas John Carlyle Davies, 1st Welsh, of Main Street, Pembroke, seated front left. (*Courtesy of Dr Frances Hurd*)*

avid cricketer. On leaving Llandovery he briefly attended Clare College, Cambridge but left prematurely on the declaration of war to attend officer cadet training at the Royal Military College, Sandhurst and was subsequently commissioned in the 1st Welsh. He was posted as wounded and missing during the fighting in Little Willie trench and it was some time before his parents received confirmation that he was presumed dead. The 20-year-old is commemorated on the Loos Memorial.

The 6th Welsh had suffered three officers – Lieutenant Colonel Lord Ninian Crichton-Stuart, Captain Reginald Gordon Snell Browning and Second Lieutenant Donald Burnie – and thirty-one men killed, and Lieutenant H.C. Hawkins and twenty-eight men wounded. Captain C.A.S. Carleton assumed command of the 6th Welsh and Captain W. Owen of the 1st Welsh when Lieutenant Colonel Hoggan was invalided to England.

Lord Ninian Crichton-Stuart was born on 18 May 1883, the third of the four children of John Patrick Crichton-Stuart, 3rd Marquess of Bute, and his wife Gwendoline. He was educated at Harrow and Christ Church, Oxford and travelled widely before being commissioned in the Scots Guards in 1905. He left the army after two years in order to concentrate on politics and agriculture and on 16 June 1906 he married the Honourable Ismay Lucretia Mary Preston, the only daughter of the Viscount Gormanston. In 1910 he was elected Member of Parliament for Cardiff and was still MP when he led the 6th Welsh to France and ultimately to his death on 2 October. Lord Ninian is commemorated by William Goscombe John's fine statue in front of the National Museum in Cardiff, on the Grangetown War Memorial and also in a fine oil painting that hangs in Cardiff Castle, his former home. He was buried with full military honours on 7 October in Béthune Town Cemetery.

Lieutenant Colonel Lord Ninian Edward Crichton-Stuart, CO of the 6th Welsh, killed during a desperate battle near the Hohenzollern Redoubt on 2 October 1915. He was the second son of John Patrick, 3rd Marquess of Bute, and Gwendoline, Marchioness of Bute. Crichton-Stuart was Member of Parliament for Cardiff from 1910 to 1915 and Justice of the Peace for County Fife. He is buried in Béthune Town Cemetery.

On 3 October the Germans recaptured the whole of the Hohenzollern Redoubt but not Big Willie Trench. The loss of the redoubt threatened the British positions opposite the Quarries, so Sir Douglas Haig reorganized his forces to retake the Quarries and the Hohenzollern Redoubt, placing XI Corps back into the line.

The 12th Division was to recapture the Quarries and the Guards Division the Hohenzollern Redoubt. The assault, which was to be supported by all the artillery of the First

The grave of Lieutenant Colonel Lord Ninian Edward Crichton-Stuart in Béthune Town Cemetery.

Army and assisted by gas and smoke, was planned to take place on 9 October and so the Guards Division relieved the 28th Division on 3 October in readiness for the operation.

The Welsh Guards, after receiving drafts from England, moved back to Vermelles on 3 October, relieving the 9th Highland Light Infantry. Battalion HQ was at Notre Dame de Consolation.

The Hohenzollern Redoubt was a notorious place that had already seen much bloodshed and the troops were not looking forward to more fighting over its desolated position. After two days of hard work linking up the old British and German trenches and carrying gas cylinders into the line, the Welsh Guards moved back to Vermelles for a rest on the night of 5/6 October. As the *History of the Welsh Guards* states:

> The billets in Vermelles were anything but comfortable. The gunners with their cheering weapons were all over the ruins, and, although one likes to hear the sound of British guns, no one wants to lie down by the side of them to rest. The Germans had a naval gun which fired armour-piercing shells with what seemed a retarded action and they searched with this gun for the British batteries amongst the ruins. This went on all day and night and there were a good few casualties.

The men also detested the carrying of gas canisters. This feeling was not helped by the knowledge of the large number of casualties suffered by the British from their own gas on 25 September, but carrying these dangerous cylinders was in itself a hazardous and tiring occupation. The maze of trenches around the Hohenzollern Redoubt was very confusing and several parties got lost in them.

Before the British had chance to launch their offensive, on 8 October the Germans launched a big attack stretching from the Hohenzollern Redoubt to Loos. Despite their large numbers, the Germans were easily repulsed and their attack quickly ground to a halt and the British attack was called off. On 12 October the Welsh Guards moved back to billets at Sailly la Bourse, while the 2nd Welsh, back in the line again, suffered another sixteen men killed and fourteen wounded by shellfire. Twelve of these men were buried in Crucifix Cemetery but this was destroyed by later shelling and most of the graves were lost. As a result, while the graves of two of these men were subsequently identified and reinterred in Dud Corner Cemetery, twelve more of them are commemorated by special memorials within the cemetery. Two of the men are commemorated on the walls of the Loos Memorial that surrounds the cemetery.

Private William Jenkin Greenwood (13105), 2nd Welsh, the son of William and Margaret Greenwood, of Llanarthinna, Quarry Road, Brynamman. He was killed at Loos on 12 October 1915 aged 23.

The special memorial to Private William Jenkin Greenwood (13105), 2nd Welsh, at Dud Corner Cemetery. Greenwood was originally buried in Crucifix Cemetery, near Loos but when the cemetery was destroyed by gunfire in further fighting in the area, his grave was lost. He is now commemorated by this special memorial in Dud Corner Cemetery.

Crucifix Cemetery, Loos Special Memorial marker stone.

Private Edward Bevan (1919) of the 2nd Welsh, the son of John and Jane Bevan, of Fern Cottage, Penllergaer, Swansea. He was killed at Loos on 10 October 1915 and was another of the men buried in Crucifix Cemetery who is now commemorated on a special memorial within Dud Corner Cemetery.

Meanwhile the 1st Monmouths had moved into the battle area with the 46th (North Midland) Division, taking over from the Guards Division in front of the Hohenzollern Redoubt. The Welsh Guards had been hard at work in the preparations for the offensive, digging in the front line and carrying gas cylinders and material into position ready for the attack. While carrying out this work on 6 October a small party of men working in No. 2 Sap lit an abandoned German stove that they had discovered in order to cook their breakfasts. Unbeknown to them the stove had been booby-trapped and it exploded, killing two men – Private Arthur Harold Richards (732) of Cathays, Cardiff and Private Richard Williams (1114) of Penygroes, Caernarfonshire – and wounded three others. The two men are buried in Philosophe British Cemetery, Mazingarbe.

The grave of Private Arthur Harold Richards (732), Welsh Guards, of Cathays, Cardiff, killed by a booby-trapped German stove.

The 46th Division was a Territorial division and had been given orders to clear the redoubt, along with the 12th Division. They planned to attack on 13 October (the attack of 9 October was postponed due to the German attack) using 137 Brigade on the right from Big Willie Trench, to advance across the trench towards Dump Trench, skirt the southern side of the dump and then to capture Fosse Alley on the far side. The rest of the division would follow in support.

Again the gas discharge proved to be ineffective as it hung over no man's land, but it had also alerted the Germans to the impending attack and when the 5th South Staffs moved from their trench at 2 pm on the 13th they were mown down by machine-gun fire. The 5th North Staffs also suffered terrible casualties while moving towards Big Willie Trench and the advance here immediately broke down.

To the left, 138 Brigade was to cross the Hohenzollern Redoubt and then take up a position in the Corons on the north side of the Dump, which was not being directly assaulted by either brigade, but when assembling to attack a German shell fell on some of the gas cylinders in their positions. Corporal James Lennox Dawson of the 187th Company, Royal Engineers won the VC for dragging three leaking cylinders over the parapet and rolling them away to a safe distance before shooting holes in them with rounds from his rifle.

Despite this drama, at 2.05 pm the 5th Leicesters attacked on the right, with the 5th Lincolns on the left, supported by the 4th Lincolns. The 1st Monmouths were standing by ready to bring up supplies and to consolidate any positions gained. With the attack of 137 Brigade having already stalled, 138 Brigade was isolated and suffered heavy casualties. Some men reached Fosse Trench but they could not hold on. As night fell the survivors were ordered to pull out of the eastern face of the redoubt and dig a new trench just behind it. An attempt by the Germans to reach the western face of the redoubt was beaten off by Sherwood Foresters of 139 Brigade, who had been in reserve.

The division had lost 3,763 officers and men during one afternoon and took months to recover. The 1st Monmouths had worked tirelessly to move up supplies and to dig the new trench but had suffered heavy casualties in doing so. Four officers – Major Oswald Michael Williams, Second Lieutenants Henry John Ballinger and Louis Herbert Collin Smith, and George Widowfield – and twenty-six men had been killed.

Lady St David's lost the second of her brothers killed during the day. Captain Paulyn Charles James Reginald Rawdon-Hastings was born on 27 November 1889, the elder son of the Honourable Paulyn Francis Cuthbert Rawdon-Hastings and Lady Maud Rawdon-Hastings, of 14 Stafford Mansions, Buckingham Gate, London. He was educated at Eton and Oxford before being commissioned in the 1st/5th Leicesters. The battalion moved to France on 3 March 1915 as part of 138 Brigade, 46th (North Midland) Division and moved to Hooge, east of Ypres, where it saw the Germans' first use of flame-

Major Oswald Michael Williams, Monmouths, of Th Mount, Caerleon, was killed at Hohenzollern Redoubt on 13 October 1915.

280

Second Lieutenant Henry John Ballinger, 1st Monmouths. Ballinger was the son of John and Amy Amelia Ballinger, of Sherborne House, Aberystwyth. Educated at Cowbridge School and St Paul's School, he enlisted at the outbreak of war in the Royal Welsh Fusiliers. He was commissioned on 22 April 1915 in the Monmouthshire Regiment and went to France on 19 July 1915, where he was posted to the 1st Monmouths. He was killed while attempting to manoeuvre some captured German machine guns into position. He was 19 years old and is commemorated on the Loos Memorial.

throwers on 30 July. The division then moved south to the Loos sector, to take part in the assault on the Hohenzollern Redoubt. Rawdon-Hastings was killed while leading A Company in a bayonet charge on the redoubt on 13 October 1915. His commanding officer wrote: 'We all miss your son grievously and the men in the company know that they have lost a good officer and friend. The example of a perfect life led by

Captain Paulyn Charles James Reginald Rawdon-Hastings, 1/5th Leicesters.

your son has left its impression on us and the men.' He was 25 years old and is commemorated on the Loos Memorial. He was heir to his uncle, the Earl of Loudon.

Two days later a Grenadier Guardsman from St Bride's Major was killed. Private Thomas Ace (9628) served with the 1st Grenadier Guards. He had felt loyal to his regiment so had not volunteered to transfer to the Welsh Guards, preferring to stay with his comrades.

Ace was a very highly-respected man at St Bride's Major. After completing his term of service in the army he returned home and became captain of the local air-rifle shooting club. He was also a renowned horseman and taught many locals to ride. He had rejoined his old regiment at the outbreak of war and was killed at Loos on 15 October. Lieutenant Howard Paget of the Grenadier Guards wrote the following:

In reply to yours of the 31st ult. re Tom Ace, he was shot through the neck and died instantaneously while in the execution of his duty in the trenches. The trenches had been recently taken from the Germans and were near the Hohenzollern Redoubt. He was buried with all possible care.

Private Thomas Ace (9628) of the 1st Grenadier Guards, a reservist from St Bride's Major.

Loos British Cemetery. The cemetery contains the graves of nearly 3,000 men who fell during the Great War, the majority from the Battle of Loos, as well as a small number of Second World War casualties. Over two-thirds of the burials are unidentified. Ace was identified by his small ID tag, so has a marked headstone.

He was one of our two sanitary men for No. 2 Company, in which capacity he is irreplaceable. I may say I have fought beside him for five months and deeply regret his loss, as he was in every way a most valuable man. Please convey my deepest sympathy to his mother.

Ace was originally buried near Loos-en-Gohelle (map reference 44a.G.5.b.4.9) on part of the Hohenzollern Redoubt, along with at least two other men from his unit. On 23 July 1920 his grave was among a number of others exhumed from the area and he was identified by his disc before being reburied in the vast Loos British Cemetery.

Another Welshman serving with the Grenadier Guards was Private Daniel Hewitt, a police sergeant with the Flintshire Constabulary, stationed at Hawarden Bridge Ironworks before the war, who lived at Connah's Quay. Hewitt was awarded the DCM for his conduct at Loos:

This honour is in recognition of his destruction of an enemy machine-gun which he discovered in a house at Puits Bis on September 28th. Without hesitation and regardless of all risk, he rushed out and threw bombs into the window until he had destroyed the gun and all the crew. (*London Gazette*, 16 November 1915.)

One of the first ever Welsh rugby internationals, the third and eldest of thirteen killed during the war, lost his life at Loos on 25 September. Richard Davies Garnons Williams was born at Llowes, Radnorshire on 15 June 1856, son of the Reverend Garnons Williams. He was educated at Magdalen College School, Oxford and at Trinity College, Cambridge. He had played at forward for Cambridge University, Brecon and Newport and was selected in the first ever Welsh international team to play against England in 1881. He was already serving in the army, having been commissioned in the 38th Foot in 1876; in the following year he transferred to the 7th Foot. He retired in 1892, although he continued to serve with the 1st (Brecknockshire) Volunteer Battalion, South Wales Borderers. He resigned from the volunteers in 1906 but he volunteered again after the outbreak of war to serve as a major with the 12th Royal Fusiliers. Williams was 59 years old when he was killed at Loos on 25 September and is commemorated on the Loos Memorial.

For the bulk of the Welsh units in France the Battle of Loos was at an end and the routine of trench warfare in the sector resumed; but fighting continued to rage in Gallipoli.

Chapter 18

Gallipoli:
The Final Months and the
Evacuation

W hile the Battle of Loos was waning, the campaign in Gallipoli had also
stalled since the August offensives at Cape Helles, Suvla and Anzac. While
the Welsh units on the peninsula were dug in to their rocky trenches, the
Welsh Horse Yeomanry had been preparing for its move to the Mediterranean.

After its formation in Cardiff and period of training at Sophia Gardens, the Welsh
Horse left Wales on 10 November 1914 for Diss, in Norfolk. Here it was brigaded with
the Norfolk Yeomanry and Suffolk Yeomanry to form the 1st/1st Eastern Mounted
Brigade. For a range of political reasons the regiment's ties with Cardiff were also
severed and a regimental depot was established in Newtown, Montgomeryshire, even
though most of the recruits were South Walians.

This move caused much furore throughout South Wales but all complaints fell on
deaf ears and the Welsh Horse would, in time, become associated with the Royal Welsh
Fusiliers.

The Welsh Horse were still in Norfolk when, in September 1915, they were warned
for a move overseas and entrained for Liverpool, where the regiment, commanded by
Lieutenant Colonel Hugh Edwardes (Lord Kensington), embarked upon the SS
Olympic with the Eastern Mounted Brigade, 54th Division. The *Olympic* arrived at
Mudros on 1 October and the troops disembarked before re-embarking aboard the
smaller HMS *Partridge* and on 8 October 1915 the Welsh Horse Yeomanry landed at
Walker's Pier, Anzac Cove. The regiment moved to Burnt Gully camp, where it awaited
the arrival of the remainder of the 54th Division on 10 October.

That day the Welsh Horse were appointed as Pioneer Battalion to 163 Brigade and
moved up to the line to carry out extensive sapping and mining operations in the
vicinity of Hill 60. Men who had cheerily enlisted to serve as cavalry were now just
pioneers, armed with shovel and pick. The first casualty suffered by the regiment at
Gallipoli occurred on 21 October. Private Roderick Donald McCrae (679) was from
44 Denmark Street, Diss, in Norfolk and had enlisted in the Welsh Horse after seeing
them on parade in his village. McCrae died of a bullet wound on 21 October and is
commemorated on the Helles Memorial.

At the end of the month Lord Kensington wrote home to his wife:

The scene at Lancashire Landing after a gale.

We landed on a fearsome night. A terrible squall of rain and wind sprang up just as we were getting on to the lighter and we had a great game making the pier in the dark. We landed in sheets of rain and got wet through to the skin. Then we had a three-mile walk in single file through saps inches thick in slimy mud and eventually fetched up at the mouth of our gully, which was at once named 'Rhondda Valley' by the men and is so officially known now. The next day was spent digging our dug-outs deep into the gully. During the night of our arrival my orderly-room sergeant had the bad luck to be shot right through both arms by a flying bullet – really bad luck and he was taken off to hospital before he had been twelve hours on the peninsula. The regiment on arrival was immediately snapped up for mining operations and fancy trench digging to the front. The men entered upon their duties in the best of spirits and are really doing fine work. We have had a few shrapnel casualties in the front trenches, but nothing serious. A few men are in hospital with dysentery, otherwise the regiment is as fit as possible. Unfortunately Major Powell has been taken off to hospital with double pneumonia, contracted during the night we arrived. Last night (October 29) we had bad luck. Our excellent, hard-working, cheery Farrier-Major Kennaugh was found halfway up the gully with his neck broken. Poor old chap. He is supposed to have fallen down on the side of the gully in the dark. His death is felt by all, as he had gained the respect and affection of all ranks and to die in such a way amidst so many other daily risks is bad luck.

The dead farrier was Frank Stanley Kennaugh (346), the 47-year-old son of John and Susannah Kennaugh of the Isle of Man. He had served for twenty-three years with the 13th Hussars and had enlisted at Cardiff. He is buried in 7th Field Ambulance Cemetery.

As pioneers the Welsh Horse were not usually in the firing line, but suffered a further two men killed before tragedy struck the regiment. On 20 November a party of men of the Welsh Horse were at work digging an underground gallery when the Turks blew a defensive charge, burying Lieutenant Renwick and eight men. Renwick managed to dig himself out but the eight men were dead.

Private Philip Davies of the Welsh Horse Yeomanry.

Private Philip Davies (182), the son of Mary Davies, of 32 Wern Road, Llanelli who had served for seven years with the Royal Engineers prior to 1914 and is commemorated on the Helles Memorial.

Lance Corporal Llewellyn Evans (136), the husband of Mary Evans, of 8 Railway Terrace, Henllan, who is buried in the 7th Field Ambulance Cemetery.

Lance Corporal Llewellyn Evans of Welsh Horse Yeoma

The grave of Private Llewellyn Evans, Welsh Horse Yeomanry, at the 7th Field Ambulance Cemetery.

Private Edward John Humphreys (18), of Griffithstown, Monmouth who is commemorated on the Helles Memorial.

Private George Augustus Jones (246), of Abertillery, who is commemorated on the Helles Memorial.

Private Llewellyn Jones (540), the son of Mrs Jones of Llainwen, Llangeler, who is buried in the 7th Field Ambulance Cemetery.

Private William Cooper Lewis (137), the husband of Rhoda Jane Lewis of Yew Tree Cottage, Leaton Heath, Shrewsbury who is buried in the 7th Field Ambulance Cemetery.

Troopers Llewellyn Jones and William Cooper Lewis of the Welsh Horse Yeomanry, killed during the explosion of a Turkish mine on 20 November 1915.

Private Albert Lovegrove (79) of Newport who is commemorated on the Helles Memorial.

Private Rhys Rees (322), the son of Margaret Rees of 1 Castle Street, New Quay, Cardiganshire, who is also commemorated on the Helles Memorial. Rees's mother was incorrectly told that her other son, John James Rees, who had enlisted with Rhys, had been killed and as a result it was his name that was placed on the New Quay War Memorial when in fact he survived.

While the Welsh Horse continued in their new role as pioneers, the other Welsh units on the peninsula were affected from higher and higher rates of sickness due to the effects of the weather, swarms of flies, fatigue and a poor diet. The weather deteriorated sharply on 27 November when strong gales and heavy rainstorms battered Gallipoli, flooding men and equipment out of their trenches and even washing corpses from shallow graves. The sea was whipped up into such a frenzy that supply proved impossible. The rain was followed by a fierce blizzard and many men froze to death in the trenches while countless others were brought down by frostbite and sickness. Fortunately for the troops at Anzac, a series of underground caves and galleries constructed by Australian and New Zealand troops during the summer months provided some shelter, unlike at nearby Suvla, where 5,000 cases of frostbite were recorded and some 200 men drowned or were found frozen to death. Fortunately the weather conditions soon improved and on 30 November the sun broke out.

With the allies outnumbered by the Turks, Sir Ian Hamilton had sent for reinforcements but the British had suffered heavily at Loos and needed men there, while on 20 September Bulgaria had joined the war on the side of the Germans. The

Germans and Austrians had advanced into Serbia, and Greece came into the war on the allied side. Troops were needed for a fresh campaign in Salonika. Lord Kitchener had asked Sir Ian Hamilton to estimate losses if the peninsula were to be evacuated. Hamilton had declared an evacuation unthinkable, so General Sir Charles Munro was sent out to report on the situation while Sir Ian Hamilton was replaced as commander-in-chief by General Birdwood.

Munro decided that the campaign was doomed and proposed evacuation, a course that was ultimately agreed upon after a visit by Kitchener himself. The evacuation was ordered on 8 December, while casualties incurred in evacuating troops from open beaches in the face of an active enemy were estimated as likely to be between 15 and 50 per cent. At Anzac and Suvla alone there were an estimated 83,000 men, 5,000 horses and mules, 2,000 carts, 200 guns, supplies for 30 days, engineering and medical stores and baggage to evacuate, so planning began in earnest.

The evacuation of the troops from Suvla was made easier by the flooding of the salt lake following the storm of 27 November, forming an easily-defended front. On the remainder of the front three lines of entrenchment were dug and wired. The embarkation was to take place from the north and south points of Suvla Bay, so a small harbour was created and a steamer run aground to serve as an embarkation pier.

The 53rd (Welsh) Division was the first of the Welsh units to leave on 11 December, the 13th Division, including the 8th Welsh, on 19 December.

The second-last member of the Welsh Horse to die at Gallipoli wrote his last letter home just before the storm hit. Private Thomas Henry Morris (233) was a miner at the Bwlfa Colliery prior to the war and lived with his wife and two children at 23 High Street, Aberdare. He was killed at Hill 60, Anzac on 13 December 1915 when a shell fragment struck him in the head. His last letter arrived at the home of his elderly mother at 5 Wern Row, Gadlys:

> We may not see one another again, but I hope we shall someday. I wish the war were over. We are under fire all day long. Yesterday they shelled us out of our dug-outs. I am looking forward to the day that I shall come home. I have seen some heart-breaking scenes out here. We have left England 10 weeks and have had no news yet. It is more like a hell than anything else here, only shot and shell and blood and thunder.

Private Thomas H. Morris (233) of the Welsh Horse Yeom a miner at the Bwl Colliery prior to the war.

Morris is buried in the 7th Field Ambulance Cemetery. The very last member of the regiment to die on the peninsula was Corporal Herbert Clay (48) of Newport, who died of wounds on 21 December 1915 and is commemorated on the Helles Memorial. Just the day before the Welsh Horse had been among the last troops to be evacuated from Anzac, so Clay probably died on a hospital ship and was then buried at sea.

By 20 December the last troops had left Suvla Bay. The last parties left in the trenches lit candles that burned strings tied to the triggers of rifles and set off small explosions, keeping the Turks completely in the dark about the situation. The evacuation of Helles was conducted from late December until 9 January 1916.The withdrawal was successfully accomplished without the loss of a single life, the 29th Division (2nd SWB) being among the last to leave.

Winston Churchill, a principal architect of the campaign, was angered by Monro's decision to evacuate and later wrote the famous words: 'He came, he saw, he capitulated'.

Over 480,000 troops had participated in the Gallipoli campaign. Casualty figures are not an exact science. The broad consensus suggests that Turkey suffered around 175,000 casualties, of which at least 56,000 were killed; the British 120,000 casualties, including over 34,000 killed; France 27,000 casualties, with almost 10,000 killed; Australia 28,000 casualties, and almost 9,000 were killed; New Zealand 7,500 casualties, over 2,700 of which were dead; India 4,000 casualties, over 1,350 of them dead; and Newfoundland 142 casualties, 49 of which were dead.

The majority of the troops evacuated moved to Egypt, where another campaign would soon be waged.

The last individual casualties suffered by Welsh units at Gallipoli were:

5th RWF: Private Evan Rowland Williams (2162), the son of Thomas and Elizabeth Williams, of Tanrallt Isa, Mochdre, Colwyn Bay, Denbighshire. Died on 29 November 1915 and commemorated on the Helles Memorial.

6th RWF: Private Adolphus Wood (2876), the son of Benjamin and Caroline Wood, of Llanerchymedd, Anglesey. Died on 30 November 1915 and buried in Lala Baba Cemetery.

7th RWF: Private Frederick Morris (2513), of Towyn, Merioneth. Died on 11 December 1915 and commemorated on the Helles Memorial.

8th RWF: Private William Hughes (12152), the son of Mrs H. Hughes, of Henefail, Llanfaethlu, Anglesey. Died on 8 January 1916 and buried in Twelve Tree Copse Cemetery. Corporal Percy Wyndham Matthews (4619) of Tonypandy also died on the same day and is commemorated on the Helles Memorial.

2nd SWB: Sergeant Thomas Lavender (10992), the son of Mr and Mrs Lavender, of 157 Shaftesbury Street, Newport. Died on 7 January 1916 and commemorated on the Helles Memorial.

4th SWB: Private Edwin Nisbeck (12721) of Newport. Died on 8 January 1916 and commemorated on the Helles Memorial. Lance Corporal Thomas Rudd (11282) of Wigan also died on the same day and is commemorated on the Helles Memorial.

4th Welsh: Private David Daniels (3867), the son of Benjamin and Ann Daniels, of 9 Box Terrace, Llanelli. Died on 10 December 1915 and commemorated on the Helles Memorial. Private William Alfred James (969), the son of John and Ann James, of Seaside, Llanelli, also died on the same day and is commemorated on the Helles Memorial.

5th Welsh: Private James Peacock (2494), the son of James and Annie Peacock, of 21 Mill Street, Llangefni, Anglesey. Died on 8 December 1915 and commemorated on the Helles Memorial.

8th Welsh: Private Leonard Isherwood (34425), the son of John and Jemima Isherwood, of 16 Bowness Street, Higher Openshaw, Manchester. Died on 16 December 1915 and buried in Hill 10 Cemetery.

Of course, other men from these units died later of wounds or sickness suffered at Gallipoli in hospitals in Malta, Egypt and Britain, but the above were the last ones to die or be commemorated on the peninsula itself.

After the evacuation the 53rd (Welsh) Division (5th RWF, 6th RWF, 7th RWF, 4th Welsh and 5th Welsh) and the Welsh Horse remained in the Middle East, while the 13th Division (8th RWF, 4th SWB and 8th Welsh) were destined for service in Mesopotamia. The 29th Division (2nd SWB) would move to France.

Sir Ian Hamilton wrote of the August offensives that ultimately led to the failure of the entire campaign in his third Gallipoli despatch, which was published in the *London Gazette* of 6 January 1916. Of the Welsh units in action, the 4th SWB gained special praise:

The right assaulting column had entered the two southerly ravines – Sazli Beit Dere and Chailak Dere – by midnight. At 1.30 a.m. began a hotly-contested fight for the trenches on the lower part of Rhododendron Spur, whilst the Chailak Dere column pressed steadily up the valley against the enemy. The left covering column, under Brigadier-General Travers, after marching along the beach to No. 3 Outpost, resumed its northerly advance as soon as the attack on Bauchop's Hill had developed. Once the Chailak Dere was cleared the column moved by the mouth of the Aghyl Dere, disregarding the enfilade fire from sections of Bauchop's Hill still uncaptured. The rapid success of this movement was largely due to Lieutenant-Colonel Gillespie, a very fine man, who commanded the advance guard consisting of his own regiment, the 4th South Wales Borderers, a corps worthy of such a leader. Every trench encountered was instantly rushed by the Borderers until, having reached the predetermined spot, the whole column was unhesitatingly launched at Damakjelik Bair. Several Turkish trenches were captured at the bayonet's point and by 1.30 a.m. the whole of the hill was occupied, thus safeguarding the left rear of the whole of the ANZAC attack. Here was an encouraging sample of what the New Army, under good auspices, could accomplish. Nothing more trying to inexperienced troops can be imagined than a long night march exposed to flanking fire, through a strange country, winding up at the end with a bayonet charge against a height, formless and still in the starlight, garrisoned by those spectres of the imagination, worst enemies of the soldier.

That same day, 10th August, two attacks, one in the morning and the other in the afternoon, were delivered on our positions along the Asmak Dere and

Damakjelik Bair. Both were repulsed with heavy loss by the 4th Australian Brigade and the 4th South Wales Borderers, the men of the New Army showing all the steadiness of veterans. Sad to say, the Borderers lost their intrepid leader, Lieutenant-Colonel Gillespie, in the course of this affair. By evening the total casualties of General Birdwood's force had reached 12,000 and included a very large proportion of officers. The 13th Division of the New Army, under Major-General Shaw, had alone lost 6,000 out of a grand total of 10,500.

Whilst one campaign came to an end, on the Western Front the flow of men to strengthen the BEF continued. More Welsh units arrived, but undoubtedly chief amongst them was Wales' very own division, the 38th, which arrived in France in time for Christmas.

Chapter 19

The Western Front:
After Loos and the Arrival of the
38th (Welsh) Division

Following the fierce fighting at the Battle of Loos, the BEF's front was 'quiet' for the remainder of the year, although trench warfare took a continuous toll of casualties. Welsh soldiers continued to perform outstanding acts of gallantry along the front. Temporary Lieutenant Evan Bonnor Hugh Jones, the son of Llewellyn Hugh Jones, official receiver in bankruptcy for North Wales and a nephew of the principal of Colet House, Rhyl, was serving with the 96th Field Company, Royal Engineers. He was awarded the Military Cross for his gallantry in October:

> For conspicuous gallantry at Fauquissart on the night of October 8th-9th, when he placed charges of gun-cotton in the German wire. Although badly wounded, he continued to try to fire the charges at point-blank range and under heavy fire and only retired when the 'lighter' proved useless and two of his four men had been hit.

On 19 November an English soldier of Polish heritage, who later made his home in Blackwood, South Wales carried out a deed of such gallantry that he became the sixth man with Welsh links to be awarded the Victoria Cross.

Samuel Meekosha was born in Leeds on 16 September 1893, the son of a Polish immigrant and an English mother. He served with the 1st/6th Battalion, West Yorkshire Regiment (the Prince of Wales's Own). The citation for his award reads:

> On 19 November 1915 near the Yser, France, Corporal Meekosha was with a platoon of about 20 NCOs and men holding an isolated trench. During a very heavy bombardment six of the platoon were killed and seven wounded, while the rest were more or less buried. When there were no senior NCOs left in action Corporal Meekosha took command, sent for help and in spite of more big shells falling

Corporal Samuel Meekosha who won the Victoria Cross for his gallantry under shellfire on the Yser.

within 20 yards of him, continued to dig out the wounded and buried men in full view of and at close range from the enemy. He was assisted by Privates Johnson, Sayers and Wilkinson who were all awarded the DCM. Their courage saved at least four lives. (*London Gazette*, 22 January 1916.)

Meekosha was later commissioned in the West Yorkshire Regiment. After the First World War he worked for the tobacco company John Player and served again with the regiment during the Second World War. He died at his home in Oakdale, Blackwood, Monmouthshire on 8 December 1950.

The Battle of Loos officially ended in mid-October. The initial successes of the first day were countered by the immense loss of life and the Germans' ability to counter-attack to recoup their lost ground. It also showed that partially-trained troops such as the Territorial and New Army divisions, however brave, could not be effective in this new warfare. In addition, it proved the importance of developing new weapons, such as the Mills bomb (hand grenade), which could have been put to great use if enough had been available for trench fighting. Gas discharged from cylinders was proven to be unreliable at best and the British learned many lessons about how to conduct further attacks of this nature.

Loos also proved to be the end of the military career of the commander of the BEF, Sir John French. His reputation already tarnished by the 'shell crisis' at Neuve Chapelle, the failure to break through at Loos and his alleged mishandling of the reserves, coupled with a lot of political machination, and this led to him resigning his command on 18 December and it passed to his main critic, Sir Douglas Haig.

After the Battle of Loos the 28th Division was withdrawn into billets at Béthune and in November left France for Salonika, the 1st Welsh embarking at Marseilles on 24 November aboard HMAT *Shropshire*, while the 6th Welsh were transferred to 3 Brigade, 1st Division, joining the 1st SWB and 2nd Welsh.

The 1st Division (1st SWB, 2nd Welsh and 6th Welsh) remained at Loos over the winter, tours of duty in the trenches alternating with rest and training in the Lillers area. The division was reviewed by King George on 28 October and many of the men were awarded honours in the New Year's

Sir John French.

Honours List. At the end of December a party under the command of Second Lieutenant George Howard Jones, 2nd Welsh, cut a belt of 12 yards of German wire, 6 yards deep and only 5 yards from the enemy parapet, an experiment in the possibility of cutting wire by hand before a raid. For this exploit Jones was awarded the MC, 'For conspicuous gallantry when in command of a patrol. He successfully cut the enemy's wire under circumstances of great difficulty and danger.' Private Thomas Evan James (27478) of the 2nd Welsh and Private John Henry Thomas (2370) of the 6th Welsh were awarded the DCM, the latter being the first in the 6th Welsh: 'For conspicuous gallantry in volunteering to cut through the enemy's wire within a few yards of his parapet and carrying out his objective in spite of his patrol being seen and fired on.' (*London Gazette*, 15 March 1916.)

On 25 November the 2nd RWF transferred with the remainder of 33 Brigade to the 33rd Division, losing the 1st Middlesex and 2nd Argyll and Sutherland Highlanders, who were replaced by the 18th Royal Fusiliers and 20th Royal Fusiliers. The division spent the winter on the Béthune front near St Venant and moved to positions at Cambrin at the end of December.

The 10th RWF of the 3rd Division remained at Ypres in the trenches at Bellewaarde, before moving south. The battalion was struck by tragedy when one of its men, Private Charles William Knight (15437), shot and killed another member of the battalion, Private Alfred Edwards (15461), while drunk in their billets on 3 November. Knight was the son of Mrs Eliza Knight, of 25 Filton Street, Fulham, London. He was sentenced to death for murder and was executed on 15 November 1915. He is buried in Le Grand Hasard Military Cemetery. The victim, Edwards, is buried in Eecke Churchyard and was the son of Elizabeth Samuels, of Stone Cottages, Avongoch, Ruabon, Denbighshire.

The grave of Private Charles William Knight (15437) in Le Grand Hasard Military Cemetery. He was shot dawn on 15 November 1915.

The 4th Division (2nd Monmouths) were also at Ypres.

The 7th Division (1st RWF) did a tour of duty in the Cuinchy sector until 23 November before beginning a move southwards and in January 1916 took up positions near Fricourt, on the Somme.

The 19th Division (9th RWF, 5th SWB and 9th Welsh) spent the winter in trenches and reserve in the Neuve Chapelle and Laventie areas, the squalid conditions being somewhat compensated for by the attractions of Béthune.

The 22nd Division (11th RWF, 7th SWB, 8th SWB and 11th Welsh) began to embark for Salonika on 27 October and would remain there for the duration of the war.

The 25th Division (6th SWB) landed in France on 26 September 1915 and were posted to the Vimy area.

The 28th Division (1st Welsh) sailed to Egypt during October and the following month moved to Salonika, where it also remained.

The 47th Division (4th RWF) was relieved by the 1st Division on 15 November and moved back to the familiar Tillers area, to billets at Auchel, Allouagne and Burbure where it rested for a month before moving back into the line for the winter.

The 46th Division (1st Monmouths) had lost heavily at Loos; it was rebuilt over the winter before moving to positions facing Gommecourt on the Somme.

The 49th Division (3rd Monmouths) remained at Ypres, positioned north of the city along the canal. The 3rd Monmouths suffered a catastrophic loss of life here on 29

Private David Thomas (1470) of the 3rd Monmouths, one of forty-two men of the battalion killed by shellfire near Boesinghe on 29 October 1915. Thomas was the son of John Thomas of Tredegar and the grandson of Evan Thomas of 64 Lammas Street, Carmarthen. He is one of the men buried in the mass grave at Ferme-Olivier Cemetery.

Sergeant Herbert William Preen (2202) of the 3rd Monmouths, one of forty-two men of the battalion killed by shellfire near Boesinghe on 29 October 1915. Preen worked for the L. & N.W. Railways at Abergavenny prior to the war. He is one of the men buried in the mass grave at Ferme-Olivier Cemetery.

December when the battalion was assembling to move into the front line. A single naval shell fired from Houthulst Forest hit the parade, causing sixty-nine casualties. Thirty-seven men were killed outright, five died later in the day, some died of their wounds over the coming days. It must have been a heart-wrenching sight for the men to have seen so many of their comrades shattered by this huge shell, yet the survivors had to retain their composure as they buried their comrades in the nearby Ferme-Olivier Cemetery. Most of the men are buried in what is marked as Plot 2, Row E, Grave 2; essentially one large mass grave due to the nature of their deaths but all have named headstones, albeit with two men named on each.

The Guards Division (Welsh Guards) remained in the Loos sector until December, when it moved to Calais.

The other units who had fought in Gallipoli were, in the process of being evacuated to Egypt.

To the background of political intrigue, the 38th (Welsh) Division, now under the command of Major General Sir Ivor Philipps MP, had completed its training and was ready for service overseas. The men of the division had made a name for themselves during their time there. The *Cambrian News* of 15 October 1915 reported:

The headstone of Sergeant Herbert William Preen (2202) and Lance Sergeant Stanley Plummer (2913) in Ferme-Olivier Cemetery.

An Eisteddfod, to Welsh soldiers in training at Winchester, was held at the Guildhall last week, under the presidency of Brigadier-General Horatio J. Evans, the conductor being Lance-Corporal Gomer Evans and the adjudicators Dr Prendergast (organist of Winchester Cathedral) for the musical competitions, Elfed, Chaplains Ll. R. Hughes, R. Peris Williams and Herbert Davies for the literary items and Lieutenant Maclean for the art section. The Eisteddfod lasted five hours. The principal competitions were for choirs of Welsh soldiers, the prizes for which were £5 and a baton for the conductor. In the competition for choirs of sixteen the Cardiff City Battalion, conducted by Corporal J.H. Davies, were the winners with their singing of *The Soldier's Chorus* from *Faust*. In the competition for choirs of thirty members and over the 13th Royal Welsh Fusiliers, the conductor of which was Private Albert Roberts, were placed first for their interpretation of the test piece, De Rille's *Destruction of Gaza*. The prize for the englyn to the President was divided between Private S.J. Phillips, 16th R.W.F. and Private Alun Mabou, 13th R.W.F. The latter also won the prize for the pryddest on *The Soldier's Life*, and was accorded bardic honours. He was crowned with a wreath of laurel by Mrs Pryce, wife of Lieut-Colonel H.E. Pryce, D.S.O. who, with Lieutenant G. Lloyd George, A.D.C. was the treasurer. Other awards were: Quartette, Bombardier Jenkins's party; baritone solo, Sergt. O. Lydford; bass solo, Private Emlyn Kemp; first tenor solo, Private Watt Phillips; second tenor solo, Signaller T.E. Griffiths; Welsh recitation, Lance-corporal Gideon Roberts; chief tenor solo, Co moral Watt Phillips duet, Private Emlyn Kemp and Bombardier Jenkins; Welsh essay on the war, Lance-Corporal Joseph Davies; second bass solo, Private D. Griffiths; cartoon, Private Howard Ll. Roberts; chief bass solo, Sergeant David Williams. Lance-Corporal G.H. Rees, 13th R.W.F., and Chaplain P. Jones Roberts were the secretaries.

The men not only gained friends for their fine Welsh singing during their regular eisteddfods and at church services but also caused a few headaches due to occasions of drunkenness in the town. The Welshmen of the 38th Division gained themselves quite a reputation during their stay at Winchester, as Stanley Richardson of Winchester recalled years later:

> I recall the riots in the 1914–1918 war. The Welsh were the worst. They attacked the police station in the Broadway, smashed all the windows and tried to get out one of the Welshmen who had been arrested. But they were beaten off, or held back by the police and then the Rifle Brigade from the depot marched down the High Street with fixed bayonets – straight down the High Street in line abreast to clear it – and the Welsh went out one end while the Rifle Brigade came in the other. I actually saw that happen. (*Winchester Voices*, Sarah Bussy.)

The division was reviewed at Crawley Down by Queen Mary on 29 November 1915 and the parade was captured on camera. That afternoon the men of the division gathered around Winchester Cathedral for a service. The *Hampshire Chronicle* reported:

> Last Sunday afternoon a Welsh service was held by the Divisional Chaplain near King Alfred's statue in the Broadway when 3,000 soldiers attended. The band of the R.W.F. played selections and the hymns. An eisteddfod was also

The former Slope Road, renamed the Road of Remembrance, at Folkestone; a road walked upon by countless thousands of men and women destined to serve in France and Flanders.

held on Thursday evening, 'Agored I'r byd'. The organisation of this was admirably carried out by Captain Anthony of Kidwelly, the Divisional Chaplain, Rev. P.J. Roberts, Lance Corporal Rees and Private W.J. Owen. Dr Prendergast, organist of Winchester Cathedral, was the musical adjudicator and the Reverends P.J. Roberts, Divisional Chaplain R. Jones (Llandinam) and Arthur Hughes (Carmarthen) adjudicated on the recitations and poetical compositions.

Just days later, on 2 December 1915, the first parties of the 38th (Welsh) Division entrained at Winchester, bound for Folkestone, and marched down Slope Road (later renamed the 'Road of Remembrance' a tribute to the thousands of soldiers who trod its path) to the harbour, often in pouring rain. For many this would be their last steps on British soil but, even with this knowledge, the men were still cheery and looking forward to their adventure.

The first troops of the division to embark were the 13th RWF, 14th RWF, 15th RWF, 16th RWF, 17th RWF, 10th Welsh, 13th Welsh and 19th Welsh. Two days later came the 14th Welsh, 15th Welsh, 16th Welsh, 10th SWB and 11th SWB. The divisional artillery followed some days later.

After safely disembarking in France, the various units assembled at Boulogne and Le Havre before entraining for Aire in northern France. Here the 38th (Welsh) Division came under the command of XI Corps, under Lieutenant General Sir Richard Haking KCB DSO. A soldier of the 15th Welsh described the journey:

The staff officers of the 38th (Welsh) Division just prior to embarkation for France.

Came the day when we marched to the station, to the cattle vans all labelled *40 Hommes, 8 Chevaux*, I think it was. What a journey it was, now December and cold. There was no heating of course and the train crawled along with frequent long stops. Even when the train was in motion we could run up to the engine, beg some boiling water to make tea, then wait till until your van came along, hand up your dixie and jump aboard. There were several trains ahead, I suppose, for it took the train two days to travel there although it could not have been seventy or eighty miles. We arrived at the rail head at midnight, men shouting 'All out, all out' and it was pitch dark. No preparations were made for the reception of the troops.

We got out of the van, half frozen with cold and all left there miserable, hungry and cold, wandering and stumbling in the dark. I at last crept into a space in a huge stack of timber but not for long, for it was too cold. So another search and at last I opened the door into a long wide timber hut. By the light of candles alight here and there I could see the whole area was covered with sleeping men. Seeing just enough space for me to lay down, I was soon down and asleep. (Private William Shanahan, Llanelli.)

The train was indeed made up of cattle wagons, built to take eight men or eight horses, as the name suggests. After disembarking from these cattle trucks at Aire the weary

The ubiquitous French cattle wagon, marked 40 Hommes, 8 Chevaux.

men marched 2 miles west through the pleasant French countryside, to billets in the village of Rincq, about 30 miles behind the British front line, where they settled down for a welcome night's sleep.

The situation on the Western Front at the end of 1915 was far from encouraging. The British and French had failed to break through the German defences in their attempts in the spring and autumn, while the Germans had forced the British into a tight salient at Ypres. The Gallipoli expedition had been a failure and the British forces in Egypt were on the defensive. In Mesopotamia General Townshend's force had been surrounded and was besieged in the town of Kut on 6 December. General Sir William Robertson had become CIGS (Chief of the Imperial General Staff) in place of General Sir Archibald Murray, who went to command the Egyptian Expeditionary Force, while several divisions had been sent to Salonika from France. In France there were now nearly a million British troops, in Salonika 93,000, in Egypt 157,000, in Gallipoli 40,000, in Mesopotamia 47,000, in East Africa 18,000, in South Africa 12,000 and in India 175,000.

The Allies realized that the only chance for a successful outcome to the war was closer coordination of operations by all of them, including Italy and Russia. Sir Douglas Haig was instructed to co-operate with Marshal Joffre in a big offensive in 1916. The allied commanders-in-chief agreed on the Somme area and to enable the French to assemble their full forces, in January Sir Douglas Haig commenced to relieve the French Tenth Army that was holding a front of 20 miles south of Loos in-between the British First and Third Armies.

XI Corps held the right of the Second Army from Laventie on the north to Givenchy on the south. The 38th (Welsh) Division was to move into this sector for trench familiarization and training alongside the Guards Division and the 19th Division; many friends would meet up for the first time in many months when the division moved into the line to learn from their now experienced Welsh compatriots.

The 38th (Welsh) Division received orders to the effect that, from 10 December 1915 to 6 January 1916, battalions of the division were to be attached in turn to units of the two divisions in the front line to learn the dark arts of trench warfare. Although there had been many months of training for the 38th Division in Britain, the reality of modern war in the field had to be faced.. Lieutenant Wyn Griffith, 15th RWF, part of 113 Brigade, wrote of his feelings as his battalion awaited their move into the trenches:

> Less than twenty-four hours stood between us and the trenches; there were two kinds of men in the world – those who had been in the trenches and the rest. We were to graduate from the one class to the other, to be reborn into the old age and experience of the front line, by the traversing of two miles over the fields of Flanders. (*Up to Mametz.*)

The 38th (Welsh) Division had lost fifty-three men dead while in training in Britain even before it had tasted war. Its first casualties in France occurred on 11 December 1915 when Private Willie Hughes (18178) of the 16th RWF was killed by a shell while working on a communication trench. Two other men were wounded. Hughes was the son of William and Mary Hughes, of 9 Pantglas Road, Bethesda, near Bangor. He is buried in Rue-du-Bacquerot (13th London) Graveyard, Laventie. Three days later the

15th Welsh lost two men killed: Private Frederick Ward (16995) of Pentre and Private William John Waite (26803) of Mardy were both shot dead by a sniper. Waite is buried in St Vaast Post Military Cemetery, Richebourg-l'Avoué, while Ward's grave was lost and he is commemorated on the Loos Memorial.

While the 38th (Welsh) Division was settling into trench life, a Welsh airman became the seventh victim of the renowned German aviator, Max Immelmann, dubbed the 'Eagle of Lille'. Charles Edward Tudor-Jones was the son of Edward Tudor-Jones and Maria Glyn Tudor-Jones (née Griffith), who hailed from Caernarfonshire. He was born in Swindon on 23 June 1895 and had been educated at Shrewsbury and at King's College, Isle of Man. He passed out of Sandhurst in May 1915 but decided to join the RFC and embarked for France on 23 September 1915 as an observer with 3 Squadron. On 15 December 1915 he was flying aboard a Morane-Saulnier L Parasol, Serial No. 5087, piloted by Lieutenant Alan Victor Hobbs, when it was shot down by Immelmann near Valenciennes, killing both men. Tudor-Jones and Hobbs are buried in Raismes Communal Cemetery.

The grave of Private Willie Hughes (18178) of Bethesda. A member of the 16th RWF, Hughes was the very first casualty suffered by the 38th (Welsh) Division in France.

The wreckage of Morane-Saulnier L Parasol 5087 of Second Lieutenant Charles Edward Tudor-Jones.

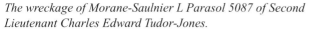

To the north, Lieutenant Wilfred Webster Tait of the 10th Welsh became the first officer casualty suffered by the division when he was killed at Croix Barbée on 19 December. Tait was the son of Francis and Edith Tait of Chester and had worked for the tax office at Rhyl prior to the war. He married Dorothy Pickersgill, of 22 West Parade, Rhyl, after receiving his commission in the 10th Welsh on 20 November 1914. He was severely wounded while attached to the 7th South Lancs of the 19th Division for training and died the same day. He was 24 years old and is buried in Vieille-Chapelle New Military Cemetery, Lacouture. His CO, Lieutenant Colonel Percy E. Ricketts, wrote to his widow:

Your husband was in the front trenches on the night of the 18th December when a bullet struck him in the head. He was removed to the ambulance at once, but died shortly afterwards. It was only his second night in the trenches. I personally have lost a friend as well as a good officer. I had only recently learnt to appreciate him at his true value and the day before his death had asked him to undertake the duties of intelligence officer and assistant adjutant, in addition to those of signalling officer, which shows the

The grave of Lieutenant Wilfred Webster Tait of th 10th Welsh.

estimate I placed upon his abilities. He was always keen and energetic and no man tried harder to do his duty. I shall miss him intensely and so will all his brother officers.

On Christmas Day 1915, their first in France, the entire 38th (Welsh) Division was given the day off, with voluntary religious services for all denominations catered for. Private Alun Lewis of the 13th RWF wrote a brief letter home to his parents at Tower House, Machynlleth to inform them that Christmas greetings had been exchanged with the Germans opposite and that he was thoroughly enjoying the experience. During the previous night the divisional artillery began to arrive from England and the assembly of the entire division was finally completed by 27 December 1915.

Sergeant Tom Williams (12444) of the 6th Battery, Motor Machine-Gun Service, wrote to a friend at Llandrindod Wells to describe his Christmas:

I did not have a very pleasant time, but that does not matter for I shall make up for it next Christmas, with a bit of luck. We kicked off by having no rations on Christmas Eve, but that did not upset me much. What we did not have, we could not eat and we had it to come. The next trouble was that we did not get any letters for three days, but I knew they would not hold the mail up just for fun, so had to keep smiling. On Christmas Day we had rather a lively time, but the following day I got my own back on 'Fritz'. I got a rifle and spent an hour or two sniping, but I had to change my position pretty often, owing to 'Fritz' being more active than usual. But I must have done a bit of damage, judging by the way they were firing at me. Our trenches were only 70 yards away from the Huns in some places, so you see I was able to have a good bit of fun. The trenches are in a cruel state, as there is three or four feet of water in them, but I have got pretty well used to getting wet by this time, but, really, if it rains much more I shall have to get myself an ark. We had another warm time before the New Year was two hours old, but this time we covered ourselves with glory by doing what others have tried for twelve months to do, but we were engaged in an attack which commenced very early on the 1st inst. The Huns had a very powerful searchlight, which we suppressed in double-quick time or our attacking party would have been mown down by machine-gun fire, so the only light they could get was from star shells. I was in a very hot quarter with three guns and I can assure you that we had our work cut out to keep them going – I was very pleased when it was all over. We brought all our boys out without a scar, but some of them had some very narrow shaves.

Towards the end of the year another naval tragedy would see a large number of Welshmen killed. The *Warrior*-class armoured cruiser HMS *Natal* was launched on 30 September 1905 and had gained worldwide fame while escorting the Royal Yacht to India in 1911, taking King George V to attend the Delhi Durbar. At the outbreak of war the *Natal* was assigned to the 2nd Cruiser Squadron of the Grand Fleet and was refitted at Cromarty before taking part in patrols in the North Sea. Following a brief refit at Birkenhead on 22 November, she rejoined the 2nd Cruiser Squadron at Scapa Flow before sailing for Cromarty Firth, where she anchored.

At around 3.15 pm on 30 December a series of huge explosions tore through the ship, which capsized in five minutes. Tragically, at the time the captain of the *Natal*, Eric Back, was entertaining a number of wives and children of his officers, as well as some nurses, who were being treated to a film show. Official casualty lists showed that 390 of her crew were lost in the sinking, but this has since been revised to 421 to include the civilians aboard. A subsequent investigation into the disaster found that the explosions had probably been caused by faulty cordite charges that had overheated and self-detonated, setting up a series of explosions.

Of the 390 crewmen killed, thirteen were from Wales, four of whom were Royal Marines. Only two of these Welshmen have known graves: Able Seaman Owen Owens (175241(CH)), of Colwyn Bay, who is buried in Cromarty Cemetery; and Benjamin Weatherall (Mechanician), of Holyhead, who is buried in Rosskeen Parish Churchyard Extension.

One of the officers lost aboard the *Natal* was her navigation officer, Lieutenant Commander Richard Edward Lewis Treweeks. He was born at St Mary's, Pembroke on 25 April 1893, the son of Major Richard and Mrs Gertrude Treweeks. He had served with the Mercantile Marine for several years prior to the war and married Dorothy Martha Caistor in Manchester in December 1914, having transferred to the Royal Navy on 1 April 1913. He was posted aboard HMS *Natal* in the rank of lieutenant and was 32 years old when he was lost in her sinking. He is commemorated on the Chatham Naval Memorial, Kent. In July 1916 his parents erected a memorial tablet to his memory in St Mary's Church at Pembroke.

The hull of the *Natal* served as a visible reminder of the disaster for several years in Cromarty Firth before being salvaged for scrap to prevent it becoming a hazard to navigation.

The very last day of 1915 saw the loss of five more Welshmen, all from different units: Lance Corporal William Charles Clarke (8500), 2nd Welsh, of Llandaff; Private Walter James Evans (38098), 8th Welsh, of Penydarren; Private William John Humphreys (24052), 16th Welsh, of Garden Village; Private William Ernest Lewis (12268), 6th KSLI, of Oswestry; and Lance Corporal Reginald Thomas Tapp (25015), 1st SWB, of Weston-super-Mare.

The memorial to Lieutenant Commander Richard Edward Lewis Treweeks of HMS Natal *at St Mary's Church, Pembroke.*

Conclusion

The first sixteen months of the war had proved very costly for Wales, with at least 8,942 Welshmen or men of Welsh units having died. Among the number are at least sixteen women and several children, mainly victims of the *Lusitania* disaster.

Breaking the casualties down into units, the following identified Welsh servicemen fell in the period from the Battle of Mons until the end of 1915:

Australian forces:	88
Belgian forces:	3 (Belgians died and buried in Wales)
British army:	8,190
British, Royal Flying Corps:	8
British, Royal Marines:	56
British, Royal Naval Air Service:	1
British, Royal Navy, RNR and RNVR:	293
Canadian forces:	96
Civilians (including nursing staff):	40
Indian forces:	7
Mercantile Marine:	136
New Zealand forces:	24

The Welsh units that had taken part in the fighting in the early days of the war had given a good account of themselves, especially on the Marne and during the First Battle of Ypres, but had suffered catastrophic casualties, which meant that these battalions were no longer the well-trained, experienced troops that they had once been and had been rebuilt with special reservists and volunteers. As a result, morale was low in some units and this can be seen from the number of 'shot at dawn' cases in the 2nd Welsh, who had suffered a more torrid time than most.

The failed Gallipoli campaign caused the resignation of the expedition commander, Sir Ian Hamilton, while the command failures of the Battle of Loos cost the job of Sir John French, who resigned as commander-in-chief on 17 December 1915. The war, it was now clear, would be a long and costly affair. The shell shortage that had partly ruined the career of Sir John French led to David Lloyd George moving from Chancellor of the Exchequer to Minister for Munitions in May 1915. It was this role more than any other that built his reputation and led to him becoming prime minister in December 1916.

The introduction of the Canadians and ANZACs to the Western Front helped add steel to the allied cause, while 1916 would also see the arrival of South African troops in France. The first New Army divisions, including our own 38th (Welsh) Division arrived on the Western Front, whilst the Territorials, including the 53rd (Welsh) Division, had also shown their worth, especially during the ill-fated Gallipoli campaign.

While the battles of 1914–15 had seen the Western Front settle into a stalemate, the war had turned into a global conflict, with fighting in Gallipoli, East Africa, China and Aden. The following year would see the fighting extend into Egypt, Mesopotamia and Salonika, while our Italian allies fought in the mountains of northern Italy against the Austrians.

The Royal Navy still stood firm guarding our waters against incursion by the German High Seas Fleet; 1916 would see the greatest naval battle in history – the Battle of Jutland – and the loss of dozens of Welsh lives.

The coming year would be the bloodiest in the history of the British army. The 38th (Welsh) Division was bloodied in the most horrific way during its attack on Mametz Wood. Other Welsh troops would also play a very active part in all these future campaigns and their stories will be covered in the next two books in this series: *The Welsh at War – The Grinding War: The Somme and Arras*; and *The Welsh at War – Through Mud to Victory: Third Ypres and the 1918 Offensives*. The latter will also cover the commemoration of the fallen in Wales as well as providing casualty statistics and the fate of the Welsh units after the Armistice. The three volumes should be read in conjunction with one another to appreciate the history of the *The Welsh at War* during the First World War.

Bibliography

Memoirs and Regimental Histories

Anon, *A Short History of the 19th (Western) Division*

Adams, Bernard, *Nothing of Importance: A Record of Eight Months at the Front with a Welsh Battalion, October 1915 to June 1916*

Atkinson, Captain C.T., *History of the South Wales Borderers 1914–1918*

Blunden, Edmund, *Undertones of War*

Churchill Dunn, Dr James, DSO, MC, DCM, *The War the Infantry Knew*

Clayton, Charles Pritchard, *The Hungry One*

Depree, Major General H.D., *38th (Welsh) and 33rd Divisions in the Last Five Weeks of the Great War*

Dudley Ward, Major Charles Hamlyn, *History of the Welsh Guards*

—, *History of the 53rd (Welsh) Division*

—, *Regimental Records of the Royal Welch Fusiliers, Vol III, 1914–1918. France and Flanders*

—, *Regimental Records of the Royal Welch Fusiliers, Vol IV, 1915–1918. Turkey – Bulgaria – Austria*

—, *The 74th (Yeomanry) Division in Syria and France*

Gaffney, Angela, *Aftermath: Remembering the Great War in Wales*

Gillon, Captain Stair, *Story of the 29th Division*

Graves, Robert, *Goodbye To All That*

Griffith, Wyn, *Up to Mametz*

Henshaw, Trevor, *The Sky Their Battlefield*

Hughes, Colin, *Mametz: Lloyd George's Welsh Army at the Battle of the Somme*

James, Brigadier E.A., *British Regiments 1914–1918*

Marden, Major General Sir Thomas O., *History of the Welch Regiment, Part Two, 1914–1918*

Munby, Lieutenant Colonel J.E., *History of the 38th (Welsh) Division*

Richards, Frank, DCM, MM, *Old Soldiers Never Die*

Sassoon, Siegfried, *Memoires of a Fox-Hunting Man*

—, *Memoires of an Infantry Officer*

St Helier Evans, Lieutenant M., *Going Across: With the 9th Welsh in the Butterfly Division*

Various, *De Ruvigny's Roll of Honour*

Wyrall, Everard, *History of the 19th (Western) Division*

Secondary Sources

Major and Mrs Holt's Battlefield Guide to Gallipoli

Major and Mrs Holt's Battlefield Guide to the Somme
Major and Mrs Holt's Battlefield Guide to the Western Front (North)
Major and Mrs Holt's Battlefield Guide to the Western Front (South)
Major and Mrs Holt's Battlefield Guide to Ypres

Historical Sources
Unit War Diaries (various), The National Archives, Series WO95
Welsh Newspaper Archives (various), The National Library of Wales,
Cymru1914.org

Newspapers and Other Periodicals
Abergavenny Chronicle
Amman Valley Chronicle
Bedford Times
Brecon and Radnor Express
Brecon County Times
Cambrian Daily Leader
Cambrian News
Carmarthen Journal
Flintshire Observer
Glamorgan Gazette
Hampshire Chronicle
Haverfordwest and Milford Haven Telegraph
Llais Llafur
Llangollen Advertiser
London Gazette
Monmouth Guardian
North Wales Chronicle
Pembroke County Guardian
The *Welshman*
Western Mail

Online Sources
Ancestry.com
Findmypast

Index

312

313

Grenfell, Gerald William (Second Lieutenant) 8th Rifle Brigade, 171

Grenfell, Julian Henry Francis, DSO (Captain) 1st (Royal) Dragoons, 164, 171

Grenfell, Pascoe St Leger (Baron), 23, 52–3, 164

Grenfell, Riversdale Nonus (Captain) 9th Lancers, 23, 52

Grierson, James (General), 27

Griffith, Wyn (Lieutenant) 15th RWF, 300, 307

Griffiths, Christopher William (*Lusitania*), 197

Griffiths, Gwilym (Rifleman, S/1596) 8th Rifle Brigade, 172

Griffiths, J (Major) Welsh Horse (RAMC attached), 39

Griffiths, John (Private, 6843) 4th RWF, 128

Griffiths, Mansell David (Trooper, 621) 8th Light Horse, 221

Griffiths, Rhys Emlyn (Private, 428) 7th AIF, 185

Griffithstown, Monmouthshire, 34, 286

Grimwood, James (Lieutenant Colonel) 7th SWB, 250

Gronow, William John (Corporal, 13925) 4th SWB, 238

Groves, Francis Neville (Lieutenant) 3rd Monmouths, 161

Guilsfield, Welshpool, 207

Gully Ravine, 189–90, 192, 217–18

Gun Trench, Loos, 258, 266

Gunn, Arthur (Second Lieutenant) Welsh Horse, 39

Gwent Glee Singers (*Lusitania*), 194, 197–9

Gwyer, Charles Percy (Captain) 8th Welsh, 226

Gwynn, Reginald Snow (Lieutenant Colonel) 1st SWB, 265

Habershon, Cyril Bernard (Captain) 2nd SWB, 192

Hadley, Reginald Bracebridge (Lieutenant) 1st SWB, 90

Haggard, Mark (Captain) 2nd Welsh, 48–51, 57

Haig, Sir Douglas, 20, 100, 210–11, 254, 256, 263–4, 277, 293, 300

Haking, Sir Richard, KCB, DSO (Lieutenant General), 118, 297

Halford, George (RSM, 13852) 4th SWB, 218

Hall, Geoffrey (Second Lieutenant) Welsh Horse, 39

Hallowes, Rupert Price, VC, MC (Second Lieutenant) Middlesex Regiment, 270–1

Hambrough, Basil Tudor Vincent Beauchamp (Second Lieutenant) Welsh Guards, 138, 267

Hamilton, Sir Ian (General), 176–7, 186, 217, 221, 227–8, 230, 233, 236, 287–8, 290, 305

Hancock, Ralph Escott, DSO (Lieutenant) 2nd Devons, 84

Hand, Samuel (Private, 9155) 2nd RWF, 170

Hansbeke, 64

Harding, William Arthur (Captain) 8th Welsh, 226

Harisoirs, 206

Harker, Thomas Hubert (Lieutenant Colonel) 7th RWF, 172

Harlech, 139, 268

Harries, George Edward (Waiter) MN (*Lusitania*), 197

Harrington, John Joseph (Air Mechanic 1st Class) RFC, 96

Harris, Richard Thomas (Bandsman, 317) 6th Welsh, 167

Hart, William (Private, 38168) 9th Welsh, 252

Hartrey, Thomas (Rifleman, S/1028) 8th Rifle Brigade, 172

Harvey, John Julian Boyd (Second Lieutenant) Welsh Horse, 39

Harvey, William (Lance Sergeant, 6064) 2nd Welsh, 127

Haute Deule Canal, 255, 261

Havard, Samuel Thomas (Private, 1268) Welsh Guards, 270

Havard, Stephen Ebenezer (Private, 2281) 4th AIF, 176

Haverfordwest, 11, 15, 17, 22, 35, 115, 175, 201

Hawarden, 130, 144, 282

Hawkesworth, Francis Henry Stanley (Second Lieutenant) 2nd Welsh, 127

Hawkins, Hervery Carleton (Lieutenant) 6th Welsh, 277

Hay, Archibald (Lieutenant Colonel) 8th RWF, 172

Hayes, Hughie Job (CSM, 5019) 2nd Welsh, 125, 131

Hazebrouck, 123, 245

Hazeldene, John Turner Clough (Second Lieutenant) 4th RWF, 205

Helles, 177–80, 182, 185–6, 191–3, 218–20, 227, 284, 289

Hellfire Corner, 165

Hellings, Frank Howell (Corporal, 1298) 6th Welsh, 81

Hendy, Percy, DCM (Private, 9929) 2nd SWB, 188

Hengoed, 221

Henllan, Cardiganshire, 75, 286

Herbert, Horace Falkland (Lieutenant) 1st Welsh, 148

Hereford, 16, 88

Hereford Regiment, 15, 108–10

Herenthage Wood, 93

Herzeel, 162, 164

Het Sas, 150

Heuringhem, 94

Hewett, Edward Vincent Osborne (Lieutenant Colonel) 6th SWB, 252

Hewett, William George, MC (Lieutenant) 2nd Welsh, 96, 127, 269

Hewitt, Daniel, DCM (Private, 12657) Grenadier Guards, 282–3

Hill 10, Gallipoli, 222, 224, 227, 229

Hill 236, Gallipoli, 182

Hill 60, Gallipoli, 236, 238–9, 284, 288

Hill 60, Ypres, 129–30, 134–6, 147–9, 156, 158

Hill 70, Loos, 254, 257, 258, 264–70, 274

Hill, Frank (Private, 8407) 2nd Welsh, 55

Hill, William Spencer (*Lusitania*), 197–8

Hills-Johnes, Sir James, VC, GCB, 113

Hindenburg Line, 120, 153

Hinges, 206

Hingette, 206

Hoare, Arthur Henry (Private, 20225) 10th CEF, 151

Hobbs, Alan Victor (Lieutenant) Royal Flying Corps, 301

Hobbs, Arthur Harold (Major) 1st Welsh, 275–6

Hogg, Henry (Private, 9983) 2nd SWB, 177

Hogg, Lewis Stephen (Captain) 9th RWF, 259

Hoggan, George Peter (Lieutenant Colonel) 1st Welsh, 131, 275, 277

Hohenzollern Redoubt, 254, 261, 266, 274, 277–82

Hold, Hubert John Edwin (Sapper, 7112) Royal Monmouth RE, 219

Hollingsworth, Frank William (Lieutenant) 2nd Welsh, 105

Holloway, Edward Leigh (Lieutenant Colonel) 10th Welsh, 112

Holyhead, 7, 33, 197, 200, 202, 221, 226, 234, 303

Holywell, 34

Homfray, John Richards (Lieutenant) 1st SWB, 95

Hong Kong, 63

Hooge, 77, 85, 89–90, 93, 96, 156, 165, 168, 170–2, 208, 216, 270–1, 273, 280

Hooge Château, 90, 170

Hooper, Henry James (Private, 11036) 1st RWF, 70

Hopkins, David Taraulis (*Lusitania*), 197

Hopkins, Thomas (Private, 13182) 1st Welsh, 169

Hopkins, William Henry (Private, 9886) 2nd SWB, 61

Hore, Percy Standish (Captain) 52nd Sikhs, 142

Hore, Ruthven Pomfret (Second Lieutenant) 1st Welsh, 203, 272

Hore-Ruthven, Alexander Gore Arkwright (Captain) Welsh Guards, 138

Hoskyns, Edwin Cecil Leigh (Lieutenant) 1st RWF, 70–1

Hospitals, 25–6, 33–6, 42, 47, 53–6, 61–2, 88, 91, 105, 125, 135, 151, 153, 160, 164, 177, 183, 185, 208, 218–19, 226, 229, 232, 234–5, 239, 242–3, 253, 258, 260, 265, 271, 285, 290

Hospitals, Albany Road Military, Cardiff, 242

Hospitals: Netley Military Hospital, 35, 61

Hospitals: St. John's Hospital, Chester, 91

Hôtel de France, 247

Houthulst Forest, 72–3, 76

Howard, Alfred Hayward (Captain) 4th Welsh, 230, 233

Howard, Philip Granville James Fitzalan (Second Lieutenant) Welsh Guards, 267

Howard, Sir Stafford, 113

Howatson, Thomas Charles (Lieutenant) AVC, 39

Howell-Price, Owen Glendower (Second Lieutenant) 3rd AIF, 176

Howells, William John (Captain) 8th Welsh, 226

Hoyle, Basil William Edmond (Captain) 9th RWF, 259

Hubbard, Thomas Stanley (Sergeant, 29521), 16th CEF, 147

Hughes, Elwy (Private, 7508) 4th RWF, 103

Hughes, Robert Thomas (Private, 7284) 4th RWF, 256

Hughes, Thomas Owen (Storekeeper) MN (*Lusitania*), 197

Hughes, William (Private, 12152) 8th RWF, 289

322

Laventie, 78, 141, 144, 173, 203, 246, 248–9, 294, 300
Lawrence, William Lyttleton, DSO (Major) 1st SWB, 90-1
Le Bizet, 94, 98, 145
Le Cateau, 22, 26-8
Le Fayel, 121
Le Havre, 14–15, 80, 94, 123, 248, 297
Le Maisnil, 203
Le Plantin, 102
Le Rutoire Farm, 258
Le Sart, 252
Le Touquet, 98–9, 141
Le Touret, 210
Leach, Edmund Henry Burley (Lieutenant Colonel) 1st SWB, 12, 88–90
Leach, Harold (Sergeant, 7309) 2nd SWB, 63
Leask, James Allan Gordon (Second Lieutenant) 2nd Welsh, 127
Leek, 139
Leland, John Henry Frederick (Second Lieutenant) 5th RWF, 233
Lens (Village), 254, 257, 259, 261, 264-6
Leschelles, 20
Lewis Gun, 214, 251
Lewis, Alun (Private) 13th RWF, 302
Lewis, Charles William (Drummer, 2/4528) 2nd SWB, 63
Lewis, Henry Clifford (Corporal, 27223) 15th CEF, 151
Lewis, Idwal (Third Officer) (*Lusitania*), 199
Lewis, Ike (Private) 4th SWB, 218
Lewis, John Nicholas (Lieutenant) 8th Welsh, 226
Lewis, Rupert Wyndham (Captain) Welsh Guards, 138, 267
Lewis, Thomas Edward (Private, 2426) 6th Welsh, 167
Lewis, Tom (Private) 9th Welsh, 271
Lewis, Trevor Edward (Captain) 5th SWB, 250
Lewis, William (Private, 2287) Brecknocks, 242
Lewis, William Cooper (Private, 137) Welsh Horse, 287
Lewis, William Ernest (Private, 12268) 6th KSLI, 304
Leycester, Robert (Lieutenant) 2nd Welsh, 123
Lieven, 254
Lille, 65–6, 301
Lillers, 216, 293
Lisburne, Earl of (Second Lieutenant) Welsh Guards, 39, 138

Little Willie Trench, Loos, 274–7
Llanbadarn, 248
Llanbedr, 34, 102
Llanbrynmair, 80
Llancarfan, 172
Llandaff, 34, 84, 304
Llandegai, 82–3
Llandernog, 34
Llandovery/Llandovery College, 33–5, 77, 224, 227, 248, 276–7
Llandrindod Wells, 15, 35–6, 39, 212–13, 302
Llandudno, 16, 33, 112, 114–17, 151, 260
Llanelli/Llanelly, 7, 19, 22–3, 34, 51, 185, 192, 197, 218, 221, 271, 286, 289–90, 298
Llanelwedd, 36
Llanerchymedd, Anglesey, 289
Llanfaethlu, Anglesey, 289
Llanfairfechan, 33, 198
Llanfihangel Glyn Myfyr, 64
Llanfyllin, 15
Llangadock, 55
Llangefni, 40, 290
Llangibby, 234
Llangollen, 113, 200
Llangyndeyrn, 89
Llanidloes, 34
Llanllwchaiarn, 134
Llanrhaeadr, 256
Llansawel, 198
Llanymynech, 207
Llewellyn-Jones, Vivian Bruford (Lieutenant) 1st Welsh, 158
Llowes, Radnorshire, 283
Lloyd George, David, 37, 110–11, 201, 216, 305
Lloyd, Gerald Aylmer (Lieutenant) 1st Welsh, 131–5
Lloyd, Sir Francis (General), 137, 139
Lloyd-George, Gwilym (Lieutenant) 6th RWF, 296
Lloyd-Jones, Edward Wynne (Captain) 7th RWF, 233
Lomax, Cyril Ernest Napier (Lieutenant) 1st Welsh, 135
Lomax, Samuel (General), 12, 54, 89–90
London, HMS, 177
London Regiment, 12th (Rangers), 158, 160, 164
London Scottish, 92, 96
Lone Pine, 184, 220–22
Lone Tree, Loos, 257–9

Roch, William Prothero (Second Lieutenant) Welsh Horse, 39

Roderick, Allan Whitlock Nicholl (Lieutenant) 4th Welsh, 230, 233

Rogers, Lewis, DCM (Private, 1946) 2nd Welsh, 127

Rosier, William Samuel (Corporal, 3/10489) 2nd SWB, 63

Rosser, David (Private, 14566) 11th RWF, 251

Rouen, 14, 24, 27, 35, 56, 91, 260

Roulers, 64, 70, 78, 158

Rowley, Samson Edwin (Corporal, 9714) 1st RWF, 213

Rowley-Conwy, Geoffrey Seymour (Major) 6th Loyals, 226–7

Royal Army Medical Corps (RAMC), 15–16, 35, 39, 63, 111, 113, 117, 205, 260

Royal Dublin Fusiliers, 179, 182, 193

Royal Edward, HMT, 235-6

Royal Engineers, 7, 110–11, 117, 203, 205, 250, 256, 286, 290
  123rd Field Company, 117
  151st Field Company, 117
  Royal Anglesey, 16, 172
  Royal Monmouth (RMRE), 7, 96, 219
  Special (Gas) Companies, 256, 280
  Welsh Field Company, 7, 273

Royal Field Artillery (RFA), 23, 27, 46, 53, 111, 149
  Caernarfonshire Battery, 7
  Cardiganshire Battery, 7, 15
  Glamorgan Battery, 7

Royal Flying Corps (RFC), 8, 40, 52, 67, 96, 100, 168, 301, 305

Royal Fusiliers, 52, 75, 131, 136, 138–9, 147, 158, 160, 162, 206, 234, 283, 294

Royal Garrison Artillery (RGA), 15, 109
  Caernarfonshire Battery, 7, 16
  Cardiganshire Battery, 7
  Glamorgan Battery, 7
  Pembroke Battery, 7, 15

Royal Horse Artillery (RHA), 7, 29, 163
  Glamorgan Battery, 7

Royal Marine Light Infantry (RMLI), 178, 192

Royal Marines, 180, 303, 305

Royal Military Academy, Sandhurst, 44, 71, 74–5, 79, 83–4, 93, 135, 144, 148, 163, 186, 206, 224, 253, 265, 277, 301

Royal Munster Fusiliers (Munsters), 27, 101–103, 122, 179, 182, 203–205, 258

Royal Naval Air Service (RNAS), 8, 40, 305

Royal Naval Dockyard, 7, 13

Royal Navy (RN), 7, 74, 97–8, 126, 180, 182, 185, 190, 194, 238, 305–306

Royal Navy, 3rd Fleet (Pembroke Reserve), 191

Royal Navy, *Amphion*, HMS, 13–14

Royal Scots, 63, 99, 166

Royal Scots Greys, 268

Royal Sussex Regiment, 111, 127–8, 228

Royal Warwickshire Regiment (Warwicks), 70, 211, 249, 261

Royal Welsh Fusiliers:
  1st Battalion (1st RWF), 13, 64–6, 67, 69–71, 83–5, 93, 97, 121, 125–6, 141, 143–5, 149, 150, 168, 210–13, 216, 256, 261, 272, 294
  2nd Battalion (2nd RWF), 12, 14, 27, 39, 44, 46, 65, 78–9, 80, 93, 118, 121, 128, 140, 145, 170, 246, 256, 262–3, 272, 294
  3rd Battalion (3rd RWF), 12, 169
  1st/4th Battalion (1/4th RWF), 13, 94, 98, 101, 103, 105, 108–109, 121–2, 127–8, 141, 143, 145, 169, 204–206, 209, 250, 256, 272, 294
  1st/5th Battalion (1/5th RWF), 10, 108, 110, 172, 229, 231–3, 289–90
  1st/6th Battalion (1/6th RWF), 108, 110, 172, 229, 231, 233, 289–90
  1st/7th Battalion (1/7th RWF), 108, 110, 172, 229, 231–3, 235, 289–90
  8th Battalion (8th RWF), 119, 172, 218–19, 222–3, 289–90
  9th Battalion (9th RWF), 120, 172, 245, 248, 250, 256, 259, 271–2, 294
  10th Battalion (10th RWF), 120, 252, 294
  11th Battalion (11th RWF), 120, 250–1, 294
  13th Battalion (13th RWF), 115, 118, 296–7, 302
  14th Battalion (14th RWF), 115, 118,
  15th Battalion (15th RWF), 115–16, 118, 297
  16th Battalion (16th RWF), 115, 118, 297, 300
  17th Battalion (17th RWF), 117–18, 297
  18th Battalion (18th RWF), 118
  19th Battalion (19th RWF), 118, 120
  24th Battalion (24th RWF), 120
  25th Battalion (25th RWF), 120
  North Wales Battalion, 112

Ruabon, 105, 126, 151, 171–2, 272, 294

Rudd, Thomas (Lance Corporal, 11282) 4th SWB, 289

Rue de l'Épinette, 210

Rue-du-Bois, 210

335